# NATURAL ENVIRONMENTS

## Studies in Theoretical and Applied Analysis

Edited by *JOHN V. KRUTILLA*

Published for
Resources for the Future, Inc.
By The Johns Hopkins University Press, Baltimore and London

Copyright © 1972 by Resources for the Future, Inc.
All rights reserved
Manufactured in the United States of America

The Johns Hopkins University Press, Baltimore, Maryland 21218
The Johns Hopkins University Press Ltd., London

Library of Congress Catalog Card Number 72-4441
ISBN 0-8018-1446-4

Library of Congress Cataloging in Publication data will
be found on the last printed page of this book.

# Acknowledgments

The papers included in this volume were first presented at a workshop sponsored by Resources for the Future in cooperation with the University of Montana School of Forestry and the U.S. Forest Service Forestry Sciences Laboratory at Missoula. I wish to acknowledge the assistance given by Arnold Bolle, Dean of the School of Forestry, and Robert Lucas, Director's Representative of the Forestry Sciences Laboratory. A large debt of gratitude is due both George H. Stankey of the Forestry Sciences Laboratory and to Robert Wambach of the School of Forestry for attending to local arrangements and helping in a myriad of other ways. We appreciate, of course, the contributions of the authors of papers published here and the contributions of J. A. Edwards, K. G. Gibbs, L. J. Guedry, and H. H. Stoevener whose paper will be published by the Oregon Agricultural Experiment Station.

A debt that is difficult to acknowledge properly is owed the discussants who prepared written comments directed toward aiding the authors in the revision of research reports preparatory to publication. Many of these discussion papers merit publication in their own right and would have been included except for the exigencies of the volume's format. While the authors acknowledge their debt to the discussants, it is nonetheless appropriate to cite them here: Blair Bower, Resources for the Future; William Burch, Yale University; Oscar Burt, Montana State University; Charles Goldman, University of California, Davis; Jon Goldstein, Joint Economic Committee; Robert Lucas, U.S. Forest Service; Cecil Law, Queen's University; David Lowenthal, American Geographic Society; Karl-Göran Mäler, University of Stockholm; Donald McCaughron,

University of Washington; James McEvoy, University of California, Davis; Clifford Russell, Resources for the Future; Vernon Ruttan, University of Minnesota; Gunter Schramm, University of Michigan; Ervin Zube, University of Massachusetts.

In addition to the written comments, many constructive suggestions were offered in a less formal way by invited guests. To all of the participants, then, I wish to accord at least symbolic authorship and to express my gratitude for their contributions to a successful workshop.

J.V.K.

# Contents

# NATURAL ENVIRONMENTS
*Studies in Theoretical
and Applied Analysis*

# Introduction

JOHN V. KRUTILLA *

The organization of economic activity in the United States stems from a system wherein property rights are vested in private parties. In spite of this and the historic policy designed to transfer lands from the public domain to private claimants as a means of national development, roughly a third of the land area of the United States remains publicly owned. Considering all federal, state, and local government lands, there are roughly three-quarters of a billion acres in public ownership. Nearly a half of this public land, however, is in Alaska where the final disposal of much federally-owned land is being undertaken currently as part of the arrangements associated with Alaska's relatively recent transition to statehood.

If we consider only the coterminous United States, approximately a fifth of the total area is federally owned. The Bureau of Land Management and the Forest Service, with 175 million and 166 million acres respectively in coterminous United States, are the two principal public land management agencies. Each one administers an area that approximates the combined area of Albania, Bulgaria, Czechoslovakia, East Germany, Hungary, and Romania. It is clear then, that the lands in federal ownership represent a significant part of the nation's total land and land-related resources.

To some extent the land remaining in the public domain has not been claimed under the Homestead Act and other land disposal programs because of the characteristics of the land itself. This is true of much of the

* Economist, Resources for the Future, Inc.

1

arid and semiarid land of the Southwest and the rugged terrain of the Sierras, Cascades, and Rockies. But there have also been specific reservations to preserve outstanding scenic or unusual natural areas. These reservations are exemplified by the National Park Service lands (16 million acres in coterminous United States) and the areas set aside as national wildlife refuges (9.9 million acres in coterminous United States) administered by the Bureau of Sport Fisheries and Wildlife.

Much of the land in federal ownership is undeveloped—largely for reasons that explain why it has not been privately claimed. It is inhospitable to homesteading or commercial food and fiber production. It also represents, in the main, the more marginal lands for silviculture. By the same token it represents the bulk of the remaining roadless areas within the country with much of the nation's scenic and wildlife attractions preserved on these lands.

There are currently 10 million acres of roadless, undeveloped land within the Forest Service holdings that have been established as part of a National Wilderness System under terms of the Wilderness Act of 1964. Another 4 million acres in lands classified by the Forest Service as "Primitive Areas" are being reviewed for possible inclusion within the National Wilderness System as are other roadless tracts of land administered by various agencies in the Department of the Interior. In the aggregate there may be as much as 50 million acres of wildland suitable for reservations under either the Wilderness Act or the Wild and Scenic Rivers Act of 1968.

Some of these unprotected *de facto* wilderness land and water areas have the capacity to serve incompatible objectives as well.[1] These lands are being looked upon to provide some of the timber for the vastly increased level of housing construction to which the Nixon Administration is committed, requiring, it is alleged, almost a doubling of the rate of timber harvest from the National Forests over the next decade. The public domain and other federal lands also represent the sites of much of the new mineral exploration. If mines are located in previously undisturbed roadless areas, they may destroy the characteristics that now make these areas suitable for consideration as additions to the protected

[1] While much of this land and its related resources are submarginal for the commercial production of natural resource commodities, there are numerous government policies that directly or indirectly subsidize the production of timber and minerals and the development of land and water resources. (Judged by free market criteria, such exploitation is uneconomic.) Examples of such subsidies can be found in the practice of "deficit sales" by the Forest Service; in allowing capital to be treated as current outlays in the "expensing" practices under tax regulations applying to mineral exploitation; and in the heavy capital subsidies reflected in interest rates used in federal and other public investment in water resource development.

wilderness system. Similarly, hydroelectric power and other multipur-
pose water resource developments often impinge on scenic areas even
when such projects are not located on wilderness tracts or wild reaches
of rivers. Furthermore, the reservation of wild rivers and lands for
recreational purposes does not necessarily eliminate the conflict over
incompatible uses, as is illustrated by the controversy over the high-
density recreation development proposed for Mineral King Valley, carried to the courts by proponents of less-developed, lower-density outdoor
recreation facilities.

Conflicts over using natural environments in ways that will destroy
their natural characteristics have increasingly been taken to the courts.
Storm King, Hells Canyon, Trans-Alaska Pipeline, Cassatot, and many
others come to mind as examples where those who wish to preserve the
value of environmental amenities have opposed land and water development, mining, or logging in natural environments. That the contro-
versies are so intense and the challenge to federal agency decisions on
proposed reallocation of natural areas so great are attributable to the
fact that it will be difficult, if not impossible, to reverse the environmental transformations that will result from such exploitation.

With so many decisions to be made about wildlands, wildlife, aquatic
environments, and scenic resources, it is important to have the best
possible information available. The evolution of methodology for analyzing such problems more adequately than has been possible in the past
may lead to research results that will support more informed administrative decisions by land management agencies—decisions that can be
defended with sufficient cogency to avoid the tortuous route through the
courts. The analytical problems are difficult ones. Yet progress is being
made, and modest though it may be, there is merit in presenting results
of the first round of concerted effort in this area.

This volume, then, addresses allocative decisions relevant to an enormous amount of land—some of it in private ownership but most of it
public land whose resources represent the outcome of a rather selective
process of public land disposal. Much of the remaining public land, as
noted earlier, does not lend itself to the commercial production of natural
resource commodities, but it does contain the preponderance of the
grand scenic areas and other sources of environmental amenities sought
by the American public.

At the root of the problem of preserving aesthetic environments are
the adverse effects of extractive industries. These effects occur when
private property resources are used in a way that impairs the quality or
availability of common property and fugitive resources. Strip mining is
a case in point. Other examples are the damming of a wild river in a

scenic stretch, and the effects on migratory waterfowl of draining wetlands in the interest of agricultural production. Static externalities of this kind constitute one of the themes running throughout the problem of managing wildlands, wildlife, and scenic resources.

Another kind of externality that presents special problems is an intertemporal externality. An action taken by one party today may have an irreversible outcome, closing out an option that would otherwise have been open to him or to another tomorrow. There is need, however, to make a careful distinction in this connection. Admittedly, almost every action has an irreversible element, and often it is no cause for concern. Even the Audubon Society, an organization dedicated to the protection and preservation of birds, can carry in its official publication a picture of a mixed bag of grouse, woodcock, and rail, along with a Parker Double used in bagging them, accompanying an article by a well-known sportsman.[2] The Society's view on hunting appears to be that not every bird, but rather every species of birds is to be protected.[3] The irreversibility is total in the demise of either the entire species or a single bird, but in the latter case there are many close substitutes represented by other members of the species. The death of the last viable mating pair, however, represents the loss of a unique element for which there is no substitute, i.e., the genetic information required for reproduction of members of the species.

The issue of irreplaceability extends beyond the survival of biological species. The question of whether Hells Canyon should be retained in its present state or developed for power turns largely on its uniqueness and scenic grandeur. One of the papers in this volume approaches this problem from an economic standpoint employing economic analysis. In other papers other disciplines are called upon. An investigation of the aesthetic dimensions of the landscape represents the application of the expertise of a landscape architect. A related paper by a psychologist tests the objective validity of the dimensions proposed by the architect. Both involve the identification, classification, and inventorying of different landscape types, ranking them in some array as a means of determining their relative scarcity, whether they lack adequate substitutes, and how this factor should be taken into account in allocating the given land area to other, and perhaps incompatible, purposes.

Not infrequently the basic information needed to form judgments about allocations is still inadequate. This is especially true of aquatic environments. One of the studies in this collection is an effort to develop means of sorting likes from unlikes as a first step toward determining

2 *Audubon*, January 1972, p. 16.
3 *Ibid.*, p. 98.

how many members of a given set of aquatic environments we have and which sets warrant the most concern because of the relative scarcity of their members.

## The Papers in Brief

The nine papers in this book are summarized below in order of their appearance. Each of them is directed toward one of the diverse problems involved in decisions about the use or management of natural areas. One of the papers represents research carried out as part of the U.S. Forest Service Wilderness Research Project, with which Resources for the Future maintains liaison. The others were undertaken directly or supported by RFF.

### Alternative Uses of Natural Environments

Some attributes of the natural environment, such as the grand scenic wonders or the genetic information of given species, are the result of evolution, the accidents of geomorphology or ecological succession measurable in time spans that far exceed the planning horizon of mankind. Decisions that irreversibly affect these features of the environment entail a special responsibility and differ in character from decisions whose consequences can be undone if hindsight shows them to be undesirable. There is always the risk of shortsightedness under circumstances of this sort, and yet the conventional criteria used for choices under such situations will involve a myopic bias. Fisher, Krutilla, and Cicchetti address this problem in their paper "Alternative Uses of Natural Environments." Employing the analytics of optimal control theory, the study develops basic decision criteria for problems involving choice between incompatible alternatives with irreversible consequences.

A related issue arises from the probability that the relative benefits from the mutually exclusive alternatives may change over time because of the differential incidence of technological progress. If a natural area, being a "gift of nature" not producible by man, provides recreational services that enter directly into the utility functions of individuals, then technological advances are not likely to be able to augment the flow of such services significantly, if at all. At the same time, the gains in technology in the producible goods and services sector represent gains in real income. There is evidence, moreover, that the demand for amenity services of natural endowments is income-elastic. Accordingly, with the demand for such services increasing, but the supply remaining substantially fixed, there are grounds for expecting that the relative prices or benefits per unit of such services will increase over time along with the gains in real income.

If we consider, on the other hand, the alternative use of a natural area for the production of intermediate goods (e.g., hydroelectric power) the results will differ significantly. Gains in technology in the production of intermediate goods, such as electric power from thermal sources, have been persistent over the past three-quarters of a century. Should these trends continue, as they are likely to under a regime of institutionalized research and development, we would expect that the cost will continue to fall relative to goods and services generally. This asymmetry in the results of technological progress leads to changes in the relationship between the annual benefits of the two incompatible uses of the natural environment. In the fourth section of the paper, the quantitative significance of this asymmetry is illustrated with reference to the controversial Hells Canyon case. Here it is indicated that even the most profitable of the possible developments is likely to yield benefits that are less than their total opportunity costs.

An interesting sidelight emerges from the analysis of the differential incidence of technological progress. When we consider the amenity services of a natural area in fixed supply confronted by a growing demand for such services, we can anticipate that their annual benefits will appreciate as their scarcity value increases over time. A rate of annual appreciation has the effect of reducing the influence of the rate of time discount to an equal extent in reckoning present value. The result is a lengthening of the relevant period over which annual benefits can be summed, and hence, a larger relative present value for the asset (or the alternative use) with the appreciating annual benefit. This effect is what Pigou may have sought to achieve in suggesting a lower discount rate for use in evaluating conservation projects.[4]

There are substantial advantages, however, in perceiving the problem as a change in relative values rather than as one to be treated by tinkering with the discount rate. First, this formulation identifies the primary influences on the respective benefit streams and thus removes the need to make arbitrary adjustments to the discount rate as suggested by Pigou. Second, the parameters of asymmetry in the effects of technological change often can be estimated from available economic data. Finally, by reflecting the appreciation in benefits of natural areas as they grow increasingly scarce, the evaluation procedure avoids the bias toward unwarranted conversion of natural environments.

The results that follow from introducing the differential incidence of technological change explicitly into the evaluation procedure are significant. But the task of estimating the numerical value of the rate of appre-

---

[4] A. C. Pigou, *The Economics of Welfare*, 4th ed. (London: Macmillan, 1952), p. 27 ff.

ciation, or of technological progress, and the rate of discount, is not to be regarded lightly. Since some of the parameters of the system are not readily observable by reference to market data, sensitivity analyses are warranted regarding the assumptions employed in estimating such values. These have been performed by the authors and the numerical results (but not the ranking of alternatives) are shown to be sensitive to the values taken by some of the parameters.

## Incidence of Technological Change

Kerry Smith in his paper, "The Effect of Technological Change on Different Uses of Environmental Resources," undertakes more intensive theoretical investigation of the relative price behavior of environmental amenities. Smith notes that in the two-good general equilibrium formulation set forth in Appendix B of the Fisher-Krutilla-Cicchetti paper the supply side of the market is not treated explicitly. In order to investigate the conditions that are assumed to hold on the production side as well as to consider the direct relationship between rate of technological advance and price behavior, Smith incorporates the supply conditions essential to deriving general equilibrium solutions.

Beginning with a highly restrictive case where the income elasticity of demand is unity for both goods, Smith discovers that the relative price behavior under technological advance in the produced-good sector depends upon whether complementarity or substitution characterizes the relationship between the two commodities. He finds that if the two goods are perfect complements, the price of the amenity services rises relative to the price of produced goods at the same rate as technology advances. If the two commodities are perfect substitutes, the relative prices of the two goods remain constant.

Because demand for amenity services is known to be responsive to changes in income, this characteristic is introduced into the formulation of a second model. Moreover, a third good is introduced into a framework that can accommodate $n$ goods. Smith assumes that the community will retain the same relative preferences (that is, amenity services will continue to be luxuries relative to the other goods); nonetheless the actual numerical value of the income elasticity for each individual good may change in response to growth in income. The resulting relative prices and commodity mixes are consistent with what one might expect. When technological advance favorably affects the two produced goods without augmenting the supply of amenity services, the relative price of the latter will increase. Furthermore, the quantity of produced goods consumed relative to the amenity service will also increase.

The objective of this exercise was to link the rate of relative price appreciation to the rate of technological advance. Two sets of influences affecting such relative price behavior are identified. The first is the direct result of technological change and is consequently roughly analogous to the vertical shifter in the Fisher-Krutilla-Cicchetti model. The magnitude of this effect is a function of the rate of technical progress as well as of parameters measuring the nature of the demand and supply conditions. The strength of this set of influences is determined by: (1) the income elasticity of the amenity service relative to the elasticities of the produced goods, (2) the relationship of the third good to each of the other two, i.e., whether complementary or substitutable, and (3) the degree to which the resource base used to derive the loci of commodity combinations may be transformed into alternative combinations of goods. Each of the factors has an effect. Consequently the character of both demand and supply affects the first determinant of the rate of relative price change. The second set of influences determines the extent to which autonomous increases in the equilibrium consumption of amenity services will increase relative prices. The same three economic factors are present: income effects, substitution effects, and supply constraints.

As a result of analysis with the three-good model, Smith establishes that under various reasonable assumptions governing the relation among goods in production and consumption, technological advance in one or more sectors will result in the appreciation of prices in the sector not benefiting from gains in technical efficiency in production.

*Wilderness Use and Users*

The valuation of a natural area when devoted to low-density recreation such as that associated with wilderness recreation depends significantly upon the intensity of use. How many recreationists should be permitted to use a wilderness area at any given time? When does intensity of use so dilute the opportunity for a wilderness experience that it no longer provides adequate recreation for the wilderness experience seeker? Should the limitation on use depend significantly on the attitudes of the recreationists in question? And whose attitudes and preferences should count in the establishment and administration of wilderness areas? The following three papers address different aspects of these questions.

*Management of Wilderness Quality.*   Is there really a need to manage wilderness areas or is the very idea a contradiction of terms? In his paper, "A Strategy for the Definition and Management of Wilderness Quality," George Stankey, after considering the extent of the remaining wilderness and the steady and rapid growth in demand for wilderness type recreation, concludes that there is no escaping the need to manage wilderness tracts if we are to preserve the diversity of opportunities for individuals to enjoy a wilderness experience among other forms of recreation. The question is rather how such areas should be administered, and in response to which set of preferences.

One of the tasks that Stankey sets for himself is identifying the preferences of the "relevant" group. He first asks what distinguishes the wilderness experience from other recreation experiences and concludes there are differences in kind rather than merely degree among them. Observing that quality resides in the perception of the individuals participating in the experience he then seeks to distinguish the individuals for whom the National Wilderness System was established by reviewing the Wilderness Act and its legislative history. The values that he finds expressed in the legislation and its history are then used to help distinguish those wilderness users who share such values from those who do not. Having selected the group that is relevant in terms of the objectives of the Wilderness Act, Stankey then considers such users' attitudes toward various situations that are encountered in a wilderness and can be controlled in some measure by management. Finally, he analyzes information from participants' questionnaire responses that he considers essential to an efficient management of wilderness areas, assuming that efficiency is defined as a response to the preference of a clientele that shares the values reflected in the objectives of the Wilderness Act.

*Optimal Capacity.*    While providing a great deal of information on the factors that should be taken into account in determining the "carrying capacity" of wilderness areas for recreational purposes, Stankey does not discuss how such capacity can be actually determined. Fisher and Krutilla in their paper, "Determination of Optimal Capacity of Resource-Based Recreation Facilities," consider the means by which carrying capacity can be defined and measured. Recognizing that a natural area may have many uses, some compatible, others incompatible with each other and with the preservation of the area in its natural state, they appreciate that an adequate analysis of the value of a tract of land requires evaluation of its benefits separately for each of its incompatible uses. Moreover, benefits from each use must be evaluated at the optimal intensity of use so that meaningful comparisons can be made.

Although the benefit-cost methodology for evaluating the net social gain from use of resources in the extractive industries has become fairly standard, the estimation of benefits and costs of low-density recreation use of wildlands has not been previously studied. Fisher and Krutilla discuss how, in principle, one would determine the optimal recreation capacity for low-density recreational facilities, and suggest some alter-

native management options for increasing capacity without eroding the
quality of the recreation service.

On the basis of findings by Stankey and others that the degree of
satisfaction obtained from a wilderness outing by the purist wilderness
user is inversely related to the number of other parties encountered in
the wilderness, Fisher and Krutilla seek to relate such "congestion costs"
to other aspects of benefits and costs experienced by the wilderness user.
At some point in the intensity of use of a given wilderness area, the addition to aggregate benefits that results from the addition of another user
will be offset by the disutility to all with whom the latter comes in contact so that no net gain is achieved. Such a point will represent the
optimal intensity for any given area.

The authors conclude that survey research is required to provide information that will relate the benefits of successive days of wilderness use
functionally to the number of encounters. The number of encounters, in
turn, can be related to the intensity of use by simulation of travel
behavior in a given area. Taking the aggregate willingness to pay for
each encounter level permits the selection of the combination of willingness to pay and intensity of use that maximizes the benefit from the
wilderness tract.

*Estimating Wilderness Demand.*   What percentage of the future population will wish to indulge an interest in wilderness experiences? The
irreversible results of converting portions of the remaining wilderness to
other uses is enough to establish the importance of this question.

Charles Cicchetti in earlier work has established, at least in a preliminary way, a relationship between the demand for various outdoor recreation experiences and the opportunities available to potential users for
indulging such interests. In his paper, "A Multivariate Statistical Analysis of Wilderness Users in the United States," Cicchetti addresses some
of the other variables relevant to the demand for wilderness recreation
by applying methods of multivariate analysis to data obtained on users
of four separate wilderness areas in the United States. Following Stankey's supposition that the wilderness system is to be administered so as to
cater to the preferences of those who share the values reflected in the
Wilderness Act, Cicchetti analyzes the relation between an individual's
purism score and various social and demographic characteristics. He
finds a strong association between the individual's educational level and
adherence to purist values regarding the wilderness. Purist values and
urban, rather than rural, residence as a child appear to be associated.
Cicchetti reminds us, however, that since his sample is preselected from
wilderness users exclusively, rather than randomly from the total popu-

lation, one cannot infer from these associations that the historical trend toward urbanization necessarily leads to an increase in the demand for wilderness recreation. We would also need to know something about non-wilderness users.

Reviewing the reaction of individuals to presence of others under various circumstances on a wilderness outing it becomes clear that purism scores and tolerance for evidence of congestion are inversely related.

While there are strong associations among some of the variables across all four wilderness areas, it is interesting to note the extent to which differences among the four areas also occur. The relation between purism and income, for example, is positive for the Bob Marshall and the Boundary Waters Canoe Area, but negative for the High Uintas. Similar differences occur in the relation between some other variables for the four wilderness areas on which data are available.

Cicchetti concludes that analyses of this sort are significant for evaluating what wildland reservations may be needed to meet the demands of the present and future. He also suggests that more intensive analyses of this sort should be undertaken in the light of the irretrievability of losses when wilderness areas are transformed by developmental or extractive activities.

*Migratory Waterfowl*

Amenity services of outdoor recreation resources are not, of course, confined to public lands. Commonly the same services are available from private lands. Moreover, in the case of migratory waterfowl, a combination of public and private lands is involved in the production and harvest of these game birds. Most of the nesting areas are privately owned, while the resting and feeding areas along the migratory routes are in large part on public lands of the wildlife refuge system. The harvesting areas, where the migratory birds are hunted, are for the most part different from the producing areas. This poses a difficult problem for the efficient management of this resource.

The problem is centered in the wetlands of the Canadian Prairie Provinces and the adjoining pothole country of the Dakotas and Minnesota in the United States. The disadvantages of marshes and ponds for the individual farmer encourage their drainage and conversion to cropland. For farmers, wetlands represent potential nuisances at best and substantial increased costs of production at worst. Yet these wetlands provide a vital part of the ecology of migratory waterfowl, which are highly prized objects of recreational hunting, viewing, and wildlife photography. The drainage of wetlands for farming thus directly affects a major outdoor recreation resource.

Such conflicts in resource use are not uncommon. For most resources, allocative decisions are guided by market prices, which reflect the valuation that producers and consumers place on additional units of resources in alternative applications. In the case of wetlands, however, a misallocation is likely because migratory waterfowl are unpriced fugitive resources subject to harvest under specified game laws and regulations. Accordingly, the value of waterfowl, and hence the value of the wetland resources used in waterfowl production, is not recorded in conventional market transactions on which the allocation decisions of farm operators owning wetlands are based.

There are grounds for believing that the incentive for wetland owners, since they cannot harvest the waterfowl crop they help produce, tends to be biased in favor of more extensive drainage than would be economic if all of the benefits and costs were properly reflected in the decisions to drain or to retain the wetlands—and the costs and gains were equitably distributed. Gardner Brown and Judd Hammack examine this issue in their paper, "A Preliminary Investigation of the Economics of Migratory Waterfowl," which undertakes the difficult task of evaluating the relative costs and gains of the production and recreational harvest of migratory waterfowl.

They first develop a demand model designed to reflect waterfowl hunters' behavior under a given initial set of conditions and the further assumption that hunters respond to these conditions so as to maximize utility from the recreation activity. Working with 2,455 usable questionnaire responses, they obtain information for each hunter on such items as the estimated number of waterfowl bagged, number of days hunted, the respondent's income, his seasonal hunting costs, and his response to a change in costs—in particular, by how much would his costs have had to increase before he would have elected to forgo his hunting. From the latter response they obtain an estimate of the total net value of the representative hunter. Fitting a log linear function to these data, they obtain a particular type of on-site willingness-to-pay function that satisfies the conditions imposed by a hypothesis derived from a priori economic reasoning. To obtain the marginal valuation of a waterfowl, then, they need only take the first partial derivative of total value with respect to the number of waterfowl bagged. This straightforward method finesses the insurmountable problems that plagued Jon Goldstein's pursuit of a demand function for waterfowl by using the travel cost method for estimating recreation demand.[5]

The authors next develop the necessary production relations. By a

[5] Jon Goldstein, *Competition for Wetlands in the Midwest, An Economic Analysis* (Washington: Resources for the Future, 1971).

blend of biological reproduction relationships and survival factors, taking into account also the predation by hunters, they develop a model which gives the number of breeders in a given year as a function of the previous year's hatch, the adult survival rate into the hunting season, and the losses to predation, along with an index of natural mortality during the winter between the autumn hunting and the spring breeding seasons. These relationships will provide the production model required for computing the allowable seasonal harvest to guide establishing the combination of season length and bag limits.

Value and production models are then combined in a theoretical analysis of the problem of how resources and constraints should be manipulated to allocate wetlands optimally to agricultural and waterfowl production. Accordingly, the problem is to select a time sequence for hunter kills and wetlands that will maximize the present on-site value less the total cost of the prerequisite wetlands. The authors point out that the information on pond productivity, costs, etc., is not available in sufficient detail to approximate a solution that could be applied with confidence. That would require extensive additional investigations by earth and life scientists as well as economists. They nonetheless estimate the optimal solution using what data are available, largely for illustrative purposes. The illustrative results suggest that the marginal benefits of waterfowl would justify substantially larger allocations of private wetlands to migratory waterfowl production before the social value product of wetland acreages would be equal at the margin for both agricultural and waterfowl production.

While the study does not yield quantitative estimates that are immediately useful for policy prescriptions or specific recommendations for changes in current practice, it does provide an analytical apparatus that identifies the key variables on which information is required and a decision model that can be elaborated to be of direct utility to resource managers. This in itself is a substantial contribution.

*Classifying Aquatic Environments*

Wildlands have been referred to above primarily as the source of such specialized recreational services as the enjoyment of outdoor recreation with the promise of solitude or gratification of interests dependent on the primeval character of the environment. The preservation of natural areas, however, serves utilitarian functions quite unrelated to recreational activities. There is yet much to be learned in the earth and life sciences from primeval natural areas. In recognition of the need to preserve the research materials found in such areas, the land management agencies of the federal government, including the Fish and Wildlife Service and the National Park Service, have designated as research natural areas over three hundred separate tracts with a total area of over a million acres.[6]

The ability to distinguish between typical classes of terrestrial communities and to identify the rare or unique cases has been aided by the permanence and dominance of vascular plants from which other characteristics of the biotic community are largely derivative. There is no similar degree of agreement regarding the classification of aquatic environments. If aquatic research areas are to be established, the system of distinguishable environments should be free from unnecessary replication, yet, sufficiently comprehensive to include all of the rare or unique examples. In his paper, "A Quantitative Approach to Classification of Inland Waters," Andrew Sheldon addresses this and related problems.

Sheldon acknowledges the futility of attempting a classification that will serve all purposes in all seasons. Given the meager data on inland lakes and streams, he concentrates more on methods and procedures than on the design of a universally valid taxonomy. He draws upon quantitative methods from numerical taxonomy and other fields where quantitative analysis has developed techniques for identifying likes and unlikes along given dimensions. He advocates the use of numerical methods on the grounds that the large mass of complex data would require machine processing and methods of multivariate analysis.

Sheldon lays out the characteristics of classification systems, describes the process of differentiating among classes and the means of rearranging subjects in terms of given characteristics using different standard methods of classification. Where he deems it desirable he introduces modifications of such methods to capture elements of interest not achieved by standard methods, or to reduce deficiencies of particular kinds where it seems warranted. He is careful to note the difficulties and weaknesses associated with each of the methods employed, but he argues that they are no worse than subjective ones in limited analyses of simple systems and that there is no practicable alternative to their use for large and complex systems.

Numerical methods and computer applications, he argues, have among their advantages: (a) rapid organization of large data sets, (b) information retrieval, (c) rapid identification of unusual or unique items in large arrays of data, and (d) objective arrangement of limnological data con-

---

[6] See *A Directory of Research Natural Areas on Federal Lands of the United States of America*, compiled by the Federal Committee on Natural Areas, 1968. Since 1968 a score or more areas have been designated by the Forest Service (see Edward P. Cliff, "Our Research Natural Areas," *American Forests*, October 1971), and some by various agencies of the Department of the Interior.

ducive to developing fresh insights. At present, he emphasizes, the greatest problem is the dearth of comparable data from large numbers of lakes and streams throughout the continent. The capabilities of modern instrumentation coupled with the taxonomic consulting services of the Smithsonian Institution's sorting center could readily and quite efficiently remedy this aspect of the problem. Accordingly, the next stage in pursuit of more comprehensive description and identification of aquatic environments should be a cooperative effort involving agencies such as the state fish and game commissions whose personnel regularly take samples of aquatic environments and the national taxonomic sorting center. An effort of this sort would hold promise of selecting an adequate preserve for research purposes. It would also provide information that, in Sheldon's words, is "adequate, accurate, and yet presented in some fashion which is also digestible" by those who make the decisions that will govern the fate of inland streams, lakes, and related water bodies.

## Landscape Aesthetics

Resource and environmental management has tended to focus on the conventional resource commodities and wildlife on the one hand, and on air and water serving as media for the discharge of urban and industrial effluents on the other. In his paper, "Aesthetic Dimensions of the Landscape," Burton Litton develops a case for recognizing the visual attributes of the landscape as resources that have a distinct value and are worthy of the same conservation concern and management accorded other resources. Modifications of the landscape that have adverse aesthetic consequences, he argues, degrade the quality of the environment no less than the more conventional examples of environmental pollution. Litton observes that the general public and, to a significant extent, the courts have become sensitized to the importance of the visual attributes of the environment, and he attempts to introduce some notions stemming from the design profession into the thinking and practices of resource managers.

He seeks to develop a way by which resource managers and members of the design profession can communicate about the visual aspects of the environment. He provides a nomenclature and rationale for the analysis of landscape attributes through his several "recognition factors," which can be used by non-design natural resource managers. Primary recognition factors are those inherent in the object of attention (i.e., form, space, etc.). Secondary recognition factors are related to the actions of the observer as his relationship to his surroundings is altered. Litton also identifies and defines a number of landscape types (e.g., panoramic landscapes, feature-dominated landscapes, etc.) to enable the layman to distinguish differences in the composition of attributes making up the landscape.

Finally, Litton discusses the qualities by which the aesthetic merit of landscapes can be judged. He recognizes that it will be difficult, if not impossible, to rank landscapes of different compositional types. On the other hand, he finds reason to believe that individuals can consistently rank landscapes *within* given compositional types as to their aesthetic quality. The ability to do this is significant if we are to accommodate aesthetic aspects of the landscape among other objectives of resource management and larger social goals.

Scenic resources, he maintains, should be amenable to description, inventorying, classifying, and recording in the same manner as other resources. Objective information of this sort could have great importance for minimizing the visual damage associated with landscape modification accompanying resource development and extraction, or in aiding the selection of routes for scenic roads and trails, and in numerous other ways. A question arises, however, about the objective validity of the Litton "aesthetic dimensions." Do these have general validity or are they the results of occupational bias and personalized perceptions?

To answer this question, Kenneth Craik in a companion study reported in the paper, "Appraising the Objectivity of Landscape Dimensions," subjects Litton's "hypotheses" to tests of validity. Craik selects five panels drawn from different populations to discover the extent to which the members of each sample perceive the visual aspects of the environment in terms substantially the same as Litton describes them. A sample of faculty and students from the School of Forestry and Conservation served as one panel. A second panel was composed of students and faculty from the Department of Landscape Architecture. A third consisted of a more representative cross-section of university students, while a fourth was drawn from a course in conservation given in the Department of Geography. All students and faculty participants were associated with the University of California, Berkeley. A sample of professional foresters comprised the fifth panel.

The participants in the test experiments perceived the visual environment in a manner remarkably consistent with the Litton perception and description. Moreover, there was no significant tendency for members of one academic group or professional affiliation to conform more closely to the hypothesized results than were members of other groups. Between-group variation was not significantly different from within-group variation, and thus the landscape dimensions developed by Litton had significant across-group reliability.

Not all of the dimensions appeared equally reliable, however, and while much which has been done by Litton will be of immediate utility in land and forest management there is much still to be done before the level of analysis and communication of results reach the stage where manipulation of the visual dimensions of the landscape will be accomplished with the confidence that characterizes the management of the more traditional resource sectors.

But this observation on landscape dimensions applies with almost equal consistency to the results of all of the research areas covered in this volume. While it may be incorrect to describe the natural environment as virgin ground for research and analysis, it remains to a remarkable degree a very fertile and only meagerly cultivated field. Most of the studies presented here serve as a fruitful point of departure for both more intensive and more extensive analysis that can lead to prescriptions for more efficient means of administering our natural environment.

# 1

# Alternative Uses of Natural Environments: The Economics of Environmental Modification

ANTHONY C. FISHER,

JOHN V. KRUTILLA, and

CHARLES J. CICCHETTI *

## I. Natural Environments as Economic Resources

Concern over the adequacy of nature's endowments has been reflected in economic literature at least from the time of Malthus. In the view of Malthus, the natural environment was simply a source of increasingly scarce resources to sustain economic activity, and, in fact, human society. Recent contributions, more or less within the Malthusian framework, have sought to develop programs for the optimal intertemporal consumption of fixed and renewable natural resource stocks.[1]

These exercises are interesting but may be of limited applicability in formulating particular resource and environmental management policies. One reason for this, developed in the studies of Potter and Christy, and Barnett and Morse, is that technological progress has so broadened the resource base that the scarcity foreseen by Malthus and assumed, for example, in the stationary utility function postulated by Plourde, has not been realized. It may make little sense, for example, to defer consumption of a particular mineral occurrence if it can be anticipated that currently inaccessible or low-quality stocks can be brought into economic production or that substitutes can be discovered or developed within a relevant time frame.

* Economists, Resources for the Future, Inc.

*Note:* A shorter version of this paper entitled "The Economics of Environmental Preservation: A Theoretical and Empirical Analysis," appeared in *American Economic Review*, vol. 62, no. 4 (September 1972).

[1] See for example, studies by Smith (1968), Plourde (1970), and Burt and Cummings (1970).

What Barnett and Morse conclude, based on the Potter-Christy data, is that over the entire industrial history of the United States, unit costs of extractive industry outputs have been falling relative to the cost of nonextractive output. These findings are inconsistent with the hypothesis of increasing natural resource scarcity in the Malthusian sense. Clearly, technological progress has had something to do with the falling costs. Yet it is equally clear that a class of costs of extractive production not accounted for in their analysis, namely, the external environmental costs (consumption of nonpriced common property resources) have been rising, perhaps even enough to offset the observed decline in private production costs. Although full social costs may not have risen, they have fallen less than private costs, and it is just this increasingly noticeable discrepancy that has stimulated the current vigorous discussion of environmental problems.

It is desirable to distinguish two (related) forms of environmental deterioration: (1) pollution, regarding which there is a relatively large and rapidly growing literature, and (2) the transformation and loss of whole environments that can result from such activities as clear-cutting a redwood forest or developing a hydroelectric project in the Grand Canyon—both, incidentally, recently under consideration. In this paper we address only the second of these forms.

Surely there are important economic issues here. But, despite a vast literature dating back to the 1930s on benefit-cost criteria for water resource development programs, economists have said virtually nothing about the environmental opportunity costs of these projects. Where reference is made to the despoliation of natural environments, "extra-economic" considerations are noted only in passing.[2] Similarly in the texts on land economics no mention is made of the economic issues involved in the allocation of wildlands and scenic resources, nor do the costs of land development include the opportunity returns forgone as a result of the destruction of natural areas.

More recently Krutilla (1967) has argued that private market allocations are likely to preserve less than the socially optimal amount of natural environments. Moreover, he concludes that the optimal amount is likely to be increasing over time—a particularly serious problem in view of the irreversibility of many environmental transformations.

In this paper we extend Krutilla's discussion in two ways. First, in Sections II and III we develop a model for the allocation of natural environments between preservation and development. Then, in Section IV, we

---

[2] See for example, *Proposed Practices for Economic Analysis of River Basin Projects*, p. 44; Krutilla and Eckstein (1958), p. 265; McKean (1958), p. 61; and Hufschmidt, Krutilla, and Margolis (1961), pp. 52–53.

apply the model to a currently debated issue: Should the Hells Canyon of the Snake River, the deepest gorge on the North American continent, be preserved in its natural state as a wild and scenic river or converted into a hydroelectric facility? More precisely, what should be the level of development of this area, not excluding the corner solution alternative of no development?

## II.  Statement and Solution of a General Model for Choosing Between Preservation and Development of a Natural Environment

Let us consider a natural area that has more than one use, and that can yield services in more than one state. For instance, a forested area can be managed for timber production, can have mineral deposits mined, or can be cleared to provide arable land, and so on. All of these uses involve some transformation of the area from its natural state. Alternatively, if preserved in its natural state, the forest may be a source of benefits from wilderness recreation, scientific research, watershed protection, and so on.[3]

Similarly, the site of a free-flowing river such as the Snake in the Hells Canyon can be converted into a source of hydroelectric power and flatwater recreation, with dams, powerhouses, and commercial recreational facilities, or left in its present state for wilderness-type big game hunting, fishing, white-water boating, and other recreation and scientific activities. Of course, interior solutions with differing levels of development and preservation will also be feasible, though not necessarily optimal, in both cases.[4]

Furthermore, a natural area may have not just one, but several alternative commercial uses as the forest example in particular suggests. We abstract from this problem by assuming allocation to the highest valued use or combination of uses via the market or through some appropriate mix of market, government intervention, and bargaining.[5]

---

[3] For a fuller description of these and other uses of a preserved natural environment, including some suggestions as to how the benefits might be measured, see Krutilla (1967).

[4] Approximately half of the Hells Canyon has already been developed with hydroelectric facilities at sites in the upstream portions of the Canyon.

[5] At least two types of externality—pollution and crowding—are likely to be significant in the commercial exploitation of a natural area. For this reason, an efficient allocation is generally unattainable without some form of government intervention or private bargaining. There is a large literature on the general externality problem, recently summarzied by Mishan, and an interesting treatment of the crowding problem by Smith in his analysis of decentralized exploitation of a common property resource such as an ocean fishery.

Similarly, an area preserved from development can be put to several different uses, but these are typically compatible, or even complementary, with the exception of expanding recreation activity, which beyond some point may impair the value of the area for other uses. In this case too we assume that the resources will be allocated to the highest valued combination of uses and that this will determine the optimal capacity of the resource for recreation.[6] Our objective at this stage, then, is to formulate a model for guiding choice between the two broad alternatives of preservation and development.

We begin in this section with a rather abstract model for the optimum use of natural environments, in its most general form. In succeeding sections a more specific methodology is developed and used to evaluate the Hells Canyon alternatives.

As a defensible definition of optimum use, we propose that use which maximizes the present value of net social returns from an area. In symbols, we propose to maximize

$$(1) \qquad \int_0^\infty e^{-\rho t} \{B^P[P(t), t] + B^D[D(t), t] - I(t)\}dt,$$

where $B^P$ and $B^D$ are flows of expected *net* social benefits (benefits minus costs) at time $t$, from $P_t$ units of preserved land (or water) area, and $D_t$ units of developed land; $I$ is the "social overhead" capital investment cost of transforming land from preserved into developed; and $\rho$ is the social discount rate. Note that the opportunity costs of development (the benefits $B^P$ from preservation), which are generally ignored in benefit-cost calculations, here enter explicitly into the expression to be maximized.

There are several constraints, imposed by nature and past development, on the maximization of (1). One is

$$(2) \qquad\qquad\qquad P + D = L,$$

where $L$ measures the fixed size of the area. A few remarks about units of measurement may be in order here. If we are measuring timber versus virgin forest acreage, for example, in the simplest case $D$ would be just the number of acres cut, and $P$ the remainder. In a more complex case, if logging in part of an area seriously interferes with the ecological balance in the rest, then $D$ would be larger than just the logged area. If, on the other hand, cutting were selective and light, $D$ might be smaller than the acreage cut. $D$ is then defined in terms of area units, such as acres, affected by the development activity, adjusted, perhaps substantially,

[6] For a detailed discussion of this problem, see the paper in this volume by Anthony C. Fisher and John V. Krutilla.

for the character of the activity. $P$ may be defined as a residual, for now, but we say more about this below.

Current and future development and preservation are constrained by past decisions:

$$(3) \qquad P(0) = P_0, \; D(0) = D_0,$$

i.e., initial values for preserved and developed portions of the area are given.

Development is a dynamic process, and irreversible. In symbols,

$$(4) \qquad \dot{D} = \sigma I,$$

and

$$(5) \qquad I \geq 0,$$

where $\sigma$ is a positive constant of transformation whose dimensions are area/money. In specifying the constraint (4) in this fashion we are assuming "constant returns" to investment in transforming the area. As for the irreversibility constraint (5), were it not effective, much of the conflict between preservation and development would vanish. It seems to us that it is precisely because the losses of certain natural environments would be losses virtually in perpetuity that they are so significant and so strenuously resisted by preservationists. On this question too we shall have more to say at a later stage, ultimately relaxing somewhat the restriction on reversibility.

Finally, we assume concave benefit functions $B^P$ and $B^D$, so that returns to increasing preservation or development are positive but diminishing; in symbols,

$$(6) \qquad B_P^P, \; B_D^D > 0$$

$$B_{PP}^P, \; B_{DD}^D < 0.$$

It is conceivable that initial stages of water resource development may be characterized by increasing returns. This will not in general be true of river systems in advanced stages of development, such as the Columbia River System, of which the Hells Canyon reach of the Snake River is a part. Accordingly, although the larger of two proposed development schemes (the High Mountain Sheep project) is more profitable than the smaller (the Pleasant Valley–Low Mountain Sheep), any increase in scale beyond High Mountain Sheep runs into severely diminishing returns as the higher pool reduces the existing developed head upstream. Moreover, though this anticipates the analysis a bit, what really matters is the behavior of development benefits *net* of opportunity costs. And the marginal opportunity costs of development, the benefits from preservation, are increasing as development increases.[7]

Again anticipating the analysis, and ignoring the dynamic irreversibility and other constraints, we can state that the problem of choosing an optimal (benefit-maximizing) level of development will have a unique solution if net benefits are always increasing at a decreasing rate. Even if they are not, as the foregoing discussion suggests might be possible, there will be an inflection point, as marginal net benefits first increase then decrease. In this case there will be one or two extrema; one will be a maximum that can be determined from the second-order conditions, though, in any application, knowledge of the benefit functions would probably make resort to second-order conditions unnecessary.

We can now proceed with solution of the problem in the general case in which no restrictions are placed on the time paths of the benefit functions. Following this, in Section III we explore the effects of certain restrictions that are plausible in a more specific context.

A problem similar in form to equations (1)–(6), that of optimal aggregate economic growth with irreversible investment, has recently been studied by Arrow and Kurz, and one nearly identical, that of a firm's optimal capital policy with irreversible investment, by Arrow—both using the techniques of control theory. Indeed, were it not for the presence of the opportunity cost term, and the crucial role it plays, the remainder of this section might consist simply in a statement of Arrow's results, slightly modified. Instead, we find it helpful to work through and adapt a portion of the Arrow analysis.

Proceeding, then, with the solution, the Hamiltonian is written

$$(7) \qquad H = e^{-\rho t} \left[ B^P(P, t) + B^D(D, t) - I(t) \right] + p(t) \, \sigma I(t),$$

where the first term on the right-hand side, namely, $e^{-\rho t} [B^P(P, t) + B^D(D, t) - I(t)]$, is the (discounted) flow of net benefits at time $t$, and $p(t)$ is the (discounted) shadow price (value of future benefits) of development. Setting $q(t) = p(t)\sigma - e^{-\rho t}$, $H$ can be simplified to

$$(8) \qquad H = e^{-\rho t} \left[ B^P(P, t) + B^D(D, t) \right] + q(t) \, I(t).$$

Note the relationship of $q$ to $p$. If technology or demand relationships are changing, then $p$, and hence $q$, will be affected.

The maximum principle of Pontryagin et al. (1962) is applied, and $I$ is chosen to maximize $H$ subject to the irreversibility restriction (5):

$$(9) \qquad H \text{ is maximized by } \quad I = 0 \qquad q < 0$$
$$I \geq 0 \qquad q = 0.$$

---

[7] This last point follows from the other half of equation (6), namely that $B_P^P > 0$ and $B_{PP}^P < 0$.

For $q > 0$, investment would have to be infinite over an interval. Quite apart from its impracticality, this possibility can be ruled out because it leads to a contradiction. Obviously, past development could not have been optimal; more should have been invested earlier.

Since, from equation (2) $P$ and $D$ are not independent, $H$ can also be written.

(10)      $H = e^{-\rho t} [B^P(L - D, t) + B^D(D, t)] + q(t) \, I\,(t)$.

Again applying the maximum principle,

(11)      $$\dot{p} = - \frac{\partial H_{max}}{\partial D}$$

$$= -e^{-\rho t} (-B_P^P + B_D^D).$$

Since equation (9) is written in $q$, not $p$, let us write

$$\dot{q} = \sigma\dot{p} + \rho e^{-\rho t}$$

(12)      $$= \sigma e^{-\rho t} (B_P^P - B_D^D) + \rho e^{-\rho t}$$

$$= e^{-\rho t} [\rho - \sigma(B_D^D - B_P^P)],$$

and

(13)      $$q(t_1) - q(t_0) = \int_{t_0}^{t_1} e^{-\rho t} [\rho - \sigma(B_D^D - B_P^P)] \, dt.$$

From (9), the optimal development path is a sequence of intervals satisfying alternately the conditions $q(t) = 0$ and $q(t) < 0$. Following Arrow, define intervals in which $q(t) = 0$ as free intervals, intervals in which $q(t) < 0$ as blocked (no investment) intervals. In a free interval, $\dot{q} = 0$, so

(14)      $$\rho = \sigma(B_D^D - B_P^P).$$

Assume, now, that investment is costlessly reversible, except for interest charges—that, if deemed desirable, an area developed as a hydroelectric project can be returned to its natural state, and the entire development complex of dam, lines, roads, etc., can be scrapped at no net cost. This, it may be noted, would be just equivalent to renting the area for this period, at a rate equal to the rate of interest. As in the related capital accumulation problem, optimal investment policy would then have the myopic property

(15)      $$\frac{\rho}{\sigma} = B_D^D(D^*, t) - B_P^P(P^*, t),$$

or        $$B_D^D(D^*, t) = \frac{\rho}{\sigma} + B_P^P(P^*, t),$$

which may be interpreted to mean that optimal investment policy equates the marginal benefits from development $B_D^D$ to the sum of direct and marginal opportunity costs $\left(\dfrac{\rho}{\sigma} + B_P^P\right)$ at any point in time.

Combining (14) and (15), we have:

(16)                              $D(t) = D^*(t)$ on a free interval.

Again, following Arrow, we define a rising segment of $D^*(t)$ as a riser. Then, since $D(t)$ is increasing on a free interval, $D^*(t)$ is increasing, and a free interval lies within a single riser.

On a blocked interval $(t_0, t_1)$ (where $0 < t_0 < t_1 < \infty$), it follows that $D(t_0) = D^*(t_0)$ and $q(t_0) = 0$, since $t_0$ is also the end of a free interval. Since $I = 0$, $D(t)$ is constant, so $D(t) = D^*(t_0)$, $t_0 \leq t \leq t_1$. Similarly, since $t_1$ is the start of a free interval, $D(t) = D^*(t_1)$, $t_0 \leq t \leq t_1$ and $q(t_1) = 0$. Summarizing, on a blocked interval $(t_0, t_1)$,

(17)                              $D^*(t_0) = D^*(t_1)$,

(18)                              $\displaystyle\int_{t_0}^{t_1} e^{-\rho t}\, r[D^*(t_0), t]dt = 0$

where                        $r(D, t) = \rho - \sigma[B_D^D(D, t) - B_P^P(P, t)]$,

(19)                              $\displaystyle\int_{t_0}^{t} e^{-\rho t}\, r[D^*(t_0), t]dt < 0$,                    $(t_0 < t < t_1)$

and

(20)                              $\displaystyle\int_{t}^{t_1} e^{-\rho t}\, r[D^*(t_0), t]dt > 0$.                    $(t_0 < t < t_1)$

Equations (18) to (20) can be given economic interpretations.

If we hold $D(t)$ equal to $D^*(t_0)$, net marginal benefits $(B_D^D - B_P^P)$ at first exceed (constant) marginal costs, since we do not invest, or push development, to the point $[D^*(t)]$ at which they are equal. As short-run optimal development $[D^*(t)]$ begins to fall, however, beyond some point there is too much development, i.e., $D(t) = D^*(t_0) > D^*(t)$. From this point, marginal benefits are less than marginal costs. Equation (18) says that over the full interval $(t_0, t_1)$ the sum of (discounted) marginal costs just equals the sum of (discounted) marginal benefits. Equation (19) says that, over an interval starting at $t_0$ and ending at any time $t$ short of $t_1$, marginal benefits exceed marginal costs. Equation (20) is, of course, not independent of (18) and (19), and says that, over an interval starting at any time $t$ beyond $t_0$ and ending at $t_1$, marginal benefits are less than marginal costs.

Myopic $(D^*)$ and "corrected" $(D)$ optimal development paths are shown in Figure 1.1. Note that at a point such as $t_0$, where $D^*$ is rising but will soon be falling, the present value of benefits may be low enough

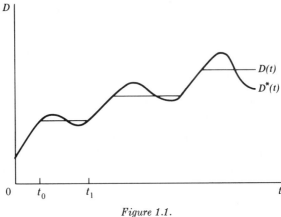

*Figure 1.1.*

for $q < 0$, and investment should cease [equation (9)] until $t_1$ [equation (17)]. We should observe, then, an alternating sequence of rising segments and plateaus in the path of optimal growth of the stock of developed land over time. The divergence of this corrected path from the myopic is a crucially important result. It says that it will in general be optimal to refrain from development, even when further development is indicated by a comparison of current benefits and costs, if "undevelopment" or disinvestment, which are impossible, would soon be indicated.[8]

### III. THE EFFECT OF SUGGESTED RESTRICTIONS ON THE TIME PATHS OF THE BENEFIT FUNCTIONS

In the foregoing analysis no restrictions were placed on the patterns of time variation of the benefit functions. But when we come to consider the Hells Canyon project, and quite probably other similar cases, both theoretical and empirical considerations suggest that benefits from development are likely to be decreasing, whereas benefits from preservation are likely to be increasing. The former, at least, may seem implausible. After all, shouldn't the demands of a growing economy increase the benefits from development of a natural area such as a hydroelectric power site? In this section we first explore this question, and the related one concerning the time pattern of benefits from preservation, then go on to show how the suggested restrictions affect optimal policy.

The traditional measure of the benefits of a hydroelectric power project at any point in time is simply the difference in costs between the most

[8] This result was anticipated by Krutilla (1967), who noted "our problem is akin to the dynamic programming problem which requires a present action (which may violate conventional benefit-cost criteria) to be compatible with the attainment of future states of affairs" (p. 785).

economic alternative source and the hydro project. This assumes, of course, that the amount of power provided by the project will be provided in any event, so that gross benefits are equal and the net benefit of the project is the saving in costs.[9] However, over the relatively long life of a hydro project, costs of the (best) alternative source of energy will continuously decrease as plants embodying new technologies come to replace the shorter-lived obsolete plants in the alternative system. This means that the benefits from developing the hydro project are correspondingly decreasing over the life of the project.[10] In the traditional benefit-cost analysis this adjustment is not made. Benefits are calculated as of the construction date, implicitly assuming that the technology of alternative sources is fixed over the entire life of the project. For purposes of discussion in this section, a simplified process of technical change and replacement involving some constant rate of decrease of benefits is considered. The implications of a more complicated and realistic process are derived in Appendix A, and applied in our computations in the next section.

Benefits from not developing, on the other hand, appear to be increasing over time. The benefit, at any point in time, from a non-priced service such as wilderness recreation in the Hells Canyon is the aggregate consumer surplus or area under the aggregate demand curve for the service.[11] Much evidence suggests a rapid growth in the demand for wilderness recreation in general, and for the Hells Canyon area in particular. This growth is due perhaps to growing population and per capita income, with the extra income used by consumers in part to "purchase" more leisure for themselves. Rising education levels, which seem to be associated with increasing preferences for taking this leisure in a natural environment doubtless also account for the rapidly growing demands.[12] Growth in demand can be broken down into two components: a horizontal and a vertical shift. The effect of population growth, for example, given unchanging distributions of preferences and income, would be to increase the quantity demanded by the same percentage at any given "price," or willingness to pay.

[9] For a fuller discussion of this point, see Steiner (1965).

[10] The decline in the alternative cost of energy can occur before any replacement is required provided that the system is growing and that new plants, operating at higher plant factors than the system load factors, are used to displace production from older plants during off-peak periods.

[11] For this conclusion to be consistent with the treatment given to the development alternative above, it is necessary to assume that there are no available suitable alternatives at the existing relative prices. These assumptions will be clarified below and have been described in detail in Appendix B of this paper.

[12] For an illustration of the rapid growth in wilderness recreation, see the figures for National Forest wilderness, wild and primitive area recreation, reported by Hoch (1962).

Changes in technology that affect the prices of goods that cannot be produced by man, relative to prices of goods that can, as well as changes in consumer incomes, would seem most plausibly to shift the price of any given quantity of the nonproduced environmental service upward. In Appendix B we derive, following Hicks and Allen, sufficient conditions for this to occur. That analysis can be summarized as follows. The "price" or value of the nonproduced services in fixed supply will increase over time relative to the price of the produced goods at those levels of use short of the point at which congestion externalities occur *if* (a) present services of the environmental resource have no good substitutes among produced goods; (b) income and initial price elasticities of demand for present services are larger than for produced goods in general; and (c) the fraction of the budget spent on the nonproduced services in fixed supply is smaller than for produced goods in general.

Changes in consumer preferences clearly can affect both the horizontal and the vertical shift parameters. For example, population might initially grow at, say, 1.5 percent per year, but the quantity of recreation days demanded at zero price might grow at 10 percent per year. However (the horizontal component of) growth in demand might eventually reflect only further growth in population, rather than an increase in the proportion of the population participating, as a "saturation level" is reached. This point is discussed further in Section IV.

Suppose, now, that the demand for wilderness recreation in the Hells Canyon is expanding at one rate in the horizontal dimension, owing perhaps to changes in population and preferences, and at another rate in the vertical dimension, owing perhaps to changes in income and technology. Then total benefits will be increasing at a rate equal to the sum of these rates, assuming a linear imputed demand function.[13]

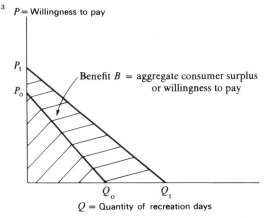

[13]    $P$ = Willingness to pay

$P_t$

$P_o$

Benefit $B$ = aggregate consumer surplus
or willingness to pay

$Q_o$        $Q_t$

$Q$ = Quantity of recreation days

(footnote continued on page 29)

It is easily seen that as benefits from preservation increase relative to benefits from development, the optimal short-run level of development $D^*(t)$ decreases.[14]

We can now show, in the analytical framework of the preceding section, the effect of this trend on optimal policy. If $D^*(t)$ is monotone decreasing, then there is in effect an infinite blocked interval. Development is either frozen at the initial level $D(0)$, or jumps, at $t = 0$, to some higher level $\bar{D}$, and is then frozen. If there is some initial investment, obviously $q(0) = 0$. Also, $\lim_{t \to \infty} q(t) = 0$, because

---

Let $P_t$ = the vertical intercept at time $t$,

$Q_t$ = the horizontal intercept at time $t$,

$r_y$ = rate of growth in willingness to pay (vertical shift),

$\gamma$ = rate of growth in quantity (horizontal shift),

$B_t$ = benefits at time $t$.

Then

(1)
$$B_t = \tfrac{1}{2} P_t Q_t,$$
$$= \tfrac{1}{2} (P_0 e^{r_y t}) (Q_0 e^{\gamma t}),$$
$$= \tfrac{1}{2} P_0 Q_0 e^{(r_y + \gamma) t}.$$

The increment over a very short period is

(2)
$$\frac{dB_t}{dt} = \tfrac{1}{2} P_0 Q_0 e^{(r_y + \gamma) t} (r_y + \gamma),$$

and the rate of increase is

(3)
$$\frac{\dfrac{dB_t}{dt}}{B_t} = \frac{\tfrac{1}{2} P_0 Q_0 e^{(r_y + \gamma) t} (r_y + \gamma)}{\tfrac{1}{2} P_0 Q_0 e^{(r_y + \gamma) t}},$$
$$= r_y + \gamma.$$

Of course, if the rates $r_y$ and $\gamma$ themselves also depend upon time ($t$), then $(dB_t/dt)/B_t$ would be a variable represented by $r_{yt} + \gamma_t$.

---

[14] If investment is ignored, total benefits at any time $t$ from an area of size $L$, where $L = P + D$, and benefits $B^P$ from the preserved area $P$ are increasing relative to benefits $B^D$ from developed area $D$ at a rate $\alpha'$, are

(1)
$$B = B^P(P, t) e^{\alpha' t} + B^D(D, t)$$
$$= B^P(L - D, t) e^{\alpha' t} + B^D(D, t)$$

Optimal $D$, $D^*$, is found by differentiating with respect to $D$ and setting equal to zero:

(2)
$$\frac{\partial B}{\partial D} = -B_P^P e^{\alpha' t} + B_D^D = 0,$$

or

$$B_D^D = B_P^P e^{\alpha' t}.$$

As $t$ increases, $e^{\alpha' t}$ increases, so that $B_P^P$ (the marginal benefits of preservation) must be decreasing, implying that $P^*$ is increasing—and $D^*$ decreasing.

(21) $$-e^{-\rho t} \leq q(t) = \sigma p(t) - e^{-\rho t} \leq 0,$$

and

(22) $$\lim_{t \to \infty} -e^{-\rho t} = 0.$$

On the blocked interval $(0, \infty)$ then, $D(t) = \bar{D}$, with

(23) $$D(0) \leq \bar{D},$$

(24) $$\int_0^\infty e^{-\rho t} r(\bar{D}, t) dt \geq 0,$$

(but the strict inequality cannot hold in both) and

(25) $$\int_t^\infty e^{-\rho t} r(\bar{D}, t) dt > 0, \qquad\qquad 0 < t < \infty$$

For the projected development in the Hells Canyon, the meaning of the analytical results is that it should be undertaken immediately, if at all. In symbols, if

(26) $$\int_0^\infty [B^P(L - \bar{D}, t) + B^D(\bar{D}, t) - I(t)] \, e^{-\rho t} \, dt$$

$$> \int_0^\infty \{B^P[L - D(0), t] + B^D[D(0), t] - I(t)\} \, e^{-\rho t} \, dt,$$

where $\bar{D} > D(0)$, then some initial development, to a level of $\bar{D}$, will be optimal. If the inequality is reversed, then no further development beyond $D(0)$ should be undertaken. In the next section, a partial and approximate evaluation of these present value integrals is attempted, with $\bar{D}$ corresponding to the most profitable level of development, the High Mountain Sheep project.

Before proceeding with the evaluation, a few qualifying remarks about the theoretical propositions will be made. First, although a particular program (in this case no development) may be indicated given current anticipations, it can be revised (in the direction of further development) at any time following the emergence of new and unanticipated relationships in the economy, as for example, a reversal of the historic decline in energy costs. Or, though a particular level of development, corresponding say to High Mountain Sheep in the Hells Canyon, may be optimal for the purposes of power generation, a higher level may be indicated by the inclusion of another purpose, for example, flat-water recreation. In fact, this is not now true for development in the Hells Canyon, because the separable costs of high-density recreation facilities would exceed their benefits. However, some change in the pattern of trends in recreation demand could reverse this result, leading to further development of the area at some future date.

Second, the somewhat abstract nature of the development measure $D$ might be reemphasized. $D$ can increase, for example, by developing additional sites along the river, by constructing facilities to accommodate larger numbers of flat-water recreation seekers, by building roads in virgin sections, etc.

Third, to what extent, if any, has the case for preservation been overstated by the absolute restriction on reversibility, and can the restriction be relaxed? Our view, as stated earlier, is that the irreversibility of development is fundamental to the problem. This does not, however, mean that it must be absolute. Two kinds of reversal are possible, or at least conceivable. One is the restoration of an area by a program of direct investment. This would seem to have little relevance for the sorts of phenomena with which we are mainly concerned: an extinct species or ecological community that cannot be resurrected; a flooded canyon that cannot be replicated; an old-growth redwood forest that cannot be restored. Hence, we have nothing further to say about restoration here.[15]

The other kind of reversal is the natural reversion to the wild, which, though also seemingly of little relevance to our main concerns, is easily fitted into the analytical framework. Suppose some (constant, though this is not necessary) non-zero rate of reversion, $\delta$. Then, $D'(t) = D(t) e^{-\delta t}$, where $D'(t)$ is development subject to reversion. It is not clear how much additional flexibility this gives to investment policy. Even in situations in which $\delta$ is significantly different from zero, it may be much smaller than the desired rate of reversion, which is determined by changes in technology and demand and unconstrained by nature.

## IV. An Empirical and Computational Application of the Model to the Hells Canyon Case

In this section we present some numerical results of a combined empirical and computational model of the costs and benefits associated with preservation and development of the Hells Canyon.[16] The value of some of the services that a natural area of this sort can provide has become measurable by advances in economic analysis, e.g., the value of some outdoor recreation resources; the value of others is as yet intracta-

[15] This is not to deny its relevance in some contexts, as shown for example, in the cleanup and revegetation of certain naturally unremarkable former coal mining areas in the Midwest.

[16] The material of this section draws on the *Testimony of Dr. John V. Krutilla, In the Matter of: Pacific Northwest Power Company and Washington Public Power Supply System*, in hearings before the Federal Power Commission (1970), and especially Exhibit R-671. For a discussion of the computational model, also see the *Testimony of Dr. Charles Cicchetti*, Exhibit R-667.

ble to economic measurement, e.g., the option value of preserving rare scientific research materials. Since we do not know how to measure the present value of all the services that would be yielded by the Canyon if preserved in its present condition, we use an indirect approach. We ask what the present value would need to be to equal or to exceed the present value of the developmental alternative. To simplify the exposition, we have restricted the calculation to the base year and determined the annual benefit for preservation to have a present value equal to or greater than the developmental alternative. This latter step is of considerable practical assistance given the asymmetry in the behavior of the value of the output streams from the two incompatible uses of the site as technology, income, and the structure of demand change over time. We show this in simplified, discrete form for illustrative purposes in equation (27).

$$(27) \qquad b_p^m = \sum_{t=1}^{T} \frac{b_0/(1 + r_t)^t}{(1 + i)^t} \bigg/ \sum_{t=1}^{T'} \frac{1(1 + \alpha_t)^t}{(1 + i)^t},$$

Where: $b_p^m$ = the minimum initial year's benefit required to make the present value of benefits from preserving the area equal to the present value of the development benefits,

$b_0$ = the initial, or base year's, development benefits,

$T$ = the relevant terminal year for the development alternative,

$T'$ = the relevant terminal year for the preservation alternative,

$i$ = the discount rate,

$r_t$ = the simplified representation of the technological change adjustment for development benefits derived in Appendix A.

$\alpha_t$ = the rate of growth in annual benefits as described above and in footnote 13. See also Appendix B.

$T$ and $T'$, the terminal years for each choice, are determined by the years in which the discounted annual benefit falls to zero. They need not and probably would not be the same. Any change in the relative annual values of the incompatible alternatives would result in different relevant time horizons.[17] For convenience in computation, we will select $T$ and $T'$ as the years in which the increment to the present value of net benefits of each alternative falls to $0.01 per $1.00 of initial year's benefits.

[17] Since control theory has not previously been applied to investment problems in the public sector, the time horizons in benefit-cost studies have hitherto been selected in an essentially arbitrary manner.

Although the initial year's development benefits may be quite large, the initial year's preservation benefits $(b_p^m)$ may need to be only very modest, given the inverse relationship between $r_t$ and $\alpha_t$. What we wish to do, then, is to compute the present value of one dollar's worth of initial year's preservation benefits for use in determining what the initial year's preservation benefits would need to be to equal or exceed the present value of developmental benefits. We do this by dividing the present value of \$1.00 of initial year's benefits growing at a variable rate $\alpha_t$ into the present value of development benefits falling at a variable rate $r_t$. This calculation yields the initial year's preservation benefits required to make the two alternatives equivalent and (26) a strict equality.

In the case of the technological change development model the quantitative results will depend on investment per unit capacity of the alternative thermal source, itself partly depending on the interest rate. In addition, the results will depend on the cost per kilowatt hour of thermal energy. Finally, the rate of advance in technical efficiency itself enters into the calculation of the difference between the results obtained both when technological advance is introduced explicitly into the analysis and when it is not. The adjustment factors for introducing the influence of technological change into the analysis are computed by the model presented in Appendix A and numerical estimates are shown in Table 1.1.[18]

The present value of a dollar's worth of initial year's preservation benefit (Table 1.2) is a function of both the rate of growth in annual benefits, $\alpha_t$, and the discount rate.

In the preceding section, and especially in footnote 13, we suggested that $\alpha_t$ is a constant, equal to $r_y + \gamma$. This is plausible, however, only so long as the capacity of the area for recreation activity is not reached. If

[18] It should be mentioned that the model used for computational purposes is derived from a technology involving fossil fuels and is not entirely relevant to the yet unspecified changes in technology of the future. Nevertheless while this model would doubtless differ from one using future technology, the effects of technological change on future costs will be of the same or greater order of magnitude, and these effects should not be ignored because we lack the ability to accurately specify future changes. Our model is also relevant to a case, like the Hells Canyon, where the power system is exclusively hydroelectric and the next hydro plant must be compared with an alternative thermal source of energy. Were we considering a mixed hydro-thermal system or a predominantly thermal system, the thermal alternative would be credited with the benefits of displacing uneconomic thermal energy from older plants with available off-peak economy energy immediately, rather than only gradually over time as in our model.

In this analysis the estimated costs of dealing with thermal pollution have been included; however, the uncertain externalities of radioactive waste disposal have not been included.

Table 1.1. Overstatement of Hydroelectric Capacity and Energy Values
by Neglecting Influence of Technological Advances

| Discount rate per year[a] | Techno- logical advance, rate/year[b] | Capacity value[c] | Conventionally estimated costs of the alternative as a percent of the costs of the alternative when adjusted for influence of technological advance, for various capacity and energy costs[d] | | |
|---|---|---|---|---|---|
| | | | (Percent at 0.98 mills per kwh) | (Percent at 1.22 mills per kwh) | (Percent at 1.28 mills per kwh) |
| $(i)$ | $(r_t)$ | $(\$/kw)$ | | | |
| | 0.03 | | 107.4 | 107.9 | 108.0 |
| 0.08 | 0.04 | $27.43 | 109.0 | 109.6 | 109.7 |
| | 0.05 | | 110.2 | 110.9 | 111.1 |
| | 0.03 | | 105.9 | 106.4 | 106.5 |
| 0.09 | 0.04 | $30.08 | 107.2 | 107.7 | 107.8 |
| | 0.05 | | 108.2 | 108.8 | 108.9 |
| | 0.03 | | 104.8 | 105.1 | 105.2 |
| 0.10 | 0.04 | $32.89 | 105.8 | 106.2 | 106.3 |
| | 0.05 | | 106.5 | 107.1 | 107.2 |

*Source:* FPC hearings (1970), *In the Matter of: Pacific Northwest Power Company and Washington Public Power Supply System*, Exhibit R–670, Table 1, p. 3, testimony of John V. Krutilla.

*Note:* See Appendix A for computational model.

[a] See Eckstein (1968), Harberger (1968), and Seagraves (1970).

[b] Data on technological change computed from Electrical World's biennial "Steam Station Cost Surveys," 1950–68.

[c] Testimony of FPC witness Joseph J. A. Jessell, FPC hearings (cited above in Source), and Exhibit R–54–B.

[d] Testimony of FPC witness I. Paul Chavez, FPC hearings (cited above in Source), and Exhibit R–107–B.

demand for the wilderness recreation services of the area is growing, congestion externalities eventually will arise. That is, a point will be reached beyond which use of the area by one more individual per unit of time will result in a diminution of the utility obtained by others using the area. For purposes of this analysis, this point is taken as the "carrying capacity" of the area. If the benefits of additional use exceeded the congestion costs, total benefits could be increased by relaxing this constraint.[19] But we seek here to define a quantity of constant quality services, the value of which will be a lower bound for preservation benefits. Let $k$ be the year (counting from zero) in which use of the area reaches capacity, $d$ the rate of decay of $\gamma$ (the horizontal component of demand shift), and $m$ the year in which $\gamma$ falls to the rate of growth of population.

Beyond some point, then, annual benefits do not grow at a uniform

[19] For a detailed discussion of this and other considerations in determining the capacity of a natural area for recreation activity, see the Fisher and Krutilla paper that appears later in this book.

Table 1.2. Present Value of One Dollar's Worth of Initial Year's
Preservation Benefits Growing at $\alpha_t$

| $r_y$ | $\gamma = 7.5\%$ <br> $k = 25$ years | $\gamma = 10\%$ <br> $k = 20$ years | $\gamma = 12.5\%$ <br> $k = 15$ years |
|---|---|---|---|
| $i = 8\%$, $m = 50$ years | | | |
| 0.04 | $134.08 | $169.86 | $173.90 |
| 0.05 | 211.72 | 263.49 | 262.12 |
| 0.06 | 385.10 | 467.30 | 449.00 |
| $i = 9\%$, $m = 50$ years | | | |
| 0.04 | $ 93.67 | $120.07 | $125.89 |
| 0.05 | 136.12 | 172.35 | 176.25 |
| 0.06 | 214.76 | 267.10 | 264.49 |
| $i = 10\%$, $m = 50$ years | | | |
| 0.04 | $ 69.28 | $ 89.45 | $ 95.71 |
| 0.05 | 95.15 | 121.91 | 127.68 |
| 0.06 | 138.17 | 174.85 | 178.66 |

Where: $i$ = discount rate,

$r_y$ = annual rate of growth of price for a given quantity,

$\gamma$ = annual rate of growth of quantity demanded at given price,

$k$ = number of years after initial year in which carrying capacity constraint becomes effective,

$m$ = number of years after initial year in which $\gamma$ falls to rate of growth of population.

rate over time but depend upon the values taken by $\gamma$, $r_y$, $k$, $d$, and $m$. Since $k$ represents the time period when "recreational carrying capacity" is reached and is given by the capacity of the area to accommodate recreation seekers without eroding the quality of the recreational experience, $k$ and $\gamma$ are related. The particular values taken, i.e., $\gamma$ of 10 percent and $k$ of 20 years, with alternative assumptions for purposes of sensitivity analyses, were chosen for reasons given elsewhere.[20] A discount rate of 9 percent with alternatives of 8 and 10 percent was the result of independent study.[21] The selection of the value of $m$ of 50 years, with alternative assumptions of 40 and 60, was governed by both the rate of growth of general demand for wilderness or primitive area recreation, and the estimated "saturation level" for such recreational participation for the population as a whole. Finally, the range of values for $r_y$ was taken from what we know about the conventional income elasticity of demand for this kind of recreation activity (as reinterpreted in the light of the expected lack of substitutes both in the present and over time)[22] and growth in per capita income over the past two or three decades.

[20] Testimony of Krutilla, FPC hearings (1970).

[21] See Eckstein (1968), Harberger (1968), and Seagraves (1970).

[22] See Cicchetti, Seneca, and Davidson (1969).

Now, what do the computational models tell us that the traditional benefit-cost analysis of comparable situations requiring the allocation of "gifts of nature" between two incompatible alternatives does not? Let us take for illustration, subject later to sensitivity analysis, the computed initial year's preservation benefit (Table 1.3) corresponding to $i$ of 9 percent, $r_t$ of 0.04, $\gamma$ of 10 percent and $k$ of 20 years, $m$ of 50 years and $r_y$ of 0.05; namely, \$80,122. Might we expect this amount to be equaled or exceeded by the first year the hydroelectric project would otherwise go into operation? In many cases we would have only the sketchiest information and would have to make such a comparison on the basis of judgment. In the case of Hells Canyon, we obtained better information and shall return to the matter subsequently. But for now, we have the sum of \$80,000, which is necessary to justify on economic grounds the allocation of the resource to uses compatible with retention of the area in its present condition. This sum of \$80,000 compares with the sum of \$2.9 million, which represents the "annualized" benefit from

Table 1.3. Initial Year's Preservation Benefits (Growing at the Rate $\alpha_t$) Required in Order to Have Present Value Equal to Development

| $r_y$ | $\gamma = 7.5\%$ <br> $k = 25$ years | $\gamma = 10\%$ <br> $k = 20$ years | $\gamma = 12.5\%$ <br> $k = 15$ years |
|---|---|---|---|
| $i = 8\%$, $m = 50$ years, $r_t = 0.04$, $b_d' = \$18,540,000*$ | | | |
| 0.04 | \$138,276 | \$109,149 | \$106,613 |
| 0.05 | 87,568 | 70,363 | 70,731 |
| 0.06 | 48,143 | 39,674 | 41,292 |
| $i = 9\%$, $m = 50$ years, $r_t = 0.04$, $b_d' = \$13,809,000*$ | | | |
| 0.04 | \$147,422 | \$115,008 | \$109,691 |
| 0.05 | 101,447 | 80,122 | 78,336 |
| 0.06 | 64,300 | 51,700 | 52,210 |
| $i = 10\%$, $m = 50$ years, $r_t = 0.04$, $b_d' = \$9,861,000*$ | | | |
| 0.04 | \$142,335 | \$110,240 | \$103,030 |
| 0.05 | 103,626 | 80,888 | 77,232 |
| 0.06 | 71,369 | 56,397 | 55,194 |

* From FPC hearings (1970), *In the Matter of: Pacific Northwest Power Company and Washington Public Power Supply System*, Exhibit R–671.

Where: $i$ = discount rate,

$r_y$ = annual rate of growth in price for a given quantity,

$\gamma$ = annual rate of growth of quantity demanded at given price,

$k$ = number of years following initial year upon which carrying capacity constraint becomes effective,

$m$ = number of years after initial year upon which $\gamma$ falls to rate of growth of population,

$b_d'$ = present value of development (adjusted),

$r_t$ = annual rate of technological progress in the development case.

the hydroelectric development when no adjustments have been made for technological progress in hydroelectric power value computations and no site value (i.e., present value of opportunity returns foreclosed by altering the present use of the Canyon) has been imputed to costs. Typically then, the question would be raised whether or not the preservation value is equal to or greater than the $2.9 million annual benefits from development.

Let us now consider the readily quantifiable benefits from current uses of the Canyon. These are based on user-day studies conducted by the Fish and Game Departments of Oregon and Idaho, in collaboration with the U.S. Forest Service and an observer representing the applicants for the FPC license, and on our imputation of values per user day. (See Table 1.4.) The day values are necessarily imputed since there is no market for the recreational services of the Canyon. Although we have not been able to conduct systematic studies of imputed demand for the several kinds of services provided, our estimates of willingness to pay are very conservative, considering observed charges in similar circumstances. The imputed value of $5 per day is taken as a lower bound on the average willingness to pay for the types of angling experiences provided in this environment. We observe, for example, that where property rights to fish and game are vested in private individuals, these rights are leased at prices of anywhere from $15 to $200 per rod day for Atlantic Salmon fishing, depending upon the country and the stream. When we consider that the largest proportion of angler days in the headwaters of the Canyon involves fishing for steelhead, thought to be genetically related to Atlantic Salmon in evolutionary antiquity, we have some notion of the magnitude of the values involved. The $25 per day for big game hunting comes from fees charged for deer hunting on private ranches in parts of Texas where the game and surroundings are much inferior to those of the Canyon and its environs. Out estimates, then, are conservative.[23]

From Table 1.4 one could argue, for example, that the preservation

[23] See also Brown, Singh, and Castle (1965), Mathews and Brown (1970), and Pearse (1968) for a more systematic evaluation of the Oregon and Washington Steelhead-Salmon Fisheries and other big game resource values, and the estimated willingness to pay. On the basis of all the evidence available to us the imputation of values in the Hells Canyon case appears to be most conservative. It should be noted, however, that two assumptions are made in order that the values appearing in Table 1.4 represent net benefits, consistent with the benefits estimated for the hydro development. One assumption is that there are no adequate substitutes of like quality, i.e., other primitive scenic areas are either congested or being rationed, conditions that are widely encountered in national parks and over much of the wilderness system. Secondly, it is assumed that the demand unsatisfied by virtue of the transformation of the Hells Canyon would impinge on the margin in other sectors of the economy characterized by free entry and feasibility of augmenting supplies, i.e., incremental costs will equal incremental benefits.

Table 1.4. Illustrative Opportunity Costs of Altering Free Flowing River and Related Canyon Environment by Development of High Mountain Sheep

| Losses | Recreation days 1969[a] | Visitor days 1969[b] | Visitor days 1976 |
|---|---|---|---|
| Stream-based recreation:[c] | | | |
| Total of boat counter survey | 18,755 | 28,132 | 51,000 |
| Upstream of Salmon–Snake confluence | 9,622 | 14,439 | 26,000 |
| Nonboat access: | | | |
| Imnaha–Dug Bar | 9,678 | 14,517 | 26,000 |
| Pittsburgh Landing | 9,643 | 14,464 | 26,000 |
| Hells Canyon downstream: | | | |
| Boat anglers | 2,472 | 1,000 | 1,800 |
| Bank anglers | 9,559 | 2,333 | 4,000 |
| Total stream use above Salmon River | 40,974 plus[d] | 46,753 plus[d] | 84,000 at $5.00/day = $420,000 |
| Hunting, Canyon area[e] | | | |
| Big game | 7,050 | 7,050 | 7,000 at $25.00/day = $175,000 |
| Upland birds | 1,110 | 1,110 | 1,000 at $10.00/day = $10,000 |
| Diminished value of hunting experience[f] | 18,000 | 18,000 | 29,000 at $10.00/day = $290,000 |
| Total quantified losses................................$895,000 ± 25% | | | |

Unevaluated losses:

A. Unmitigated anadromous fish losses outside impact area.
B. Unmitigated resident fish losses: Stream fishing downstream from High Mountain Sheep.
C. Option value of rare geomorphological-biological-ecological phenomena.
D. Others.

a "Recreation day" corresponds to definition in *Supplement 1, Senate Document No. 97*, namely, an individual engaging in recreation for any "reasonable portion of a day." In this particular study, time involved must be minimum of one hour, as per letter, from Monte Richards, Coordinator, Basin Investigations, Idaho Fish and Game Department.

b "Visitor day" corresponds to the President's Recreational Advisory Council (now, Environmental Quality Council) *Coordination Bulletin No. 6* definition of a visitor day as a twelve-hour day. Operationally, the total number of hours, divided by twelve, will give the appropriate "visitor day" estimate.

c Source: *An Evaluation of Recreational Use on the Snake River in the High Mountain Sheep Impact Area*, Survey by Oregon State Game Commission and Idaho State Fish and Game Department in cooperation with U.S. Forest Service, Report dated January 1970, and Memorandum, W. B. Hall, Liaison Officer, Wallowa-Whitman National Forest, dated January 20, 1970.

d Scenic flights and trail use via Saddle Creek and Battle Creek Trails were not included in the survey. Thus, estimates given represent an underreporting of an unevaluated amount.

e "Middle Snake River Study, Idaho, Oregon and Washington," Joint Report of the Bureau of Commercial Fisheries and Bureau of Sports Fisheries and Wildlife, in *Department of the Interior Resource Study of the Middle Snake*, Tables 10 and 11.

f The figure of 18,000 hunter days is based on witness William E. Pitney's estimate at FPC hearings of 15,000 big-game-hunter days on the Oregon side, and an estimate of 10,000 hunter days on the Idaho side (provided in letter from Monte Richards, Coordinator, Idaho Basin Investigations, Idaho Fish and Game Department, dated February 13, 1970), for a total of 25,000 hunter days (excluding small game, i.e., principally upland birds) in the Canyon area, less estimated losses of 7,000 hunter days. This provides the estimated 1969 total of 18,000 hunter days, which growing at estimated 5 percent per year for deer hunting and 9 percent per year for elk hunting, would total 29,000 hunter days by 1976.

benefits shown are roughly only a third ($0.9 to $2.9 million) as large as would be required in comparisons based on traditional analysis of similar cases. By introducing the differential incidence of technological progress on the mutually exclusive alternative uses of the Hells Canyon and the growth in demand for these uses, we reach quite a different conclusion. The initial year's preservation benefit, subject to reevaluation on the bases of sensitivity tests, appears to be $900,000, an order of magnitude larger than the $80,000 it needs to be to have a present value equaling or exceeding the present value of the development alternative. Thus we get results significantly different from traditional analysis.

What about the sensitivity of these conclusions to the particular values that were given to the variables used in our two simulation models? Sensitivity tests can be performed with the data in tables 1.1 and 1.2, along with additional information available from computer runs performed. Some of these checks are displayed in Table 1.5.

Given the estimated user days and imputed value per user day, it follows that the conclusions regarding the relative economic values of the two alternatives are not sensitive, within a reasonable range, to the particular values chosen for the variables and parameters used in the computational models.

There is need, however, for another set of tests when geometric growth rates are being used. We might regard these as "plausibility analyses." For example, the ratio of the implicit price to the projected per capita income in the terminal year was examined and found to equal $2.5 \times 10^{-3}$. At today's per capita income level this is comparable to a user fee of approximately $10.00. Similarly, the ratio of the terminal year's preservation benefit to the GNP in the terminal year is found to be $4.0 \times 10^{-7}$ in the present example. This value compares with a ratio of the total revenue of the Applicants for the FPC license in 1968 to GNP of $5.0 \times 10^{-4}$. The year at which the growth rate in quantity of wilderness-type outdoor recreation services demanded falls to the rate of growth of the

Table 1.5. Sensitivity of Estimated Initial Year's Required Preservation Benefits to Changes in Value of Variables and Parameters (at $i = 9\%$)

| Variable | Variation in Variable | | Percent change | Percent change in preservation benefit |
| | From | To | | |
| --- | --- | --- | --- | --- |
| $r_y$ | 0.04 | 0.05 | 25 | 39 to 49 |
| $r_t$ | 0.04 | 0.05 | 25 | 25 |
| $k^a$ | 20 yrs. | 25 yrs. | 25 | 30 to 40 |
| $\gamma$ | 10% | 12.5% | 25 | −4 to +7 |
| $m$ | 40 yrs. | 50 yrs. | 25 | 3 |

a The 25 percent change in years before carrying capacity is reached translates into a 40 percent change in carrying capacity at the growth rate of 10% used here.

population must also be checked to ensure that the implicit population participation rate is something one would regard as plausible. Such tests were performed in connection with the Hells Canyon case in order to avoid problems that stem from use of unbounded estimates. We found that our assumed initial rate of 10 percent, appropriately damped over time, was a realistic value.

Finally, since the readily observed initial year's benefits from preservation appear to be higher than the minimum required to have their present value exceed the present value of developmental benefits, the computation is concluded at this point. Since the analysis relies implicitly on the price compensating measure of consumer surplus and does not include consideration of option value, or other meaningful representation of the effects of uncertainty, the resulting estimate would be for these reasons, as well as the restricted carrying capacity, a lower bound estimate of the preservation value. Preliminary findings as to the effect of uncertainty on environmental costs and benefits suggests, for example, that in important cases a downward adjustment of benefits from development relative to preservation is indicated.[24] Should the present value of the output stream from the developmental alternative exceed that of the preservation alternative as calculated above, a question might then still arise as to whether the allocation to irreversible developmental purposes can be justified on economic grounds.


## V. Conclusions

In section II of this study, where we proposed a model for the allocation of natural environments between preservation and development, we showed that it will generally be optimal to refrain from some development indicated by current benefits and costs if "undevelopment," which is impossible, would soon be indicated. In section III we showed that if, as in the case of the proposed development in the Hells Canyon, benefits from development are decreasing over time relative to benefits from preservation, it will be optimal to proceed with the development immediately, if at all.[25] In section IV we considered this question in detail for the case of the Hells Canyon, and showed that it will not, in fact, be optimal to undertake even the most profitable development project there. Rather the area is likely to yield greater benefits if left in its natural state.

---

[24] See Cicchetti and Freeman (1971) and Arrow and Fisher (forthcoming).

[25] This is consistent with the differences in views held by members of affluent societies and less-developed countries on these and related environmental issues.

## *Appendix A*

### TECHNOLOGICAL CHANGE ADJUSTMENT MODEL

Over the first 30-year period, taken as the useful life of a thermal facility, let $PVC_t$ represent the present value of annual costs per kilowatt of the thermal alternative in year $t$:

$$PVC_1 = C_1 + E(8760F),$$

$$PVC_2 = \left\{C_1 + [E\ 8760(F - k)] + \frac{E}{(1 + r)}\ (8760k)\right\}\left(\frac{1}{(1 + i)}\right),$$

$$\cdot$$
$$\cdot$$
$$\cdot$$

$$PVC_n = \left\{C_1 + E[8760\{F - (n - 1)k\}] + \frac{E}{(1 + r)^{n-1}}\ [8760(n - 1)k]\right\}$$

$$\times \left(\frac{1}{1 + i}\right)^{n-1} \text{ for } 1 < n < 30,$$

where $C_1$ = capacity cost/kw/yr during first 30-year period,

$\quad\quad E$ = energy cost/kwh,

$\quad\quad F$ = the plant factor (0.90),

$\quad\quad k$ = a constant representing the time decay of the plant factor (0.03),

$\quad\quad i$ = the discount rate,

$\quad\quad r$ = the annual rate of technological progress.

Writing out the $n^{\text{th}}$ term yields:

$$PVC_n = \frac{C_1}{(1 + i)^{n-1}} + \frac{8760EF}{(1 + i)^{n-1}} - \frac{8760Ek(n - 1)}{(1 + i)^{n-1}} + \frac{8760Ek(n - 1)}{[(1 + r)(1 + i)]^{n-1}}.$$

These terms can be summed individually using standard formulas for geometric progressions,[1] and then factored to form:

$$PVC_{1,\cdots,30} = \sum_{n=1}^{30} PVC_n = (C_1 + 8760EF)\left[\frac{1 - a^{30}}{1 - a}\right] - \frac{8760Ek}{i}$$

$$\times \left\{\frac{1 - a^{29}}{1 - a} - 29a^{29}\right\} + \frac{8760Ek}{(1 + r)(1 + i) - 1}\left\{\frac{1 - b^{29}}{1 - b} - 29b^{29}\right\},$$

[1] See p. 357 of the *C.R.C. Standard Mathematical Tables*, 12th ed. (Cleveland: Chemical Rubber Publishing Co., 1961).

where
$$a = \left(\frac{1}{1+i}\right)$$

$$b = \frac{1}{(1+r)(1+i)}.$$

Over years $31, \ldots, T$ the cost expressions are similar except that we are dealing with only a 20-year additional period and all terms thus get discounted by a factor of $[1/(1+i)^{30}]$. Hence, using similar formulas for the sum of geometric series the present value of annual costs per kilowatt from this latter period is determined to be:

$$PVC_{31,\ldots,T} = \sum_{n=31}^{T} PVC_n = \left(\frac{1}{1+i}\right)^{30}\left\{(C_2 + 8760E'F)\left[\frac{1-a^{20}}{1-a}\right]\right.$$

$$\left. - \frac{8760E'k}{i}\left[\frac{1-a^{19}}{1-a} - 19a^{19}\right] + \frac{8760E'k}{(1+r)(1+i)-1}\left[\frac{1-b^{19}}{1-b} - 19b^{19}\right]\right\}$$

where
$$C_2 = \frac{C_1}{(1+r)^{30}}$$

$$E' = \frac{E}{(1+r)^{30}}.$$

The overall present value is:

$$PVC_{1,\ldots,T} = PVC_1 + \ldots + PVC_{30} + PVC_{31} + \ldots + PVC_T.$$

Traditional analyses are based essentially on the model given below.

$$K = \sum_{n=1}^{T} \frac{[C_1 + E(8760F)]}{(1+i)^{n-1}} \quad \text{or, which is equivalent,}$$

$$= [C_1 + E(8760F)]\left[\frac{1-a^T}{1-a}\right] \quad \text{to be consistent with previous notation.}$$

The adjustment factors in Table 1.4 are obtained as follows:

$$K/PVC_{1,\ldots,T} = \sum_{t=1}^{T} \frac{b_0}{(1+i)^t} \bigg/ \sum_{t=1}^{T} \frac{b_0/(1+r_t)^t}{(1+i)^t}$$

$$= T \bigg/ \sum_{t=1}^{T} \frac{1}{(1+r_t)^t}$$

# *Appendix B*

## AN ECONOMIC DESCRIPTION OF A TWO-GOOD WORLD, WHEN ONE GOOD IS NONPRODUCIBLE

*Charles J. Cicchetti**

The situation considered in this appendix is a two-good world in which supply is fixed for one good (which is not producible) and expandable for the other (which represents all manufactured goods). The purpose of the analysis is to consider the set of conditions that will lead to an increase in the price of the good in fixed supply when (a) technological change is exogenously introduced and reduces the relative price of the manufactured good; (b) the good in fixed supply is a relative luxury, its income elasticity exceeding that of the manufactured good; and (c) a smaller portion of the representative consumer's budget is spent on the good in fixed supply.

### DEFINITION OF TERMS USED IN THE ANALYSIS

$F$ = good in *fixed* supply; $P_f$ = price of good in fixed supply;

$M$ = all *manufactured* goods; $P_m$ = price of manufactured goods;

$e_{P_f F}$ = price elasticity of demand for good $F = \dfrac{\partial \log F}{\partial \log P_f}$ ;

$e_{P_m M}$ = price elasticity of demand for good $M = \dfrac{\partial \log M}{\partial \log P_m}$ ;

$k_f$ = percent of budget spent on good $F$;

$k_m$ = percent of budget spent on good $M$;

$I$ = income = $P_f F + P_m M$;

$e_{IF}$ = income elasticity of good in fixed supply $= \dfrac{\partial \log F}{\partial \log I}$ ;

$e_{IM}$ = income elasticity of manufactured goods $= \dfrac{\partial \log M}{\partial \log I}$ ;

$e_{P_f M} = \dfrac{\text{cross elasticity of demand for manufactured}}{\text{goods and the price of good in fixed supply}} = \dfrac{\partial \log M}{\partial \log P_f}$ ;

* My special thanks to Robert H. Haveman who collaborated on an earlier draft of this model.

$$e_{P_mF} = \frac{\text{cross elasticity of demand for good in fixed}}{\text{supply and the price of manufactured goods}} = \frac{\partial \log F}{\partial \log P_m};$$

$$\sigma = \frac{\text{elasticity of substitution between the good in}}{\text{fixed supply and the manufactured good; that is,}}$$

$$= \frac{\dfrac{d\,(F/M)}{(F/M)}}{\dfrac{d\,(MRS_{FM})}{MRS_{FM}}}$$

where $$MRS_{FM} = -\frac{dF}{dM} = \frac{\text{marginal utility of } M}{\text{marginal utility of } F} = \frac{\dfrac{\partial U}{\partial M}}{\dfrac{\partial U}{\partial F}}$$

where $U$ = utility.

Note: $0 \le \sigma \le \infty$ ; $\sigma = 0$; $F$ and $M$ are not substitutable; and $\sigma = \infty$ when $F$ amd $M$ are perfect substitutes.

## General Equilibrium Conditions for a Two-Good World

In 1934, Hicks and Allen derived a set of four independent equations that may be used to describe the consumption side of two-good economies under appropriate conditions.[1] Their system, in which community preferences can be analyzed by considering a representative individual, is represented by equations (1) to (4).

*Hicks-Allen Equations:*

(1) $$k_f\, e_{IF} + k_m\, e_{IM} = 1\,,$$

(2) $$k_f + k_m = 1\,,$$

(3) $$k_f\, e_{P_fF} + k_m\, e_{P_fM} = -k_f\,,$$

(4) $$k_f\, e_{P_mF} + k_m\, e_{P_mM} = -k_m\,.$$

Equations (1) to (4) may be further combined to form equations (3') and (4'), which we designate as the Slutsky-Schultz Equations. These equations, along with equations (1) and (2), express an equivalent system of four independent equations.

[1] There are several major sources for the relationships designated Hicks-Allen and Slutsky-Schultz. For example, see H. Wold and L. Jureen, *Demand Analysis* (New York: John Wiley & Sons, 1953); J. R. Hicks and R. G. D. Allen, "A Reconsideration of the Theory of Value," *Economica*, New Series, 1934.

*Slutsky-Schultz Equations:*

$$(3') \qquad\qquad e_{IF} + e_{P_fF} + e_{P_mF} = 0$$

$$(4') \qquad\qquad e_{IM} + e_{P_fM} + e_{P_mM} = 0$$

If the economy is in equilibrium, the system represented by equations (1) to (4)—or by (1), (2), (3'), and (4')—can be converted to a system that is analogous to the income and substitution effects of microeconomics by adding another factor—the elasticity of substitution ($\sigma$). The set of four independent equations so derived is labeled Hicks-Allen II and shown in equations (5) to (8).

*Hicks-Allen II:*

$$(5) \qquad\qquad -e_{P_fF} = k_f\, e_{IF} + (1 - k_f)\sigma,$$

$$(6) \qquad\qquad -e_{P_fM} = k_f\, e_{IM} - k_f\sigma,$$

$$(7) \qquad\qquad -e_{P_mF} = k_m\, e_{IF} - k_m\sigma,$$

$$(8) \qquad\qquad -e_{P_mM} = k_m\, e_{IM} + (1 - k_m)\sigma.$$

Equations (5) to (8) plus equation (1) comprise the Hicks-Allen II model, which has nine parameters and five equations (instead of eight parameters and four equations as in the two preceding systems). Four parameters must be prespecified in order to determine a unique equilibrium solution for the remaining five parameters.

As Hicks and Allen point out, the elasticity of substitution in a two-good world is restricted in sign. According to their definition, goods can only be competitive in a two-good world; consideration of complementary relationships requires at least a three-good world. The restriction (i.e., $0 \leq \sigma \leq \infty$) is a definite limitation on all two-good worlds. It should be noted, however, that the signs of $\partial F/\partial P_m$ and $\partial M/\partial P_f$ need not be positive.[2] If the elasticity of substitution ($\sigma$) is numerically large, i.e., if it is more important than the income elasticities ($e_{IF}$ and $e_{IM}$), the cross-partial derivatives will be positive. Such cases are normally expected. However, if the income elasticities are at least as important in magnitude as the elasticity of substitution ($\sigma$) the cross-partial derivatives can be of either sign, and need not agree in sign.

[2] For a further discussion and clarification of this point, see: J. M. Henderson and R. Quandt, *Microeconomic Theory* (New York: McGraw-Hill Book Company, 2nd edition, 1971).

## Technological Change and Its Effect on the
## Price of Goods in Fixed Supply

The case examined here is an economy with two goods. The supply of one of these goods is fixed; the supply of the other is expandable. Technological change is exogenously introduced, and it reduces the relative price of the manufactured good, $M$. The good in fixed supply, $F$, has an income elasticity greater than that of the manufactured good and in these circumstances is a luxury good relative to $M$. A smaller portion of the representative consumer's budget is spent on the good in fixed supply; i.e., $k_f > k_m$. Since there are only two goods, the equations discussed above apply.

If income (money) is assumed to be constant and entirely expended on goods $M$ and $F$, and if the price of manufactured goods falls, economic theory indicates that there will be a movement along the demand curve for manufactured goods (from $A$ to $B$ in Appendix Figure B.1). The amount of money spent on $M$ after such a price change depends upon the price elasticity of demand for good $M$. If $|e_{P_m M}|$ equals one, there will be no change in the percentage of income $(k_m)$ spent on good $M$ and therefore on $F$. If $|e_{P_m M}|$ is less than one, total expenditure on good $M$ will decline; therefore $k_m$ will decline and [from equation (2)] $k_f$ will increase. If $k_f$ increases, this implies that the demand curve for $F$ will shift out from the origin. Note that the opposite effect will also hold if $|e_{P_m M}|$ exceeds one.

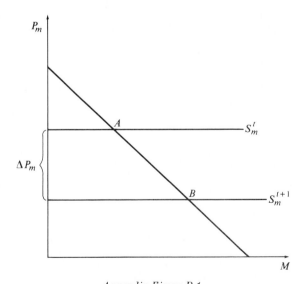

*Appendix Figure B.1.*

*Summary of Conditions for $dP_F > 0$:*

If                    $e_{P_m M} < 1$        and        $dP_m < 0$,        (assumption 1)

then                                $\Delta k_f > 0$

and                              $\Delta$ demand for $F > 0$.

In other words this result means that if there are two goods in the economy and the one with a price-inelastic demand experiences a price decline, the demand for the second good will increase.

Two additional determinants of relative shifts in demand schedules
are the two income elasticities of demand for the two goods. If good $F$ is
a relative "luxury good" in the sense that $e_{IF} > 1$, it follows from equation (1) (assuming that $k_f$ and $k_m$ are not zero) that $e_{IM} < 1$ (assumption
2). Recalling equation (4') and using the case in which the producible
good has an inelastic price elasticity (assumption 1), the following conditions can be derived:

(4')                        $e_{IM} + e_{P_f M} + e_{P_m M} = 0$

$$e_{P_f M} = -e_{IM} - e_{P_m M},$$

since:                            $0 < e_{IM} < 1$                    (assumption 2)

$$-1 < e_{P_m M} < 0$$                    (assumption 1)

then:

(a) if    $e_{IM} = |e_{P_m M}|$,    $e_{P_f M} = 0$,

(b) if    $e_{IM} < |e_{P_m M}|$,    $e_{P_f M} > 0$,

(c) if    $e_{IM} > |e_{P_m M}|$,    $e_{P_f M} < 0$.

When $e_{P_f M} > 0$ [case (b)], it follows that an increase in the quantity of $M$
purchased is accompanied by an increase in the willingness to pay for
good $F$. Therefore the demand for the good in fixed supply shifts away
from the horizontal or quantity axis. In other words when a manufactured good has a price decline and an income elasticity that is smaller in
absolute value than its price elasticity, the demand for the good in fixed
supply is induced to increase.

If an additional assumption is considered, namely, that a greater portion of the budget is spent on manufactured goods, i.e., $k_m > k_f$ (assumption 3), then $e_{P_m F}$ can be analyzed. Consider equation (4):

(4)                        $k_f\, e_{P_m F} + k_m\, e_{P_m M} = -k_m$

(4*)    $\therefore$                    $k_f(e_{P_m F}) = -k_m(1 + e_{P_m M}).$

From assumption 1:

$$-1 < e_{P_m M} < 0.$$

Therefore:
$$1 > (1 + e_{P_m M}) > 0,$$

From assumption 3:

$$k_m > k_f > 0,$$

Substituting in equation (4*):

$\therefore$
$$e_{P_m F} < 0,$$

and

$$|e_{P_m F}| > |1 + e_{P_m M}|.$$

If $k_f$ is small relative to $k_m$ and $e_{P_m M}$ is inelastic, then $e_{P_m F} < 0$, and a decline in the price of good $M (dP_m < 0)$ results in an increase in the demand for the good in fixed supply ($F$).

It should be noted that the three assumptions are interdependent because the systems are simultaneous partial differential equation systems. Consideration can now be given to two important parameters that have been ignored since early in the discussion: the price elasticity of demand for the good in fixed supply ($e_{P_f F}$) and the elasticity of substitution between $F$ and $M$ ($\sigma$). These parameters, whose magnitudes are implicitly restricted by the values and signs of the parameters used in the three assumptions, are considered below.

Consider equation (3):

(3)
$$k_f\, e_{P_f F} + k_m\, e_{P_f M} = -k_f,$$

(3*)   $\therefore$
$$e_{P_f M} = \frac{-k_f(1 + e_{P_f F})}{k_m}.$$

When the conditions described above hold:

$$k_f < k_m$$

and

$$e_{P_f M} > 0.$$

By substituting these conditions into equation (3*), it follows that:

$$|e_{P_f F}| > 1.$$

Therefore, the price elasticity of demand for the good in fixed supply is implicitly assumed to be price elastic when the three assumptions represented by the conditions considered above are explicitly made in a two-good world.

Furthermore, this information may be used to determine the size of $e_{P_fF}$ relative to $e_{IF}$ under these conditions. Using equation (3′), the following expression can be derived:

$$(3') \qquad\qquad e_{IF} + e_{P_fF} + e_{P_mF} = 0,$$

$$\therefore \qquad\qquad e_{P_mF} = -e_{IF} - e_{P_fF}.$$

Since $\qquad\qquad e_{IF} > 1,$

and $\qquad\qquad e_{P_fF} < -1,$

when $\qquad\qquad e_{P_mF} < 0,$

then $\qquad\qquad 1 < |e_{P_fF}| < e_{IF}.$

By using equation (4′) we can similarly deduce under these conditions that:

when $\qquad\qquad e_{P_fM} > 0,$

$$1 > |e_{P_mM}| > e_{IM}.$$

Finally, the magnitude of $\sigma$, the elasticity of substitution, implied by these conditions can be considered. Using equation (5), the following expression can be derived:

$$(5) \qquad\qquad -e_{P_fF} = k_f\, e_{IF} + (1 - k_f)\sigma.$$

Since $\qquad\qquad k_f < (1 - k_f) = k_m$

and $\qquad\qquad e_{IF} > 1,$

then $\qquad\qquad \sigma > 0.$

Furthermore,

since $\qquad\qquad -e_{P_fF} > 1$

and $\qquad\qquad e_{IF} > -e_{P_fF}$

$$k_f + (1 - k_f) \equiv 1,$$

then $\qquad\qquad e_{IF} > \sigma.$

In order to compare $e_{IM}$ and $\sigma$, consider equation (6):

$$(6) \qquad\qquad -e_{P_fM} = k_f\, e_{IM} - k_f\sigma$$

$$= k_f(e_{IM} - \sigma).$$

If $\qquad\qquad -e_{P_fM} < 0,$

and $\qquad\qquad e_{IM} > 0,$

$$\sigma > 0.$$

Additionally, it follows that:

$$\sigma > e_{IM},$$

∴                    $$e_{IF} > \sigma > e_{IM}.$$

By way of summary, in a two-good world when one good is a relative luxury good and nonproducible and the two goods are at least partially substitutable (i.e., $\sigma \neq 0$), a drop in the price of the producible good will cause a shift in the demand for the good in fixed supply in both the price and quantity dimensions when:

(a)                    $$k_m > k_f,$$

(b)                    $$e_{IF} > \sigma > e_{IM},$$

(c)            $$e_{IF} > |e_{P_fF}| > 1 > |e_{P_mM}| > e_{IM}.$$

Finally, it should be pointed out that these conditions, although sufficient, need not be necessary. That is, if some of the components of the shift in the demand for the good in fixed supply $(D_f)$ were negative and others positive, the net result could still be a positive shift in $D_f$. The case considered above was extreme in the sense that all the factors considered resulted in a positive shift in the demand for good $F$. This was done deliberately, as stated at the outset. To understand an economy with a nonproducible good more fully, it is, however, more important to extend the analysis to the more realistic case of an $n$-good world in which complementary and independent goods may exist than to consider other cases in a two-good world in which there are conflicting positive and negative forces, which may act upon $D_f$. (For a more detailed discussion of such systems, see the following paper by V. Kerry Smith.)

## REFERENCES

Arrow, K. J. 1968. "Optimal Capital Policy with Irreversible Investment," in J. N. Wolfe, ed., *Value, Capital, and Growth*. Chicago: Aldine-Atherton. Pp. 1–20.

———, and A. C. Fisher. "Environmental Preservation, Uncertainty, and Irreversibility," *Quarterly Journal of Economics* (forthcoming).

———, and M. Kurz. 1970. "Optimal Growth with Irreversible Investment in a Ramsey Model," *Econometrica*, vol. 38 (March 1970), pp. 331–44.

Barnett, H. J., and Chandler Morse. 1963. *Scarcity and Growth*. Baltimore: Johns Hopkins Press for Resources for the Future.

Brown, W. G., A. Singh, and E. N. Castle. 1965. "Net Economic Value of the Oregon Salmon-Steelhead Sport Fishery," *Journal of Wildlife Management*, vol. 29 (April 1965), pp. 66–79.

Burt, O. R., and R. Cummings. 1970. "Production and Investment in Natural Resource Industries," *American Economic Review*, vol. 60 (September 1970), pp. 576–90.

Cicchetti, C. J., J. J. Seneca, and P. Davidson. 1969. *The Demand and Supply of Outdoor Recreation*. Washington, D.C.: U.S. Bureau of Outdoor Recreation.

———, and A. M. Freeman III. 1971. "Option Demand and Consumer Surplus," *Quarterly Journal of Economics*, vol. 85 (August 1971), pp. 528–39.

Eckstein, Otto. 1958. *Water Resource Development*. Cambridge, Mass.: Harvard University Press.

———. 1968. In *Economic Analysis of Public Investment Decisions: Interest Rate Policy and Discounting Analysis*. Hearings before the Joint Economic Committee, 90th Cong. 2 sess. Washington, D.C.

Federal Power Commission. 1970. *In the Matter of: Pacific Northwest Power Company and Washington Public Power Supply System*. Hearings before the Federal Power Commission. Washington, D.C.

Harberger, A. 1968. In *Economic Analysis of Public Investment Decisions: Interest Rate Policy and Discounting Analysis*. Hearings before the Joint Economic Committee, 90th Cong. 2 sess. Washington, D.C.

Hicks, J. R., and R. G. D. Allen. 1934. "A Reconsideration of the Theory of Value," *Economica* (February 1934), New Series 1.

Hoch, Irving. 1962. "Economic Analysis of Wilderness Areas," in *Wilderness and Recreation: A Report on Resources, Values, and Problems*. ORRRC Study Report No. 3. Washington, D.C., pp. 203–64.

Hufschmidt, M. M., J. V. Krutilla, and J. Margolis. 1961. "Standards and Criteria for Formulating and Evaluating Federal Water Resources Developments." Report to Bureau of the Budget. Washington, D.C.

Krutilla, J. V. 1967. "Conservation Reconsidered," *American Economic Review*, vol. 57 (September 1967), pp. 777–86.

———, and Otto Eckstein. 1958. *Multiple Purpose River Development*. Baltimore: Johns Hopkins Press for Resources for the Future.

Mathews, S. B., and G. S. Brown. 1970. *Economic Evaluation of the 1967 Sport Salmon Fisheries of Washington*. Washington Department of Fisheries Technical Report 2.

McKean, R. N. 1958. *Efficiency in Government Through Systems Analysis*. New York: Wiley.

Mishan, E. J. 1971. "The Postwar Literature on Externalities: An Interpretive Essay," *Journal of Economic Literature*, vol. 9 (March 1971), pp. 1–28.

Pearse, P. H. 1968. "A New Approach to the Evaluation of Non-Priced Recreation Resources," *Land Economics*, vol. 44 (February 1968), pp. 87–99.

Plourde, C. G. 1970. "A Simple Model of Replenishable Natural Resource Exploitation," *American Economic Review*, vol. 60 (June 1970), pp. 518–22.

Pontryagin, L. S., et al. 1962. *The Mathematical Theory of Optimal Processes*. New York: Interscience.

Potter, N., and F. T. Christy, Jr. 1962. *Trends in Natural Resource Commodities.* Baltimore: Johns Hopkins Press for Resources for the Future.

*Proposed Practices for Economic Analysis of River Basin Projects.* 1958. Report to the Inter Agency Committee on Water Resources, prepared by the Subcommittee on Evaluation Standards. Washington, D.C.

Seagraves, J. A. 1970. "More on the Social Rate of Discount," *Quarterly Journal of Economics,* vol. 84 (August 1970), pp. 430–50.

Smith, V. L. 1968. "Economics of Production from Natural Resources," *American Economic Review,* vol. 58 (June 1968), pp. 409–31.

Steiner, P. O. 1965. "The Role of Alternative Cost in Project Design and Selection," *Quarterly Journal of Economics,* vol. 79 (August 1965), pp. 417–30.

U.S. Senate. 1962. *Policies, Standards, and Procedures in the Formulation, Evaluation, and Review of Plans for Use and Development of Water and Related Land Resources.* Prepared under the direction of the President's Water Resources Council. Senate Document No. 97, 87 Cong. 2 sess. Washington, D.C.

———. 1964. "Evaluation Standards for Primary Outdoor Recreation Benefits." Supplement No. 1, Ad Hoc Water Resources Council. Washington, D.C.

Wold, H., and L. Jureen. 1953. *Demand Analysis.* New York: Wiley.

# 2
# The Effect of Technological Change on Different Uses of Environmental Resources

V.  KERRY  SMITH [*]

Natural endowments that are given and fixed—combined with accumulating knowledge and skills—provide the sources of all the goods and services on which the community depends. While the fixity of natural resources lay at the bottom of Malthus's concern, his predictions seem not to have been borne out. As Barnett and Morse (1963) have argued, the advances in scientific knowledge and mastery of techniques have been sufficiently pervasive and rapid to allow for an ever expanding supply of natural resource commodities at constant or falling supply prices. Technical change has thus provided the means with which to increase per capita production and consumption of final goods in the United States in spite of an increasing population. But increases in the standard of living have not dispelled a nagging anxiety that the quality of life may not necessarily be improved (Barnett and Morse, p. 252).

A reason for this paradox, suggested by Krutilla (1967), is that technological progress may not have the same effect on each use to which the natural endowments are put. The services of natural endowments may serve as factor inputs and be subjected to further processing into final consumption goods. Or they may function as sources of amenity services, providing opportunities for recreation, viewing wildlife or scenery or

* Economist, Resources for the Future, Inc.

*Author's note.* The research reported in this paper was supported by a grant from Resources for the Future, Inc. to the author at Bowling Green State University. Clifford Russell and Karl-Göran Mäler provided a careful and penetrating review of the paper. Thanks are also due John V. Krutilla, Charles J. Cicchetti, and Vernon Ruttan for their comments on earlier drafts. All remaining errors rest with the author.

even for breathing clean air, which enter directly into the utility function of final consumers. Advances in production technology will tend to impinge on produced goods and services but not on amenity services, which are gifts of nature and depend on the accidents of biological evolution, geomorphology, and ecological succession and are not producible by man (Krutilla, Cicchetti, Freeman, and Russell, 1972). Since the supply of amenity services derived from natural areas is not generally capable of augmentation, these services remain fixed in the sense perceived by Malthus. Further, if they are to remain of constant quality, there is no scope for technological advance to provide for their expansion or for their replacement if the environment on which they depend is irreversibly altered. Herein lies an asymmetry in the implication of technological progress for the value of natural endowments when their services are used for mutually exclusive purposes.

This proposition has been employed in the evaluation of the two incompatible alternative uses of a scenic area, i.e., the Hells Canyon reach of the Snake River in Idaho and Oregon (see the preceding paper by Fisher, Krutilla, and Cicchetti). One alternative is represented by the possibility of developing the hydroelectric potential of the Canyon by damming the river in that reach. The other is represented by preserving the area for its several amenity services. The benefits from preservation are measured, using conventional notions of consumer surplus, by the area under the aggregate demand curve for the services rendered by the Canyon preserved in its current state. Over time, shifts in demand are postulated to occur. The quantity of services demanded is assumed to increase owing to changes in tastes and growth in population. Also, upward shift in prices, or a vertical shift in the demand function, is assumed to be related to technical change, which results in increases in per capita income.

The postulated upward shift in prices of amenity services relative to goods and services generally is predicated on three conditions that are sufficient to guarantee such price behavior (see Fisher, Krutilla, Cicchetti, App. B). These conditions are: (1) there are no good substitutes for the amenity services in question; (2) income and initial price elasticities of demand are larger for amenity services than for produced goods; and (3) a smaller fraction of the budget is spent on nonproduced services in fixed supply than on produced goods. These conditions are derived from a general statement of the character of demand in a two-good model. But, as the model does not address the nature of the supply side of the market for goods and services, it is not possible to infer a direct relationship between the rate of price appreciation and the rate of technological change. In addition, it is difficult to assess the overall sensitivity of price behavior to each of the separate conditions derived. But an equally serious limitation of this two-good model is that it permits neither an adequate investigation of the effects of substitutes on the price behavior of the amenity services nor the variation of income, price, and cross elasticities of demand as the level of community income changes. In some cases, this may not be significant, but in others it may.

The objective of this paper is to integrate these factors within a complete general equilibrium framework in an analysis of the price behavior of amenity services. Accordingly, both supply and demand influences are included in the equilibrium solutions. While general equilibrium models are easy to formulate in concept, they are often difficult to work with.

In order to avoid operational difficulties, the models presented in this paper will be cast from a similar mold. The approach taken herein will be to work with "summary functions" for the demand side and supply side of the market. Since the primary interest is with the effect of demand and supply parameters upon relative prices, an attempt is made to choose a community utility function that will provide the most "realistic" pattern of elasticities. This approach assumes that the community's actions conform to the assigned utility function. However, it does not necessarily follow that this function is derived by aggregating individual preferences. On the supply side, in lieu of specifying individual production relationships and considering firm structure and factor market complexities, I have chosen a summary of the outcome of all the processes, which enumerates what may be derived from them. Thus, we have a general equilibrium solution without many of its "headaches." However, this all comes at some cost. We must assume the supply mechanism works so as to give our summary function. This assumption is also true of demand. Then, without stating the origin of technical change in the complex of production procedures, I merely discuss its effect upon the summary function. The analysis is comparative static with a one-period time horizon. Thus, questions of an optimal control character are not considered.

As noted earlier, the solutions are sensitive to the specification of the "summary functions." A number of alternative specifications have been considered. However, two functional forms are explicitly presented. One of these is a homogeneous function with two commodities. Since the effects of this specification do not change with increases in the number of goods, it can serve two functions: (1) it illustrates, when compared with the second model, the general limitations of a two-good model; (2) it indicates the severe restrictions homogeneity of degree one imposes upon the nature of demand. The second model is a three-good model, which can be generalized to $n$-goods. The community utility function is nonhomogeneous. Moreover, it has as one specific case Houthakker's (1960) additive preferences demand structure. The first two sections of the paper describe each of the models and the equilibrium solutions they imply. Section III derives the rate of change in relative prices given asymmetric technical change in each model. The last section summarizes the results and their implications.

## I. The Two-Good World

*Assumptions and Framework*

The simplest method for analyzing the asymmetric implications of technology is to consider their effects in the context of a two-commodity model.[1] Krutilla (1967) has provided the framework and key components that must be considered in such a conceptualization. Assume one of the two goods consists of the services of unspoiled natural endowments. An example of such an environmental resource might be a wilderness area with unique attributes such as Hells Canyon. When the area is used for certain recreation pursuits or for scientific purposes, its services cannot be expanded or reproduced.[2] Increased productivity as a result of technological change is *not* possible with such goods. The supply of services of homogeneous quality from these natural endowments is inelastic and unchanging with time. In contrast, if we assume the second commodity in the two-sector world is a fabricated or manufactured good whose production may be augmented by technical change, a dichotomy is established on the supply side of the model. The supply of manufactured goods responds to changes in technology through the increased productivity they engender, while the ability to supply additional wilderness experiences does not. In order to model the impact of this asymmetry several restrictive assumptions shall be made. The outputs of both sectors will be assumed to be homogeneous and infinitely divisible through time. The world is assumed to be "neoclassical," and production and consumption externalities are considered nonexistent.[3] Thus we are not allowing intertemporal production externalities. The supply of factor

---

[1] Gannon (1967) has attempted a graphic model of this problem with little definite results. Also see Smith and Krutilla (forthcoming).

[2] See Baumol (1967) and Kelso (1971).

[3] This assumption ignores the fact that production decisions may have irreversible consequences as noted by Krutilla (1967). In effect a decision in period $t$ to produce a fabricated good may prevent the community from deciding to alter its consumption pattern in $t + k$ to natural endowments. The reasoning is straightforward. The decision to produce the fabricated good made irreversible reduction in the supply of services of the natural endowment. For some initial analysis of this problem see Smith and Krutilla (forthcoming).

inputs for the production of the manufactured good will be assumed constant, so that increases in the commodity's supply are solely the result of technology. All factor inputs will be fully employed and the locus of production possibilities for the community under study is the maximum level of output for each commodity combination with the existing technology. If we assume the factor inputs underlying the transformation function are allocated efficiently, then the convexity property of the locus is upheld (see Kelly, 1969), and may be represented in Figure 2.1 as contour $AB$. Along the vertical axis we have measured the amenity services derived from natural endowments ($F$) and available for direct consumption. The horizontal axis measures the quantity of the manufactured good ($M$) available. The transformation curve is a picture of the best a community can achieve with its existing technology and factor supplies. For our purpose, the specification of both the production functions and the factor markets will be assumed to be such that they yield the neoclassical production possibility frontier.

Technical change will be exogenously given in this model and will be disembodied from the factor inputs. That is, we are assuming all tech-

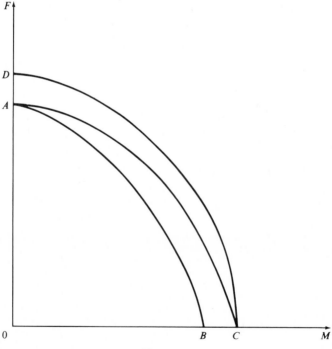

*Figure 2.1.*

nological change consists of better methods of production and organization that improve the efficiency of all factors, without regard to their age.[4] The focus of attention will be upon the results of technology for each of the two commodities. Consequently the effects of a changing technology upon the nature of the productive structure and the underlying production decisions is left unexplained, subsumed in the specified path of the production possibility frontier.

The demand side of this commodity model will be described in terms of community indifference curves (CIC). The use of this approach does not necessarily require that the utility function be derived directly from that of the individuals within the community. Rather, we need only assume that the society acts *as if* the function describes its behavior. If we choose to link the community function directly with those of its individual members, we must assume identical tastes. Therefore the social utility of the last dollar of income is the same across all individuals. Baumol (1949–50) and Samuelson (1956) have discussed these conditions so that further elaboration is unnecessary. The link between the community's utility function and the resulting demand structure is found in the work of Hicks and Allen (1934). Before presenting the relationships between income, price, and cross elasticities, a few definitions must be stated. First, the elasticity of substitution ($\sigma$) between $F$ and $M$ is defined to be the percent change in the production mix ($M/F$) relative to the percent change in the marginal rate of substitution ($MRS_{MF}$). Equation (1) expresses this definition mathematically.

$$(1) \qquad \sigma = \frac{d(M/F)}{M/F} \cdot \frac{\dfrac{dM}{dF}}{d\left(\dfrac{dM}{dF}\right)} = \frac{d\left(\dfrac{F}{M}\right)}{\dfrac{F}{M}} \cdot \frac{\dfrac{dF}{dM}}{d\left(\dfrac{dF}{dM}\right)}.$$

The curvature of the CIC contours assures that the elasticity will be greater than zero. It is seen to be independent of the units of measurement of $F$ and $M$ as well as symmetrical. This parameter is an index of the curvature of a single indifference curve. A measure of the distance between indifference curves can be obtained through the Hicks-Allen coefficients of income variation, defined in (2a) and (2b).

$$(2a) \qquad \rho_F = -\frac{M}{MRS_{FM}} \cdot \frac{\partial}{\partial M}(MRS_{FM}),$$

$$(2b) \qquad \rho_M = \frac{F}{MRS_{FM}} \cdot \frac{\partial}{\partial F}(MRS_{FM}).$$

[4] See Ferguson (1969) and Hamberg (1971) for discussion of this.

Both coefficients cannot be negative. In the case of normal (e.g., non-Giffen goods) they will be positive. It is possible to define the income elasticities as well as the price and cross elasticities in terms of these three indexes and the proportions of the budget spent on each good. Thus in equations (3a) and (3b) we define the income elasticities of demand:

$$(3a) \qquad E_Y(F) = \frac{Y}{F} \cdot \frac{\partial F}{\partial Y} = \rho_F \cdot \sigma,$$

$$(3b) \qquad E_Y(M) = \frac{Y}{M} \cdot \frac{\partial M}{\partial Y} = \rho_M \cdot \sigma,$$

where $Y$ = income (money).

The price and cross-elasticities may also be defined by making use of an equilibrium condition $[K_F E_Y(F) + K_M E_Y(M) = 1]$:

$$(4) \qquad E_{P_F}(F) = K_F E_Y(F) + (1 - K_F)\,\sigma,$$

$$(5) \qquad E_{P_F}(M) = K_F E_Y(M) - K_F\sigma,$$

$$(6) \qquad E_{P_M}(M) = K_M E_Y(M) + (1 - K_M)\,\sigma,$$

$$(7) \qquad E_{P_M}(F) = K_M E_Y(F) - K_M\sigma,$$

where: $\quad P_F$ = price of $F$,

$\qquad\qquad P_M$ = price of $M$,

$$K_F = \frac{P_F \cdot F}{Y},$$

$$K_M = \frac{P_M \cdot M}{Y},$$

$$E_{P_F}(F) = -\frac{P_F}{F} \cdot \frac{\partial F}{\partial P_F} = \text{price elasticity of demand for } F,$$

$$E_{P_M}(M) = -\frac{P_M}{M} \cdot \frac{\partial M}{\partial P_M} = \text{price elasticity of demand for } M,$$

$$E_{P_F}(M) = -\frac{P_F}{M} \cdot \frac{\partial M}{\partial P_F} = \text{cross elasticity } M \text{ for } F,$$

$$E_{P_M}(F) = -\frac{P_M}{F} \cdot \frac{\partial F}{\partial P_M} = \text{cross elasticity } F \text{ for } M.$$

For any functional form assumed for the CIC mapping it is possible to derive the three indexes and therefore to structure the underlying pattern of community demand.

*The Model with a Constant Elasticity of
Substitution (CES) Utility Index*

A comparative static analysis of the model is straightforward. Summary measures are specified for the consumption side of the market and then of the production side. Once these are given, it is possible to establish a general equilibrium solution to the system, given the absence of imperfections. Such a solution calls for the equality of the marginal rate of transformation of the goods ($M$ and $F$) from production to the marginal rate of substitution in consumption. Assume that the CIC mapping is defined by a set of constant elasticity of substitution ($\sigma$) indifference curves (CES), given in equation (8).

$$(8) \qquad U = D\left[F^{\frac{1+B}{B}} + CM^{\frac{1+B}{B}}\right]^{\frac{B}{1+B}},$$

where:  $U$ = level of community welfare,

$D$ = neutral utility shift parameter,

$C$ = biased utility shift parameter,

$B = -\sigma$, elasticity of substitution; $\sigma > 0$.

The form of this function is similar to that used by Arrow, Chenery, Minhas, and Solow (1961) in their study of international production patterns.[5] In order to derive the equilibrium commodity mix and price ratio it is convenient to assume a specific functional form for the locus of production possibilities. Powell and Gruen (1969) have specified one useful form for such a frontier. They define it as the constant elasticity of transformation production possibility curve. The elasticity of transformation is defined in an analogous fashion to that of the elasticity of substitution. However, the elasticity is negative because of the curvature of the production contour. Equation (9) defines the elasticity, which is also symmetrical with respect to $M$ and $F$. As the absolute value of the elasticity increases, the frontier approaches a downward-sloping straight line. Accordingly, it is a measure of the curvature of the production possibility locus.

$$(9) \qquad \tau = \frac{d(M/F)}{\frac{M}{F}} \cdot \frac{\frac{dM}{dF}}{d\left(\frac{dM}{dF}\right)}, \qquad (\tau < 0)$$

[5] Inada (1968) has employed a Cobb-Douglas utility function for a one-sector growth model to demonstrate the relationship between traditional growth theory results and analysis of the character described herein.

A shift in the curve away from the origin indicates, in our case, a change in technology. However, it is possible to allow for quality change. Suppose the units of measure for $F$ and $M$ include a quality dimension as well as quantity dimension; then a reduction in the quality of one good would be interpreted as a lessening in its effective supply. The functional form for the Powell-Gruen frontier is given in equation (10).

(10)
$$\frac{1}{A} \cdot M^{1-1/\tau} + F^{1-1/\tau} = R\left(1 - 1/\tau\right),$$

where:         $A$ = bias shift parameter,

                    $R$ = neutral shift parameter,

                    $\tau$ = elasticity of transformation; $\tau < 0$.

An increase in the parameter $A$ may be interpreted as a pivoting in the production frontier similar to that depicted in Figure 1 from contour $AB$ to $AC$. Alternatively a change in $R$ exhibits a parallel shift in the locus similar to the movement from $AB$ to $DC$.

When equation (8) is solved for the marginal rate of substitution and equation (10) for the marginal rate of transformation, equations (11) and (12) result.

(11)
$$MRS_{MF} = -\frac{dM}{dF} = \frac{1}{C}\left[\frac{M}{F}\right]^{1/\sigma},$$

(12)
$$MRT_{MF} = -\frac{dM}{dF} = A\left[\frac{M}{F}\right]^{1/\tau}.$$

The equilibrium conditions call for equality of (11) and (12). Thus the corresponding commodity mix and price ratio are:

(13a)
$$\frac{M}{F} = [CA]^{\gamma}, \qquad\qquad\qquad (\gamma > 0)$$

(13b)
$$\frac{P_F}{P_M} = A^{\delta}\, C^{r}, \qquad\qquad\qquad (\delta > 0,\ r < 0)$$

where:
$$\gamma = \frac{\tau \cdot \sigma}{\tau - \sigma},$$

$$\delta = \frac{\tau}{\tau - \sigma},$$

$$r = \frac{\sigma}{\tau - \sigma}.$$

The comparative static solutions for both price ratio and commodity ratio are related to the bias parameters in consumption ($C$) and produc-

Table 2.1. Single Period Biased Technical Change

| | Period $t$ | Period $t+1$ |
|---|---|---|
| Commodity ratio $(M/F)$ | $C^\gamma A_0^\gamma e^{\gamma g t}$ | $C^\gamma A_0^\gamma e^{\gamma g t} e^{\gamma g}$ |
| Price ratio $(P_F/P_M)$ | $C^r A_0^\delta e^{\delta g t}$ | $C^r A_0^\delta e^{\delta g t} e^{\delta g}$ |

tion $(A)$ and the respective elasticities. This conclusion becomes quite important if the incidence of technical change is not uniform across both goods. That is, if technology through time favors the production of $M$ and not $F$, as we have suggested earlier, then the terminus of the production contour on the $M$ axis will shift out while that of $F$ remains stationary. The change from contour $AB$ to $AC$ is an example. Increases in the bias parameter in production $(A)$ will provide the same result. If we assume a time path for the bias parameter $A$, then the effects of asymmetric change may be illustrated. Consider the specification in equation (14).

(14) $$A = A_0 e^{gt},$$

where:  $A_0$ = initial level of bias,

$g$ = rate of growth in bias,

$t$ = time,

$e$ = base of natural logarithm system.

(15) $$\frac{\frac{dA}{dt}}{A} = g.$$

The commodity mix in period $t$ relative to $t+1$ and corresponding price ratios are given in Table 2.1.

The equilibrium commodity mix will increase. Moreover the relative price of $F$ will increase. In the limit as $t$ is allowed to grow without bound we find that the consumption of $M$ will also grow without bound and the relative price of $F$ will increase as well.[6] An important implicit assumption

---

[6] Clifford Russell and Karl-Göran Mäler have pointed out in this case the quantity of $F$ consumed as $t$ is allowed to grow may be different from zero.

Substituting from equation (13a) into the transformation function (10), it is possible to derive an expression for $F$ solely as a function of the parameters of the system.

$$F = \left[ \frac{R\left(1 - \frac{1}{\tau}\right)}{1 + C^\gamma \left(1 - \frac{1}{\tau}\right) \cdot A^{\frac{\tau(\sigma-1)}{\tau-\sigma}}} \right]^{\frac{\tau}{\tau-1}}$$

The limit of this expression as $t$ gets large can be determined by examining the exponent of $A$ (since this is the parameter we are allowing to grow over time). $F$ will approach zero only if the commodities $M$ and $F$ are substitutes, i.e., $\sigma > 1$. In the

Table 2.2. Nature of Demand with a CES Utility Map

| Commodity | $E_{P_i}(M)$ | $E_{P_i}(F)$ | $E_Y(i)$ |
|---|---|---|---|
| Manufactured($M$) | $K_M(1 - \sigma) + \sigma$ | $K_M(1 - \sigma)$ | 1 |
| Environmental service($F$) | $K_F(1 - \sigma)$ | $K_F(1 - \sigma) + \sigma$ | 1 |

of this conclusion is that the produced or manufactured good, $M$, is perishable in a given time period, so stocks may not be accumulated. In addition to this assumption there is a more important consideration. Implicit in the behavior of the system are the demand characteristics corresponding to the CES utility function. Accordingly, Table 2.2 presents the relationship of the price, income, and cross elasticities of demand corresponding to this utility function. They are derived from equations (1) through (7).

Since the utility functions imply unitary income elasticities, all Engel's curves are linear. Moreover the commodities are undistinguishable in terms of relative preferences, for given prices, as income increases. Thus the homogeneity specification is important. Additionally, the value of the elasticity of substitution is one determinant of the price and cross elasticities. Following Irving Fisher (1925) and Donald Katzner (1970), we can define the degree to which two goods are complementary in terms of the size of $\sigma$. All commodities are partially complements and substitutes, thus $\sigma$ measures degree of either characteristic which dominates. For example, a value of zero for the elasticity implies that the two goods are perfect complements; an infinitely large value implies that the two goods are perfect substitutes; and a value of one implies that they are independent. Substituting into the table with $\sigma = 1$, we find both cross elasticities become zero as we might suspect and both price elasticities are always unity. Most empirical research investigating the nature of the demand for the amenities derived from natural endowments in their preserved state indicates that a specification of unitary income elasticities is untenable. [7] Moreover, the overall rigidity in the price and cross elasticities gives little scope for variation when the attributes and therefore the uses of a particular environmental resource diverge.

## II. The Three-Good World

*Definitions*

Assume the economy now has three sectors that provide goods to enter the community's preference function. Two of these will retain the labels

cases where they are independent, $\sigma = 1$, or complementary, $\sigma < 1$, $F$ will have a non-zero limit. Further, in the independent case, $F$ will be a constant through time.

[7] See Cicchetti, Seneca, and Davidson (1969).

we used previously: the fabricated good ($M$) and the services of unique natural environments ($F$). The third commodity may take on a number of roles and will be designated $X$. For example, $X$ may be another manufactured good which is a good substitute for $M$, or it might function as artificially produced recreational amenity substituting for certain types of $F$. Alternatively $X$ might be a manufactured good that is a complement to $F$. For example, a boat and a river or lake are both required for boating. Less rigid complementary relationships are also possible. The equipment used in camping and backpacking exhibits a substantial variation across individuals.[8]

The utility index that is chosen to describe the community's preferences for these three goods will have a decided effect upon our ability to alter the nature of good $X$. For example, a homogeneous function would imply unitary income elasticities for all three goods and a fairly rigid structure of price and cross elasticities. A three-sector model requires some additional definitions and some increasing complexity.

First, the elasticity of substitution in a two-good world is both an index of the curvature of a given CIC curve at any point and a measure of the degree to which those goods are complements or substitutes. However, when we introduce another commodity we must distinguish the two. We are interested in paired comparisons for establishing the degree to which any two commodities are substitutes, and in the case of curvature we would like an index that would take into account curvature in all three planes at any point. Thus, we shall define the partial elasticity of substitution as the index for paired comparisons. This elasticity, defined in equation (16), is also equivalent to the negative of the Hicks-Allen elasticity of complementarity.

$$(16) \qquad \sigma_{ij} = \frac{X_1 f_1 + X_2 f_2 + \ldots + X_n f_n}{X_i X_j} \cdot \frac{R_{ij}}{R},$$

where:  $X_1, \ldots, X_n$ = commodities,

$f(X_1, \ldots, X_n)$ = utility function,

$f_i = \dfrac{\partial f}{\partial X_i},$

$f_{ij} = \dfrac{\partial^2 f}{\partial X_j\, \partial X_i}.$

[8] Preliminary results with a sample of recreationists at the Spanish Peaks wilderness area reinforce this observation.

$$
R = \det \begin{bmatrix}
0 & f_1 & f_2 \ldots f_n \\
f_1 & f_{11} & f_{12} \ldots f_{1n} \\
f_2 & f_{21} & f_{22} \ldots f_{2n} \\
\cdot & \cdot & \cdot \ldots \cdot \\
\cdot & \cdot & \cdot \ldots \cdot \\
\cdot & \cdot & \cdot \ldots \cdot \\
f_n & f_{n1} & f_{n2} \ldots f_{nn}
\end{bmatrix}
$$

$R_{ij}$ = determinant of the $ij$<sup>th</sup> cofactor of the bordered Hessian above.

In order to describe the curvature of the CIC utility surface, it is necessary to define the following index.

$$
(17) \quad \sigma' = \frac{MRS_{FM} \cdot MRS_{FX}}{F \cdot X \cdot M} \cdot \frac{F + MRS_{FM} \cdot M + MRS_{FX} \cdot F}{G},
$$

where: $MRS_{FM} = -\dfrac{dF}{dM}$ for constant $X$,

$MRS_{FX} = -\dfrac{dF}{dX}$ for constant $M$,

$$
G = \det \begin{bmatrix}
1 & MRS_{FM} & MRS_{FX} \\
\dfrac{\partial}{\partial F}(MRS_{FM}) & \dfrac{\partial}{\partial M}(MRS_{FM}) & \dfrac{\partial}{\partial X}(MRS_{FM}) \\
\dfrac{\partial}{\partial F}(MRS_{FX}) & \dfrac{\partial}{\partial M}(MRS_{FX}) & \dfrac{\partial}{\partial X}(MRS_{FX})
\end{bmatrix}
$$

The index $\sigma'$ indicates the mutual substitutability of $X$, $F$, and $M$. In contrast, the partial elasticity of substitution $\sigma_{ij}$ categorizes the degree of substitutability for particular cross-sections of the utility contour. For example, suppose we wanted to measure the degree of substitution between $M$ and $X$. We can measure in three different cross-sections, two of which may be represented by the partial elasticities of substitution. First we can measure along the $FM$ direction holding $X$ constant. This is partial elasticity $\sigma_{FM}$. Alternatively we can measure along the $XF$ direction holding $M$ constant. This is partial elasticity $\sigma_{FX}$. Finally we can measure along the $MX$ direction holding $F$ constant. We denote this index as $_{MX}\sigma_{MX}$ and define it in terms of the partial elasticities and portions of the budget spent on each good. For the three-good world, Hicks and Allen define twelve indexes of the complex of preferences. Given the specification of a utility function (the Hicks-Allen integrability condition), these twelve indexes can be reduced to nine.[9] Three relate to

[9] Hicks and Allen (1934) demonstrate the solution for this elasticity. However for our purposes it is not necessary to do so.

substitution between pairs of goods, three to the degree of complementarity, and three to the spacing of utility contours. In the two-good world the two indexes referring to the spacing of CIC surfaces were defined as coefficients of income variation. Once the model is generalized to include another commodity, it becomes necessary to generalize these definitions as in equations (18) through (20).

$$(18) \quad \rho_F = \frac{M \cdot X}{MRS_{FM} \cdot MRS_{FX}} \cdot \begin{vmatrix} \dfrac{\partial}{\partial M}(MRS_{FM}) & \dfrac{\partial}{\partial X}(MRS_{FM}) \\[2mm] \dfrac{\partial}{\partial M}(MRS_{FX}) & \dfrac{\partial}{\partial X}(MRS_{FX}) \end{vmatrix}$$

$$(19) \quad \rho_M = -\frac{F \cdot X}{MRS_{FM} \cdot MRS_{FX}} \cdot \begin{vmatrix} \dfrac{\partial}{\partial F}(MRS_{FM}) & \dfrac{\partial}{\partial X}(MRS_{FM}) \\[2mm] \dfrac{\partial}{\partial F}(MRS_{FX}) & \dfrac{\partial}{\partial X}(MRS_{FX}) \end{vmatrix}$$

$$(20) \quad \rho_X = \frac{F \cdot M}{MRS_{FM} \cdot MRS_{FX}} \cdot \begin{vmatrix} \dfrac{\partial}{\partial F}(MRS_{FM}) & \dfrac{\partial}{\partial M}(MRS_{FM}) \\[2mm] \dfrac{\partial}{\partial F}(MRS_{FX}) & \dfrac{\partial}{\partial M}(MRS_{FX}) \end{vmatrix}$$

All three coefficients are independent of the units of measurement and are positive in the normal case (non-Giffen goods). There can be at most two "Giffen" or inferior goods in a three-commodity world. It is possible to define the $_{MS}\sigma_{MS}$, $_{FX}\sigma_{FX}$ and $_{FM}\sigma_{FM}$ in terms of equations (21) through (23).

$$(21) \quad (1 - K_F)\,\frac{\sigma'}{_{MX}\sigma_{MX}} - K_M\sigma_{FM} - K_X\sigma_{FX} = 0,$$

$$(22) \quad (1 - K_M)\,\frac{\sigma'}{_{FX}\sigma_{FX}} - K_F\sigma_{FM} - K_X\sigma_{MX} = 0,$$

$$(23) \quad (1 - K_X)\,\frac{\sigma'}{_{FM}\sigma_{FM}} - K_F\sigma_{FX} - K_M\sigma_{MX} = 0,$$

where: $\sigma_{FX}$, $\sigma_{MX}$, and $\sigma_{FM}$ are the partial elasticities of substitution,

$\sigma'$ is defined in equation (17),

$K_F$, $K_M$, $K_X$ are the proportion of the budget spent upon each commodity.

The income elasticities of demand are related to the coefficients of income variation in the same manner as the two-good world. That is, $E_Y(i) = \sigma' \cdot \rho_i$ for $i = F$, $M$, and $X$. However, we must replace $\sigma$ by $\sigma'$. Hicks and

Allen derive the general relationships between the price and cross elasticities for one of the three goods in terms of the indexes and income elasticities. In equations (24) through (32) the equations for all three goods are
presented.

$$(24) \quad E_{P_F}(F) = K_F E_Y(F) + (1 - K_F) \cdot \frac{\sigma'}{_{MX}\sigma_{MX}},$$

$$(25) \quad E_{P_F}(M) = K_F E_Y(M) - K_F \cdot \sigma_{FM},$$

$$(26) \quad E_{P_F}(X) = K_F E_Y(X) - K_F \cdot \sigma_{FX},$$

$$(27) \quad E_{P_M}(M) = K_M E_Y(M) + (1 - K_M) \cdot \frac{\sigma'}{_{FX}\sigma_{FX}},$$

$$(28) \quad E_{P_M}(F) = K_M E_Y(F) - K_M \sigma_{FM},$$

$$(29) \quad E_{P_M}(X) = K_M E_Y(X) - K_M \sigma_{XM},$$

$$(30) \quad E_{P_X}(X) = K_X E_Y(X) + (1 - K_X) \cdot \frac{\sigma'}{_{FM}\sigma_{FM}},$$

$$(31) \quad E_{P_X}(F) = K_X E_Y(F) - K_X \sigma_{FX},$$

$$(32) \quad E_{P_X}(M) = K_X E_Y(M) - K_X \sigma_{MX},$$

where:       $Y$ = money income,

$P_F$ = price of $F$,

$P_M$ = price of $M$,

$P_X$ = price of $X$,

$K_F$ = proportion of income spent on $F$,

$K_M$ = proportion of income spent on $M$,

$K_X$ = proportion of income spent on $X$,

$$E_{P_F}(F) = -\frac{\partial F}{\partial P_F} \cdot \frac{P_F}{F},$$

$$E_{P_M}(M) = -\frac{\partial M}{\partial P_M} \cdot \frac{P_M}{M},$$

$$E_{P_X}(X) = -\frac{\partial X}{\partial P_X} \cdot \frac{P_X}{X},$$

$$E_{P_F}(M) = -\frac{\partial M}{\partial P_F} \cdot \frac{P_F}{M},$$

$$E_{P_F}(X) = -\frac{\partial X}{\partial P_F} \cdot \frac{P_F}{X},$$

$$E_{P_M}(F) = -\frac{\partial F}{\partial P_M} \cdot \frac{P_M}{F},$$

$$E_{P_M}(X) = -\frac{\partial X}{\partial P_M} \cdot \frac{P_M}{X},$$

$$E_{P_X}(F) = -\frac{\partial F}{\partial P_X} \cdot \frac{P_X}{F},$$

$$E_{P_X}(M) = -\frac{\partial M}{\partial P_X} \cdot \frac{P_X}{M}.$$

Once the CIC function is specified it is possible to characterize the demand relationships that the specification implies in much the same way as was done in the two-good model. Thus, while the procedure for deriving these characteristics has become more complicated, our objectives have not changed.

On the supply side of the model it is necessary to generalize the CET transportation locus. Moreover, distinctions between indexes might be defined in the generalization,[10] but this refinement of supply will not be developed because the focus of this study is upon the character of demand and the equilibrium time path of commodity mix and price ratio. Rather, we define a constant partial elasticity of transformation production frontier. In this case the two indexes will coincide for all commodity combinations. The function is a generalization of the two-good function first derived from Powell and Gruen (1969). The partial elasticity of transformation may be defined in a fashion analogous to that of the partial elasticity of substitution.

(33) $$\tau_{ij} = \frac{x_1 g_1 + x_2 g_2 + \ldots + x_n g_n}{x_i x_j} \cdot \frac{H_{ij}}{H}$$

where: $x_1, \ldots, x_n$ = commodities,

$g(x_1, \ldots, x_n)$ = production transformation frontier,

$$g_i = \frac{\partial g}{\partial x_i},$$

$$g_{ij} = \frac{\partial^2 g}{\partial x_j \partial x_i},$$

[10] In this case, however, we are measuring the degree of jointness in supply.

$$H = \det \begin{bmatrix} 0 & g_1 & g_2 \cdots g_n \\ g_1 & g_{11} & g_{12} \cdots g_{1n} \\ g_2 & g_{21} & g_{22} \cdots g_{2n} \\ \cdot & \cdot & \cdot \cdots \cdot \\ \cdot & \cdot & \cdot \cdots \cdot \\ \cdot & \cdot & \cdot \cdots \cdot \\ g_n & g_{n1} & g_{n2} \cdots g_{nn} \end{bmatrix}$$

$H_{ij}$ = determinant of $ij^{\text{th}}$ cofactor of the bordered Hessian above, $\tau_{ij} < 0$.

In general $\tau_{ij}$ will be less than zero, while $\sigma_{ij}$ will be greater than zero as a result of the concavity of one contour and the convexity of the other. The functional form of the constant partial elasticity of transformation frontier is similar to Uzawa's (1962) constant partial elasticity of substitution production function. It is given in equation (34) for our three-commodity model.

(34)     $\alpha_1 F^{1-1/\tau} + \alpha_2 M^{1-1/\tau} + \alpha_3 X^{1-1/\tau} = K'(1 - 1/\tau)$

where $\tau_{FM} = \tau_{MX} = \tau_{FX} = \tau$, and $M$, $F$, and $X$ are the commodities previously defined.

Technical change is assumed to be disembodied, as in the two-good world, and may be introduced by altering $K'$ in the case of neutral change, or the relative sizes of $\alpha_1$, $\alpha_2$, and $\alpha_3$ in the nonneutral cases. With neutral change, the production transformation surface shifts out in a parallel contour. Since the transformation contour now exists in three-space, nonneutral change requires a specification of the relative variation in $\alpha_1$, $\alpha_2$, and $\alpha_3$. The reasoning is straightforward. The production transformation contour may pivot along either of two axes while remaining fixed on the $F$ axis. If the ratio $\alpha_2/\alpha_1$ is increasing faster than $\alpha_3/\alpha_1$, technical change favors $F$ the most, then $X$, and then $M$. Clearly this example is an unrealistic case. We are interested in only those cases in which the effects of technical change upon $F$ are negligible relative to that upon $M$ and $X$. Consider the problem in terms of Figure 2.2. The production possibility contour in period $t$ is $ADB$. Technical change causes the frontier to pivot in the next period to $AEC$. The movement of the locus in the $F–M$ plane is greater than in the $F–X$ plane. This point is easily seen in the diagram, since $BC$ exceeds $ED$ and the contour retains its neoclassical shape.

In order to conveniently represent the alternatives, assume that we specify technical change in terms of time functions for $\alpha_2/\alpha_1$ and $\alpha_3/\alpha_1$. We assume that each ratio is changing at a constant rate.

(35)
$$\left(\frac{\alpha_2}{\alpha_1}\right)_t = m_1\, e^{gt}$$

(36)
$$\left(\frac{\alpha_3}{\alpha_1}\right)_t = m_2\, e^{rt}$$

where:          $m_1$ and $m_2$ are constants.

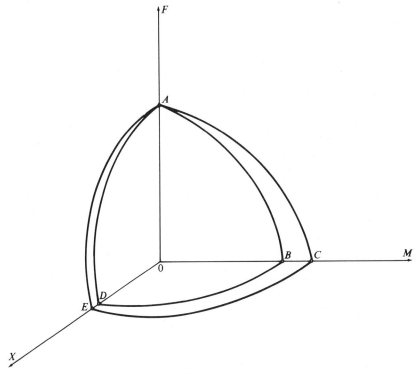

*Figure 2.2.*

The condition depicted by Figure 2.2 requires both $g < 0$, $r < 0$ and $|g| > |r|$. In general our attention will focus upon those cases where technology favors $M$ and $X$ but not $F$. Accordingly, in terms of Figure 2.2 the production frontier in the $X$–$M$ plane will be shifting out from one period to the next, as movement from $DB$ to $EC$ depicts. The absolute magnitude of $r$ and $g$ determines whether it is parallel ($|r| = |g|$), favors $M(|r| < |g|)$, or favors $X(|r| > |g|)$.

*The Model with a Non-Homogeneous Utility Function*

Since the functional form of the utility index describing community preferences is directly linked to the structure of demand hypothesized, a non-homogeneous utility function with three goods will be introduced. This function is a specific form of Mukerji's (1963) general class of production functions. The utility index is a generalization of the work of Arrow, Chenery, Minhas, and Solow (1961) as well as that of Uzawa (1962). Equation (37) describes the general format for this class of functions.

$$(37) \qquad U = \alpha\left[\sum_{r=1}^{n} A_r \, X_r^{-\rho_r}\right]^{-1/\rho}$$

where:     $\alpha > 0, \; \rho > 0,$

$A_r > 0, \; \rho_r > 0$ for $r = 1, 2, \ldots, n,$

$n$ = number of commodities.

The specific version of this function used in our present model assumes $\alpha = 1$ and is given in equation (38).

$$(38) \qquad U = (a_1 \, X^{-B_1} + a_2 \, F^{-B_2} + a_3 \, M^{-B_3})^{-1/B}.$$

It should be noted that only in the case where $B_1 = B_2 = B_3$ is the function in (38) homogeneous. In general we shall assume such is not the case. The Mukerji class of functions has the property that the partial elasticities of substitution are constant in ratios. Thus, for our case, equations (39) and (40) describe the relationships between the three partial elasticities.

$$(39) \qquad \frac{\sigma_{FX}}{\sigma_{XM}} = \frac{1 + B_3}{1 + B_2} \, ; \, \sigma_{XM} = \left(\frac{1 + B_2}{1 + B_3}\right)\sigma_{FX},$$

$$(40) \qquad \frac{\sigma_{FM}}{\sigma_{FX}} = \frac{1 + B_1}{1 + B_3} \, ; \, \sigma_{FM} = \left(\frac{1 + B_1}{1 + B_3}\right)\sigma_{FX},$$

The marginal rates of substitution under this utility specification are given in equations (41) and (42), and the marginal rates of transformation in equations (43) and (44).

$$(41) \qquad MRS_{FX} = \frac{a_1}{a_2} \cdot \frac{B_1}{B_2} \cdot \frac{F^{1+B_2}}{X^{1+B_1}},$$

$$(42) \qquad MRS_{FM} = \frac{a_3}{a_2} \cdot \frac{B_3}{B_2} \cdot \frac{F^{1+B_2}}{M^{1+B_3}},$$

$$(43) \qquad MRT_{FX} = \frac{\alpha_3}{\alpha_1}\left[\frac{F}{X}\right]^{1/\tau},$$

$$(44) \qquad MRT_{FM} = \frac{\alpha_2}{\alpha_1}\left[\frac{F}{M}\right]^{1/\tau}.$$

Equating (41) to (43) and (42) to (44) it is possible to solve for the equilibrium product mix and price ratio for each of the pairs of commodities.

$$(45) \qquad M = \left[ \frac{a_3}{a_2} \frac{B_3}{B_2} \frac{\alpha_1}{\alpha_2} \right]^{\gamma_1'} F^{\gamma_2'},$$

where:

$$\gamma_1' = \frac{1}{1 + B_3 - \dfrac{1}{\tau}} \; ; \gamma_1' > 0,$$

$$\gamma_2' = \frac{1 + B_2 - \dfrac{1}{\tau}}{1 + B_3 - \dfrac{1}{\tau}} \; ; \gamma_2' > 0.$$

$$(46) \qquad X = \left[ \frac{a_1}{a_2} \frac{B_1}{B_2} \frac{\alpha_1}{\alpha_3} \right]^{\gamma_3'} F^{\gamma_4'},$$

where:

$$\gamma_3' = \frac{1}{1 + B_1 - \dfrac{1}{\tau}} \; ; \gamma_3' > 0,$$

$$\gamma_4' = \frac{1 + B_2 - \dfrac{1}{\tau}}{1 + B_1 - \dfrac{1}{\tau}} \; ; \gamma_4' > 0.$$

These results differ from those with the homogeneous function in that the levels of consumption become important. For example, in (47) and (48) the relative prices are a function of the level of equilibrium consumption of amenity services.

$$(47) \qquad \frac{P_M}{P_F} = \left[ \frac{\alpha_2}{\alpha_1} \right]^{(1+B_3)\gamma_1'} \left[ \frac{a_3}{a_2} \frac{B_3}{B_2} \right]^{-\gamma_1'/\tau} F^{(1-\gamma_2')/\tau}$$

$$(48) \qquad \frac{P_X}{P_F} = \left[ \frac{\alpha_3}{\alpha_1} \right]^{(1+B_1)\gamma_3} \left[ \frac{a_1}{a_2} \frac{B_1}{B_2} \right]^{-\gamma_3'/\tau} F^{(1-\gamma_4')/\tau}.$$

Technical change can enter the model in four general ways, though only the fourth case is of immediate interest for our present purpose. Table 2.3

Table 2.3. Nonneutral Technical Change with a Three-Commodity Model

| Case | $M$ | $X$ | $P_M/P_F$ | $P_X/P_F$ |
|------|------|------|-----------|-----------|
| (1) $r > 0$ $g > 0$ | decrease | decrease | increase | increase |
| (2) $r < 0$ $g > 0$ | decrease | increase | increase | decrease |
| (3) $r > 0$ $g < 0$ | increase | decrease | decrease | increase |
| (4) $r < 0$ $g < 0$ | increase | increase | decrease | decrease |

summarizes the results for each of the four cases when $F$ is assumed invariant. The overall tendencies for commodity mix and price ratios remain the same as in the two-good model. However, there are important differences: First, the relative prices are a function of the level of consumption of $F$. The direction of change with changes in the level of $F$ is related to the adjusted measures of relative preferences (i.e., $\gamma_2'$ and $\gamma_4'$). The adjustments, here, indicate the extent of substitutability on the supply side of the market in each case. Consequently, our assumption of constant substitutability for all pairs of goods (i.e., constant partial elasticity of transformation) is an important restriction upon our model. Finally, the amount of $M$ and $X$ consumed is a function of the level of $F$, and this function changes with alterations in the relative preferability of $M$ and $X$ respectively (i.e., the $\gamma_1'$ and $\gamma_3'$).

The general conclusions from this three-good model are not appreciably different from those of the two good. Accordingly, it is important to outline the gains resulting from both the generalization and the specific form chosen for the utility index. Thus in what follows we will spell out the pattern of demand implied by the present specification.

The index curvature, $\sigma'$, of a CIC contour may be described in this case as in equation (49), which is directly derived from the definition given in (17).

$$(49) \quad \sigma' = \frac{1 + \dfrac{M}{F} MRS_{FM} + \dfrac{X}{F} MRS_{FX}}{\left[ (1+B_3)(1+B_1) + (1+B_1)(1+B_2)\dfrac{M}{F} MRS_{FM} \right. \left. + (1+B_3)(1+B_2)\dfrac{X}{F} MRS_{FX} \right]}$$

The Hicks-Allen coefficients are given in equations (50) through (52).

$$(50) \qquad\qquad \rho_F = (1+B_3)(1+B_1),$$

$$(51) \qquad\qquad \rho_M = (1+B_2)(1+B_1),$$

$$(52) \qquad\qquad \rho_X = (1+B_3)(1+B_2).$$

Because $B_1$, $B_2$, and $B_3$ are each assumed to be greater than zero, Mukerji's function does not allow for inferior goods. In such cases the coefficients of income variation would have to be less than zero. Substitution from (50) through (52) into (49) yields another formulation of $\sigma'$.

$$(53) \qquad \sigma' = \frac{1 + \dfrac{M}{F} MRS_{FM} + \dfrac{X}{F} MRS_{FX}}{\rho_F + \rho_M \cdot \dfrac{M}{F} MRS_{FM} + \rho_X \cdot \dfrac{X}{F} MRS_{FX}}.$$

With the results of the index of curvature of a utility contour and the Hicks-Allen indexes of income variation it is possible to enumerate the income, price, and cross elasticities of demand implicit from this utility specification. Table 2.4 presents these results. The first thing to be noted is the relationship between the income elasticities of demand and the partial elasticities of substitution [given in equations (39) and (40)].

$$\text{(54a)} \qquad \frac{\sigma_{FX}}{\sigma_{XM}} = \frac{1 + B_3}{1 + B_2} = \frac{E_Y(F)}{E_Y(M)},$$

$$\text{(54b)} \qquad \frac{\sigma_{FM}}{\sigma_{FX}} = \frac{1 + B_1}{1 + B_3} = \frac{E_Y(M)}{E_Y(X)}.$$

Since the partial elasticities of substitution may be used to indicate both the relationships between pairs of commodities in a Fisher-Katzner framework, and the relative income elasticities, some "base" partial elasticity must be chosen for the determination of the price and cross elasticities of demand. In addition, the index of curvature also enters into both the price-related and income-related elasticities. One important advantage of the nonhomogeneous specification is that the demand elasticities reflect the level of equilibrium consumption. That is, the magnitudes of the elasticities change with alterations in the commodity mix. This approach has some substantial advantages over the two-good, homogeneous model, which will become more apparent with an examination of the rate of change in relative prices resulting from technical change in each case.

## III.  THE RATE OF RELATIVE PRICE CHANGE

Our analysis has revealed that under fairly general conditions both models predict an increase in the price of amenity services $(F)$ relative to the prices of commodities affected favorably by technical change. This result should not be surprising. It was derived by Baumol (1967) in a simple supply model. Furthermore, it is precisely the behavior postulated by Fisher, Krutilla, and Cicchetti in their analysis of the preservation benefits of Hells Canyon. The amenity services of the Canyon in its preserved state represent the good that is incapable of augmentation through technological innovation. Consequently both my general equilibrium approach and their partial equilibrium analysis indicate relative price appreciation.

However, the relationship between the rate of price appreciation and the rate of technical advance can be derived in the present framework, whereas it must be approximated in the partial equilibrium model. Such a relationship permits two questions to be answered. First, it allows us

Table 2.4. Nature of Demand: Three-Good World with Nonhomogeneous Utility Function

| Commodity | $E_{Pi}(M)$ | $E_{Pi}(F)$ | $E_{Pi}(X)$ | $E_Y(i)$ |
|---|---|---|---|---|
| $M$ | $K_M(1+B_2)(1+B_1)\,\sigma'$ $+\sigma_{FX}\left[K_F\left(\dfrac{1+B_1}{1+B_3}\right)\right.$ $\left.+K_X\left(\dfrac{1+B_2}{1+B_3}\right)\right]$ | $K_M(1+B_3)(1+B_1)\,\sigma'$ $-K_M\left[\dfrac{1+B_1}{1+B_3}\right]\sigma_{FX}$ | $K_M(1+B_2)(1+B_3)\,\sigma'$ $-K_M\left[\dfrac{1+B_2}{1+B_3}\right]\sigma_{FX}$ | $(1+B_2)(1+B_1)$ times $\sigma'$ |
| $F$ | $K_F(1+B_2)(1+B_1)\,\sigma'$ $-K_F\sigma_{FX}\left[\dfrac{1+B_1}{1+B_3}\right]$ | $K_F(1+B_3)(1+B_1)\,\sigma'$ $+\sigma_{FX}\left[K_M\left(\dfrac{1+B_1}{1+B_3}\right)+K_X\right]$ | $K_F(1+B_2)(1+B_3)\,\sigma'$ $-K_F\sigma_{FX}$ | $(1+B_3)(1+B_1)$ times $\sigma'$ |
| $X$ | $K_X(1+B_2)(1+B_1)\,\sigma'$ $-K_X\left[\dfrac{1+B_2}{1+B_3}\right]\sigma_{FX}$ | $K_X(1+B_3)(1+B_1)\,\sigma'$ $-K_X\sigma_{FX}$ | $K_X(1+B_2)(1+B_3)\,\sigma'$ $+\sigma_{FX}\left[K_M\left(\dfrac{1+B_2}{1+B_3}\right)+K_F\right]$ | $(1+B_2)(1+B_3)$ times $\sigma'$ |

to determine the effect that a specified rate of growth in output per unit of input in the fabricated goods sector will have upon the relative prices of goods fixed in supply. Second, and equally important, by isolating the parametric relationships between the two rates it may be possible to specify the conditions under which a partial equilibrium model will yield a "good enough" approximation of the behavior of relative prices.

Consider, our first case, the two-commodity model. The income elasticities of demand are equal for both manufactured and fixed goods. In addition the price and cross elasticities are symmetrically related to the elasticity of substitution (see Table 2.2). The price ratio $(P_F/P_M)$ was found to be a function of the parameter indicating biased changes in technology $(A)$ and of that indicating any nonneutral changes in preferences $(C)$.

$$(55) \qquad\qquad \frac{P_F}{P_M} = A^\delta C^r. \qquad\qquad (\delta > 0;\, r < 0)$$

Recall that increases in $A$ represent a situation in which technology is progressively favoring the fabricated goods $(M)$ sector. If we assume, for convenience, that such change is progressing at an exponential rate, $g$, [equation (14)], then it is possible to derive the relationship between the rate of change in the price ratio and that of technology.

$$(56) \qquad\qquad \frac{d\left(\dfrac{P_F}{P_M}\right)}{dt} \Bigg/ \left(\dfrac{P_F}{P_M}\right) = \frac{\dfrac{dP_F}{dt}}{P_F} - \frac{\dfrac{dP_M}{dt}}{P_M} = \delta g.$$

If we let $\cdot = \dfrac{d}{dt}$, and substitute for $\delta$, then (56) becomes (57).

$$(57) \qquad\qquad k_0 = \frac{\left(\dfrac{P_F}{P_M}\right)^{\cdot}}{\left(\dfrac{P_F}{P_M}\right)} = \frac{\tau}{\tau - \sigma}\, g. \qquad\qquad (\tau < 0;\, \sigma > 0)$$

Since $\delta$ will generally be less than or equal to one, the rate of price appreciation can not exceed $g$. Consider the reasons why this might be the case. Suppose $M$ and $F$ were always used together in a fixed way. That is when the two goods are perfect complements in consumption.[11] We would then expect the rate of relative price appreciation to equal the rate of technological change. Thus when $M$ and $F$ are perfect comple-

---

[11] Given the types of activities or goods we are representing by $M$ and $F$ this case seems unlikely, but it does serve as a boundary example.

ments in consumption then $\sigma = 0$ and $k_0 = g$. Alternatively, suppose that $\sigma$ approaches infinity. In this case $M$ and $F$ are perfect substitutes and exchange at a constant marginal rate of substitution for all possible levels of consumption of $F$ or $M$. There is no price appreciation in this case ($\delta \to 0$).

The effects of the nature of goods (complements versus substitutes) and of income upon the nature of demand are not necessarily separable. That is, whether or not two goods are substitutes will affect their respective income elasticities of demand as well as their price and cross elasticities. Consequently it is not easy to attribute certain price behavior solely to one component of the total picture. In the present case, the community preference function presupposes unitary income elasticities for both goods, so that the character of the goods is the key determinant of the rate of price appreciation.

Moreover, supply considerations are found to be as significant as those of demand. The elasticity of transformation, $\tau$, measures the changes in the rate of transformation that we must be prepared to accept with changes in the desired commodity mix. That is, at any level of consumption of fabricated commodities ($M$), we must be prepared to forgo some of the manufactured goods if we wish to have additional amenity services ($F$). The index $\tau$ measures the curvature of the transformation frontier, and thus it also measures how the marginal rate of transformation changes with changes in the commodity mix. Suppose for a constant $\sigma$ we allow the absolute value of $\tau$ to increase without bound. As a result, our ability to reallocate resources under such circumstances implies a constant tradeoff (downward-sloping straight line transformation frontier), and the rate of price appreciation, $k_0$, will equal $g$, the rate of technical advance. This case is similar in its effects to the perfect complements case of demand.

Alternatively $\tau$ may approach zero. In economic terms, such a limiting process means a fixed amount of $F$ and $M$ may be produced and no other combinations are possible. Relative prices will not appreciate in this case.[12]

The limitations of this two-good homogeneous model have been outlined previously. They are briefly: (a) unitary income elasticities, (b) failure to consider substitutes for the amenity services, (c) rigid cross elasticity effects, and (d) an overly simplistic division of the supply side

---

[12] These results are derived using L'Hospital's rule $\lim_{\tau \to -\infty} \dfrac{\tau}{\tau - \sigma} g$ as an indeterminate form. However application of the aforementioned rule allows us to see $\lim_{\tau \to -\infty} \dfrac{\tau}{\tau - \sigma} g = g$. Alternatively $\lim_{\tau \to 0} \dfrac{\tau}{\tau - \sigma} g = 0$.

of the market into two classes of goods.[13] Consequently we will consider the most general of the four models—the three-good model with a non-homogeneous preference function. In this case two price ratios are necessary to define completely relative price movements. Equations (58) and (59) repeat the functions reported in (47) and (48). It should be noted that for mathematical convenience we have inverted the price ratios and are measuring $P_M$ and $P_X$ relative to $P_F$. This change allows us to conveniently assess the movement of $P_M$ relative to $P_X$. We expect now to speak of declines in $P_M/P_F$.

$$(58) \qquad \frac{P_M}{P_F} = \left[\frac{\alpha_2}{\alpha_1}\right]^{(1+B_3)\gamma_1'} \left[\frac{a_3}{a_2}\frac{B_3}{B_2}\right]^{-\gamma_1'/\tau} F^{(1-\gamma_2')/\tau},$$

$$(59) \qquad \frac{P_X}{P_F} = \left[\frac{\alpha_3}{\alpha_1}\right]^{(1+B_1)\gamma_3'} \left[\frac{a_1}{a_2}\frac{B_1}{B_2}\right]^{-\gamma_3'/\tau} F^{(1-\gamma_4')/\tau}.$$

Differentially biased technical change (case 4) was introduced in this model with changes in the ratios $(\alpha_2/\alpha_1)$ and $(\alpha_3/\alpha_1)$. Again let us assume their time path is described by exponential time functions. Technical change that favors $M$ most, then $X$, and not $F$ is given by specifying that the rates of change in these ratios are less than zero and that equation (60) describes their mutual relationship.

$$(60) \qquad \frac{\left|\dfrac{d\left(\dfrac{\alpha_2}{\alpha_1}\right)}{dt}\right|}{\left(\dfrac{\alpha_2}{\alpha_1}\right)} > \frac{\left|\dfrac{d\left(\dfrac{\alpha_3}{\alpha_1}\right)}{dt}\right|}{\left(\dfrac{\alpha_3}{\alpha_1}\right)}$$

or

$$(61) \qquad |g| > |r|.$$

Consider first $\left(\dfrac{\dot{P}_M}{P_F}\right) \Big/ \left(\dfrac{P_M}{P_F}\right)$ and its relationship to $r$ and $g$.

$$(62) \qquad k_1 = \frac{\left(\dfrac{\dot{P}_M}{P_F}\right)}{\left(\dfrac{P_M}{P_F}\right)} = (1 + B_3)\,\gamma_1'\,g + \frac{(1 - \gamma_2')}{\tau}\left(\frac{\dot{F}}{F}\right).$$

Making use of the definitions of $\gamma_1'$ and $\gamma_2'$ and the equilibrium demand relationships given in Table 2.4, it is possible to express equation (62) in more meaningful terms. First, equations (63) and (64) define the parameters.

---

[13] All of these demand effects are interdependent and are isolated individually only for emphasis.

$$(63) \qquad \gamma_1' = \frac{1}{1 + B_3 - 1/\tau},$$

$$(64) \qquad \gamma_2' = \frac{1 + B_2 - 1/\tau}{1 + B_3 - 1/\tau}.$$

Substituting into (62) and simplifying we derive:

$$(65) \qquad k_1 = \left(\frac{(1 + B_3)}{1 + B_3 - 1/\tau}\right)g + \frac{(1 + B_3) - (1 + B_2)}{\tau(1 + B_3 - 1/\tau)}\left(\frac{\dot{F}}{F}\right).$$

Three relationships allow a more meaningful economic representation of equation (65): (1) the income elasticity of $F$ in equilibrium, $[E_Y(F) = (1 + B_3)(1 + B_1)\sigma']$; (2) the income elasticity of $M$ in equilibrium, $[E_Y(M) = (1 + B_2)(1 + B_1)\sigma']$; and (3) the degree to which $M$ and $X$ are substitutes or complements relative to $F$ and $M$ $[(\sigma_{MX}/\sigma_{FM})(1 + B_1) = 1 + B_2]$.

$$(66) \quad k_1 = \frac{E_Y(F)g}{E_Y(F) - \dfrac{E_Y(M)\sigma_{FM}}{\tau\sigma_{MX}(1 + B_1)}} + \frac{E_Y(F) - E_Y(M)}{\tau E_Y(F) - \dfrac{E_Y(M)\sigma_{FM}}{\sigma_{MX}(1 + B_1)}}\left(\frac{\dot{F}}{F}\right).$$

There are a number of factors that will influence $k_1$; however, several observations are possible. First, if the income elasticities of $F$ and $M$ are equal, we need only consider the first term. Since $\tau$ is less than zero, the denominator will in general be larger than the numerator. The extent to which it is larger depends upon the nature of the second term in the denominator. Accordingly, we should attempt to decipher the potential sources for variation in its size. The term consists of the income elasticity of demand for $M$ adjusted by two effects. The first of these

$$[\sigma_{FM}/\sigma_{MX}(1 + B_1)]$$

is a demand adjustment. The magnitude of this term depends upon the nature of the relationship between the goods $F$ and $M$ relative to $X$ and $M$, and we would expect the term to be larger if $F$ and $M$ are closer substitutes than $X$ and $M$ are. We might say that this term provides a taxonomic index of the three-good interrelationships in demand. We found in the two-good world that the strength of the relationship between the commodities $F$ and $M$ (substitutes versus complements) affected the rate of relative price appreciation. Now the question is somewhat more complex. We must consider which pair of goods has the strongest substitution tendencies. For example, if $F$ and $M$ are closer substitutes than $X$ and $M$, this should somewhat offset technical change biased in favor of $M$ relative to $F$. The reasoning is straightforward. We are more likely to substitute $M$ for $F$ than for $X$. A situation where $X$ and $M$ were the closer substitutes would imply, for given $\tau$, that the first term in (66) would be close in size to $g$; in economic terms, the rate of price appreciation of $F$ relative to $M$ would be closer to the rate of technical advance.

Consider the second adjustment to $E_Y(M)$. If the elasticity of transformation, $\tau$, increases, we may, by reallocating our resources, more easily obtain alternative commodity mixes. In the limit as $\tau$ approaches negative infinity, the first term will equal $g$. The other polar case would be a condition where our production possibilities are inflexible and $\tau$ approaches zero. The first term of (66) will then, *ceteris paribus*, approach zero.

The second term of equation (66) accounts for the effect of an increasing rate of consumption of $F$. Suppose the community chooses to consume more amenity services over time. Such behavior will also affect the rate of price appreciation. Heuristically, we might compare the first term to the "vertical shifter" of the demand curve in the Fisher, Krutilla, Cicchetti paper and the second term to the "horizontal shifter."[14] That is, the first indicates the rate at which the vertical intercept is changing $D_1 D_1'$ in Figure 2.3A, and the second indicates the rate at which a given rate of change in the horizontal intercept, $F_0 F_1$ in Figure 2.3B, will affect the rate of relative price increase. A closer examination of this term indicates that if the income elasticity of $F$ equals that of $M$, then only the first effect is important. In addition, the denominator of the second term is somewhat different than the denominator of the first term of (66) and will always be negative (for non-Giffen goods). Hence this second term, for positive $\dot{F}/F$, will oppose or complement the first effect depending upon the relative magnitude of the two income elasticities. If $E_Y(F) > E_Y(M)$ then the second term will complement the effect of technical change. Furthermore the denominator of the fraction indicates a balancing of the supply effects, $\tau$, and demand effects, $\dfrac{\sigma_{FM}}{\sigma_{MX}(1+B_1)}$. That is, suppose they are equal (and opposite in sign); the overall expression may then be rewritten as:

[14] I would caution the reader that this simplification is made *only* for ease of exposition. It does *not* mean the model presupposes linear demand functions. Rather I seek to relate the general equilibrium results in an approximate sense to the effects described by Fisher, Krutilla, and Cicchetti. The rate of increase in $F$ is the equilibrium consumption and not, strictly speaking, the rate of movement of the horizontal intercept. Furthermore, the construction of two-dimensional demand relationships is a partial equilibrium framework, and the relationship described in (66) is derived under a general equilibrium model. I am indebted to Charles Cicchetti for pointing up this analogy.

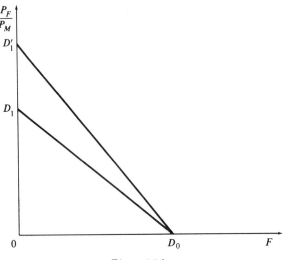

*Figure 2.3A.*

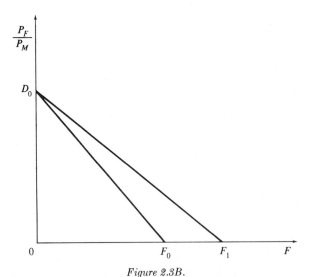

*Figure 2.3B.*

(67)    $$k_1 = \frac{E_Y(F)g}{E_Y(F) + E_Y(M)} - \frac{E_Y(F) - E_Y(M)}{|\tau|[E_Y(F) + E_Y(M)]}\left(\frac{\dot{F}}{F}\right)$$

where    $$|\tau| = \frac{\sigma_{FM}}{\sigma_{MX}(1 + B_1)}.$$

This expression clearly puts major emphasis upon the relative magnitudes of the income elasticities. In this simplification we have assumed that supply tradeoffs, $\tau$, equal our measure of the degree to which we can substitute between goods, $\sigma_{FM}/\sigma_{MX}(1 + B_1)$.

How important are supply effects? This question is legitimate in light of the Fisher, Krutilla, Cicchetti supply assumptions (perfectly inelastic supply). Consider one polar case. Let $\tau$ approach zero. The first approaches zero, but the second term does *not*. Consequently, $k_1$ is not necessarily zero. In the two-good model we found that $k_0$ did approach zero as $\tau$ did.

Table 2.5 presents a summary of several supply and demand assumptions and their effects upon the relative price appreciation of amenity services. All six of the cases are the polar cases for supply with alternative demand assumptions. In order to get an idea of nonpolar cases, we select our assumed behavior of $\dot{F}/F$ and then the income elasticity relationship. The terms reported are bounds on price behavior. For example, if we assume that $\dot{F}/F > 0$ and $E_Y(F) > E_Y(M)$, then we can see that the two

Table 2.5. Relative Price Behavior in a Three-Good World: $\dfrac{\left(\dfrac{\dot{P}_M}{P_F}\right)}{\dfrac{P_M}{P_F}}$

| Case | $E_Y(F) > E_Y(M)$ | $E_Y(F) = E_Y(M)$ | $E_Y(F) < E_Y(M)$ |
|---|---|---|---|
| (1) $\tau \to 0$ $\dfrac{\dot{F}}{F} > 0$ | $-\dfrac{E_Y(F) - E_Y(M)}{\left(\dfrac{E_Y(M)\ \sigma_{FM}}{\sigma_{MX}(1 + B_1)}\right)}\left(\dfrac{\dot{F}}{F}\right)$ (declining) | $0$ (no change) | $-\dfrac{E_Y(F) - E_Y(M)}{\left(\dfrac{E_Y(M)\ \sigma_{FM}}{\sigma_{MX}(1 + B_1)}\right)}\left(\dfrac{\dot{F}}{F}\right)$ (increasing) |
| (2) $\tau \to 0$ $\dfrac{\dot{F}}{F} = 0$ | $0$ (no change) | $0$ (no change) | $0$ (no change) |
| (3) $\tau \to 0$ $\dfrac{\dot{F}}{F} < 0$ | $-\dfrac{E_Y(F) - E_Y(M)}{\left(\dfrac{E_Y(M)\ \sigma_{FM}}{\sigma_{MX}(1 + B_1)}\right)}\left(\dfrac{\dot{F}}{F}\right)$ (increasing) | $0$ (no change) | $\dfrac{E_Y(F) - E_Y(M)}{\left(\dfrac{E_Y(M)\ \sigma_{FM}}{\sigma_{MX}(1 + B_1)}\right)}\left(\dfrac{\dot{F}}{F}\right)$ (declining) |
| (4) $\tau \to -\infty$ $\dfrac{\dot{F}}{F} > 0$ | $g$ (declining) | $g$ (declining) | $g$ (declining) |
| (5) $\tau \to -\infty$ $\dfrac{\dot{F}}{F} = 0$ | $g$ (declining) | $g$ (declining) | $g$ (declining) |
| (6) $\tau \to -\infty$ $\dfrac{\dot{F}}{F} < 0$ | $g$ (declining) | $g$ (declining) | $g$ (declining) |

effects conform. That is, in both case (1) and case (4) the two terms call
for $k_1$ to be less than zero and declining. Consequently the two effects are
reinforcing. Specific parametric assumptions are necessary to compare
$k_1$ to $g$ in absolute magnitudes.

We shall not dwell upon the rate of change in $P_X/P_F$, since the same
kinds of interrelationships are present. Equation (68) specifies the nature
of the relative price change determinants.

$$(68) \quad k_2 = \frac{\left(\dfrac{\dot{P}_X}{P_F}\right)}{\dfrac{P_X}{P_F}} = \frac{E_Y(F)r}{E_Y(F) - \dfrac{E_Y(X)\sigma_{FX}}{\tau\sigma_{XM}(1+B_3)}}$$

$$+ \frac{E_Y(F) - E_Y(X)}{\tau E_Y(F) - \dfrac{E_Y(X)\sigma_{FX}}{\sigma_{XM}(1+B_3)}}\left(\frac{\dot{F}}{F}\right).$$

Once again, three factors appear to be critical to relative price appreciation of $F$ related to $X$. Assuming $r < 0$, we need to consider for $\dot{F}/F > 0$:
(1) the size of the respective income elasticities of demand for $F$ and $X$;
(2) the degree to which $X$ is a substitute for $F$ relative to whether or not
it is a substitute for $M$; (3) finally the ease with which we can transform
our resources so as to produce alternative combinations of $F$, $X$, and $M$.

## IV. Conclusions

In this paper I have presented the conditions under which technical
change that is biased in favor of manufactured commodities will result in
an increase in the relative price of the services of environmental resources
and a reduction in the quantity consumed relative to the quantity of a
manufactured or fabricated good. The model has been constructed
assuming no intertemporal production externalities; that is, no allow-
ance has been made for the irreversibilities suggested by Krutilla (1967).
Accordingly, the model considers a situation in which there is increasing
"relative scarcity" as opposed to increasing "absolute scarcity." Technological change, by increasing our ability to produce fabricated goods
and leaving untouched the available quantity of amenity services of
homogeneous quality, makes such services relatively scarce. Moreover,
the introduction of irreversibilities in the model would require the commitment of a set of resources to the production of fabricated goods for all
future time. The size of the resource commitment at any point in time
depends upon the community's past choices of the fabricated goods.

By definition, the larger the amount of fabricated goods chosen for
consumption in period $t$, the smaller the absolute amount of amenity

services available for consumption in succeeding time periods.[15] Accordingly, we must be selective in our use of environmental resources to produce fabricated commodities. Resources that are unique and irreplaceable will have appreciating value when used in producing amenity services and may have a depreciating opportunity cost if the alternative is to use them in the production of fabricated goods.

Barnett and Morse (1963) have suggested that technological change has compensated for the depletion of higher quality natural resource stocks by permitting the use of lower quality resources without significant cost increases. In many cases these lower quality resources do not have unique attributes which enhance the recreational or scientific activities compatible with use of them in their preserved state. They further suggest that technological advances may lead to a steady-state equilibrium, wherein natural resources scarcity is no longer a problem. They note:

> Advancing ocean technology could conceivably lead to a "steady state" equilibrium of a great circular flow process analogous to, but far more complex than, the carbon dioxide cycle. Equally important are the energy plateaus already created by atomic fission and eventually, perhaps, to result from nuclear fusion and solar energy devices. Once energy becomes available in unlimited quantities at constant cost, the processing of large quantities of low-grade resource material presumably can be undertaken at constant cost without further technological advance, and at declining cost with technological advance and capital accumulation (p. 239).

The model developed in this paper is very similar to the situation described above. Accordingly, our model demonstrates that the problem of providing the amenities associated with unspoiled natural environments is *not* alleviated by technological change. In contrast, in the absence of more selective judgment in our development decisions, it may be aggravated by such change.

Furthermore, the demonstration of the pricing behavior postulated by Fisher, Krutilla, and Cicchetti does not require their restrictive assumptions. We need not constrain demand as much as their conditions (in Appendix B of the Fisher, Krutilla, Cicchetti paper) would indicate. Three considerations are important: (1) the income elasticity of demand for amenity services relative to that of fabricated goods, (2) the availability of good substitutes for these services, and (3) the ability of the economy to transform its resources so as to produce alternative com-

---

[15] One convenient description of the costs associated with these effects would be to designate them public user costs. These are the costs imposed upon future consumers resulting from the intertemporal effects of current resource allocations.

modity mixes. The demand conditions are *not* independent of one another. However, it is clear that the price of amenity services will increase relative to fabricated goods in all but peculiar cases. The aforementioned conditions are the determinants of the relationship of the rate of relative price increase to that of technological change.

A fundamental question remains because the impact of irreversibilities upon price behavior has not been specified. The present model has established that, at best, irreversibilities will add to the increase in the relative price of amenity services. However, the extent of their effect may result in more dramatic increases in this price appreciation. Accordingly the preservation versus development decisions under such conditions may have fundamental effects upon the level of living of future generations.

## References

Arrow, K. J., H. B. Chenery, B. S. Minhas, and R. M. Solow. 1961. "Capital Labor Substitution and Economic Efficiency." *Review of Economics and Statistics.*

Barnett, H. J., and Chandler Morse. 1963. *Scarcity and Growth.* Baltimore: Johns Hopkins Press for Resources for the Future.

Baumol, W. J. 1949–50. "The Community Indifference Map." *Review of Economic Studies.*

———. 1967. "Macroeconomics of Unbalanced Growth: The Anatomy of Urban Crisis." *American Economic Review,* June 1967.

Bhagwati, J. 1958. "Immiserizing Growth." *Review of Economic Studies.*

Brown, M., and John De Cani. 1963. "Technological Change and the Distribution of Income." *International Economic Review.*

Cicchetti, C. J., J. J. Seneca, and P. Davidson. 1969. *The Demand and Supply of Outdoor Recreation.* Washington, D.C.: U.S. Bureau of Outdoor Recreation.

Corden, W. M. 1956. "Economic Expansion and International Trade: A Geometric Approach." *Oxford Economic Papers.*

Ferguson, C. E. 1969. *The Neoclassical Theory of Production and Distribution.* Cambridge: Cambridge University Press.

Fisher, I. 1925. *Mathematical Investigations in the Theory of Value and Prices.* New Haven: Yale University Press.

Gannon, Colin. 1969. "Towards A Strategy for Conservation in a World of Technological Change." *Socio-Economic Planning Science,* 3.

Gorman, W. M. 1965. "Production Functions in Which the Elasticities of Substitution Stand in Fixed Proportion to Each Other." *Review of Economic Studies.*

Hamberg, D. 1971. *Models of Economic Growth.* New York: Harper and Row.

Herberg, H., M. C. Kemp, and S. P. McGee. 1970. "Factor Market Distortions, the Reversal of Relative Factor Intensities, and the Relation Between Product

Prices and Equilibrium Outputs." Paper delivered to Econometrics Workshop, Michigan State University.

Hicks, J. R., and R. G. D. Allen. 1934. "A Reconsideration of the Theory of Value." *Economica*.

Hicks, J. R. 1965. *Value and Capital*. 2d ed. Oxford: Oxford University Press.

Houthakker, H. S. 1960. "Additive Preferences." *Econometrica*, 1960.

Inada, K. 1968. "On Neoclassical Models of Economic Growth." *Review of Economic Studies*.

Johnson, H. G. 1966. "Factor Market Distortions and the Shape of the Transformation Curve." *Econometrica*.

Jones, R. W. 1965. "The Structure of Simple General Equilibrium Models." *Journal of Political Economy*.

———. 1971. "Distortions in Factor Markets and the General Equilibrium Model of Production." *Journal of Political Economy*, May/June 1971.

Katzner, D. 1970. *Static Demand Theory*. New York: The Macmillan Co.

Kelly, James Stewart. 1969. "Lancaster vs. Samuelson on the Shape of the Neoclassical Transformation Surface." *Journal of Economic Theory*, 1.

Kelso, M. M. 1971. "Macroeconomics of Unbalanced Growth." Unpublished manuscript.

Krutilla, J. V. 1967. "Conservation Reconsidered." *American Economic Review*, September 1967.

———, C. J. Cicchetti, A. M. Freeman III, and C. S. Russell. 1972. "Observations on the Economics of Irreplaceable Assets." In A. V. Kneese and B. T. Bower (eds.), *Environmental Quality Analysis: Theory and Method in the Social Sciences*. Baltimore: Johns Hopkins Press for Resources for the Future.

Lancaster, K. J. 1966. "A New Approach to Consumer Theory." *Journal of Political Economy*, 74.

Lloyd, R. J. 1970. "The Shape of the Transformation Curve with and without Factor Market Distortions." *Australian Economic Papers*, June 1970.

McFadden, D. 1963. "Constant Elasticity of Substitution Production Functions." *Review of Economic Studies*.

Mukerji, V. 1963. "A Generalized S.M.A.C. Function with Constant Ratios of Elasticity of Substitution." *Review of Economic Studies*.

Nadiri, M. I. 1970. "Some Approaches to the Theory and Measurement of Total Factor Productivity: A Survey." *Journal of Economic Literature*.

Nordhaus, W. D. 1969. *Invention, Growth, and Welfare: A Theoretical Treatment of Technological Change*. Cambridge, Mass.: M.I.T. Press.

Powell, A. A., and F. H. G. Gruen. 1969. "The Constant Elasticity of Transformation Production Frontier and Linear Supply System." *International Economic Review*.

Samuelson, P. 1956. "Social Indifference Curves." *Quarterly Journal of Economics*.

Smith, V. K., and J. V. Krutilla. 1972. "Technical Change and Environmental Resources." *Socio-Economic Planning Science*, April 1972.

Uzawa, H. 1962. "Production Functions with Constant Elasticities of Substitution." *Review of Economic Studies*.

# 3

# A Strategy for the Definition and Management of Wilderness Quality

Wilderness management is in many ways a paradoxical term, for wilderness connotes an image of a landscape untouched and an opportunity for free and unconfined use, while management suggests control and planned direction. It is perhaps because of the inherently contradictory nature of the term that wilderness management is one of the more challenging and difficult tasks facing resource managers today.

This paper focuses on two topics. First, when formulating a relevant management strategy, how can the administrator most effectively utilize feedback from the wilderness visitor population? Second, what aspects of wilderness recreation use appeal to visitors whose perception of wilderness is most consistent with the concept given statutory recognition by the Wilderness Act of 1964—specifically, lands without permanent improvements, structures, or human habitation that offer man an opportunity for solitude and a challenging, primitive kind of experience, and where the forces of nature predominate?

### WILDERNESS MANAGEMENT PROBLEMS

The manager must contend with three major factors in attempting to meet the objectives of the Wilderness Act: (1) institutional constraints; (2) limited availability of the resource; (3) and the rapid growth in wilderness recreation use.

* Geographer, U.S. Forest Service.

*Institutional constraints.* The manager must make his decisions in light of the constraints and obligations that the Wilderness Act imposes. The definition of wilderness is specified by the Act, as are permissible management activities, the type of opportunity the area should provide, and other considerations. Not only must the manager subject his decisions to the test of the law, but he must also contend with the all too common burdens of poor financing and inadequate manpower. Managerial actions that might be the most economical or the most efficient can prove to be illegal. Others that are more difficult or expensive might become the only feasible alternatives open to him.

*Limited availability of the resource.* At present, about 10 million acres (almost all National Forest land) are included in the National Wilderness Preservation System. An additional 4 million acres, presently classified as National Forest Primitive Areas, are managed as though they were in the System, pending their possible reclassification in accord with the Wilderness Act. Together, these acreages constitute only 0.7 of one percent of the land in the 48 states. Estimates as to the eventual size of the Wilderness Preservation System vary widely, but probably a realistic figure is on the order of 35 million acres (about 2 percent of the conterminous United States). This would include additions from National Forest lands, National Park System holdings, and lands of the Bureau of Sport Fisheries and Wildlife.

Within the 48 conterminous states, about 50 million acres (2.6 percent) appear to possess the characteristics necessary for wilderness designation.[1] Demands for timber, minerals, and other resources also will be made on some of this acreage and will undoubtedly preclude all of it from being classified as wilderness. Therefore, the wilderness resource base is finite in scope and irreproducible, given practical considerations of time.

Classifying additional lands as wilderness (i.e., transforming them from a *de facto* to a *de jure* status) does little to add new opportunities because *de facto* wildernesses are already being used for wilderness recreation. The question remaining is how much of the present *de facto* wilderness land will be retained under statutory protection.

*Rapid growth in wilderness recreation use.* Growth in wilderness recreation use has been climbing steadily since the end of World War II, averaging approximately 10 percent per year while population has grown

[1] For details of my attempt to estimate the dimensions of the resource base from which additional wilderness proposals could be made, see George H. Stankey, "Myths in Wilderness Decisionmaking," *Journal of Soil and Water Conservation*, vol. 25, no. 5, p. 187.

only about 2 percent per annum. In 1959 the Wildland Research Center projected a nearly ten-fold increase in visits to wilderness by the turn of the century, equivalent to about a 6 percent annual growth rate.[2] In the decade since that report, however, use has continued to increase at the 10 percent per year level.

Simple projections do not tell the whole story. Wilderness users tend to be disproportionately drawn from higher-income groups, professional and technical occupational categories, urban areas, and the college and postgraduate ranks.[3] Moreover, these characteristics apply to a steadily increasing proportion of the population. If indeed some causal relationship exists between any or all of these variables and wilderness use, then the possibility of future increases in wilderness use is further enhanced.

Burch and Wenger have suggested that a disproportionately high number of persons who participated in automobile camping as children move into a more primitive style of recreation later in their life cycle.[4] Although we can only speculate as to the exact nature and scope of this "learning-by-doing" process, it could represent a potentially significant source of future increases in wilderness use.[5]

Finally, *de facto* wilderness opportunities are declining—primarily because of continuing road construction in hitherto undeveloped areas. This will probably cause those who have been using these areas to seek out *de jure* wilderness areas.

In summary then, we have an increasing number of people seeking a primitive kind of recreational experience in a type of area that is limited in supply and whose reproduction is largely beyond our technical-economic capabilities. The issue is further complicated by the institutional constraints of the Wilderness Act: these preclude the options of either letting use continue unabated or totally restricting use. The objectives of this Act necessitate managerial action; the question confronting us concerns the specific nature of that action.

[2] Wildland Research Center, *Wilderness and Recreation: A Report on Resources, Values, and Problems,* Outdoor Recreation Resources Review Commission Study Report No. 3 (Washington, D.C.: Government Printing Office, 1962), p. 236.

[3] Most outdoor recreationists tend to be atypical in their socioeconomic characteristics when compared with the U.S. population. The above statement does not in any way suggest that a high income, a professional occupation, etc., are sufficient factors to explain recreational behavior.

[4] William R. Burch, Jr., and Wiley D. Wenger, Jr., *The Social Characteristics of Participants in Three Styles of Family Camping,* U.S. Forest Service Research Paper PNW-48, 1967, p. 18.

[5] The "learn-by-doing" hypothesis was put forward by Paul Davidson, F. Gerard Adams, and Joseph Seneca, "The Social Value of Water Recreational Facilities Resulting from an Improvement in Water Quality; The Delaware Estuary," in Allen V. Kneese and Stephen C. Smith (eds.), *Water Research* (Baltimore: The Johns Hopkins Press for Resources for the Future, 1966), p. 186.

## WILDERNESS MANAGEMENT OBJECTIVES

Although the wilderness experience is typified as free and spontaneous and the physical environment in which it takes place as wild and natural, there is considerable evidence that opportunities for such experiences might gradually disappear without some managerial controls. The issue is not whether management action is needed, but what the specific nature of the management goal should be. Traditionally, the basic question to which we have addressed our attention is "What is the acceptable level of physical-biological change that we can allow in our wildernesses?"

The Wilderness Act commits us to the dual objective of use and preservation. This objective also unalterably commits us to accept a wilderness environment that is less than totally unmodified because *any* use occurring in an ecosystem results in change. The relationship between use and change is not a simple linear function; in some areas, fairly low levels of use might cause substantial changes in the ecosystem. Frissell and Duncan found that over 80 percent of the groundcover at campsites in the Quetico-Superior area was lost despite only light recreational use (defined as up to 30 days of use per season).[6] Similarly, Wagar concluded "In wilderness situations even a little direct contact by recreationists might cause marked changes in plant composition and appearance."[7]

This should not be taken to mean that continuing increases in use will not cause further resource change. Rather, we need to recognize that even low levels of use can produce fairly substantial amounts of change and thus compromise the objective of maintaining a "natural" ecosystem (above and beyond the extent to which it is compromised by global-wide pollution).

Davis suggests that "The question of carrying capacities too often sounds like a physical problem when its heart is really a matter of interpersonal quality effects."[8] Thus, the question of "the acceptable level of physical-biological change" becomes a problem of defining the critical thresholds of sensitivity of wilderness users to various congestion costs: crowding, environmental change, and so forth. Answers will be arbitrary unless we know how people perceive and respond to the environment or how they define their goals and objectives.

Despite an array of administrative and legislative edicts, wilderness remains largely a function of human perception. Consequently, the wil-

---

[6] Sidney S. Frissell, Jr., and Donald P. Duncan, "Campsite Preference and Deterioration," *Journal of Forestry*, vol. 63 (1965), p. 258.

[7] J. Alan Wagar, *The Carrying Capacity of Wildlands for Recreation*, Forest Science Monograph 7, 1964, p. 18.

[8] Robert K. Davis, "Recreation Planning as an Economic Problem," *Natural Resources Journal*, vol. 3, no. 2, p. 248.

derness user is an important source of information for managers faced
with decisions regarding the appropriate utilization of the wilderness.
However, there is little face-to-face communication between user and
manager in wilderness and little opportunity for managers to observe
users in a systematic, unbiased fashion. Nevertheless, a growing body of
information has been developed over the past decade from survey
research efforts. We now have a description of characteristics and attitudes of a considerable number of wilderness visitors, although the
results are disparate in space, time, and definitions of variables.

Incorporating visitor attitudes and opinions into the wilderness deci-
sion-making process is not a simple or straightforward exercise. Wilderness visitors are not in any sense a uniform or homogeneous population;
on the contrary, we have substantial evidence suggesting considerable
diversity among these people in terms of prior wilderness experience,
socioeconomic background, and motivation.[9] Represented among wilderness visitors are value systems that cover a wide and often conflicting
range. As a consequence, visitor attitudes about some potential management action can be expected to vary considerably; views on trail standards, for example, might range from those favoring no trails at all to those
favoring a rather elaborate system of well-maintained paths. How does
the wilderness manager judge which value system is most relevant to his
decision needs?

The premise that certain wilderness visitors' attitudes should weigh
higher in the social welfare function for wilderness areas seems to be consistent with the direction and objectives embodied within the Wilderness
Act and the decisions of the Congress and the President to foster the
development of the National Wilderness Preservation System.[10]

The wilderness manager is charged with providing a specific type of
recreational opportunity. His concern is with the quality of that particular activity, which may be said to represent a point along a continuum
of recreational activities, not a continuum of recreational quality. Too

[9] John C. Hendee et al., *Wilderness Users in the Pacific Northwest: Their Char-
acteristics, Values, and Management Preferences*. Pacific Northwest Forest and Range
Experiment Station, Portland, Oregon, 1968; Robert C. Lucas, "Wilderness Percep-
tion and Use: The Example of the Boundary Waters Canoe Area," *Natural Resources
Journal*, vol. 3, no. 3 (1964), pp. 394–411; George H. Stankey, "The Perception of
Wilderness Recreation Carrying Capacity: A Geographic Study in Natural Resources
Management," Ph.D. dissertation, Department of Geography, Michigan State Uni-
versity, 1971.

[10] Refer to the next paper in this book, "Determination of Optimal Capacity of
Resource-Based Recreation Facilities," by Anthony C. Fisher and John V. Krutilla,
for further discussion of measurement problems involving the intensity of users'
preferences.

often the term "high quality recreation" is equated with "wilderness recreation." Wilderness recreation does not represent a polar position on a *quality continuum* having some intensive or commercial activity such as a "Coney Island" at the other end. The quality of wilderness recreation can be judged only by examining the extent to which the motivations and objectives of the visitor who seeks the type of opportunity provided by wilderness are fulfilled. For example, interaction with the pristine environment appears to be an important component of the wilderness experience. To the extent this opportunity is impeded (e.g., by the presence of litter, the loss of vegetation due to excessive use, etc.), the quality of the wilderness trip is lost. Conversely, the wilderness trip in a pristine setting where visitors enjoy complete or near solitude would legitimately be described as "high quality." Consequently, it is possible to define, perhaps rather specifically, the nature of wilderness quality and to make the provision of a "high quality wilderness experience" a realistic, pragmatic management objective.

However, the practical significance of such a definition of quality is contingent upon identifying the portion of the wilderness user population that specifically seeks the opportunities that wilderness is defined as providing. As suggested earlier, wilderness visitors are not a homogeneous group that subscribes to any easily identifiable image of wilderness. Thus, if visitor attitudes are to be a useful guide for the wilderness manager, we need to define those people in the wilderness user population whose needs and motivations are most nearly fulfilled by the wilderness opportunity.[11]

The alternative to giving more weight to the attitudes of certain wilderness users would be to assume that all people have similar tastes and preferences, which is simply not true, whether one is talking about food, clothing, or recreation.

If we try to manage wilderness for all, we will find ourselves bound on a course having equally unpalatable possible outcomes. "The cost of taking everyone's preferences into account may be paralysis," Wildavsky writes, "Worse, it may result in grand opportunities foregone or in irreversible damage to the environment."[12] Treating wilderness visitor responses in an undiscriminating fashion could lead to both inequitable and inefficient allocations. Only those visitors whose needs and tastes lie

[11] This assumes an equitable distribution of other types of recreational opportunities to meet the needs and desires of the nonwilderness recreationist.

[12] Aaron Wildavsky, "Aesthetic Power or the Triumph of the Sensitive Minority Over the Vulgar Mass: A Political Analysis of the New Economics," *Daedalus*, vol. 96, no. 4 (1967), p. 1127.

"on the average" would be satisfied, and it is precisely this type of visitor who can most easily be accommodated elsewhere. Furthermore, there is probably a high degree of substitutability among alternatives associated with this type of visitor's preferences. At the same time, we would fail altogether to allocate opportunities for those who seek an experience associated only with environments of a near natural state—locations that are of limited availability and beyond our capability at present to reproduce.

Moreover, the preservation values that wilderness possesses (e.g., a reservoir of germ plasm, a source of yet undiscovered medicinal values in flora and fauna, an ecological bench mark, etc.) could be easily lost if a management strategy were adopted that permitted essentially unlimited use.

The fundamental thesis of this paper is tied to the notion that wilderness represents one type of opportunity within a broad spectrum. We should not try to manage wilderness for all. By ensuring the provision of this entire spectrum of opportunities, we might achieve a more equitable distribution of social benefits. The proportions that other recreation opportunities would represent in the full spectrum would reflect both the demand for them and the extent of substitutability between the different types of experiences they provide. Our attention here, however, is focused on the wilderness component of the recreation spectrum and how benefits of this particular opportunity can be optimized.

The question remains, however, of how one defines those wilderness visitors whose attitudes are most relevant for the wilderness manager. Given the wide disparity of views as to what constitutes wilderness, how can a strategy be formulated that will provide managers with guidelines to weigh visitor input in the most appropriate manner?

## A Proposed Strategy for Defining the Relevant Wilderness Visitor Population

Other investigators have recognized the multimodal nature of tastes found among wilderness visitors and have attempted to control for this variation in their analyses. Lucas[13] approached the problem by differentiating users in the Boundary Waters Canoe Area (BWCA) by method of travel, noting that paddling canoeists held more rigid and demanding concepts of wilderness than motorboaters. The Wildland Research Center[14] utilized prior wilderness experience "as a rough and admittedly

---

13 "Wilderness Perception and Use," p. 408.
14 *Wilderness and Recreation*, p. 135.

partial measure of commitment." More recently, Hendee et al.[15] developed a scale to differentiate users on the basis of the underlying values that governed their attitudes and motivations regarding wilderness use.

During the summer of 1969 a survey was undertaken to investigate the question of wilderness recreation carrying capacity.[16] Four wildernesses were included in the study: The Bob Marshall Wilderness in Montana, the Bridger Wilderness in Wyoming, the High Uintas Primitive Area in Utah, and the Boundary Waters Canoe Area in Minnesota. Building upon previous work by Hendee et al., an attitude scale was designed to measure the extent to which a respondent's perception of wilderness coincided with the institutional objectives embodied in the Wilderness Act.

Each respondent was asked to consider the 14 items listed below. The first ten concern three basic characteristics of wilderness defined within the Wilderness Act: a natural ecosystem, minimal human development, and primitiveness of recreational activity. The remaining four items relate to other qualities of the wilderness environment—solitude, little evidence of other visitors, remoteness from urban areas, and size of the area.

   A.   Absence of man-made features, except trails,

   B.   Lakes behind small man-made dams,

   C.   Gravel roads,

   D.   Private cabins,

   E.   Stocking the area with kinds of game animals that are not native to the area,

   F.   Developed campsites with plank tables, cement fireplaces with metal grates, and outhouses,

   G.   Lots of camping equipment to make camping easy and comfortable,

   H.   Stocking the area with kinds of fish that are not native to the area,

   I.   No motorized travel by visitors,

   J.   Forests, flowers, and wildlife much the same as before the pioneers,

   K.   Solitude (not seeing many other people except those in your own party),

   L.   Covers a large area (at least 25 square miles),

---

[15] *Wilderness Users in the Pacific Northwest,* p. 23.

[16] For a discussion on the sampling scheme, questionnaire administration, and other methodological aspects of this study, see Stankey, "The Perception of Wilderness Recreation Carrying Capacity," Chapter 3.

M.  Remote from towns or cities,
N.  Little evidence of other visitors before you.

Respondents were asked to consider each item *in the context of wilderness*, and rate it on a five-point scale, ranging from "very undesirable" to "very desirable." Responses were accorded values from one to five, and scoring was arranged so that a person who held strong "purist" ideas about wilderness would score high while the person with less intense notions would score low. For example, a "very undesirable" response to "gravel roads" was accorded five points as was a "very desirable" response to "no motorized travel by visitors." The possible range for total scores was between 70 and 14. From the individual scores it was possible to rank respondents along a continuum ranging from a strong purist concept of wilderness to a less rigid one. This, in turn, made it possible to evaluate user attitudes toward levels and types of use and potential management alternatives in light of the degree of correspondence between the respondent's definition of wilderness and that of the Wilderness Act.

The respondents were classified into groups on the basis of their overall "purism" score. Four groups were established: strong purists (scores between 60 and 70 on the scale); moderate purists (scores from 50 to 59); neutralists (scores from 40 to 49); and nonpurists (scores of less than 40). Table 3.1 shows the percentage distribution of these groups among the four study areas.

The boundaries of the groupings were somewhat arbitrary. To be classified as a "strong purist," for example, a respondent had to rate each item in a manner reflecting close agreement with the institutional definition of wilderness. The major difference between the "strong purist" and "moderate purist" groupings is one of strength of agreement. For the purposes of this paper the "strong purist" (hereafter referred to

Table 3.1. Distribution of Purist Groups

| Study area | Total no. | Strong purists (70–60) | Moderate purists (59–60) | Neu- tralists (49–40) | Non- purists (39–14) |
|---|---|---|---|---|---|
| | | *Percent of all respondents in each area* | | | |
| Boundary Waters Canoe Area | 206 | 20 | 49 | 25 | 6 |
| Bob Marshall | 120 | 53 | 39 | 7 | 1 |
| Bridger | 144 | 67 | 23 | 10 | * |
| High Uintas | 154 | 31 | 49 | 18 | 2 |
| Total | 624 | 40 | 41 | 16 | 3 |

* Less than 0.5%.

simply as the "purist") will be treated as the most relevant user for the wilderness manager's decisions.[17]

### The "Purist" Concept

Theorists commonly recognize three components of attitude: how a person *feels* about some object (affective component); what he *knows* about the object (cognitive component); and how he might actually *behave* in regard to an object (behavioral component).

The attitude scale utilized here measures how the respondent feels about "wilderness" as defined by the Wilderness Act. This approach is both purposive and pragmatic because it is the Wilderness Act that will in the end judge the legitimacy of any management decision. Of course the Act could be changed; if it were, the attitudes of respondents toward the new definition would need to be measured.

By summing the individual scores of each item in the scale and utilizing this sum as a measure of purism we assume that "purism" is unidimensional, whereas it is almost certainly multidimensional.[18] The significance of the undisturbed ecosystem, the challenge of the recreational activity, and freedom from congestion are all separate dimensions about which people could hold a purist disposition. And, a purist disposition on one dimension would *not necessarily* presuppose a similar stance on another dimension.

The scale has an intuitive rather than an empirical foundation. It taps a multidimensional domain because it seeks to measure the extent to which the respondent's definition of wilderness coincides with that presented by the Wilderness Act, *a definition which is also multidimensional.* To have factor-analyzed the scale to derive a unidimensional scale would have destroyed this intuitive foundation. Purism, as used in this paper, is a purposively created unit of analysis, which, it is argued, holds particular relevance for the wilderness manager operating within the con-

---

[17] At the risk of being charged with setting up a "straw man" type of argument, I should point out that focusing on the "strong purist" who represents only 40 percent of the total sample does not in any way imply that the remainder of the sample should be ignored. On the contrary, the remaining 60 percent is vitally important, especially in terms of efforts to develop new recreational opportunities and the relative mix of these opportunities. Moreover, eventual decisions regarding wilderness management might reflect the attitudes of this segment of the sample more than the strong purists; this remains the decision of the wilderness administrator. A complete discussion of the remaining three purist groups can be found in Stankey, "The Perception of Wilderness Recreation Carrying Capacity."

[18] Hendee et al., "Wilderness Users in the Pacific Northwest," and Thomas A. Heberlein, "Some Relationships Between Theoretical and Applied Issues in Attitude Research: The Case of Wilderness," paper presented to the Annual Meeting of the Rural Sociological Society, August 1971, Denver, Colorado.

straints of the Wilderness Act. It does not represent either some intrinsic environmental quality or a homogeneous attitude domain.

## A Conceptual Framework for the Study of Carrying Capacity

The "preserve" and "use" dichotomy of the Wilderness Act has created a situation that leaves virtually no alternatives for the wilderness manager to consider other than establishing some "carrying capacity" for wilderness. As Figure 3.1 shows, simply restricting all use is an untenable course of action, at least according to the objectives set forth by the Act. Similarly, allowing use to continue to increase unabated violates the preservation directive promulgated by the Wilderness Act.

As the previous discussion indicated, we can identify two relatively distinct domains where carrying capacity is a legitimate concept: the first focusing on the ecological parameters of wilderness; and the second, on the sociological aspects. Determining the ecological carrying capacity of wilderness involves primarily an investigation of the change in the physical-biological regime brought about by both natural processes, such as erosion, siltation, etc., and human impacts, such as fire suppression or recreational impacts. Determining the sociological carrying capacity of wilderness requires focusing our attention on the manner in which use, in all its parameters, affects satisfaction. As Figure 3.1 indicates, impacts stem from each of the use parameters (e.g., type of use encountered) as well as from the many complex interactions of these parameters.

Together, these two interdependent considerations comprise what is typically and simplistically referred to as wilderness carrying capacity. Melding input from the ecological and sociological domains is a complex task. The objective of this present paper is not to delve into this process, but rather to examine something of the nature of the sociological dimension of the capacity problem.

Much of our knowledge of the effects of the interaction between wilderness users is conjectural and intuitive. By and large we have operated with a generalized and universalistic model of carrying capacity that drew a simple linear relationship between use and recreational quality. The conceptual work of Wagar and the empirical studies of Lucas have cast doubt as to the validity of that model. Thus, we need to turn our attention to the development of a more particularistic model that weighs a variety of use parameters and the interactions between these parameters.

The development of such an analytic framework permits us to investigate some of the more significant conceptual issues. For example, regard-

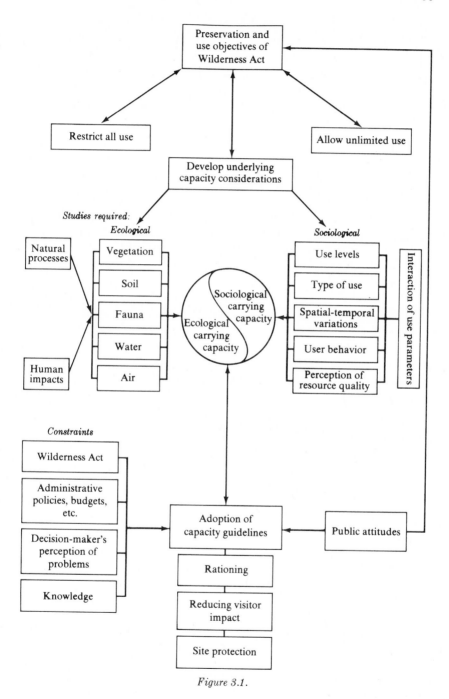

*Figure 3.1.*

ing the level of use one might encounter, do thresholds of sensitivity exist, levels of use beyond which visitor satisfaction rapidly diminishes? Is socializing an important aspect of the wilderness experience and how does it vary in significance between inter- and intra-group contacts?

We need to address ourselves to the interactions between travel methods. What role does exposure and expectation play and do these factors moderate or accentuate potential conflict?

Spatial-temporal variations in use might very well have an important influence on the visitors' reactions. Does the location of an encounter affect user satisfaction? Do visitors develop "mental maps" of wilderness that describe certain patterns of use as appropriate in some locations (e.g., on trails) and not in others (e.g., campsites)?

Finally, the whole range of individual human behavior plays an important role in the social carrying-capacity system—a role that is perhaps the most difficult for us to grasp. Are there accepted social norms that govern wilderness behavior and to what extent do violations of these norms affect other users?

The interaction between man and the physical environment offers an intriguing area of investigation as well (Figure 3.1). However, it has not been included in the present study.

Eventual decisions regarding the capacity standards for wilderness will need to accommodate the different aspects of use as well as the ecological aspects. Moreover, eventual decisions will be under various constraints—legal, administrative, and behavioral.

## Visitor Satisfaction and Wilderness Use

In this study we examined four broad parameters of wilderness use: (a) intensity of use; (b) character of encounters; (c) spatial-temporal aspects of use; and (d) destructive visitor behavior. The basic question asked about each of these was how it affected satisfaction for the wilderness user, especially the purist.

### Intensity of Use: Number of Encounters

This first parameter involves a number of items designed to probe visitor response to varying intensities of use ranging from the abstract concept of solitude to questions involving specific levels of use.

Solitude, the "quality or state of being alone" is commonly used to describe the wilderness experience. However, it is an abstract and amorphous term, subject to widely varying interpretation.

When wilderness visitors were asked if "solitude—not seeing many other people except those in your own party" was desirable, 82 percent of the overall sample responded in a positive fashion. Among the purists, 96 percent felt solitude was desirable; none thought it undesirable. Thus, as a conceptual characteristic of wilderness, it appears to be an extremely important quality to most users, regardless of their position on the purism scale.

This finding does little more, however, than lend substance to what most people have intuitively felt all along. The intent of this particular item was to delineate an image of the wilderness environment in terms of the visitor's perception of use levels in a normative sense. Although solitude was an important quality visitors ascribed to wilderness, did they *expect* to find conditions consistent with this quality? How much of an effect did encounters with others have upon satisfaction?

The whole aspect of "expectation" is intriguing. If a person expects to find a beach quiet and uncrowded he might experience considerable disappointment if it is not. If, on the other hand, he expects it to be crowded, bustling with people, and it is in fact, he might not be happy with the situation, but his expectations have probably tempered his reaction even though he would have preferred to find it uncrowded.

Visitors were asked whether they agreed or disagreed with the proposition "It is reasonable to expect that one should be able to visit a wilderness area and see few, if any, people." Nine out of 10 purists agreed with this statement, as did nearly 80 percent of the visitors to the three western wildernesses. But in the BWCA, where use intensity was the highest of all the areas studied, only 67 percent agreed. It appears that where the chance of seeing others was greater, visitors found it less reasonable to expect not seeing some others.

The response obtained in the BWCA could also be interpreted as evidence of the congestion costs associated with increasing use. As use has increased in the BWCA, those persons seeking solitude might have been turning to other areas or have stopped visiting wilderness altogether. That is, in response to conditions that prohibit their achieving certain personal objectives (in this example, solitude), they "drop out." In turn, they are replaced by persons whose interest in solitude might not be so great. Thus, surveys such as this may be tapping an altogether different clientele than that of some years ago. One can only speculate at present on this possibility, but well-designed longitudinal studies should be initiated to document whether or not such a process is occurring.

Do some people view the wilderness environment as an arena for enhanced opportunities for social interaction? If a person truly desires solitude, we might expect to find him traveling alone. Few do travel alone, however. Only 2 percent of the respondents in this study were traveling by themselves. However, one need not think this leads directly to the conclusion that people who say they want solitude adopt a strategy that precludes it. Rather, contacts between the members of one's own group are probably much different from those with other groups. The strengthening of feelings of camaraderie and the sharing of a special kind of experience with members of one's own party probably do not infringe greatly upon an individual's search for solitude. Members of one's own group "belong," members of other groups are "strangers" who invade the experience.[19]

The data obtained in this study substantiate the reasoning that, for the purist, the primary interaction is with the environment and his close companions. To probe the role of wilderness as an opportunity for social interaction, visitors were asked to comment on the following three items: (a) "Meeting other people around the campfire at night should be part of any wilderness trip"; (b) "It's most enjoyable when you don't meet anyone in the wilderness"; and (c) "You should see at least one group a day in the wilderness to get the most enjoyment out of your trip."

An interesting pattern of responses was discovered. To all three items, only one out of 10 purists responded in a fashion that would support the premise that intergroup social interaction is an integral part of the wilderness experience. Moreover, the statistical association between purist score and response was relatively strong; gamma[20] equaled $-0.39$, 0.41, and $-0.42$, respectively, for the three items.

The responses of the overall sample to these items departed markedly from those of the purists. Nearly half (45 percent) responded positively to the idea that meeting other people around the campfire was an important part of the wilderness experience. One out of four persons disagreed with the proposition that it is most enjoyable when you don't meet anyone in the wilderness, and a similar percentage agreed with the item that you should see at least one other group each day.

Two other items were investigated to test the reactions of visitors to various use intensities: (a) meeting many people on the trail, and (b) meet-

---

[19] Hendee et al. (1968), p. 31, concur with this; they note "(we do not) . . . suggest that wilderness users are actively antisocial. The fact that most wilderness use is by family or friendship groups suggests . . . an aversion only to the kind of depersonalized human encounters so common to modern life."

[20] Gamma indicates the proportional reduction in error (PRE) in predicting category response to the dependent variable possible from knowledge of the independent variable category over that which would occur under random conditions. It ranges in value from $+1.0$ to $-1.0$. Because only a few respondents were at the nonpurist end of the scale there were few low scores to balance the analysis, and the possibility of obtaining high gamma values (e.g., $\pm 0.75$) was reduced. We must therefore focus our attention on the *relative* strength of associations rather than the absolute strength.

ing no one all day. Visitors were asked to indicate the degree to which these situations would bother them or add to their enjoyment.

About one out of four persons, excluding the purists, enjoyed encountering others on the trail; substantial variations occurred among the four areas. In the BWCA, almost 33 percent responded positively to this situation; in the western areas, only 14 percent expressed enjoyment. Because trails are by their very nature arteries for the movement of people, contacts with others are expected; apparently for many people if such contacts do not involve excessive numbers, they can be tolerated. However, purists reacted differently: 60 percent indicated they would be bothered to some degree, 30 percent were neutral, and only 10 percent said they would enjoy meeting others.

Evidence (from the item on solitude) would lead us to hypothesize that the experience of meeting *no one* all day should be considered highly desirable. However, the strength of support was less for this item than for solitude. Forty percent of the "nonpurists"[21] responded that they would enjoy it; 21 percent said it would bother them. Of the purists, nearly three out of four indicated they would enjoy meeting no one all day; and only 3 percent indicated such a situation would bother them. Considerable consistency was found among the responses of purists in each of the study areas. The only marked deviation occurred in the BWCA where only 60 percent of the purists indicated they would enjoy no encounters; 36 percent said they did not care.

Why did purists not express wholehearted agreement with some of these items? Why, for example, did less than 100 percent of the purists indicate they would enjoy a situation involving no encounters? We hypothesize that the answer lies in the fact that capacity, or the purists' definition of a satisfactory experience, is not a simple function of numbers encountered. Other factors come into play. As one woman noted, "it's not how many people you meet, it's how they behave."

*Character of Encounter: Mode of Travel and Party Size*

Wilderness visitors viewed low intensities of use, involving few or no encounters, as an important dimension of the wilderness experience, but it is impossible to generalize beyond this and say that purists are simply and unequivocally opposed to encounters. Thus, it is necessary that we shift our focus from a model of capacity dependent on a universal rejection of all people to a more particularistic model that considers how variations in behavior affect a wilderness user's perception of capacity.

[21] As used here, "nonpurists" includes those classified as moderate purists, neutralists, and nonpurists in Table 3.1.

*Method of travel.* In the BWCA, Lucas found that canoeists were more disturbed by a single motorboat than by the presence of three other canoes.[22] His results suggested that factors other than numbers of encounters should be considered in determining carrying capacity.

Initially, an effort was made in this study to provide some measure of purists' attitudes toward different methods of travel. In the three western areas, visitors were generally in accord with the proposition "both backpacking and horseback travel are entirely appropriate ways to travel in wilderness areas"; 97 percent agreed in the Bob Marshall, 71 percent in the Bridger, and 83 percent in the High Uintas. The percentages appear linked to the predominant method of travel in each area: highest in the Bob Marshall where 65 percent of visitors travel on horseback and lowest in the Bridger where 85 percent of the use is on foot.

In the BWCA, where "paddling" was substituted for backpacking and "using an outboard motor" for horseback travel, only about one in three purists (36 percent) agreed that both methods of travel were appropriate. The primary cause of rejection was an aversion to outboard motors; 83 percent of the purists were paddling canoeists.

Visitors were also asked to indicate which method of travel they preferred to meet (or not meet) in the area they were visiting. In the BWCA, purists (a) demonstrated a marked preference for seeing canoes (76 percent), (b) displayed a surprising ambivalence toward motor canoes (52 percent did not care if they met them), and (c) emphatically rejected seeing motorboats (85 percent preferred not to meet them). Less then 10 percent of the purists expressed a preference for seeing either motor canoes or motorboats.

This clear rejection of a travel method had no equivalent in the western areas except in the Bridger where two-thirds of the purists indicated a preference for not meeting groups accompanied by horses. In the other two areas, however, purists demonstrated tolerance toward the various travel methods; they either expressed a preference for seeing them or were neutral.

The favorable attitude of purists in the BWCA toward canoeists is an entirely predictable and understandable situation. Evidence has already been presented that motors are considered inappropriate in the purist's concept of wilderness. Moreover, the purists are, by and large, canoeists. In the West, purists display a basically positive attitude toward horses, regarding them as legitimate and appropriate in wilderness. The purists were a more mixed group in the West—54 percent were backpackers and the remainder were either on horseback or hiking and leading stock.

[22] Robert C. Lucas, *The Recreational Capacity of the Quetico-Superior Area.* U.S. Forest Service Research Paper LS-8, 1964, p. 23.

*Party size.* Another obvious variable in seeking to pin down sources of use conflict is party size. Commonly, the wilderness trip is undertaken by a small group composed of family or friends. (Two-thirds of this study's sample were traveling in parties of four people or less.) But large outfitted horse parties are also common. Typically, these parties include from 15 to 30 guests, a work crew of perhaps a half dozen, and, on the average, one pack animal per guest.

Such parties might have serious impacts on user satisfaction in any or all of three ways: (a) other users might regard such groups as simply an inappropriate use of wilderness; (b) such groups might inflict severe ecological damage upon the resource; (c) such groups contribute to feelings of crowding.

To determine how users reacted to large parties, visitors were asked to respond to the statement "Seeing a large party reduces the feeling that you're out in the wilderness."

Substantial uniformity in response to this item occurred, unlike several of the past statements where considerable geographic variation was found. About 80 percent of the purists overall expressed agreement with the statement. Only in the BWCA and the Bob Marshall was any substantial disagreement found; 20 percent of the purists in each of these areas disagreed. Nevertheless, there was still substantial agreement to this item by purists in the BWCA (74 percent) and the Bob Marshall (72 percent).

The distribution of use encounters over time is typically uneven. One might go for some time without seeing anyone else; then, several parties might pass by in short succession. To discover whether the spacing of these encounters has an influence on visitor satisfaction, visitors were asked to express a preference for one of the options in each of the following situations:

A. "Seeing one large party of 30 people during the day and no one else *or* one small party of three people during the day and no one else?"
B. "Seeing one large party of 30 people during the day and no one else *or* five small parties of three people each spaced through the day and no one else?"
C. "Seeing one large party of 30 people during the day and no one else *or* 10 parties of three people each spaced through the day and no one else?"

The responses on these items were noteworthy in two regards. First, the majority of users (purists and nonpurists) in the four areas expressed a preference for the small parties in all three situations, except in the

Bob Marshall, where nearly half favored the single large party over 10 small parties. The reaction to situations A and B were not surprising. The choice between one large party and one small party seemed obvious: only 2 percent favored the former. Choosing between the alternatives posed in situation B also seemed predictable: only 17 percent favored the large party, ranging from 16 percent in the Bridger to 28 percent in the Bob Marshall.

When the responses to item C were examined, however, the hypothesis that users, especially purists, would trade off their dislike of large parties for the increased opportunity for solitude they would have by expressing a preference for the large party was found to be incorrect. Even though meeting 10 small parties a day would mean about one encounter per hour, visitors in all areas except the Bob Marshall displayed a decided preference for the 10 small parties. This leads us to speculate that large parties have a particularly deleterious impact upon visitor satisfaction although they compose only a small percentage of total use in most areas (in this study, only 2 percent were in parties larger than 15).

The second feature regarding response to these items concerns the relatively high degree of consistency among visitors to the BWCA, Bridger, and High Uintas and between purists and nonpurists in each area. The following tabulation shows responses to the three items for each area broken down for purists and nonpurists; specifically, it shows percentages favoring a varying number of small parties over one large party.

| Party/parties | BWCA | Bridger | High Uintas |
| | Purist/ nonpurist | Purist/ nonpurist | Purist/ nonpurist |
| --- | --- | --- | --- |
| One small party | 88/70 | 94/88 | 82/73 |
| Five small parties | 65/59 | 66/66 | 65/57 |
| Ten small parties | 54/48 | 55/55 | 32/43 |

The small party represents conventional wilderness behavior, and apparently visitors, whether in the BWCA or Bridger, or whether purist or nonpurist, support this understood norm.

*Use and Satisfaction*

In attempting to determine how use affects visitor satisfaction, we must look at both the amount and the character of use encountered. Visitors were therefore asked to indicate how they felt about encountering an increasingly larger number of specific kinds of other parties. Responses were recorded along a five-point scale ranging from "Very pleasant" to "Very unpleasant." The period during which the encounters occurred was held constant at one day. Visitors were first asked their feelings about meeting no other parties of any kind during the day, then one party of backpackers, two, and so forth, up to a total of nine. The same process was repeated for parties on horseback. In the BWCA, references were to paddling canoeists, motor canoeists, and motor boaters. All the parties were described as small groups, having a maximum of five people in each.

From this data it was possible to construct a series of "satisfaction curves" regarding the various methods of travel a visitor might encounter (see Figure 3.2). These curves were computed by determining the percentage of all respondents who indicated "Very pleasant" or "Pleasant" reactions to the various encounter situations. Thus, the slopes of the curves represent the changes in the percentage of persons responding in a favorable manner to increased levels of use. They do not represent *aggregate* measures of satisfaction. There are three aspects of Figure 3.2 that bear comment.

(a) Compared to the overall sample, a greater proportion of the purists consistently demonstrate a preference for the zero encounter situation. Just over 80 percent of the purists in each of the four areas reacted positively to a situation involving no other encounters.

(b) The number of persons responding positively declines as use increases. This concurs with most of the past hypotheses regarding use and visitor satisfaction in wilderness.[23] In all cases, the curves derived for the purists show a steady decline from no encounters; curves for the overall sample in three of the cases show an increase in response for up to two or three parties of backpackers. In the Bob Marshall and the High Uintas, a majority of persons appear to find encounters with others (both backpackers and horseback riders) enjoyable. In the Bridger, however, purists demonstrate a strong antipathy toward horseback parties. The Bridger supports only limited horse use while horse parties comprise over half the use in the other areas. In the Bob Marshall and the High Uintas, the traditional character of recreation use and the characteristics of the landscape have fostered a norm supporting horse travel; in the Bridger, the relative harshness of the physical-biological regime and the consequent scarcity of horse parties have resulted in a norm of travel method that does not include the horse.

In the BWCA, less than half the sample responded positively to a situation of no encounters. Purists did not differ appreciably from others in their reaction to one or two encounters with canoeists. The most

[23] For example, see "The Carrying Capacity of Wildlands for Recreation," p. 7.

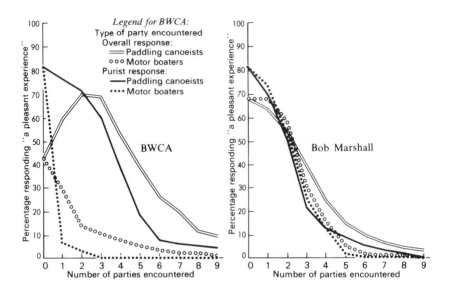

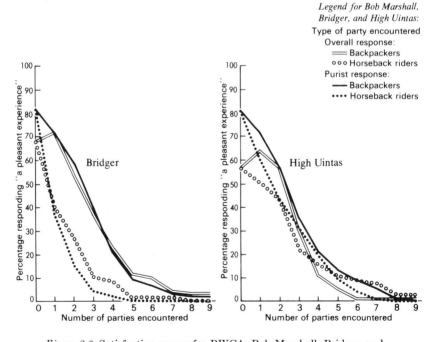

*Figure 3.2.* Satisfaction curves for BWCA, Bob Marshall, Bridger, and High Uintas.

dramatic impact on purist satisfaction comes when motorboats are considered. The percentage of purists indicating a pleasant reaction drops from 82 percent (with no encounters) to 7 percent with one encounter with a motorboat; this clearly delineates the degree to which such craft are perceived as being inappropriate in wilderness. The negative evaluation of these boats is less widely held by the overall sample.

(c) Except for the reaction to motor craft in the BWCA—and despite widely varying resource characteristics and different patterns, types, and intensities of recreational use in the four areas—there is a high degree of consistency among purists in their perception of what constitutes inappropriate levels and types of use.

## Location of Encounters

Encounters in a wilderness occur not only on the trail, where meeting others might be expected, but also at campsites, where solitude and privacy might be especially important. To test whether visitors differentiate between encounters on the trail and those at campsites, they were asked to state their preference on the following: "Seeing a lot of people within the first few miles or so from the road and no one else the rest of the trip *or* several other parties in the area where I expect to camp and no one else."

Over 80 percent of the purists favored the situation that involved trail encounters. In all four areas, less than one in 20 expressed a preference for seeing others in the vicinity of their camp.

To test the notion that the campsite represents a place where new acquaintances and friendships are developed, respondents were asked the extent to which they agreed with the proposition "When staying out overnight in the wilderness it is most enjoyable not to be near anyone else."

About 90 percent of the purists and about two-thirds of the nonpurists agreed that the wilderness campsite should provide complete solitude. The idea that the campsite is an area where intergroup contacts should be developed was rejected (gamma equaled 0.43). The more purist that users were, the more they were inclined to agree with the statement.

If attitudes toward other parties are influenced by the campsite location, we might expect to find modifications in expected behavior.[24]

[24] The relationship between an individual's attitude about some object and his subsequent behavior toward that object is a poorly understood process. Several studies have reported low or even negative correlations between attitude and behavior (e.g., see Irwin Deutscher, "Words and Deeds: Social Science and Social Policy," *Social Problems*, vol. 13 [1966], pp. 235–54). However, in their review of the literature on the attitude-behavior relationship, Tittle and Hill concluded that the predictive quality of attitudes relative to behavior was a function of (a) the measurement tech-

Respondents were asked to consider a situation where, after they set up camp in an isolated location, two or three other parties arrive on the scene. Several behavioral reactions were included as possible responses.

Among the purists in the four areas, between 70 percent and 83 percent indicated that their enjoyment would be adversely affected by others camping near them. Many indicated they would cut short their visit. Nearly half of the purists in the Bob Marshall and Bridger indicated they would attempt to find another campsite.

We felt that the strongly expressed displeasure about having others near one's campsite ought to be reflected in the purist's preference for a campsite location in terms of its spatial relationship to other camps. To determine what factor spatial relationships play in a user's selection of a campsite location, respondents were asked to indicate their preference for one of the following: (a) "a spot out of sight and hearing of all other campers"; (b) "a place some distance away from others; seeing or hearing them, however, would not bother me"; and (c) "a place near other campers."

Purists in the Bob Marshall and Bridger were heavily in favor of a location offering complete solitude (85 percent in both areas). The intensity of expressed preference for such locations was somewhat less in the BWCA (70 percent) and the High Uintas (75 percent). In none of the areas did *any* purist opt for a location where he would be more likely to meet others. The association between purist score and preference for a location out of sight and hearing of others was high (gamma = 0.52). For the four areas together, less than two out of 10 purists desired a location where others could be seen or heard even if they were some distance away.

Apparently, the opportunity to escape from others is an important characteristic of the camping site. Within the camping zone the primary interaction involves man and the physical environment; interaction with other parties is unwanted.

*Destructive Behavior Aspects of Capacity*

What effect does evidence of man's presence—not actual encounters—have upon purists' satisfaction levels? What does the evidence of previous use have on the purist's perception of carrying capacity?

nique used; (b) the degree to which the criterion behavior constituted action within the individual's common range of experience; and (c) the degree to which the criterion behavior represented a repetitive behavioral configuration (Charles R. Tittle and Richard J. Hill, "Attitude Measurement and Prediction of Behavior: An Evaluation of Conditions and Measurement Techniques," *Sociometry*, vol. 30, no. 2 [1967], pp. 199–213). The extent to which wilderness behavior fits (b) and (c) above is conjectural, but the findings of Tittle and Hill suggest that the measurement of attitudes can, under certain conditions, reduce the range of uncertainty regarding predictions of user behavior.

In a wilderness environment (where the works and evidence of man are generally minimal), the evidence of destructive behavior is particularly noticeable. Destructive behavior, as used in this paper, describes behavior that might violate institutional restrictions, accepted social norms, or both. Our attention was focused on two consequences of destructive behavior: littering and campsite deterioration. In many ways, campsite deterioration is an ecological dimension of the carrying capacity problem. However, it was included because it is often aggravated and accelerated by human behavior and because it can greatly impair the quality of a wilderness trip.

*Campsite overuse.* Any use of an ecosystem results in some physical change, and this is particularly true at a campsite where use is concentrated within a relatively small space. We hypothesized that visual evidence of campsite "wear and tear" would have a strong effect on visitor satisfaction because our findings had suggested the campsite environment was an especially important part of the wilderness experience.

This hypothesis was substantiated to a much greater degree than expected. There is a wide range in the inherent capabilities of sites to withstand change and a wide variation in both the type and intensity of use at different sites. Nevertheless, there was uniform and emphatic purist concern with sites that evidenced wear and tear. Virtually all those responding (98 percent) to a question concerning reactions to such sites indicated they would be dissatisfied.[25]

Even though people say they don't like beat-up campsites, it is apparent they still use them. One might argue this is further evidence that behavior and attitude are poorly related. However, we must recognize that very often a party has little choice and has to take what is available. Also, the fact that a party is occupying a particular site does not in itself justify the conclusion that its members derive a satisfactory experience from that location.

*Littering.* A central contention in this study is that carrying capacity is a function of several different dimensions. Virtually all respondents, regardless of their attitudes toward wilderness, expressed strong negative reactions to finding litter in the wilderness. But evidence also has been presented that an excessive number of encounters is important in visitor definitions of capacity. To test how these two elements of the capacity problem were related, visitors were asked the extent to which they

---

[25] One could legitimately argue here that there was no other socially acceptable response to such a question. It is apparent that questionnaire-type surveys do not lend themselves to certain types of investigations.

agreed with the statement "Seeing too many people in the wilderness is more disturbing than finding a littered campsite."

Overall, two-thirds of the purists disagreed with the statement; there was a remarkable consistency in response among the four areas, ranging from 64 percent in the Bridger to 73 percent in the High Uintas. The "moderate purists" group (see Table 3.1) actually showed a slightly higher level of disagreement than the purists. Responding to this particular statement was probably a difficult task for the purists. It was essentially a question of which was "the lesser of two evils." The uniform pattern of response, however, suggests that certain values are widely held. Also noteworthy is the uniformity of response stimulated by "too many people."

### IMPLICATIONS OF PURIST ATTITUDES FOR WILDERNESS MANAGEMENT

Inasmuch as a wilderness management philosophy consistent with the objectives of the Wilderness Act is impossible under a "manage for all" approach, we need some technique to differentiate users in a manner that most nearly meshes visitor needs and motives with opportunity. The purist, as defined in this paper, serves this function.

In a capsule version, what do the attitudes of the purist imply for the wilderness manager?

First, we are talking about a wilderness environment involving a low intensity of use. Design, variations in the timing of travel, and other modifications in the actions of managers and visitors might make it possible to increase total use in some areas, perhaps substantially over what it is now. However, use limitations will almost certainly need to be instituted eventually in order to protect both the environmental qualities of wilderness and the recreational opportunities these areas provide.

Second, conflicts between the traditional small party and the large group are serious and should be dealt with. Conflicts between the different travel methods in the three western wildernesses do not appear especially serious, and there is probably not a large payoff in increased aggregate satisfaction associated with a decision to zone backpackers away from small horse parties. Nevertheless, there might be good and sufficient biological reasons to close off some or all of certain wildernesses to horse travel.

Conditions in the BWCA are entirely different. There is a serious conflict between canoeists and those using motorboats. The latter craft are perceived as inappropriate and destructive to the wilderness setting. Elimination of motors within the BWCA rather than their exclusion from certain areas probably is needed.

Third, being able to locate an isolated campsite is important to most visitors. Management efforts to provide more information about opportunities to locate such sites could carry rather substantial positive benefits.

Fourth, there is a clear and unequivocally negative reaction on the part of purists to the more obvious effects of ill use. I would speculate that purists espouse a wilderness philosophy where man is subordinate to nature, and that evidence of man's disregard for nature—litter, campsite destruction, and so forth—is especially annoying for them. Again, efforts to control or eliminate these problems probably will yield substantial gains in relation to costs.

Finally, on many aspects of wilderness use, there is little to distinguish the purists' responses from those of the undifferentiated overall sample except the purists' more intense reaction. However, there are certain dimensions of the wilderness experience to which purists ascribe a significantly different set of values than others do; it is in these situations that the preferences of the purists should be followed in an effort to ensure both the preservation of the natural character of wilderness lands and the maintenance of a recreational experience that is largely nonsubstitutable.

One of the aspects of this study that was especially interesting was the pattern of purists' responses. Purists, who were defined to possess similar conceptual attitudes about wilderness, responded in a fairly uniform way to questions about what the wilderness should be like. Solitude, for example, was rated highly whether the respondent was from the BWCA or the Bridger.

Attitudes toward actual conditions of use, however, tended to reflect local customs and varied from area to area. Attitudes toward horses for example, were most favorable in the Bob Marshall, where horses are more common. Similarly, large parties were regarded more tolerantly in areas where such groups are common. As both the study by Hendee et al. and the ORRRC Report 3 concluded, the appeal of wilderness is probably a generic one, but individual area differences result in certain modifications of this appeal.

## Purists and Wilderness Management

A standard argument for not using visitor attitudes as a means of formulating wilderness management strategies is that public attitudes as to what constitutes solitude, the pristine, or the natural will become less discriminating as population rises, urban densities increase, and so forth.

The idea that attitudes about what is "pure wilderness" will weaken in the future might be a classic example of a self-fulfilling prophecy. If we orient wilderness management along a line designed to accommodate gradually less-demanding tastes, we will almost certainly attract a clientele that, in time, will hold a less demanding concept of wilderness. Burch writes "The trajectory of the future is not determined by the future, but by our present conception of it."[26]

The external stimuli with which the citizen of tomorrow will have to contend are largely beyond the control of the wilderness management agencies—traffic, population, design of cities, and so forth. However, the internal stimuli (the conditions the visitor encounters within the wilderness) are elements of the environment that the managing agencies can manipulate and control. Developing a management orientation with which purists acquiesce will probably foster the continued existence of purist attitudes.

The data herein suggest that local or unique sets of conditions can modify attitudes; exposures breed tolerance to some degree. Unfortunately, we lack the rigorous kinds of longitudinal studies needed to fully support this contention, but there is a strong probability that it is correct. A wilderness management strategy that is uncompromising in its effort to fulfill the intent of the Wilderness Act will probably enjoy sound purist support in the future. Gradually reducing the rigorousness of guidelines for wilderness management will not only result in the eventual deterioration of the unique environmental qualities these areas possess, but will also result in the loss of a special kind of experience for which there is little substitute. Although the Canadian Northland and the Amazon Basin might represent opportunities for certain special kinds of experiences, they cannot logically be considered either realistic or sufficient alternatives for tomorrow's wilderness enthusiast. The remoteness of these areas and the expense of reaching them would largely preclude the present pattern and style of wilderness use and would therefore narrow the spectrum of opportunities discussed earlier in this paper. Most wilderness trips are of short duration, averaging only two or three days. Also, many wilderness visitors take several trips each season. If we seriously believe in the necessity for a "Conservation Ethic," then we need to consider the value of preserving the richness and diversity of the resources and experiences still available in our American wildernesses.

---

[26] William R. Burch, "Fishes and Loaves: Some Sociological Observations on the Environmental Crises," in Francois Mergen (ed.), *Man and His Environment: The Ecological Limits of Optimism* (New Haven: Yale University Press, 1970), p. 41.

# 4

# Determination of Optimal Capacity of Resource-Based Recreation Facilities

ANTHONY C. FISHER and
JOHN V. KRUTILLA*

## I. GROWING DEMAND AND CONGESTION IN OUTDOOR RECREATION

There are roughly three-quarters of a billion acres of land in public ownership in the United States, a substantial part of which represents wild or undeveloped lands such as those found in the National Wilderness System, and also in the National Forest, National Park, and National Refuge Systems. Some of this land is reserved for uses incompatible with raw material exploitation by extractive industries. Examples are the Wilderness and Refuge System lands. Some is *de facto* wilderness; i.e., land available for inclusion in the Wilderness System under terms of the Wilderness Act of 1964. Such tracts as yet unprotected by legal wilderness status are also subject to logging, mining, conversion to cropland, and other extractive purposes pending determination of their status.

Demand for the services that wildlands provide in their natural state

* Economists, Resources for the Future, Inc.

*Note:* This paper was published in slightly different form in *Natural Resources Journal,* vol. 12, no. 3 (1972).

*Authors' note.* We are indebted to George Stankey and Robert Lucas for providing much of the information on wilderness users' attitudes and behavior, and to Blair Bower, Gunter Schramm, and Robert Lucas for a critical review of an earlier draft of this paper. Acknowledgment is also due Charles Cicchetti for much help in the preparation of the paper and to Kerry Smith, Walter Spofford, Robert Barro, and John Brown for comments on an earlier draft. We retain the responsibility for any remaining misconceptions or errors.

Table 4.1. Visits to National Parks and National Forests, Selected Years, 1904–1964
*(thousands of visits)*

| Year | National Parks | National Forest Lands | |
|------|------|------|------|
| | | Areas improved by public funds | Other areas[a] |
| 1904 | 121 | — | — |
| 1924 | 1,424 | 3,460 | 1,200 |
| 1946 | 8,991 | 8,763 | 9,478 |
| 1954 | 17,969 | 19,747 | 20,557 |
| 1964 | 34,048 | 35,629 | 81,062 |

Source: Marion Clawson, *The Federal Lands Since 1956* (Washington, D.C.: Resources for the Future, Inc., 1967), pp. 60, 95.

[a] Unimproved areas, e.g., wilderness areas and a few public areas improved by non-federal means.

has grown phenomenally since the early years of this century. Table 4.1 shows the trends in the recreational use of National Park and National Forest lands. Perhaps most striking are the figures for use of the "other," largely unimproved areas of the National Forests. Rapid as the increase in use of all National Park and National Forest lands has been, it appears that the increase in use of just some of the more nearly natural areas has been several times more rapid. Also suggestive are figures for man-days of use of National Forest Wilderness Areas alone. Over a period of just 12 years, from 1947 to 1959, use increased by 356 percent.[1] Disaggregated figures for recent years show a continuation of these trends.[2]

This rapid and sustained growth in demand for wildlands recreation seems likely to continue, and poses some problems regarding the allocation of lands among the various uses. In most instances, the problem is one of determining the most efficient allocation of land. Should it be used by an extractive industry to produce mineral, forest, or agricultural products, or preserved in its natural state to provide recreational and other services? A related problem, perhaps a sub-problem, involves the allocation of land between low-density and high-density recreational uses. In either case we wish to compare the benefits from a given use with those from an incompatible alternative use to which the resources

[1] Wildland Research Center, *Wilderness and Recreation: A Report on Resources, Values, and Problems*, Outdoor Recreation Resources Review Commission Study Report No. 3 (Washington, D.C.: Government Printing Office, 1962), pp. 226–29.

[2] See monthly reports, U.S. Department of the Interior, National Park Service, *Public Use of the National Parks*, for 1967–69; also U.S. Forest Service statistics on Recreational Use of National Forests, available from the U.S. Department of Agriculture, Forest Service.

may be directed. Since use of resources for one purpose precludes their use for any incompatible purpose or purposes, the benefits forgone are in effect the opportunity costs of the selected use and must be added to any direct costs associated with that use.[3]

Typically we would anticipate that the value of the services a tract of land would yield, and hence the value of the land and associated resources, would differ depending on the use to which it was put. The value of a site would then depend on its resource endowment and the elasticities of demand and supply for the respective services it might yield. From the standpoint of economic efficiency the objective would be to allocate wildlands and scenic resources in such a way as to maximize the value of the services they yield, i.e., to allocate them to their most highly valued uses over an appropriately long time horizon.

While highly developed markets tend to achieve an efficient allocation in this sense in some areas of the economy, allocation of wildland resources to the production of various goods and services has in large measure been handled by extra-market devices in the public sector.[4] Under these circumstances, market transactions do not serve as a measure of benefits and costs, and a variety of estimating techniques have been developed as part of the apparatus of resource management.

Generally speaking, rather traditional benefit-cost analysis in conjunction with a wide array of inputs from the various resource management disciplines can provide reasonably good estimates of benefits and costs of various extractive activities. Even the art of estimating the demand for, and value of, resource based non-priced outdoor recreation services has developed in a promising way during the past decade or so.[5] Perhaps somewhat less well understood and correspondingly less developed is the methodology for evaluating the benefits from preserving unique natural phenomena, particularly those that will be reserved for or devoted to low-density recreational uses. One of the reasons in the latter case, of course, turns on the problem of optimal density for low-

[3] Not all uses are mutually exclusive, however. Logging in mature stands may improve light conditions for the production of understory browse for ungulates thus improving recreational hunting, for example. As some kinds of extractive and recreational activities are complementary to a point, the problem in its largest dimensions may be the specification of the optimal product mix where joint products are involved. While complementary uses represent an aspect of the total problem, we abstract from that aspect in the paper.

[4] For a summary of these, see John V. Krutilla and Jack Knetsch, "Outdoor Recreation Economics," *The Annals of the American Academy of Social and Political Sciences,* May 1970; and John V. Krutilla, "Conservation Reconsidered," *American Economic Review,* September 1967.

[5] T. L. Burton and M. N. Fulcher, "Measurement of Recreation Benefits: A Survey," *The Journal of Economic Studies,* 1967, review the state of the art as of 1967.

density recreational activities. Maximizing the value of a particular
tract of wildland allocated, by whatever means, to the provision of low-
density recreational services will require that an optimal density be
chosen.[6] This is only another way of saying that an optimal capacity
needs to be defined. The development of operational concepts for defining
optimal recreational capacity for low-density recreational wildlands is
the objective of this paper. The significance of having operational concepts for determining recreational capacity will become obvious in the
course of the analysis.

## II. THE MEANING OF CAPACITY

Two concepts of recreational capacity should be clarified at the outset.
The first, which we refer to as the ecologist's carrying capacity, is
basically a biological or physical relationship between a given resource
stock and its maximum sustained yield, i.e., the maximum number of
individuals of a species that can be supported by a given habitat under
conditions of maximum stress. The second is the economist's conception
of capacity. This, too, is usually given in a physical measure but in
terms of a product of constant quality. When we speak of a wilderness
experience as the product or service sought, we recognize that solitude
as well as primeval setting are dimensions of the quality of the service.
With a sufficient amount of wilderness area relative to the demand for
the services, it is conceivable that an unvarying quality of wilderness
experience can be realized. However, at some point an increase in the
number of wilderness recreationists will involve some trail and camp
encounters impinging on the privacy and solitude sought. At this point
one would anticipate an erosion of the quality of the recreation experience. Quality deterioration through what is referred to as the external
effects of congestion may exceed the permissible level for optimal intensity of use, in an economist's sense, substantially before the carrying
capacity in the ecologist's sense is reached. Conversely, for some areas
supporting fragile ecosystems the use constraint may need to be set
before significant congestion costs are experienced if the ecological integrity of the area is to be protected. It is important, then, to note the
distinction between these concepts of capacity and to distinguish them
in our treatment of the problem in what follows below.

Following Stankey,[7] albeit using an economic rationale, we shall consider a low-density recreation use of a differentiated product catering to

----

[6] This assumes, of course, that growth in demand will continue posing problems of
congestion and value reduction if some capacity constraints are not enforced.

[7] George H. Stankey, "The Perception of Wilderness Recreation Carrying Capacity: A Geographic Study in Natural Resources Management," Ph.D. thesis, Michigan
State University, 1971.

a relatively specialized clientele or sub-market. (This use is hereinafter referred to as a wilderness experience.) Stankey has employed a rationale based on an extra-market allocative device (political process) for selecting his "public," or "clientele" (in our terms, the relevant "customer"). We can, like Stankey, assume that the wildland tract in question has been designated as a *de jure* wilderness area, and our interest could center on determining what intensity of use would maximize the value of the service flow. On the other hand, we can select for analysis a given tract in order to determine whether its value as a wilderness recreation resource would exceed its value as a high-density recreational resource or, alternatively, as a source of natural resource commodites exploited in a manner incompatible with retaining its integrity as a natural area.[8] In the latter case we would wish to establish the benefit of the tract when retained in its wild state by fixing the intensity of use at the level that would maximize the value of the preservation alternative. This value would then be compared with the opportunity returns forgone by precluding the higher density development or the incompatible extractive alternatives.

Our analysis assumes a multi-modal distribution of tastes in recreation pursuits. That is, we are taking it for granted that those who elect to devote a significant portion of their leisure time to outdoor activities in the remote backcountry and those who devote vacation periods to more gregarious situations *tend* to cluster in mutually exclusive groups.[9] The task of allocating resources to cater to the various preferences of those seeking outdoor recreation is one the market would fail to perform efficiently, thereby justifying public intervention. But if intervention is to succeed in improving the efficiency with which resources are allocated, it must make provision for the entire range of tastes in proportion to the number of consumers involved and the elasticities—price and income, current and projected—of their demand.

From this point forward we examine only that segment of the outdoor recreation market represented by the unambiguous wilderness experience seeker for whom solitude is a desired objective: i.e., the satisfaction or utility gained from the wilderness experience tends to be inversely related to the number of other parties he meets during a wilderness outing.[10]

[8] A situation where the latter type of analysis would be appropriate is the remaining portion of Hells Canyon where there is controversy over whether to preserve it in its present condition as a wild and scenic recreational resource or develop the Snake River in this reach as a hydroelectric project. See the paper by Fisher, Krutilla, and Cicchetti, in this book.

[9] The person who likes to spend his vacation backpacking in the wilderness in search of solitude is unlikely to spend any time at a high-density vacation spot. But he is not necessarily antisocial throughout the year.

[10] See Stankey, "The Perception of Wilderness Recreation Carrying Capacity," and his paper in this book.

### III. A Simple Model for Determining Optimal Capacity

In this section we review the analytics of determining an optimal recreation capacity for low-density recreational use facilities. Let us consider a relatively homogeneous group of recreationists who wish to enjoy a wilderness recreation experience. We assume that, for all members of the group, an increase in the probability of encountering others on a wilderness outing is attended by diminished utility from the outing. For simplicity, we assume also a uniform distribution of recreationists over the recreation season. A season in this context can be segmented into as many intervals as necessary—a summer backpacking season, the autumn hunting season, and so on.

With these assumptions we present in Figure 4.1 a rather special set of schedules of aggregate demand or willingness to pay. On the horizontal axis, use intensity is represented by the quantity of recreation days (or recreationists) per unit time. Thus $q_1$ represents a density half as great as $q_2$, a third as great as $q_3$, etc., and the expected encounter rate is peculiar to the use intensity in question. Along the vertical axis we have represented the price, or willingness to pay, per recreation day. For convenience of diagrammatic exposition, let us assume momentarily that there are thresholds, and that changes in intensity of use within ranges demarcated by such thresholds do not result in any congestion costs, but that changes between one threshold and another, moving from the origin to the right, are attended by quantum jumps in utility-diminishing congestion effects. Accordingly, for any intensity of use within the range of 0 to $q_1$, we consider the quality of the wilderness experience constant. This experience, being free of adverse congestion effects, represents the range of highest unit value wilderness experience and is represented by the highest demand schedule $D_1 D_1'$. The total value of the recreation service flow per unit of time with capacity fixed at $q_1$ (and fully utilized) is represented by the area under the demand schedule $D_1 D_1'$, here $0 P_1 D_1' q_1$.[11]

Admission of additional unambiguous wilderness experience seekers would be attended by the addition of utility enjoyed by them. But an increase in the density of recreationists would result in a deterioration of the quality of the experience as compared with the experience at the lower encounter level. The relevant demand schedule might then be drawn as $D_2 D_2'$ for a service with a quality now fixed by the use intensity represented by $0 q_2$. The demand curve for the changed quality of service

---

[11] For a summary discussion, see Jack L. Knetsch and Robert K. Davis, "Comparison of Methods for Recreation Evaluation," in Allen V. Kneese and Stephen C. Smith (eds.), *Water Research* (Baltimore: Johns Hopkins Press for Resources for the Future, 1966).

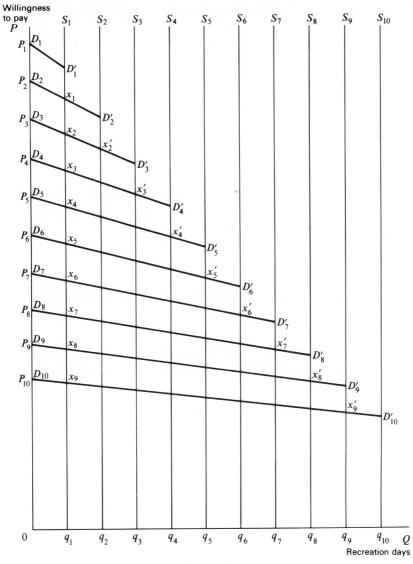

*Figure 4.1.*

being lower, represents the diminution of utility per unit previously enjoyed by those who experienced the wilderness with no adverse congestion effects. Accordingly, the gain in utility enjoyed by the additional
numbers participating would be represented by the area $q_1 x_1 D_2' q_2$. The
loss is represented by the area $P_2 P_1 D_1' x_1$. As long as the gain from ad-

mitting additional numbers exceeds the loss due to congestion costs, aggregate net benefits will increase. Beyond a point the congestion costs exceed the gains experienced by the additional recreationists and total net benefits diminish. On the diagram, this occurs in the neighborhood of $q_6$.

Now if there are no costs other than the so-called "externalities" or adverse effects of congestion, the maximum net total benefit level of use would also define the optimal recreation capacity for such a low-density recreation facility or natural area. But normally there will be other costs as well—for example, the cost of potential environmental degradation of the sort Brandborg has alluded to, where recreational pressure may exert an adverse effect on the ecological environment.[12] Moreover, as Wagar and others have noted, costs in the form of operating expenditures may be incurred to reduce, modify, or eliminate the adverse effects of congestion.[13] Further, costs in the form of investment outlays to expand the intensive margins (e.g., laying out a duplicating but nonintersecting trail system to reduce or eliminate the probability of increased encounters with increased recreational density) may, and in the normal situation would, qualify for consideration in a well-managed wilderness area or system. Accordingly, the maximum total benefit as defined above is not likely to indicate the optimal recreation capacity for the wilderness tract in question. The reasons will be: (a) ecological degradation costs will not have been taken into account, and (b) the possibility of incurring expenditures to augment capacity must be considered at any time—and over time—in determining optimal recreation capacity for a given tract of land.

To take account of these factors in our diagrammatic analytics, we need to return to Figure 4.1, and from the basic notions contained therein, derive an additional set of geometric relationships.

If we now change our assumption that we experience constant quality recreation services within appreciable ranges limited by discrete threshold values and assume that these ranges can be made appropriately small, we can postulate a total net benefit function as shown in Figure

---

[12] Stewart M. Brandborg, "On the Carrying Capacity of Wilderness," *Living Wilderness*, vol. 82 (1963), p. 28. See also R. Burnell Held, Stanley Brickler, and Arthur T. Wilcox, *A Study to Develop Practical Techniques for Determining the Carrying Capacity of Natural Areas in the National Park System*, Center for Research and Education, Colorado State University, November 1969, for a more extended discussion of the inevitable adverse ecological effects, which range from the negligible effects from the first footstep to the severe effects from such activities as overgrazing and the trampling of fragile alpine meadows by pack stock.

[13] J. Allan Wagar, *The Carrying Capacity of Wildlands for Recreation*, Forest Service Monograph 7, 1964. See also Marion Clawson, "Philmont Scout Ranch, An Intensively Managed Wilderness," *American Forests*, May 1968.

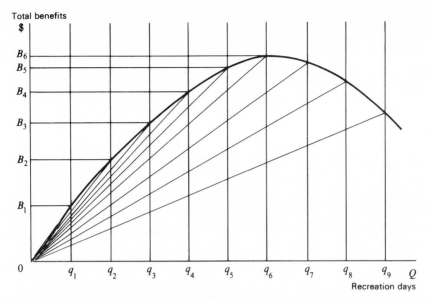

*Figure 4.2.*

4.2. Here we have the benefit measured along the vertical axis with the quantity of recreational services (user days) measured along the horizontal axis. All points on the total benefit function measured by the vertical distance, divided by the corresponding quantity (given by the perpendicular dropped from a given point to the horizontal axis) will yield the average benefit, represented by the slopes of the chords shown in Figure 4.2.

These average benefit computations can be represented in an average benefit curve such as the one $B/q$ of Figure 4.3, and the relation of the incremental (or marginal) benefit to the average and total is represented in standard textbook form as the dashed line in Figure 4.3. We note in passing that the point of maximum net benefit (use intensity represented by $q_6$) is the point at which the cost of incremental congestion disutilities just equals the benefit of incremental gains to utility; hence, the net marginal or incremental benefit function at that point equals zero.

If there were to be no costs other than those associated with congestion, the optimal capacity would be at the point at which the total benefit was a maximum and the incremental or marginal benefit was zero. With the introduction of, say, ecological degradation costs, adjustment to the use intensity for purposes of defining the optimal capacity may be required. Conceivably one could argue that the adverse impact on the area's environment would be reflected in diminished utility to the wilder-

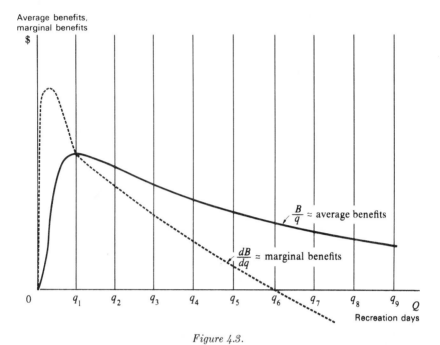

*Figure 4.3.*

ness user, and thus should be incorporated, as were congestion disutilities in the net marginal benefit function. However, in some cases—for example, if the damage to an area is extensive or permanent, or if a particular species is endangered—wilderness users are not the only ones who suffer a loss. Society as a whole has lost the opportunity to view an example of untrammeled natural environment.[14] Accordingly, it is desirable to distinguish these costs from the more conventional disutilities associated with congestion. We do so in Figure 4.4 by means of a separate marginal cost of ecological damage function $(MC_d)$, representing the adverse impact of wilderness users on the ecology of the wilderness areas as the intensity of use increases. If such ecological damage effects should occur before the maximum total net benefit (excluding this latter consideration) is reached, $MC_d$ would intersect the net benefit schedule short of the $q_6$ intensity of use level. Thus ecological damage as the effective constraint or "limiting factor" would determine optimal use at a level rep-

[14] This option value will be of utility to an individual as long as he or his heirs can exercise the option. For a discussion of this, see Burton Weisbrod, "Collective Consumption Aspects of Individual Consumption Goods," *Quarterly Journal of Economics*, August 1964; Charles J. Cicchetti and A. Myrick Freeman III, "Consumer Surplus and Option Value in the Estimation of Benefits," *Quarterly Journal of Economics*, August 1971.

Marginal benefits,
marginal costs

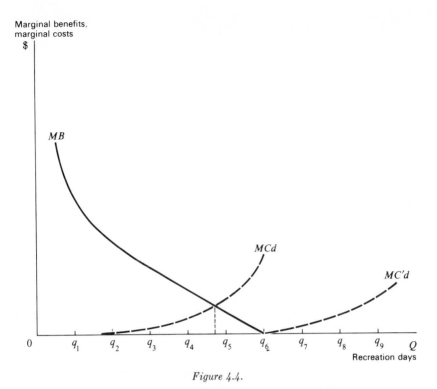

*Figure 4.4.*

resented by the intersection of a perpendicular dropped from the intersection of the $MC_d$ and $MB$ functions to the horizontal, i.e., just short of
level $q_5$ in Figure 4.4. However, if the ecological damage effects did not
occur until after the maximum benefit capacity was reached (where
$\Delta B = \Delta C$), the ecologist's concept of carrying capacity would not serve
as the effective constraint. This situation is represented by the curve
$MC_d'$.

We need to attend to another practical matter before considering expenditures made by public land management agencies to augment capacity. We have assumed implicitly that the costs of restricting entry to the
wilderness tract in question were negligible. In a practical sense this is
not likely to be true. Thus, some consideration of administrative costs is
required for defining optimal capacity, other things remaining equal. In
Figure 4.5, where the ecological damage cost is assumed to be negligible
within the relevant range (between 0 and $q_6$), the net benefit will not be
maximized at $q_6$, as when administrative costs were taken to be zero, but
at an intensity of use at a point short of $q_6$. This point is given by the
intersection of the marginal benefit function (net of congestion costs) and

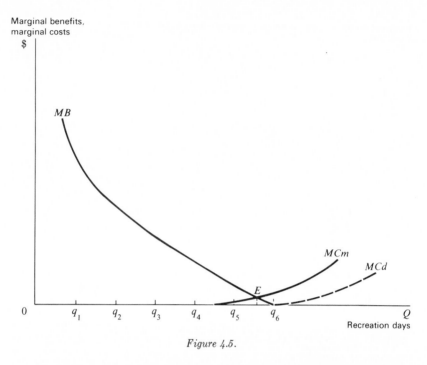

*Figure 4.5.*

the marginal cost of administering the intensity of use ($MC_m$), which is indicated by the new efficiency point $E$.[15] The administrative cost here reflects simply an attempt to ration use, without affecting the spatial or temporal distribution of users.

We can also consider the possibility of using more labor-intensive management methods to redistribute use and thus increase the capacity of a given facility without reducing the quality of experience.[16] We show this in Figure 4.6. Here the $MC_m'$ curve represents the increase in management expenditures devoted to the more intensive management of the *recreationists* in order to provide a less-congested wilderness experience. The incremental cost shift from $MC_m$ to $MC_m'$ has the effect, as well, of shifting the marginal benefit schedule (net of congestion disutility) from

[15] Since the services are provided independently of costs incurred for rationing, the equating of $MB$ and $MC_m$ is only a partial criterion. The direct and opportunity costs of rationing must be less than the reduction in congestion costs that they are intended to achieve. Otherwise, no rationing is justified. We have more to say about this in section III.

[16] See Marion Clawson, "Philmont Scout Ranch," for an interesting discussion of the use of advance reservations, period of orientation, and dissemination of information to Boy Scout backpack groups at the Philmont Ranch in order to increase the aggregate number of recreation days without proportional deterioration of the wilderness experience.

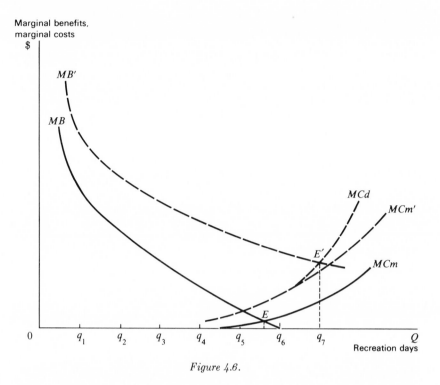

*Figure 4.6.*

$MB$ to $MB'$ and providing all wilderness users with a higher-valued wilderness experience. This follows from the manner in which the $MC'_m$ expenditures have shifted $MB'$, the marginal benefit function (net of congestion disutility). But the benefit was achieved, by assumption, at an increase in both ecological damage costs ($MC_d$) for the increased level of use and of direct public agency management expenditures ($MC'_m$). We now have the optimal level shifting from a use intensity something short of $q_6$ to one in the neighborhood of $q_7$, i.e., below $E'$, the intersection of the $MB'$ and the vertical sum of the $MC'_m$ and $MC_d$ curves.

An alternative would be to reduce congestion by investment, e.g., by additions to the trail system that would increase capacity without a proportional increase in encounters. This method would involve a trade-off between more labor-intensive (current) expenditures and capital improvements. It might also eliminate the element of "regimentation," which regulating the time and place of wilderness use would undoubtedly have for some. To show the effect of capital improvements, however, it might be best to return to the form of the total benefit curve in Figure 4.2, which is reproduced in Figure 4.7 as the $TB$ curve (compressed along the horizontal dimension). From any given investment cost level $OM$

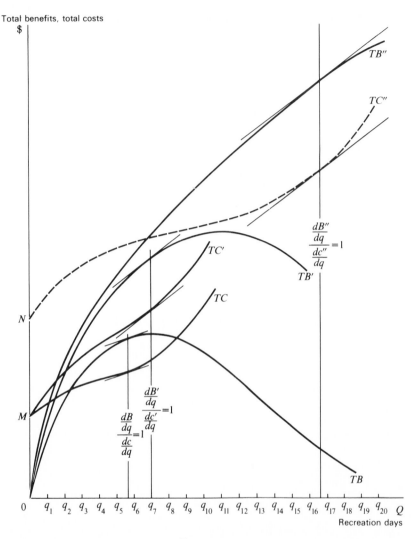

*Figure 4.7.*

(i.e., the present value of the opportunity returns forgone by precluding an alternative use of the tract), a total cost curve, *TC*, will trace both the fixed and variable costs, and the slope of the *TC* curve will give the marginal cost. The optimal capacity (at *E*, Figure 4.5) would be shown on Figure 4.7 where the slopes of the *TB* and *TC* curves were equal— where marginal benefits equal marginal costs—just short of $q_6$. The optimal capacity (at $q_7$) resulting from the shift in the total benefit curve

$TB$ to $TB'$ due to additional expenditure on more intensive management (represented by the shift of $TC$ to $TC'$) is shown similarly, paralleling the exposition in Figure 4.5 and Figure 4.6. But Figure 4.7 can illustrate in addition the effects of an investment, say, as an alternative to more labor-intensive expenditures to increase the capacity in question.

Consider then an increase in the investment of an amount corresponding to $MN$. Assume first that this is associated with an expanded but nonintersecting trail system that could accommodate larger numbers of individuals without increasing the probability of encounters. The increased capacity[17] is reflected by the change in the position of the total benefit curve from $TB$ to $TB''$. The difference between the two total benefit curves ($TB$ and $TB''$) at any $q$ represents the diminution of congestion disutilities due to the increased capacity of the trail system. To obtain the optimal intensity of use for the enlarged facility, we would trace the total cost curve $TC''$ beginning at $q_0$ from $ON$, and find the point at which the first derivative of the total cost curve $TC''$ equaled the first derivative of the total benefit curve $TB''$, namely where the marginal benefits and costs were equal. In Figure 4.7, this would be in the neighborhood of $q_{17}$.

Of course, for any level of investment to be considered as optimal, it must be such that the difference between the total benefit and total cost curves is at a maximum at the points at which their first derivatives are equal, i.e., it must be the optimal mix of current and capital expenditures. Moreover, if we are going to optimize, we need to compare not only the gains from current and from capital expenditures (operating maintenance expenditures versus capital improvements), but also the gains to capital outlays from augmenting capacity by investment within a given wilderness tract as compared with investment in additional wildlands (either additional land for the wilderness tract in question or for land elsewhere in the wilderness system).

A decision about how to expand capacity is complicated because the option of adding de facto wilderness land to the system may be lost if deferred. De facto wilderness unprotected by wilderness status and subject to depletion by other incompatible uses may suffer irreversible damage and lose its value as wilderness land, or the opportunity costs of holding wilderness tracts could rise so much that some might counsel disinvesting in extensive tracts. In either case, the option to invest in internal improvements remains open.

The problem of defining criteria for choice involving irreversibilities

---

[17] Defined as an increase in the number of recreation days that can be accommodated for any given probability of encounter—or, alternatively, as a gain (reduction) in utility (disutility) for any given number of recreation days.

and uncertainty is one that merits separate investigation. Here, we simply draw it to the reader's attention.[18] Given the above qualifications, we now summarize the optimality conditions by the following expressions:

$$(1) \qquad \qquad \pi = B - (C_d + C_m + C_k)$$

where: $\pi$ = net benefits,

$B$ = benefits (net of congestion disutilities),

$C_d$ = cost of damage to ecological environment,

$C_m$ = current expenditures,

$C_k$ = capital expenditures, i.e., the relevant interest and amortization charges (or depreciation charges), the latter fixed by the relevant time horizon (or physical life of capital improvements).

Our criterion for optimal use of the area, maximization of $\pi$, is achieved by differentiating with respect to $q$, and setting equal to zero. Thus:

$$(2) \qquad \frac{d\pi}{dq} = \frac{dB}{dq} - \left( \frac{dC_d}{dq} + \frac{dC_m}{dq} + \frac{dC_k}{dq} \right) = 0, \text{ and } \pi > 0,$$

or, letting

$$MB = \frac{dB}{dq}, \text{ etc.,}$$

$$MB = MC_d + MC_m + MC_k,$$

i.e., the marginal benefits from an increase in recreational services ($MB$), whether quantity, quality, or the combination, must equal the sum of the marginal costs whether increased management expenditures (current costs), damage to the ecological environment, or investment in improvements (capital costs). These are generally well-understood considerations in the area of benefit-cost analysis. The problem lies in applying the principles.

## IV. SOME PROBLEMS IN MAKING THE MODEL OPERATIONAL

Let us consider how the benefit and cost constructs specified in equations (1) and (2) can be made operational. As noted above, (total) benefits from a non-priced service are conventionally measured as the area under an imputed demand curve for the service (see Figure 4.8). This demand is the marginal benefit introduced in the preceding section. The

---

[18] For a rigorous treatment of this problem see the first paper in this book, "Alternative Uses of Natural Environments," by Fisher, Krutilla, and Cicchetti.

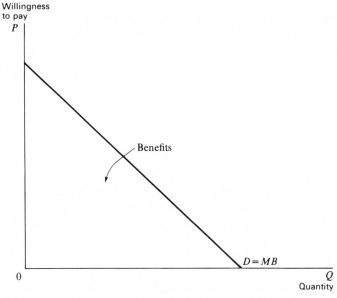

*Figure 4.8.*

area under the curve is also known as the consumers' surplus, the sum of the amounts each consumer of the resource would be willing to pay in order to continue consuming.[19] Our problem, then, is in part the familiar one of finding a way to observe and aggregate consumer willingness to pay for recreation, but we are also concerned with capturing the effects of varying levels of congestion on this willingness to pay. Thus the marginal benefit curve of Figure 4.8, like similar curves in Figures 4.4 to 4.6, represents benefits *net* of congestion costs. In our judgment, supported by a brief discussion of costs later in this paper, estimating this curve for a particular recreation season at a particular site constitutes the heart of the optimal capacity problem.[20]

Before we proceed with our proposals for estimating the marginal benefit curve, let us try to indicate why a monetary measure, such as willingness to pay, is the preferred measure of benefits. Suppose, first,

[19] For a detailed discussion of the concept of consumer surplus, including mention of an alternative definition, see Charles J. Cicchetti and A. Myrick Freeman III, "Consumer Surplus and Option Value in the Estimation of Benefits."

[20] Our definition of "recreation season" is a fairly loose one. Essentially, it is designed to avoid lumping in various activities with dissimilar congestion effects, such as summer backpacking, fall hunting, and winter skiing, that might be undertaken over the course of a single year in an area. We owe this point to Gunter Schramm's discussion of an earlier draft of the paper.

that benefits could be measured and then aggregated in some agreed-upon non-monetary, arbitrary utility units (AUs). Suppose, further, that ecological damage costs are not significant. From the discussion summarized in equation (2), it can be seen that efficient utilization of the environmental resources for recreation requires a balancing of marginal AUs against the marginal dollar expenditures of the management agency. If marginal benefits were observed to be negative when there was no restriction on use, some restriction might seem to be desirable. But there would be no way of knowing how much, as there would be no way of comparing incremental changes in benefits measured in AUs with incremental changes in the costs of restricting use measured in dollars.

Moreover, it is generally understood that there is no legitimate way to aggregate intensities of preferences (the AUs) across individuals, as would be required for the above procedure.[21] Even if we assume that some cardinal measure of utility is associated with a particular wilderness outing for each individual, it seems that aggregation would require further assumptions of a dubious nature. To see this, let us assume that there exists for each individual a function relating the "percent of complete satisfaction" from a wilderness outing to its degree of congestion. Now in order to aggregate, say, 90 percent satisfaction (90 AUs) for one individual with 90 percent satisfaction (90 AUs) for another to get a total of 180 AUs for a given outing, we would need to make interpersonal comparisons. This would involve assuming that both individuals have an equal capacity for enjoying the outing and, moreover, that both have an equal proportion of their welfare associated with it. To appreciate that this would not, in general, be true we can imagine two individuals, one having a keen interest in the outing with high expectations associated with it, and the second only mildly enthusiastic. Both may have their expectations realized to the same degree, and would indicate the same percentage of complete satisfaction, yet the amount of utility each would derive from the experience would differ. This difference should be reflected in any measure of aggregate benefits.

On the other hand, if it could be learned from each individual what he would be willing to pay for a day of wilderness recreation characterized by a given degree of congestion, intensities of preferences would be reflected in an easily aggregated measure. Of course, even this measure is not free from interpersonal considerations, as it is dependent on the existing distribution of income. There are, however, several possible

[21] This is a very old problem in welfare economics. Some notion of the difficulties can be obtained by consulting Kenneth J. Arrow and Tibor Scitovsky, *American Economic Association, Readings in Welfare Economics*, Homewood, Illinois: Richard D. Irwin, Inc. for AEA, 1969.

answers to objections on distributional grounds to a monetary measure of recreation benefits. First, we might assume an exogenous, socially sanctioned distribution of income, affected perhaps by explicit policies for redistribution such as a negative income tax. This is the tack generally taken by economists focusing on the efficiency of a particular allocative scheme. Second, we might note the positive relation between participation in wilderness recreation and income (and education), and that such recreation can be classed as a "luxury" good, i.e., one for which demand rises more than proportionally with income.[22] Finally, we have been considering the monetary measure merely as a conceptual device for benefit evaluation. So far, nothing has been said about instituting user charges.

Use of a monetary measure makes possible the solution of another aggregation problem as well. Individual demand may encompass willingness to pay for not just a single day in the wilderness, but for several days. Thus if we know that an individual is willing to pay, say, $10 for one day, and $15 for two days, then the marginal value of the first day is obviously $10, and of the second, $5. The total value of an area for a recreation season is the sum of all such marginal day values over all participating individuals.

The problem of conformable units is also encountered in assessing the costs of ecological damage. Although uncertainty about benefits from future recreation activity in an area is likely to make precise evaluation impossible, significant costs might be associated with such irreversible losses as destruction of the scenic or wildlife resources on which the recreation activity is based. For our purpose we want to identify a region of discontinuity or rapid rise in the $MC_d$ curve within which optimal capacity would fall—so long as congestion costs were not yet significant.[23]

Let us turn now to our suggestions for measuring consumer surplus benefits net of congestion costs. A prerequisite for any discussion of this problem is the definition of an operational measure of congestion. As we hinted in our earlier discussion, we propose for this purpose the number of encounters, $E$, of recreationists with each other over a fixed period, say a day. Different types of encounters, in different circumstances, will have different effects on recreationists' utility. An encounter at a trailhead,

---

[22] See, for example, Charles J. Cicchetti, Joseph J. Seneca, and Paul Davidson, *The Demand and Supply of Outdoor Recreation* (Washington, D.C.: Bureau of Outdoor Recreation, 1969).

[23] Professor Robert Ream, a plant ecologist with extensive backcountry experience, has suggested that in most cases extensive ecological damage from wilderness use will not occur until after the congestion constraints become effective. There may be an exception to this observation, we would imagine, if pack stock is used as a mode of travel in wilderness areas.

for example, is less distasteful to the wilderness solitude seeker than one
at his backcountry campsite. There might be even greater variation in
the costs of encounter if the definition were broadened to include "encounters" with evidence of other recreationists, such as litter, trampled
vegetation, and so on.[24]

Ideally, then, we are interested in information of the following sort:
what are the amounts each individual would be willing to pay for a single
recreation day characterized by a given set of encounters; similarly for
two such days, and so on. In symbols, individual $i$'s willingness to pay
can be represented (for any given number of days) as

(3) $$P_i = f(E, \bar{O}, \bar{T}_i)$$

where $E$ is a column vector of different types of encounters, $E_1, E_2, \ldots$,
and $\bar{O}$ and $\bar{T}_i$ are, respectively, other characteristics of the recreation
experience and the individual's tastes, both taken as exogenously determined.

Assuming we can get this information, how is it related to level of use?
That is, how is the vector of encounters determined? To answer this question, we propose a model to simulate the travel behavior of recreationists
through the wilderness tract, coupled with an assumption about the time
pattern of use over the recreation season. For the purpose at hand we
assume for simplicity, with no loss in generality, a uniform distribution
of recreation days over the season. This gives the number of individuals
present on any one day as $R/n$, where $R$ is the total number of recreation
days over the season and $n$ is the length of the season (in days). Using
the simulation model, we can relate this number $R/n$ to the numbers of
(different types of) encounters expected. Of course, the number of different types of encounters that can be handled in this fashion will depend
upon the complexity built into the simulator. In principle, an indefinitely
large number could be considered, though in a first application perhaps
only four types—say, trail and campsite and two modes of travel (foot
and horseback)—may be attempted.[25] For the remainder of this discussion we speak simply of encounters, recognizing that this may refer to
anything from undifferentiated encounters to a vector of different types
of encounters. The information obtained would appear much as shown
in Table 4.2.

Let us return now to the question of how the required information on
willingness to pay is to be obtained. In the absence of the ordinary market

[24] This broad view of the encounter phenomenon we owe to Blair Bower's discussion
of an earlier draft of this paper.
[25] Work on a somewhat more complex model is currently going forward in the
Natural Environments Program at RFF.

Table 4.2. Expected Encounters as a Function of Intensity of Use

| Use (recreation days) | Encounters | Probabilities | Expected encounter |
|---|---|---|---|
| 10,000 | 0 | .75 | 0.4 |
| | 1 | .15 | |
| | 2 | .05 | |
| | 3 | .03 | |
| | 4 | .02 | |
| 19,500 | 0 | .50 | 0.8 |
| | 1 | .31 | |
| | 2 | .10 | |
| | 3 | .06 | |
| | 4 | .03 | |
| 28,500 | 0 | .20 | 1.4 |
| | 1 | .40 | |
| | 2 | .25 | |
| | 3 | .10 | |
| | 4 | .05 | |
| 37,000 | 0 | .10 | 2.0 |
| | 1 | .25 | |
| | 2 | .35 | |
| | 3 | .20 | |
| | 4 | .10 | |
| 45,000 | 1 | .10 | 3.0 |
| | 2 | .25 | |
| | 3 | .35 | |
| | 4 | .20 | |
| | 5 | .10 | |
| 52,500 | 2 | .10 | 3.9 |
| | 3 | .25 | |
| | 4 | .35 | |
| | 5 | .20 | |
| | 6 | .10 | |
| 59,500 | 3 | .10 | 5.0 |
| | 4 | .25 | |
| | 5 | .35 | |
| | 6 | .20 | |
| | 7 | .10 | |
| 66,000 | 4 | .10 | 6.0 |
| | 5 | .25 | |
| | 6 | .35 | |
| | 7 | .20 | |
| | 8 | .10 | |

price data, there are essentially two possibilities: (1) an explicit set of questions put to individuals requesting them to state the value of the experience; or (2) indirect inference of the value from some aspect of their observed behavior. For reasons we shall indicate shortly, economists have traditionally favored the latter approach, at least in principle. Clawson and Knetsch have shown how an aggregate demand schedule can be inferred from recreationists' observed travel costs, and then used to calculate their consumers' surplus benefits.[26] Unfortunately, there is no obvious way to extend the technique to treat congestion externalities, which are our main concern.

Since we are constrained to adopt the first approach and seek to learn directly from individuals what they are willing to pay for a recreation experience characterized by a given degree of congestion, we should note the possible pitfalls. Two reasons have been suggested why a response to a hypothetical question of this sort may be unreliable. First, as Samuelson has pointed out, the individual has an incentive to understate his willingness to pay for a publicly provided good, as he may reckon he can continue to enjoy it without being assessed his full consumer surplus.[27] To eliminate this general bias, an interview procedure formulated by Davis specifically for outdoor recreation studies is very useful.[28] The idea is to have the individual react to the possibility that he can be excluded—for failure to pay a sufficient price—a possibility that is plausible in this, if not in the typical public good, case. In Bohm's recent controlled experimental study of the consistency of consumer responses to questions concerning their willingness to pay for entertainment services, the expected bias did not appear.[29]

The second objection to the interview procedure is that, even where there is no dissimulation, response to a hypothetical situation cannot be assumed to correspond exactly to behavior in a real situation. An individual's response might not be influenced by his income constraint, whereas his behavior will be. Accordingly, there might be a tendency to overstate willingness to pay in the hypothetical situation. Indeed, one explanation of the experimental results reported by Bohm may be found in the relatively small amounts of money involved. However, if the purpose of a willingness to pay question is to estimate benefits from recreation for comparison with benefits from alternative uses of a tract of wildland, an income-constrained estimate may itself have a downward bias because it corresponds to the Hicksian "price-compensating" measure of

[26] Marion Clawson and Jack L. Knetsch, *Economics of Outdoor Recreation* (Baltimore: Johns Hopkins University Press for Resources for the Future, 1966).

[27] Paul A. Samuelson, "The Pure Theory of Public Expenditures," *Review of Economics and Statistics*, November 1954.

[28] Robert K. Davis, "The Value of Outdoor Recreation: An Economic Study of the Maine Woods," Ph.D. thesis, Harvard University, 1963.

[29] Peter Bohm, "Estimating Demand for Public Goods: An Experiment," *Swedish Journal of Economics*, forthcoming.

Table 4.3. Willingness to Pay for Two-Encounter Recreation Days for Five Different Categories of Individuals

| Number of days | Willingness to pay by category | | | | |
|---|---|---|---|---|---|
| | A | B | C | D | E |
| 1 | $10 | $12 | $ 9 | $ 7 | $ 5 |
| 2 | 18 | 19 | 17 | 12 | 9 |
| 3 | 25 | 25 | 23 | 16 | 12 |
| 4 | 31 | 30 | 28 | 19 | 14 |
| 5 | 36 | 34 | 32 | 21 | 15 |
| 6 | 40 | 37 | 36 | 22 | — |
| 7 | 43 | 39 | 39 | — | — |
| 8 | 45 | 41 | 41 | — | — |
| 9 | 46 | 42 | 42 | — | — |
| 10 | 47 | 43 | — | — | — |

consumer surplus, whereas the "price-equivalent" measure may be more relevant when a change from *de facto* wilderness to an incompatible use is contemplated.[30] Since the difference between the two measures is related to the presence or absence of the income constraint, what appears to be an upward bias in response to a question regarding willingness to pay in a hypothetical situation may simply be a reflection of a more appropriate measure of benefit.

## V. An Illustrative Application

Recall that, using the travel behavior simulator, we can generate an expected number of encounters per day as a function of any given total number of recreation days in a season. Given this relation, a sample from some known number of recreation visits can be questioned as to willingness to pay for one day with the expected number of encounters, two days, and so on.

For purposes of illustration, suppose the use of an area is 37,000 recreation days uniformly distributed over the season so that just two encounters could be expected on any day (see Table 4.2). Suppose further that each user could be placed in one of five different categories, corresponding to his monetary evaluation of the two-encounter day. This information might be presented as in Table 4.3.

[30] For a discussion of this point, see John V. Krutilla, Charles J. Cicchetti, A. Myrick Freeman III, and Clifford Russell, "Observations on the Economics of Irreplaceable Assets," in Allen V. Kneese and Blair T. Bower, eds., *Environmental Quality Analysis: Research Studies in the Social Sciences* (Baltimore: Johns Hopkins University Press for Resources for the Future, 1972).

Next suppose that there are 6,000 users distributed among the five categories as follows:

| Group | No. in group | Percent of total |
|---|---|---|
| A | 1,000 | 16.66 |
| B | 1,250 | 20.83 |
| C | 1,500 | 25.00 |
| D | 1,200 | 20.83 |
| E | 1,000 | 16.66 |

To compute the total benefits of the 37,000 recreation days, we start with the highest amount that a group of recreationists is willing to pay for another day of recreation (see Table 4.4). The highest amount, $12 per day, will be paid by individuals of group B, of which there are 1,250, giving an aggregate marginal and total benefit of $15,000 (1,250 multiplied by $12/day). We then proceed to the next highest "bid," which is $10 from individuals in group A; this produces a marginal benefit of $10,000 (1,000 individuals multiplied by $10/day). The third (block of) day(s) would be claimed by the 1,500 individuals in group C, who are each willing to pay $9/day, which produces a marginal benefit of $13,500. The cumulative benefit is now $38,500. A user fee might be set such that only 37,000 recreation days in total are claimed so that the encounter level would remain at the expected number of two per day. From Table 4.4, Column 4 it is apparent that the user fee should be something just over $2.00 per day, for at $2.00 something over 40,000 recreation days

Table 4.4. Computation of Benefits Based on a Two-Encounter per Day Recreation Experience

| User fee for given day (1) | Number in relevant group (2) | Number of days by group and price (3) | Cumulative number of days (4) | Marginal benefits (5) | Total (cumulative) benefits (6) | Source of marginal benefit (7) |
|---|---|---|---|---|---|---|
| $12 | 1,250 | 1,250 | 1,250 | $15,000 | $ 15,000 | B |
| 10 | 1,000 | 1,000 | 2,250 | 10,000 | 25,000 | A |
| 9 | 1,500 | 1,500 | 3,750 | 13,500 | 38,500 | C |
| . | . | . | . | . | . | . |
| . | . | . | . | . | . | . |
| 2 | 1,250 | 1,250 | 36,500 | 2,500 | 190,000 | B |
| 2 | 1,000 | 1,000 | 37,500 | 2,000 | 192,000 | A |
| 2 | 1,250 | 1,250 | 38,750 | 2,500 | 194,500 | B |
| 2 | 1,500 | 1,500 | 40,250 | 3,000 | 197,000 | C |
| 1 | 1,000 | 1,000 | 44,250 | 1,000 | 198,000 | E |

Table 4.5. Relationship of Aggregate Benefit to Number of Recreation Days

| Recreation days (1) | Expected number of encounters (2) | Aggregate willing-ness to pay, i.e., benefits (3) | Marginal benefits (4) |
|---|---|---|---|
| 10,000 | 0.4 | — | — |
| 19,500 | 0.8 | — | — |
| 28,500 | 1.4 | — | — |
| 37,000 | 2.0 | $197,000 | — |
| 45,000 | 3.0 | 239,560 | $  42,560 |
| 52,500 | 3.9 | 233,811 | −5,749 |
| 59,500 | 5.0 | 201,795 | −32,016 |
| 66,000 | 6.0 | — | — |
| 72,000 | 7.0 | — | — |

would be taken. This example illustrates the mechanism by which the expected encounters could be manipulated and hypothetical discriminating monopoly receipts could serve as an aggregate measure of benefit.

A similar exercise could be performed involving responses to questions of an identical sort when the "product" offered is an outing with the expected number of encounters per day set at three, at four, and so forth. For each set of responses to questions regarding willingness to pay for an outing with a different expected number of encounters, a computation corresponding to the total cumulative benefits (col. 6, Table 4.4) would result, giving benefits measured in monetary units for each intensity of use. From the illustrative figures we would find the maximum (net of congestion disutilities) benefit in the neighborhood of 45,000 recreation days (Table 4.5).

Returning to the aggregation problem cited earlier, it is easily seen that this procedure aggregates all of the highest valued uses of the area, even if this means adding in two or three days for some individuals before the first days for others.

Note that none of the above requires that use be rationed by money prices. Thus far we have considered monetary units only as a measure of benefits. However, there would seem to be an important advantage in employing user fees as the rationing device as well. If management set a fee equal to the willingness to pay of the last or marginal users, each of the days included would bear a higher value than each of the days excluded. Alternatively, admitting the daily ration of the first 45,000 recreation days per season on a first-come-first-served basis at a zero user fee would not ensure that the individuals who valued the wilderness tract most highly would be admitted. That would, of course, affect the value of the wilderness tract, as it would not be allocated to its highest valued use.[31] Again, this assumes that the income distribution (which affects individuals' willingness to pay) is a socially sanctioned distribution. If non-efficiency benefits from the use of wilderness would accrue to society by an alternative admissions policy, we would be able to weigh these benefits against the losses resulting from the exclusion of some willingness to pay in order to better evaluate the merits of the alternative admissions policy.[32]

Another advantage of price rationing is that any initial miscalculation could readily be corrected through subsequent price adjustment. For example, suppose management, on the basis of prior information concerning user willingness to pay, set a user fee expected to optimally restrict use to the 45,000 days in our illustration. If, following the institution of this fee, only 35,000 days are taken, then clearly the consumers' surplus measure of benefits has been overestimated, and the fee might be lowered. This sort of iterative procedure then can provide additional information about consumer tastes that should be of value to managers.

## VI. CONCLUSIONS AND DIRECTIONS OF FUTURE RESEARCH

We have now worked through a simplified example designed to illustrate how a wilderness tract might be managed in accordance with economic principles to provide maximum recreation benefits. In doing so we noted that a user travel-behavior simulator and a survey research effort were needed to provide estimates of wilderness users' responses to different circumstances as a result of the differences in intensity of use. The responses would then be registered as differences in the amounts such users would be willing to pay for differences in the quality of the experience defined in terms of the freedom from congestion. Since simulator and survey investigations are just getting under way at Resources for the Future, we can do no more at this time than say something about the character of the studies.

[31] See Joseph J. Seneca, "The Welfare Effects of Zero Pricing of Public Goods," *Public Choice* (Spring 1970), pp. 101–10.

[32] See D. Nichols, E. Smolensky, and T. N. Tideman, "Discrimination by Waiting Time in Merit Goods," *American Economic Review*, June 1971, for an argument that discrimination by waiting time is to be preferred to discrimination by money prices in certain "merit good" cases. For reasons indicated in John V. Krutilla and Jack L. Knetsch, "Outdoor Recreation Economics," *The Annals of the American Academy of Political and Social Sciences*, May 1970, this argument is applicable to population-oriented "inner city" recreation, but not to the resource-oriented wilderness recreation that is the concern of this paper. Additional analysis of the mechanism for provision of public goods is found in Charles J. Cicchetti and Robert Haveman, "Optimality in Producing and Distributing Public Outputs," unpublished manuscript.

The Spanish Peaks Primitive Area of Montana has been selected as a prototype from which data can be obtained to endow the simulator with considerable realism. Data are available on the characteristics of the area, trails, campsites, and terrain, and on the distribution of wilderness users by trailhead, routes, lengths of stay, and mode of travel for the present level of use intensity.[33] A simulator is being developed, using these data, which will mimic the behavior of existing users, registering the number of encounters by location (whether at periphery or interior of area), type of encounter (while traveling on trail or during campsite occupancy), and mode of travel (whether by foot or pack stock and horseback). Given a functioning simulator that is run for an appropriate number of times for each intensity of use postulated, estimates of the expected encounters by location, type, and mode can be developed and functionally linked to the number of recreation days of specified composition.

Concurrently a survey is being prepared to elicit information on the nature of individual users' willingness-to-pay functions under pre-assigned conditions that reflect the intensity of use. It is impossible to account for every relevant dimension of the quality of a given experience because users would have to be asked an excessive number of questions. The strategy to be employed will be to select a limited number of questions to address to each potential respondent, raising as many of the questions relevant to determining the schedule of willingness to pay as possible within our sampling constraints. This is intended to produce a scatter of observations from which we can obtain an estimate of the functional relationship between willingness to pay and encounters of various sorts for various lengths of stay by applying conventional econometric techniques.

To the best of our knowledge neither the simulation study nor the survey research proposed here has been attempted in precisely such circumstances by others, but we feel that the strategy we have outlined above is sufficiently promising to warrant the attempt. The resulting information might be of considerable value to public land managers who are faced with serious problems in administering the use of wilderness lands.

---

[33] These data represent the contribution of the Wilderness Research Project undertaken by Robert Lucas and George Stankey.

# 5
# A Multivariate Statistical Analysis of Wilderness Users in the United States

CHARLES J. CICCHETTI*

The nation's wilderness areas, which have been experiencing greatly increased use,[1] can be expected to be in even greater demand as population, income, and leisure time continue to increase. However, the supply of such areas is already limited and may become even more restricted if some of today's *de facto* wilderness areas are transformed by developmental or extractive activities. Can present wilderness areas be managed to meet present and future demands, or will additional wildland reservations be needed—and when? Simple projections of aggregate demand are not enough to answer such questions.

In this paper I attempt to shed some light on the possible scale and nature of the future increases in use by examining the preferences and behavioral patterns of wilderness users. Using Stankey's data from his surveys of wilderness users in four different recreation areas in the United States,[2] I analyze the relationship between the preferences and behavioral patterns of these users and (1) certain socioeconomic factors such as age, race, sex, income, and education; (2) childhood residential and recreational experience; and (3) conformity with the purposes of the

* Economist, Resources for the Future, Inc.

[1] Wildland Research Center, *Wilderness and Recreation: A Report on Resources, Values, and Problems*, Outdoor Recreation Resources Review Commission Study Report No. 3 (Washington, D.C.: Government Printing Office, 1962).

[2] The sample design survey research approach and data in this analysis have been developed by George H. Stankey, "The Perception of Wilderness Recreation Carrying Capacity: A Geographic Study in Natural Resources Management," Ph.D. thesis, Michigan State University, 1971, and related paper in this present volume entitled, "A Strategy for the Definition and Management of Wilderness Quality."

Wilderness Act and membership in conservation organizations. My approach is to formulate a set of behavioral hypotheses, which I then test statistically, using a multiple regression analysis.

The actual formulation of hypotheses, some of which may be interdependent, is called a structural model. To facilitate the subsequent discussion of my experimental design, I digress to clarify the definition, specification, and interpretation of structural models as such.

## The Structural Model

In general, a structural model is a mathematical presentation of the various interdependent hypotheses a researcher will test. There are three types of variables in a structural model: (1) endogenous or dependent variables, which are explained by the implied causal mechanism of the model, (2) exogenous variables which are explained outside the model, and (3) predetermined endogenous variables, which are explained at a prior point in time by the model.

The term "model" usually implies that there are two or more dependent variables whose values are determined simultaneously. Each of these "jointly determined endogenous variables" is represented by a separate structural equation, which forms a distinct hypothesis to be tested. In any given equation the hypothesis tested is that the endogenous variable on the left is dependent upon the explanatory variables on the right, which may include exogenous variables, predetermined endogenous variables, and other jointly determined endogenous variables. If a linear form is hypothesized for the model, a structural equation may have the following form:

$$(\text{Dependent variable})_{1t} = \alpha + (\beta \cdot \text{exogenous variable})$$

(1) $$+ (\gamma \cdot \text{predetermined endogenous variable})$$

$$+ (\delta \cdot \text{jointly determined endogenous variable}) + U_{1t}.$$

Where $\alpha$, $\beta$, $\gamma$, and $\delta$ are the parameters of this structural equation and $U_{1t}$ represents its error term.

There are two broadly defined approaches for testing an econometric hypothesis with a structural model. In one approach, the structural model is simultaneously estimated and all the available information is utilized. In the other, a portion of the structural model, even a single equation, is tested by using the limited information included in a particular segment of the model. I use the latter approach for two reasons. First, not enough is known about the factors that affect wilderness preferences and behavior to be able to identify all the causal and interde-

Table 5.1. Variables Used in the Wilderness Recreation Structural Equations

| Endogenous variables | Exogenous variables | Predetermined endogenous variables |
|---|---|---|
| (1) Purism score | (1) Professional person (Occupation) | (1) Auto camping as a child |
| (2) Membership in special conservation organizations | | (a) often |
| | (2) Age | (b) never |
| | (3) Sex | (c) seldom |
| (3) Membership in any conservation organization | (4) Education | (2) Hiking as a child |
| | (5) Income | (a) often |
| | (6) Residence as a small child | (b) never |
| (4) Pack up and leave when congestion occurs | | (c) seldom |
| | | (3) Other camping as a child often. |
| (5) Stay but at reduced satisfaction when congestion occurs | | (4) Age at first visit to a wilderness area |
| (6) Stay at no loss in satisfaction when congestion occurs | | |
| (7) Total number of wilderness visits | | |
| (8) First visit to a wilderness area | | |
| (9) Backpacker | | |
| (10) Horseback rider | | |
| (11) Hiking with stock | | |
| (12) Outfitted trip | | |
| (13) Organization-sponsored trip | | |

pendent relationships that might be included in a structural model for wilderness recreation. Second, in addition to knowledge of the explanatory variables to be tested, there must be information or hypotheses concerning the variance-covariance matrix of the error terms $[U_{1t}$ in equation (1)] of the structural model. Not being in a position to test an entire structural model simultaneously, I test various hypotheses on an interdependent portion of a larger structural model. (The variables used in the structural equations that are considered below are listed in Table 5.1.)

## DATA SOURCE, DESCRIPTION, AND METHODOLOGY

The data used in this study are based upon information collected under the direction of George H. Stankey[3] of the U.S. Forest Service during the summer of 1969 in four areas: The Bob Marshall Wilderness, the Bridger Wilderness, the High Uintas Primitive Area, and the Boundary Waters

[3] "The Perception of Wilderness Recreation Carrying Capacity."

Canoe Area. The first two areas are located in sparsely populated areas of Montana and Wyoming, respectively; visitors often travel by horse in the Bob Marshall, but usually backpack in the Bridger. The High Uintas Primitive Area is only about one hour's drive from Salt Lake City, Utah; day visits comprise a significant component of the area's total use. The Boundary Waters Canoe Area is located in northern Minnesota; it can be reached by good highways and draws many of its visitors from the Twin Cities and Chicago areas.

The data were collected primarily through an on-the-spot questionnaire, which focused on the following five dimensions:

(1) a description of the party;
(2) the past experience of the respondent in terms of both general outdoor recreation and wilderness;
(3) respondent attitudes and perceptions of the various parameters of use;
(4) respondent attitudes about potential management alternatives in regard to wilderness; and
(5) a standard socioeconomic description of the respondent.[4]

In an attempt to eliminate the interviewer and party leader biases of earlier studies, each person over 15 years of age was given a questionnaire and asked to complete it privately. Instead of delaying visitors in inclement weather, or late in the day, names and addresses were taken, and the questionnaire was mailed. By using follow-up letters as reminders, an overall return of 78 percent was obtained from the mailed questionnaires.[5]

All but two of the 13 endogenous variables in Table 5.1 are coded in binary form from the Stankey questionnaires. For the empirical analysis the dichotomous dependent variables were coded one (1) if the respondent indicated that he would take a particular action (for example, if he indicated that he would pack up and leave if the area became congested) and zero if he indicated that he would not.[6] Such structural equations may be interpreted as conditional probability statements. That is, if given the characteristics of an individual the probability of his acting in a certain manner (e.g., packing up) can be estimated.

The other two endogenous variables are coded as continuous variables. The "Purism Score" variable is determined by adding the response by an

[4] Ibid., p. 82.
[5] Ibid., p. 91.
[6] For a discussion of the economic and econometric implications of binary or dichotomous dependent variables, the reader is referred to C. J. Cicchetti, J. J. Seneca, and P. Davidson, *The Demand and Supply of Outdoor Recreation* (Washington, D.C.: Bureau of Outdoor Recreation, 1969).

Table 5.2. Mean Values of the Endogenous Variables by Study Area

| Variable | Bridger | Bob Marshall | High Uintas | BWCA |
|---|---|---|---|---|
| Sample Size | 144 | 120 | 154 | 206 |
| Purism score[a] | 60.0 | 59.2 | 55.5 | 52.3 |
| Membership in special conservation organizations[b] | .167 | .142 | .013 | .005 |
| Membership in any conservation organization | .417 | .317 | .286 | .141 |
| Pack up and leave when congestion occurs | .368 | .408 | .208 | .233 |
| Stay but at reduced satisfaction when congestion occurs | .326 | .325 | .429 | .335 |
| Stay at no loss in satisfaction when congestion occurs | .194 | .233 | .325 | .379 |
| Total number of wilderness visits | 13.3 | 10.3 | 13.4 | 11.6 |
| First visit to a wilderness area | .146 | .200 | .169 | .272 |
| Backpacker (paddle canoe in BWCA) | .847 | .317 | .494 | .578 |
| Horseback rider (motor canoe in BWCA) | .083 | .650 | .506 | .107 |
| Hiking with stock (motor boat in BWCA) | .069 | .033 | N.A. | .306 |
| Outfitted trip | .028 | .442 | .065 | .471 |
| Organization-sponsored trip | .063 | .050 | .201 | .141 |

[a] This score ranges from 14 to 70 and is fully explained by Stankey in "The Perception of Wilderness Recreation Carrying Capacity: A Geographic Study in Natural Resources Management," Ph.D. thesis, Michigan State University, 1971.

[b] The conservation organizations included in this variable are generally more active and purist-oriented. Included, for example, are the Sierra Club Wilderness Society, National Recreation and Parks Association, and local wilderness clubs.

individual to 14 items, to determine the individual's feelings about the wilderness and man's tamperings with nature.[7] The score ranges from a low of 14 up to a maximum of 70, with the highest scores serving as an indication of the purist wilderness user. The second continuous variable is the total number of wilderness visits the individual has previously made, and is constrained to be a non-negative integer. In Table 5.2, the means for the thirteen endogenous variables in each of the four study areas are shown.

The information in Table 5.2 is both interesting and informative, but its usefulness is restricted by the fact that tests of the data's statistical significance are limited, it is not possible to explain the levels or differences in these data, and it is not possible to predict how changing external conditions, such as increasing income, leisure time, etc., might affect these values. For these reasons, we have adopted a multivariate regression approach to test various hypotheses, which might be important for

[7] For a discussion of the questionnaire, the sampling methodology, and the technique utilized to develop the purist score, see Stankey, "The Perception of Wilderness Recreation Carrying Capacity."

explaining, in an assumed causal manner, these various dependent or endogenous variables. We will test three basic hypotheses:

*Hypothesis I.* The endogenous variables in the model depend upon the present socioeconomic characteristics of the wilderness user.

*Hypothesis II.* The endogenous variables depend upon the childhood residential and recreational experiences of the wilderness user.

*Hypothesis III.* Purism score, membership in special conservation organizations, and membership in any conservation organization are endogenous variables, which in turn affect the other jointly determined endogenous variables of the model.

In Table 5.3, the mean values and coding of the exogenous and predetermined endogenous variables are shown. These explanatory variables were used to test the above hypotheses for the endogenous variables in Table 5.2. Combined, Tables 5.2 and 5.3 form the portion of the structural model that is estimated below.

As previously indicated, a single-equation multivariate regression approach is used. If hypothesis I or hypothesis II is being tested, an ordinary least squares (OLS) regression approach is utilized. However, if hypothesis III is being tested with jointly determined endogenous variables used as explanatory variables, the ordinary least squares approach would produce biased estimates.[8] Accordingly, a two-stage least squares (2SLS) approach is used to determine statistically consistent estimators.[9]

## EMPIRICAL RESULTS

The empirical results of the multiple regression analysis of the endogenous (dependent) variables listed in Table 5.2 are presented in Tables 5.4–5.8. The three hypotheses discussed above were tested for each dependent variable and each area, and the results were separated into the following descriptive groups:

  I. Intensity of feeling or wilderness commitment,
  II. Reaction to crowdedness,

[8] Biased estimators may best be understood by realizing that the notion of "unbiasedness" is expecting to determine the true value of the coefficient on average for a small sample size.

[9] Consistency is heuristically similar to "unbiasedness." If we let $\theta'$ be an estimator of the parameter $\theta$ and $\theta'$ converges in probability as the number of observations approaches infinity, then $\theta'$ is a consistent estimator of $\theta$.

A two-stage least squares (2SLS) estimate is used to estimate structural equations in a model that has jointly determined endogenous variables as explanatory variables. When a given structural equation in the model has this property, it is biased, and a 2SLS regression approach is then utilized to achieve statistical consistency.

Table 5.3. Mean Values and Coding for the Predetermined Variables

| Variable | Code | Bridger | Bob Marshall | High Uintas | BWCA |
|---|---|---|---|---|---|
| *Exogenous* | | | | | |
| Professional person | PRO; 1 = white collar worker | .514 | .350 | .208 | .199 |
| Age | AGS; discrete | 31.4 | 38.3 | 29.6 | 25.6 |
| Sex | SEX; 1 = male | .799 | .883 | .877 | .699 |
| Education | EDS; discrete yrs. of school (8 or less count as 8) | 14.70 | 13.60 | 13.30 | 13.02 |
| Income | FAY; discrete ($\div$ $1,000) | 13.08 | 9.42 | 9.71 | 8.42 |
| Residence as a small child | RST; 1 = less than 5,000 pop. | .396 | .592 | .494 | .461 |
|  | RSC; 1 = less than 50,000 pop. | .639 | .833 | .701 | .665 |
| *Predetermined Endogenous* | | | | | |
| Auto camping as a child: | | | | | |
| Often | ACO; 1 = yes | .188 | .100 | .227 | .160 |
| Never | ACN; 1 = yes | .458 | .425 | .201 | .505 |
| Seldom | ACS; 1 = yes | .306 | .392 | .468 | .218 |
| Hiking as a child: | | | | | |
| Often | HCO; 1 = yes | .188 | .150 | .123 | .150 |
| Never | HCN; 1 = yes | .542 | .458 | .409 | .553 |
| Seldom | HCS; 1 = yes | .215 | .308 | .318 | .214 |
| Other camping often as a child | OCO; 1 = yes | .076 | .100 | .143 | .063 |
| Age at first visit to a wilderness area | AFV; discrete | 17.5 | 18.2 | 12.1 | 10.9 |

III. Wilderness experience,
IV. Mode of travel,
V. Type of trip.

*Group I—Purism Score*

In Table 5.4, the results of group I (intensity of feeling) are presented for the four recreation areas and the three dependent variables included in this category: purism score, membership in a special conservation organization and membership in any conservation organization. In columns 1 through 21, the coefficients that were found to be statistically different from zero are presented with their corresponding $t$ statistic[10] shown in parentheses immediately below. In columns 22 and 23, the coefficient of multiple determination adjusted for degrees of freedom $(\bar{R}^2)$[11] and the overall equation $F$ statistic[12] are as presented with the degrees of freedom for the corresponding equation shown below in parentheses.

To facilitate the interpretation of the equations shown in Tables 5.4 through 5.8, the first equation in Table 5.4 is discussed in some detail. This equation—the purism score for Bridger wilderness users—may be written as follows:

Purism score = 33.4061 − 2.6020 (professional person)
(Bridger)        (7.2)        (−1.9)

+ 1.2094 (age) − 0.0184 (age²)
    (3.6)              (−3.9)

+ 0.1100 (age at first visit) + 0.6526 (education)
    (2.0)                              (2.2)

[10] A $t$ statistic is utilized to test the hypothesis that a given coefficient is not significantly different from zero. It is determined by dividing the regression coefficient (minus zero) by the standard error of that regression coefficient. A $t$ value of 1.28 gives a two-tailed test of confidence, which may heuristically be considered as meaning that if this experiment were conducted with 100 samples we would expect to find this coefficient significantly different from zero 80 times. Therefore it is said that the degree of confidence is 0.80.

[11] An $\bar{R}^2$ is the coefficient of multiple determination or the square of the multiple correlation coefficient. Since it is also equal to one minus the ratio of the unexplained sample variance in a regression to the total sample variance, it is often considered as an index of how "good" a regression equation is in "explaining" the dependent variable. Great care should be taken in overinterpreting this statistic and comparing it with other equations and estimation techniques. For some detailed warnings about such overinterpretations, the reader is referred to: Cicchetti, Seneca, and Davidson, *The Demand and Supply of Outdoor Recreation.*

[12] An $F$ statistic provides a test of the hypothesis that all the coefficients in a given equation are not statistically significant from zero. As such, it is a weaker test than the $F$ statistics in multiple regressions, and in a single bivariate regression, its value is equal to the $t$ statistic squared.

− 2.9213 (population as a small child less than 50,000)
  (−2.5)

+ 3.8347 (hiking often as a small child)
  (2.7)

$$\bar{R}^2 = 0.269, \ F(7,136) = 8.5.$$

The first term is the constant term. The product of each of the other coefficients in the equation and the coded value of the corresponding variable for any given individual is added to this term to estimate the purism score of a Bridger wilderness user with similar characteristics. For example, the second term indicates that one would expect a professional person or white-collar worker to have a purism score some 2.6 points below that of a nonprofessional, who has identical characteristics for the other variables shown in this equation.

The next two variables—age and age$^2$—must be considered jointly, since they both measure the effect of a change in the age of the wilderness user on the estimated purism score. Taken together they indicate that as the age of the respondent increases the purism score increases at a decreasing rate. If the derivative of this equation is taken with respect to age and set equal to zero, we find the age–purism score effect has a maximum which occurs at age 30.4 years, since

$$\frac{d(\text{Purism score, Bridger})}{d(\text{Age})} = 1.2094 - (2) \ (0.0184)\text{age} = 0 \ ;$$

and $$\frac{d^2(\text{Purism score, Bridger})}{d(\text{age})^2} < 0.$$

Graphically, this age-purism score relationship, would be similar to the function shown in Figure 5.1.

It should be pointed out that the purism score variable may be different from the dependent variables that are used to measure actual behavioral patterns because the purism score may be a state of mind rather than a behavioral trait. After other socioeconomic factors were accounted for, the purism score at first increased with the age of the different respondents, who were interviewed at the same point in time, and then declined. For such variables as the number of wilderness visits in a season or the probability of being a backpacker, the conventional assumption is that respondents who are alike except for age can be used as a basis for predicting the effect of age changes. However, it may not be appropriate to predict purism score in such a manner since it does not require actual performance or behavior. Therefore, while an individual wilderness user might be expected to participate less as his age increases, such an assumption about a state of mind may be far from reality.

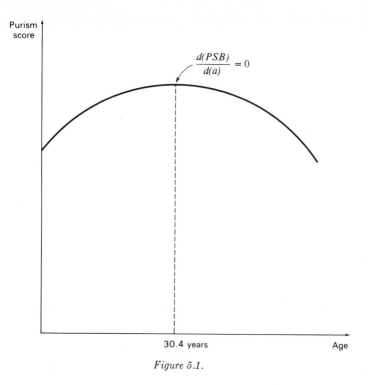

Figure 5.1.

The variable—age at first visit—indicates that the older the wilderness user was when he first visited a wilderness, the higher will be his purist score by some 0.11 point per one year of age. It is important to note that the result is consistent with the "conservation club membership" hypothesis and may indicate that the user who does not visit a wilderness at a young age may have greater expectations for a pristine experience and be more likely to view the wilderness as a resource which should be undeveloped. Lending additional support to this suggestion is the fact that several of the conservation club equations presented in Table 5.4 also show a positive relationship between "age at first visit" and conservation club membership. A related variable is education, which indicates that for each year of education beyond the eighth grade the purism score increases by approximately 0.65 point. Together, these last two variables indicate that with greater age and education a desire for a more remote or pristine experience develops.

The last two variables explicitly measure the effect of certain childhood experiences on the estimated purism score. The first indicates that growing up in a small town or a rural area has a negative effect on the

Table 5.4. Group I (Intensity of Feeling) Multiple Regression Results by Recreation Area

| Dependent variable and recreation area | Constant term | Professional person | Age | Age² | Age at first visit | Sex | Education | Income | Income² | Residence as a small child; population less than | |
|---|---|---|---|---|---|---|---|---|---|---|---|
| | | | | | | | | | | 5,000 | 50,000 |
| | (1) | (2) | (3) | (4) | (5) | (6) | (7) | (8) | (9) | (10) | (11) |
| *Purism score* | | | | | | | | | | | |
| Bridger | 33.4061 (7.2) | -2.6020 (-1.9) | 1.2094 (3.6) | -.0184 (-3.9) | .1100 (2.0) | — | .6526 (2.2) | — | — | — | -2.9213 (-2.5) |
| Bob Marshall | 51.7221 (15.2) | — | — | — | — | — | .3258 (1.5) | .4120 (1.4) | -.0115 (-1.1) | -1.8101 (-1.2) | — |
| High Uintas | 44.7080 (13.2) | — | — | — | — | 1.7515 (1.1) | .8539 (4.0) | -.1173 (-1.5) | — | -3.8132 (-3.5) | — |
| BWCA | 43.0057 (12.9) | — | -.4870 (-1.8) | .0056 (1.4) | — | — | 1.3557 (5.2) | .1690 (1.9) | — | -3.5839 (-3.1) | — |
| *Membership in a special conservation organization* | | | | | | | | | | | |
| Bridger | -.4773 (-.9) | — | — | — | — | — | — | — | — | — | -.0796 (-1.2) |
| Bob Marshall | -.2679 (-1.0) | -.1398 (-1.6) | .0140 (1.1) | -.0002 (-1.1) | .0062 (2.9) | -.1178 (-1.2) | .0198 (1.8) | — | — | -.2737 (-4.2) | — |
| High Uintas | .1535 (3.0) | — | -.0222 (-6.5) | +.0003 (7.4) | .0018 (2.2) | — | .0102 (2.9) | .0013 (1.2) | — | -.0185 (-1.2) | — |
| BWCA | — | — | — | — | This equation is not statistically significant | | | | | | |
| *Membership in any conservation organization* | | | | | | | | | | | |
| Bridger | -.4230 (-.8) | — | — | — | — | -.2226 (-2.4) | — | .0245 (1.5) | -.0009 (-1.5) | -.3274 (-4.3) | — |
| Bob Marshall | .8489 (2.6) | -.1840 (-1.6) | -.0342 (-2.0) | .0005 (2.4) | .0051 (1.9) | -.4102 (-3.3) | .0271 (1.9) | .0100 (1.8) | — | -.3726 (-4.3) | — |
| High Uintas | 1.0002 (4.3) | — | -.0362 (-2.5) | .0005 (2.4) | — | — | — | -.0224 (-1.3) | .0008 (1.3) | — | — |
| BWCA | .3000 (2.1) | — | -.0151 (-1.6) | .0002 (1.3) | .0076 (2.9) | — | — | .0168 (1.5) | -.0005 (-1.1) | -.0932 (-1.9) | — |

Table 5.4. (cont'd)

| Dependent variable and recreation area | Auto camping as a child | | | Hiking as a child | | | Other camping often as a child | Purism score | Conservation membership | | $\bar{R}^2$ | F Statistic (degrees of freedom) |
| | Often | Never | Seldom | Often | Never | Seldom | | | Special | Any | | |
| | (12) | (13) | (14) | (15) | (16) | (17) | (18) | (19) | (20) | (21) | (22) | (23) |
| *Purism score* | | | | | | | | | | | | |
| Bridger | — | — | — | 3.8347 (2.7) | — | — | — | — | — | — | .269 | 8.5 (7, 136) |
| Bob Marshall | — | 2.0100 (1.4) | — | 4.9198 (2.5) | — | — | 3.8230 (1.6) | — | — | — | .083 | 2.5 (7, 112) |
| High Uintas | — | 3.0791 (2.3) | — | — | — | — | 2.2496 (1.5) | — | — | — | .201 | 7.4 (6, 147) |
| BWCA | — | — | — | — | — | — | — | — | — | — | .209 | 11.8 (5, 200) |
| *Membership in a special conservation organization* | | | | | | | | | | | | |
| Bridger | — | — | — | .1143 (1.3) | .1317 (1.9) | — | .2336 (2.0) | .0097 (1.2) | — | — | .095 | 4.1 (5, 138) |
| Bob Marshall | — | .1297 (2.1) | — | .1917 (2.3) | — | — | — | — | — | — | .229 | 4.9 (9, 110) |
| High Uintas | — | .0619 (3.3) | — | — | — | — | — | — | — | — | .368 | 13.7 (7, 146) |
| BWCA | — | — | — | — | This equation is not statistically significant | | | | | | | — |
| *Membership in any conservation organization* | | | | | | | | | | | | |
| Bridger | .1839 (1.9) | — | — | — | — | — | — | .0167 (1.8) | — | — | .215 | 7.5 (6, 137) |
| Bob Marshall | — | — | — | .2540 (2.3) | — | — | — | — | — | — | .240 | 5.2 (9, 110) |
| High Uintas | — | −.2131 (−2.4) | — | .2073 (1.8) | — | — | — | — | — | — | .071 | 2.9 (6, 147) |
| BWCA | — | — | — | — | −.1107 (−2.2) | — | .1802 (1.8) | — | — | — | .054 | 2.5 (8, 197) |

— = variable rejected as being statistically different from zero at a confidence level of ~0.80 using the $t$ statistic for the respective coefficient.

purism score, resulting in a purist score nearly 3 points lower than that
of wilderness users who grew up in a large town or urban area. However,
since this variable like the others utilized in this study only measures
differences between those who actually visit a wilderness area, it is
inappropriate to read into this result (or any other in this study for that
matter) conclusions concerning the population as a whole. For example,
a conclusion that increases in urban population growth must result in an
increase in the demand for wilderness recreation has not been proved by
this result since we have no information about urban dwellers who do
not use wilderness areas. The result does indicate, however, that it is
incorrect to assume that wilderness "buffs" generally do not grow up in
urban areas. It also supports the conclusions of Harry, Gale, and Hendee,[13] who indicated that a rural residence may produce a "utilitarian"
view of a wilderness. They reason that because the head of a rural household is often engaged in an extractive occupation, such as lumbering,
mining, fishing, or agriculture, respondents growing up in rural areas
may be less likely to view forests as resources to be preserved.

The final variable indicates that Bridger wilderness users who hiked
often as children scored nearly 4 points higher on the purism score. This
result, which tends to confirm hypothesis II, indicates that knowledge
and experience gained from childhood hiking have a tendency to increase
the preference for a "pristine" wilderness.

Overall, the Bridger purism score equation is statistically significant
as indicated by the $F$ statistic, each coefficient is statistically significant from zero at greater than the 0.95 confidence level, and the adjusted
$\bar{R}^2$ indicates that the ratio of the "explained" variation to the total
variation is approximately 0.27.

The purism score equations for the three other wilderness and primitive areas also shown in Table 5.4 may be similarly interpreted. Sometimes, as in the Boundary Waters Canoe Area (BWCA) equation, the
age-age squared pattern may be asymmetrical with that found in the
Bridger. In the BWCA, the purism score declines at a decreasing rate
as the age of the respondent increases, and then begins to increase. (See
Figure 5.2.) One possible explanation for this finding is that the BWCA
area has relatively heavy use by middle-aged men employed in extractive
industries as miners, loggers, etc., who use the area primarily as a source
of good fishing and may be indifferent to their relatively pristine surroundings.[14]

[13] J. Harry, R. Gale, and J. Hendee, "Conservation: An Upper-Middle Class Social
Movement," *Journal of Leisure Research*, vol. 1, no. 3, 1969.
[14] I owe the interpretation of this result to the comments on an earlier draft of this
paper by Robert Lucas and George Stankey.

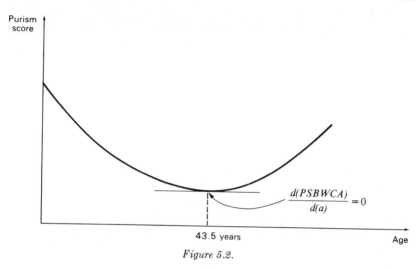

*Figure 5.2.*

The positive education effect noted in the Bridger purism score equation is a consistent pattern, appearing in all four purism score equations. A positive coefficient for the sex variable in the High Uintas purism equation indicates that male visitors to this primitive area rank higher on the purism score than women visitors. The positive income effect and negative income squared effect in the Bob Marshall purism score equation may be considered as being similar to the age-age squared effect, which is shown in Figure 5.1. As income increases for Bob Marshall wilderness users we expect the purism scores to increase but at a decreasing rate until it reaches a maximum at an income level of approximately $17,900. At income levels greater than this amount, purism score will begin to decline.

The negative effect of growing up in a rural area with a population less than 5,000 in both the Bob Marshall and BWCA purism equations is consistent with the rural-utilitarian view that a forest should be used for extractive purposes. In both the Bob Marshall and High Uintas equations, "never having auto camped as a child" has a positive purism score effect, as does "other camping often as a child." In addition, "hiking often as a child" has a positive effect in the Bob Marshall equation.

All four equations are statistically significant and most variables are significant at least at the 0.80 confidence level as indicated by a *t* value in parentheses of 1.28.

*Group I—Membership in Conservation Organizations*

Two other dependent variables presented in Table 5.4 are: "membership in a special conservation organization" and "membership in any

conservation organization," respectively. Since the dependent variable
is coded as either a 1 for members or 0 for nonmembers, the estimated
value of the dependent variable may be interpreted as a conditional
probability. Since the range of variation is restricted,[15] the absolute
value of the coefficients in these equations will be smaller than comparable coefficients in the purism score equation.

Most of the patterns identified above are repeated in these equations.
The reason for this may be that many of the factors that are important
in forming the purist preference for a pristine wilderness area also explain
membership in conservation organizations. A positive relationship between purism score and membership in conservation organizations
among Bridger wilderness users suggests that purist attitudes and conservation membership may be reinforcing variables.

Other important patterns have been found for this group of equations.
For example, as age increases up to age 35 years, the probability of being
a member of a special conservation organization increases and then
declines for Bob Marshall wilderness users. For High Uintas users, however, the probability of membership in special conservation organization
declines until age 37, and then begins to increase. This same relationship
is found in the equations for the Bob Marshall, High Uintas, and BWCA
for the probability of membership in *any* conservation organization.
Several equations also indicate a positive relationship between the probability of membership in conservation organizations and the age the
respondent first visited a wilderness.

Only about one in five respondents in the Bridger and Bob Marshall
were women. However, in these two areas the probability of membership
in conservation organizations and outdoor clubs is greater for a woman
than for a man who is similar with respect to the other statistically
significant variables in the equations.

Both education and income have a positive influence on the probability of membership in conservation organizations and outdoor clubs in
most of the equations presented in Table 5.4. Income-income squared
effects were also found in two areas. These indicate that the probability
of membership increases up to an income of $13,600 for the Bridger and
$16,800 for the BWCA, and then declines. The negative effect of having
grown up in a rural area that was identified in the purism score equations was repeated in the equations derived for the probability of mem-

---

[15] For a discussion of the statistical problems of heteroscedasticity, efficiency, and
the interpretation of $\bar{R}^2$ when binary dependent variables are utilized, see: C. J.
Cicchetti, J. J. Seneca, and P. Davidson, *The Demand and Supply of Outdoor Recreation*, and V. Kerry Smith's paper, "The Effect of Technological Change on Different
Uses of Environmental Resources," earlier in this book.

bership in conservation organizations. This last result is consistent with the pro-development stance expected from respondents raised in rural areas which we attributed to Harry, Gale, and Hendee above.

Membership in the wilderness-oriented conservation organizations is generally negatively related to "never having auto camped as a child," and positively related to "hiking often as a child," and to "other camping often as a child" for the wildernesses and primitive areas shown in Table 5.4. One exception to this pattern is in the Bridger equation, where both "hiking often" and "hiking never" are positively related to the probability of membership in special conservation organizations. This result should be interpreted as indicating that Bridger users who hiked only a few times as children have a lower probability of membership in a wilderness-oriented conservation organization.

Membership in any conservation organization or outdoor club is positively related to the "auto camping often" variable for Bridger users and "hiking often" for the other three areas. It is important to note that a negative sign for the "never hiking" variable in the BWCA equation should be interpreted as a positive "hiking as a child" effect, covering both the "some" and "often" responses. In both Bridger equations a two stage least-squares approach was utilized since the jointly determined endogenous variable purism score was used as an explanatory variable in these equations. One effect of using an explanatory variable which depends to a large extent on other explanatory variables such as age, education, and profession is that this single variable *may* replace these other socioeconomic variables, which it depends upon in the regression equation. This substitution is sometimes repeated below.

Overall, the coefficients in the probability of membership equations shown in Table 5.4 are statistically significant from zero at a confidence level of approximately 0.80 and many at a much higher confidence level. The $\bar{R}^2$ and $F$ statistics indicate good-to-acceptable results for the equations shown in Table 5.4, given the cross-section, binary variable character of the data.

### Group II—Reaction to Crowdedness

The patterns discussed above for Group I generally held for each equation in Group II, but as the dependent variable changed from purism score to membership in special conservation organizations, and then to membership in any conservation or outdoor club, the positive effects of the socioeconomic factors, previous childhood experience, and so on, were reduced or dampened, as one might expect. In Group II, reaction to crowdedness was measured by the following three dependent variables: (1) "pack up and leave," (2) "stay but at reduced satisfaction"

and (3) "stay at no loss in satisfaction." A priori we would expect purist
visitors to react to congestion in one way and users at the lower end of
the purist scale to react in an opposite fashion. Accordingly, we might
expect to find complete sign changes for the various explanatory variables
in these equations, with the "pack up" equations most like the "purism"
and "special conservation organization" equations in Table 5.4 and the
"staying at no loss in satisfaction" least like them.

The equations for these three dependent variables are shown in Table
5.5. The most important result from the standpoint of consistency with
the a priori expectations are found in columns 19 and 20. As one moves
from the "packing up" to the "staying at no loss in satisfaction" equation, the effect of purism score changes from positive to either neutral or
negative. Membership in a special conservation organization has a negative effect on "staying at no loss in satisfaction" for Bob Marshall users.
This suggests that, while members of large conservation club trips dislike congestion, they may not be able to leave the group when congestion
occurs.

The other explanatory variables generally follow patterns similar to
those described above, but there are a few exceptions. For example,
education has a negative effect on "packing up" in the Bridger, but this
is partly due to the fact that this equation also contains a positive purism
score variable. Since these two variables have been found to be very
highly associated with one another when they appear in the same equation, the effect of education can only be considered after adjusting for its
effect on purism score. Another exception to the pattern is the BWCA
"packing up" equation.

The combined results in Table 5.5 seem to indicate that the visitor
who is older when he first visits a wilderness, who has had considerable
auto camping and hiking experience as a child, who has a discriminating
view of the wilderness, and who did not grow up in a small town is the
one likely to be most upset by congestion. He may even cut short his
planned trip and return home. There are no obvious or consistent age
and income patterns for the equations presented in Table 5.5.

Overall the equations are fair to good statistically, with the BWCA
"packing up" equation an exception. In addition, most variables are
significant at the 0.80 confidence level or above. Each equation has a
significant $F$ statistic.

*Group III—Wilderness Experience*

In Table 5.6 the regression results are presented for two endogenous
variables that may be used to measure the depth of experience and the
intensity of use of wilderness areas. For the Bridger Wilderness, being a

professional person (white collar), and having higher income and education and frequent childhood experiences in auto camping and hiking all contribute positively to the number of wilderness visits by the respondents.

In the Bob Marshall equation for "total wilderness visits," there are some similar, as well as dissimilar results. For example, education has a positive influence on the number of wilderness trips. Income has an increasing effect at a decreasing rate up to an annual income of about $14,000. But both professional users and users who hiked often as children were found to have participated in fewer wilderness trips than other users. Such differences between areas may be due to the fact that they attract different clienteles. For example only about 8 percent of Bridger users were horseback riders, while 65 percent of Bob Marshall users traveled by horseback.

In both the Bob Marshall and BWCA equations, male users previously participated in about nine more wilderness visits than female users with otherwise similar socioeconomic characteristics. A somewhat surprising result for the BWCA equation is the negative education effect, unless this is attributed to those areas of relatively unique local clientele. Growing up in a small town, not having "auto camped often," and "hiking often" all had a positive influence on the total number of wilderness visits by BWCA users.

In the "first visit to a wilderness" equation, three strong patterns can be observed. First, not surprisingly, the younger the wilderness user the greater is the probability that he is visiting the wilderness for the first time. Second, women wilderness users are more likely to be visiting wilderness areas for the first time. Finally, in each area except the Bob Marshall, where the results are perhaps distinct because horseback riding is the dominant mode of travel, not having "hiked often as a child" increases the probability of visiting a wilderness for the first time. Too much should not be read into the latter result, since it may also be age dependent. A negative auto camping effect is also observed for BWCA first-time wilderness visitors. The other results in these equations follow no particular pattern. Overall, all the equations are good-to-strong statistically, most coefficients are significant at the 0.90 confidence level or above. The $F$ statistics are all statistically significant.

*Group IV—Mode of Travel*

In Table 5.7, the results are shown for the mode of travel equations. The results depend in part on the prime mode of travel in each area. As was shown in Table 5.2, about 85 percent of the Bridger users are backpackers, some 65 percent of the Bob Marshall users are horseback riders,

Table 5.5.  Group II (Reaction to Crowdedness) Multiple Regression Results by Recreation Area

| Dependent variable and recreation area | Constant term | Professional person | Age | Age² | Age at first visit | Sex | Education | Income | Income² | Residence as a small child; population less than 5,000 | 50,000 |
|---|---|---|---|---|---|---|---|---|---|---|---|
| | (1) | (2) | (3) | (4) | (5) | (6) | (7) | (8) | (9) | (10) | (11) |
| *Pack up and leave when congestion occurs* | | | | | | | | | | | |
| Bridger | -.8866 (-.3) | – | – | | – | .1267 (1.3) | -.0217 (-1.0) | – | +.0002 (1.0) | – | – |
| Bob Marshall | -1.0034 (-1.7) | – | – | | .0125 (5.0) | – | – | .0049 (1.0) | – | – | – |
| High Uintas | -.0642 (-1.3) | – | -.0218 (-1.5) | .0002 (1.2) | .0065 (1.8) | – | .0462 (3.2) | – | – | – | – |
| BWCA | .4798 (3.4) | – | .0043 (1.4) | – | – | – | -.0169 (-1.5) | -.0238 (-1.8) | .0006 (1.1) | – | – |
| *Stay but at reduced satisfaction when congestion occurs* | | | | | | | | | | | |
| Bridger | .1898 (.3) | – | – | – | – | .1666 (1.7) | .0518 (2.7) | – | – | .1253 (1.6) | – |
| Bob Marshall | .5917 (5.2) | – | – | – | -.0100 (-4.1) | – | – | – | – | – | -.2579 (-2.3) |
| High Uintas | This equation is not statistically significant | | | | | | | | | | |
| BWCA | .2123 (1.1) | .1118 (1.1) | -.0235 (-1.5) | .0003 (1.4) | – | – | .0196 (1.2) | .0168 (3.1) | – | -.1117 (-1.7) | – |
| *Stay at no loss in satisfaction when congestion occurs* | | | | | | | | | | | |
| Bridger | 1.5857 (3.4) | -.1710 (-2.3) | – | – | .0055 (2.5) | -.2111 (-2.9) | -.0250 (-1.3) | – | – | -.1291 (-2.2) | – |
| Bob Marshall | .1733 (1.5) | .2216 (2.6) | – | – | – | – | – | -.0062 (-1.2) | – | – | .1192 (1.2) |
| High Uintas | .6495 (2.9) | – | – | – | – | – | -.0401 (-2.7) | .0288 (1.7) | -.0008 (-1.3) | .1616 (2.2) | – |
| BWCA | 1.2979 (3.3) | – | .0236 (1.8) | -.0004 (-1.9) | – | -.0641 (-1.0) | – | – | – | – | – |

Table 5.5. (cont'd)

| Dependent variable and recreation area | Auto camping as a child | | | Hiking as a child | | | Other camping often as a child | Purism score | Conservation membership | | $\bar{R}^2$ | F Statistic (degrees of freedom) |
| --- | --- | --- | --- | --- | --- | --- | --- | --- | --- | --- | --- | --- |
| | Often | Never | Seldom | Often | Never | Seldom | | | Special | Any | | |
| | (12) | (13) | (14) | (15) | (16) | (17) | (18) | (19) | (20) | (21) | (22) | (23) |
| *Pack up and leave when congestion occurs* | | | | | | | | | | | | |
| Bridger | — | — | — | .1188 (1.1) | — | — | — | .0234 (1.6) | — | — | .079 | 3.4 (5,138) |
| Bob Marshall | .2502 (1.9) | — | — | — | −.2088 (−2.6) | — | — | .0204 (2.0) | — | — | .277 | 10.1 (5,114) |
| High Uintas | — | — | — | — | — | — | — | — | — | — | .076 | 4.2 (4,149) |
| BWCA | .0898 (1.1) | — | — | −.1041 (−1.2) | — | — | — | — | — | — | .025 | 1.9 (6,199) |
| *Stay but at reduced satisfaction when congestion occurs* | | | | | | | | | | | | |
| Bridger | — | — | — | — | — | — | — | −.0135 (−1.1) | — | — | .085 | 4.3 (4,139) |
| Bob Marshall | −.1761 (−1.2) | .1001 (1.1) | — | .2784 (2.2) | .1063 (1.1) | — | .1464 (1.1) | — | — | — | .202 | 5.3 (7,112) |
| High Uintas | | | | This equation is not statistically significant | | | | | | | | |
| BWCA | — | .1405 (2.2) | — | .2633 (2.8) | — | — | — | — | — | — | .114 | 4.3 (8,197) |
| *Stay at no loss in satisfaction when congestion occurs* | | | | | | | | | | | | |
| Bridger | −.1492 (−2.0) | — | — | — | — | — | — | −.0131 (−1.3) | — | — | .284 | 9.1 (7,136) |
| Bob Marshall | — | — | — | — | — | — | — | — | −.4096 (−2.0) | — | .067 | 3.1 (4,115) |
| High Uintas | — | — | — | — | −.0888 (−1.2) | — | — | — | — | — | .082 | 3.7 (5,148) |
| BWCA | — | — | — | — | — | — | — | −.0226 (−2.9) | — | — | .094 | 6.3 (4,021) |

— = variable rejected as being statistically different from zero at a confidence level of ∼0.80 using the *t* statistic for the respective coefficient.

Table 5.6. Group III (Wilderness Experience) Multiple Regression Results by Recreation Area

| Dependent variable and recreation area | Constant term | Professional person | Age | Age$^2$ | Age at first visit | Sex | Education | Income | Income$^2$ | Residence as a small child; population less than | |
|---|---|---|---|---|---|---|---|---|---|---|---|
| | | | | | | | | | | 5,000 | 50,000 |
| | (1) | (2) | (3) | (4) | (5) | (6) | (7) | (8) | (9) | (10) | (11) |
| *Total number of wilderness visits* | | | | | | | | | | | |
| Bridger | −7.6111 | 12.3673 | — | — | — | — | .9880 | −.3366 | — | — | — |
| | (−.9) | (3.6) | | | | | (1.6) | (−1.9) | | | |
| Bob Marshall | −15.482 | −8.9334 | — | — | −.1429 | 9.2644 | 1.3917 | 1.3544 | −.0485 | — | — |
| | (−2.2) | (−2.9) | | | (−1.8) | (2.4) | (3.2) | (2.6) | (−2.7) | | |
| High Uintas | | | | | This equation is not statistically significant | | | | | | |
| BWCA | 10.5578 | — | .3129 | — | — | 8.5921 | −1.2548 | — | — | 4.3913 | — |
| | (1.5) | | (2.1) | | | (2.7) | (−2.4) | | | (1.5) | |
| *First visit to a wilderness area* | | | | | | | | | | | |
| Bridger | .5678 | −.0874 | — | .0001 | −.0219 | −.0632 | — | −.0040 | — | .0548 | — |
| | (8.8) | (−1.8) | | (3.5) | (−10.0) | (−1.1) | | (−1.4) | | (1.2) | |
| Bob Marshall | 1.0030 | .2662 | — | — | −.0106 | −.1544 | −.0310 | −.0369 | .0011 | — | — |
| | (5.9) | (3.5) | | | (−5.6) | (−1.7) | (−3.0) | (−2.9) | (2.6) | | |
| High Uintas | .4603 | — | — | — | −.0214 | −.0977 | — | .0174 | −.0007 | — | — |
| | (4.8) | | | | (−8.4) | (−1.3) | | (1.5) | (−1.6) | | |
| BWCA | .6772 | .1212 | — | — | −.0311 | −.0610 | — | — | — | — | — |
| | (14.2) | (2.1) | | | (−13.2) | (−1.2) | | | | | |

Table 5.6. (cont'd)

| Dependent variable and recreation area | Auto camping as a child | | | Hiking as a child | | | Other camping often as a child | Purism score | Conservation membership | | $\bar{R}^2$ | $F$ Statistic (degrees of freedom) |
| | Often | Never | Seldom | Often | Never | Seldom | | | Special | Any | | |
| | (12) | (13) | (14) | (15) | (16) | (17) | (18) | (19) | (20) | (21) | (22) | (23) |
| *Total number of wilderness visits* | | | | | | | | | | | | |
| Bridger | 4.7160 (1.3) | — | — | 18.7769 (5.3) | — | — | — | — | — | — | .251 | 10.6 (5,138) |
| Bob Marshall | — | — | — | −6.2902 (−1.8) | — | — | — | — | — | — | .127 | 3.5 (7,112) |
| High Uintas | This equation is not statistically significant | | | | | | | | | | | |
| BWCA | −10.8047 (−2.7) | — | — | 20.4486 (5.0) | — | — | — | — | — | — | .180 | 8.5 (6,199) |
| *First visit to a wilderness area* | | | | | | | | | | | | |
| Bridger | — | — | — | −.3352 (−5.8) | — | — | — | — | — | — | .481 | 19.9 (7,136) |
| Bob Marshall | — | — | — | .1757 (2.1) | — | — | — | — | — | — | .394 | 12.0 (7,112) |
| High Uintas | — | — | — | −.1802 (−2.3) | — | — | — | — | — | — | .320 | 15.4 (7,112) |
| BWCA | −.0943 (−1.5) | — | — | −.2075 (−3.2) | — | — | — | — | — | — | .483 | 39.4 (5,200) |

— = variable rejected as being statistically different from zero at a confidence level of ∼0.80 using the $t$ statistic for the respective coefficient.

Table 5.7. (Mode of Travel) Multiple Regression Results by Recreation Area

| Dependent variable and recreation area | Constant term | Professional person | Age | Age$^2$ | Age at first visit | Sex | Education | Income | Income$^2$ | Residence as a small child; population less than 5,000 | Residence as a small child; population less than 50,000 |
|---|---|---|---|---|---|---|---|---|---|---|---|
| | (1) | (2) | (3) | (4) | (5) | (6) | (7) | (8) | (9) | (10) | (11) |
| *Backpacker* | | | | | | | | | | | |
| Bridger | .1824 (1.1) | — | — | — | .0030 (1.3) | .0842 (1.2) | .0431 (3.5) | -.0287 (-2.2) | .0010 (2.1) | — | — |
| Bob Marshall | -.2568 (-.8) | -.4122 (-3.7) | .0170 (1.1) | -.0003 (-1.5) | .0072 (2.7) | .1634 (1.4) | .0285 (2.0) | — | — | -.1190 (-1.4) | — |
| High Uintas | 1.3098 (5.0) | .1931 (1.9) | -.0501 (-3.0) | .0005 (2.0) | — | — | .0203 (1.2) | — | — | -.2167 (-2.9) | — |
| *Paddle canoe* | | | | | | | | | | | |
| BWCA | .9346 (5.2) | -.2634 (-3.0) | -.0578 (-4.0) | .0007 (3.3) | -.0047 (-1.5) | — | .0672 (4.6) | — | — | -.3945 (-5.8) | — |
| *Horseback rider* | | | | | | | | | | | |
| Bridger | .3735 (2.8) | — | — | — | -.0034 (-1.9) | .1096 (2.0) | -.0209 (-2.5) | — | — | .0733 (1.6) | — |
| Bob Marshall | 1.6206 (5.2) | .4505 (4.3) | -.0370 (-2.3) | .0006 (2.9) | -.0074 (-2.8) | -.2579 (-2.2) | -.0240 (-1.7) | — | — | — | — |
| High Uintas | -.3536 (-1.4) | -.1999 (-2.0) | .0481 (3.0) | -.0004 (-2.0) | — | — | -.0201 (-1.2) | .0088 (1.7) | — | .2318 (3.0) | — |
| *Motorized canoe* | | | | | | | | | | | |
| BWCA | .0950 (.8) | .1095 (2.1) | -.0140 (-1.8) | .0003 (2.4) | — | .0805 (1.8) | — | — | — | .1562 (3.8) | — |
| *Hiking with stock* | | | | | | | | | | | |
| Bridger | .3925 (3.4) | — | — | — | — | -.2030 (-4.1) | -.0163 (-1.9) | .0169 (1.9) | -.0006 (-1.8) | — | — |
| Bob Marshall | -.3952 (-3.3) | -.0823 (-2.0) | .0192 (3.0) | -.0002 (-3.0) | — | .0983 (2.0) | — | — | — | .0656 (1.9) | — |
| High Uintas | | | | | Not Applicable | | | | | | |
| *Motor boat* | | | | | | | | | | | |
| BWCA | -.0292 (-.2) | .2092 (2.3) | .0689 (4.6) | -.0009 (-4.2) | — | — | -.0701 (-4.6) | — | — | .1759 (2.8) | — |

Table 5.7. (cont'd)

| Dependent variable and recreation area | Auto camping as a child | | | Hiking as a child | | | Other camping often as a child | Purism score | Conservation membership | | $\bar{R}^2$ | F Statistic (degrees of freedom) |
| | Often | Never | Seldom | Often | Never | Seldom | | | Special | Any | | |
| | (12) | (13) | (14) | (15) | (16) | (17) | (18) | (19) | (20) | (21) | (22) | (23) |
| *Backpacker* | | | | | | | | | | | | |
| Bridger | .1085 (1.4) | — | — | −.1451 (1.9) | — | — | — | — | — | — | .101 | 3.3 (7,136) |
| Bob Marshall | — | — | — | — | — | — | — | — | — | — | .259 | 7.0 (7,112) |
| High Uintas | — | — | — | — | — | — | — | — | — | — | .254 | 11.4 (5,148) |
| *Paddle canoe* | | | | | | | | | | | | |
| BWCA | — | — | — | −.2067 (−2.6) | — | — | — | .0114 (.6) | — | — | .328 | 15.3 (7,198) |
| *Horseback rider* | | | | | | | | | | | | |
| Bridger | −.1054 (−1.8) | — | — | −.1088 (−1.8) | — | — | — | — | — | — | .101 | 3.7 (6,137) |
| Bob Marshall | — | — | — | — | — | — | — | — | — | — | .321 | 10.4 (6,113) |
| High Uintas | — | — | — | — | — | — | — | — | — | — | .263 | 10.1 (6,147) |
| *Motorized canoe* | | | | | | | | | | | | |
| BWCA | — | — | — | — | — | — | — | — | — | — | .163 | 9.0 (5,200) |
| *Hiking with stock* | | | | | | | | | | | | |
| Bridger | — | — | — | — | — | — | — | — | — | — | .126 | 6.1 (4,139) |
| Bob Marshall | .1501 (2.9) | — | — | −.0810 (−1.8) | — | — | — | — | — | — | .151 | 4.0 (7,112) |
| High Uintas | — | — | — | — | — | — Not Applicable — — — — | | | | | | |
| *Motor boat* | | | | | | | | | | | | |
| BWCA | — | — | — | .1919 (2.3) | — | — | — | — | — | — | .159 | 7.4 (6,199) |

— = variable rejected as being statistically different from zero at a confidence level of ∼0.80 using the *t* statistic for the respective coefficient.

backpackers and horseback riders are about equally represented in the High Uintas, and nearly 58 percent of the Boundary Waters Canoe Area users are paddling canoeists.

For the backpacking equations, higher education, being older on the first visit to a wilderness, and being a male, all contribute positively to the probability of a visitor using this mode of travel. For Bridger users the income effect is negative up to about $14,350 per year; it then becomes positive and begins to increase at an increasing rate. Since the mean income level for all Bridger users is nearly $14,100, it can be seen that the backpacking probability is much greater among visitors with upper-middle or higher incomes.

The positive effect of auto camping and the negative effect of hiking as children should be noted for the Bridger backpacking equation, along with the negative effect of hiking on the paddling canoeist equation. Living in a rural area as a child has a negative effect on backpacking and paddling canoeing, but a positive effect on horseback riding and motorized canoeing. Since those who prefer wilderness left in a pristine state are generally backpackers and paddle canoeists rather than horseback riders or those who use motor canoes, these results are consistent with those found previously. Education and age at first visit are negatively related to horseback riding. In the Bob Marshall, the negative sex effect indicates that the proportion traveling by horse is likely to be greater for women visiting the area than for men; it does not mean that most horseback riders are women because women comprise less than 12 percent of Bob Marshall users.

In the "hiking with stock" equations, a negative education, a positive income, and negative male effect should be noted for the Bridger wilderness users. In the Bob Marshall "hiking with stock" equation, nonprofessionals and older males who grew up in a rural town and camped often by car but hiked infrequently were the ones more likely to hike with stock.

Overall, the equations are good-to-strong statistically, with most coefficients significant at the 0.90 level or better and all $F$ statistics are significant.

*Type of Trip*

The results for the probability that a wilderness user will use the services of an outfitter or visit the wilderness as part of an organization trip are shown in Table 5.8. Since approximately 45 percent of Bob Marshall and BWCA visitors and fewer than 7 percent of the High Uintas and Bridger visitors use an outfitter, the results of the former two areas are the more important and statistically significant for this dependent variable. Cost differences should also be noted. An outfitted trip in the BWCA generally costs about $11 per person per day and usually involves only equipment rental and supplies, while an outfitted trip in one of the western wilderness areas usually costs $25 to $40 per person per day and involves experienced guides, cooks, and so on.

In both the Bob Marshall and BWCA "outfitter" equations, we find an age effect, which shows that the probability of using an outfitter declines until a visitor is in his early thirties and then begins to increase rapidly. Somewhat offsetting this effect is the next variable, which indicates that the older the visitor on his first wilderness visit the less likely is the probability of his using an outfitter.

In the Bob Marshall, professional persons, women, users who grew up outside a rural area, and people with incomes over $10,000 per year (the mean is $10,300) are more likely to be using outfitters. In the BWCA, higher education and not having hiked often as a child increase the probability of using an outfitter's service. However, in the BWCA the use of an outfitter usually implies a paddling canoe experience and should therefore be expected to be positively related to a purist wilderness view. In the Bridger, visitors who rank lower on the purism scale are more likely to use an outfitter. This result is consistent with a priori expectations, even though only a small percentage (3 percent) of respondents used outfitters.

In the "organization-sponsored trip" equations, the more important results are for the High Uintas and BWCA, since it is in these two areas that a significant number of visitors participate in such trips (some 20 percent of the total sample in the High Uintas and 14 percent in the BWCA). The results indicate that Bob Marshall users who participate on an organization trip are likely to be professionals visiting the wilderness for the first time and to rank high on the purist scale. It is tempting to conclude that Wilderness Society trips, which may bring members to a wilderness for the first time, are made up of people who lack wilderness experience but who both anticipate and desire a pristine setting and would therefore have a high purism score.

In the High Uintas and BWCA areas where Boy Scout trips are a significant part of the total, both lower education and not having "hiked often as a child" increase the probability of visiting the area as part of an organization-sponsored trip. In the High Uintas, age has a negative although diminishing effect, being a professional and/or a male has a positive effect, income has a negative effect (though at a diminishing rate), and growing up in a rural area has a negative effect on participating

Table 5.8. (Type of Trip) Multiple Regression Results by Recreation Area

| Dependent variable and recreation area | Constant term | Professional person | Age | Age² | Age at first visit | Sex | Education | Income | Income² | Residence as a small child; population less than | |
|---|---|---|---|---|---|---|---|---|---|---|---|
| | | | | | | | | | | 5,000 | 50,000 |
| | (1) | (2) | (3) | (4) | (5) | (6) | (7) | (8) | (9) | (10) | (11) |
| *Outfitted trip* | | | | | | | | | | | |
| Bridger | .3218 (1.7) | — | — | — | — | — | — | -.0041 (-2.6) | — | — | — |
| Bob Marshall | 1.6379 (5.8) | .3227 (3.4) | -.0624 (-4.1) | .0009 (4.9) | -.0084 (-3.4) | -.2113 (-1.9) | — | -.0258 (-1.6) | .0013 (2.4) | -.1442 (-1.8) | — |
| High Uintas | This equation is not statistically significant | | | | | | | | | | |
| BWCA | .2571 (1.4) | — | -.0620 (-4.0) | .0010 (4.1) | -.0105 (-3.1) | — | .0926 (6.6) | — | — | — | — |
| *Organization-sponsored trip* | | | | | | | | | | | |
| Bridger | This equation is not statistically significant | | | | | | | | | | |
| Bob Marshall | -.5522 (-2.0) | .1380 (3.5) | — | — | .0022 (1.9) | — | — | — | — | — | — |
| High Uintas | 1.3816 (5.9) | .1523 (1.9) | -.0318 (-2.3) | .0003 (1.8) | — | .2054 (2.4) | -.0415 (-2.9) | -.0269 (-1.9) | .0008 (1.6) | -.0993 (-1.6) | — |
| BWCA | .5737 (5.4) | — | — | — | — | -.1739 (-3.5) | -.0246 (-3.1) | — | — | — | — |

Table 5.8. (cont'd)

| Dependent variable and recreation area | Auto camping as a child | | | Hiking as a child | | | Other camping often as a child | Purism score | Conservation membership | | $\bar{R}^2$ | F Statistic (degrees of freedom) |
|---|---|---|---|---|---|---|---|---|---|---|---|---|
| | Often | Never | Seldom | Often | Never | Seldom | | | Special | Any | | |
| | (12) | (13) | (14) | (15) | (16) | (17) | (18) | (19) | (20) | (21) | (22) | (23) |
| *Outfitted trip* | | | | | | | | | | | | |
| Bridger | −.0431 (−1.3) | — | — | — | — | — | — | −.0039 (−1.2) | — | — | .063 | 4.2 (3, 140) |
| Bob Marshall | — | — | — | — | — | — | — | — | — | — | .426 | 12.0 (8, 111) |
| High Uintas | This equation is not statistically significant | | | | | | | | | | | |
| BWCA | — | — | — | −.1302 (−1.5) | — | — | — | — | — | — | .191 | 10.7 (5, 200) |
| *Organization-sponsored trip* | | | | | | | | | | | | |
| Bridger | — | — | — | — | — | — | — | .0087 (1.9) | — | — | .129 | 6.9 (3, 116) |
| Bob Marshall | This equation is not statistically significant | | | | | | | | | | | |
| High Uintas | — | — | — | −.2278 (−2.6) | — | — | — | — | — | — | .259 | 6.9 (9, 144) |
| BWCA | .1864 (3.0) | — | — | −.1370 (−2.1) | — | — | — | — | — | — | .136 | 9.1 (4, 201) |

— = variable rejected as being statistically different from zero at a confidence level of ~0.80 using the *t* statistic for the respective coefficient.

in an organization-sponsored trip. In the BWCA, women and active childhood auto campers are more likely to participate in an organization-sponsored trip.

Overall, the equations are good to strong statistically, all $t$ statistics indicate a degree of confidence at the 0.90 level or greater, and the $F$ statistics are significant for each equation.

### Summary and Conclusions

In statistical work one must keep in mind that theories or hypotheses are never proven conclusively; instead, hypotheses are rejected. We use statistics and set the level of confidence we wish to have concerning the rejection of hypotheses that might be true for the population though unsupported by the sample we have drawn. Nevertheless, several strong associations were observed and discussed above. For example, the positive relationship was observed between education and non-rural childhood residence and those dependent variables which indicated a non-extractive or non-development view of a wilderness user.

Despite the fact that the population of the United States may be moving away from rural areas, increasingly having a higher income, more education, and more awareness of the wilderness from environmental organizations, the results presented above *can not* be used to prove that increasing pressures or demands for wilderness will come in the future. However, the strength of the "associations" presented in this analysis should make rational and sober planners and policy makers realize that recent increases in wilderness use are very likely to continue into the future. Efforts to quantify and to test these tentative results more fully should begin before irreversible decisions are made and future options have been foreclosed, which could result in reduced economic welfare.

# 6

# *A Preliminary Investigation of the Economics of Migratory Waterfowl*

GARDNER MALLARD BROWN, JR., and
JUDD HAMMACK*

Hunting and fishing are major forms of recreation in the United States. Of the 148 million persons in the country 12 years old or older in 1965, approximately 22 percent fished and/or hunted for three days or more during the year. About 9 percent engaged in hunting, and one percent specifically engaged in the hunting of waterfowl.[1]

*The General Setting*

Migratory waterfowl generally nest in the northern areas of the continent in the summer and fly south to open water in the fall and winter. Some species of teal have been known to migrate as far south as Peru, but most species winter in the United States, with some making a

* Economists at the University of Washington, and at California State University, Los Angeles, respectively.

*Authors' note.* Numerous wildlife experts in both the United States and Canada provided helpful information, especially Aelred D. Geis and Charles H. Lobdell. Stimulating comments at one stage or another were offered by David R. Anderson, James A. Crutchfield, Jon H. Goldstein, Richard McDonald, and Gerald J. Paulik. Oscar Burt's review of an earlier draft was particularly helpful. Major financial support was provided by Resources for the Future, Inc. Supplementary funds received by Hammack from a National Defense Education Act Fellowship and a University of Washington summer faculty research award received by Brown are acknowledged.

[1] All of the statistics except the last one were based on data in U.S. Bureau of Census, *Statistical Abstract of the United States: 1968* (Washington, D.C.: U.S. Government Printing Office, 1968), pp. 8, 204. The last statistic was founded on M. Edwin Rosasco, David R. Anderson, and Elwood M. Martin, "Waterfowl Harvest and Hunter Activity in the United States During the 1966 Hunting Season," Administrative Report No. 138, Migratory Bird Populations Station (Laurel, Maryland: U.S. Bureau of Sport Fisheries and Wildlife, 1967), p. 25. (Mimeographed.)

circuit through Mexico. Because of their migratory nature, the birds are under the jurisdiction of the central government when in Canada, the United States, or Mexico. North American waterfowl are an international resource in both a legal and a physical sense; the birds are as dependent upon their breeding grounds in the north as they are upon their wintering grounds in the south. In general, the quantity and quality of wintering grounds are believed to be adequate, and the critical factor in sustaining waterfowl populations is the amount of nesting grounds.[2]

The rolling, pothole-pocked farmlands of central and southern Alberta, Saskatchewan, and Manitoba, together with parts of the neighboring states of North Dakota, South Dakota, and Minnesota, provide the prime duck-producing areas of the continent. The region comprises but 10 percent of the total continental breeding area, yet produces upwards of 55 percent of the total ducks in an average year.

The supply of superior nesting grounds has declined as farmers continue to drain the prairie wetlands to increase their arable land and eliminate the costs incurred in tilling around the potholes. Also, some wetlands have been claimed as refuse dumps for brush, and deeper ponds have been tapped for irrigation water.

Drainage of the more permanent wetlands has been particularly severe in the United States. According to a recent study, the average annual drainage rate since 1964 has averaged 1.9 percent of the total wetland acreage in the tristate area of North Dakota, South Dakota, and Minnesota. In a 19-county area of Minnesota 14 percent of the wetlands were drained in a recent four-year period.[3] In the Canadian prairies, drainage appears to have proceeded at a considerably slower rate.

Drainage in the prairie pothole region is a matter of considerable concern since it threatens the nesting habitat of the dabbling ducks, which with geese and diving ducks are the waterfowl of major interest to hunters. Dabblers include mallards and pintails—two highly desired and relatively abundant species—and compose a larger percentage of the total kill than either geese or diving ducks.

*Direction of the Study*

Valuation of fish and game is an important segment of the young and imperfect field of recreational resource economics. The valuing of any

[2] Walter F. Crissey, "Prairie Potholes from a Continental Viewpoint," *Saskatoon Wetlands Seminar*, Canadian Wildlife Service Report, Series No. 6 (Ottawa: The Queen's Printer, 1969), p. 167. Crissey's comment with respect to wintering grounds specifically referred to mallards. Generalization to other species, particularly dabbling ducks, seems reasonable.

[3] J. Larry Haddock and Lawrence W. DeBates, "Report on Drainage Trends in the Prairie Pothole Region of Minnesota, North Dakota and South Dakota" (U.S. Bureau of Sport Fisheries and Wildlife, 1969), p. 7. (Mimeographed.)

recreational resource provides a formidable problem for economic analysis, as most recreational resources are either not priced in a market or only partially priced through charges that are usually not set by market conditions. (Campground fees and hunting license fees are examples of partial pricing.) Hence the economist's usual tools for valuation of goods and services, based on market observations, either are of little use or require considerable modification. No fully satisfactory general analytic framework yet has been developed, but continued attempts at analysis are spurred by the lack of value figures for rational decision making and the increasing alternate-use values for many recreation sites.

Our approach is as follows: First, we formulate a theoretical model to determine the value of waterfowl to hunters and to approximate a purchase price as nearly as possible. Second, we subject the model to empirical test and derive a marginal value of a waterfowl in dollar terms. Third, we formulate a waterfowl production function and other biological relationships. Then, drawing together the economic and biological information thus obtained we show how it might be applied to the determination of the most efficient economic use of prairie wetlands.

## VALUATION OF WATERFOWL: A THEORETICAL FRAMEWORK

### Marginal Valuation of Waterfowl

For ease of exposition the following assumptions are made: (1) the hunter does not distinguish between waterfowl, i.e., the value of a bird is not influenced by its species, age, or sex; (2) the kill probabilities are constant for each hunter on each hunting site during the season, and each hunter is aware of the probabilities; (3) each hunter hunts waterfowl at but one site during the season; (4) all relevant costs are known to each hunter at the beginning of the season.

From these assumptions it follows that a representative hunter will consider any waterfowl shot by him to be equal in value to any other he might have shot. At the start of the season, he will choose the hunting ground that will maximize his total net welfare, knowing in advance the expected kill he will obtain at each site. Since all costs at the chosen site are known in advance, this will be interpreted to mean that all costs to the hunter may be regarded as variable and therefore as reflected in marginal cost curves. Furthermore, the number of days the individual will hunt is known to him at the beginning of the season. Nothing in the assumptions and their implications prohibits: (1) the kill probabilities from varying from site to site, or (2) the daily kill on an individual site from varying from hunter to hunter.

Waterfowl hunters are subject to two institutional constraints: the maximum number of waterfowl that may be bagged per day and the maximum number of days during which waterfowl may be shot.[4] In the United States these limits are primarily determined by the federal government which offers each state several combinations of bag and day limits designed to give approximately the same total kill for the season. Each state then chooses the option it prefers.

Line $AB$ in Figure 6.1 shows the income-compensated demand curve for bagged waterfowl for a representative hunter on his first day of hunting during the season.[5] The downward-sloping curve implies that each waterfowl bagged gives the hunter less satisfaction, measured in dollars, than the bird previously shot. The marginal cost of each bird is assumed constant. Since, as stated, all costs are considered variable, any costs that more conventionally would be recognized as seasonal or daily are apportioned to the marginal cost curve for bagged waterfowl.

Were the hunter subject to no constraints, he would shoot birds until he reached point $E$ in Figure 6.1, if that many birds were available on the chosen site. However, it is assumed that he is unable to reach $E$ due to the constraint imposed by the vertical line at $H$, representing either the legal bag limit or the number of birds that may be shot on the hunting ground, whichever is the lesser.

The relevant constraint may be thought of as a cost constraint becoming infinite at some point: the cost of exceeding the bag limit may be both a fine and social stigma; a hunter in Utah on land with a probable yield of two waterfowl per day may travel to California to obtain six waterfowl per day; and so on. For a first approximation, we may consider such cost infinite. Viewing the constraint as one of cost, the hunter would proceed to maximize his net benefit by equating his marginal gross benefit to marginal cost through shooting waterfowl each day up to his constraint. Thus, on each hunting day, the hunter reaches a constrained equilibrium. This should not be interpreted, however, as implying that an additional waterfowl shot per day would have no positive net value. It well may have, and the value would be represented by the amount the individual would pay for the relaxation of the constraint by one waterfowl per day. On the first day of hunting the hunter's costs are represented by the area $OJZH$, and his net benefits, or consumer's surplus, are the area $JAFZ$.[6]

---

[4] There is a third constraint, the maximum number of birds a hunter may have in his possession. The number varies from state to state but is usually either the bag limit or twice the bag limit. The possession limit here is considered relatively minor and is neglected in the analysis.

[5] For simplicity, all demand curves in Figures 6.1 and 6.2 are depicted as linear continuous functions. Strictly stated, bagged waterfowl are expressed in terms of expected values, although for simplicity of exposition the point is not emphasized.

[6] A common definition of consumer's surplus is that it measures the difference be-

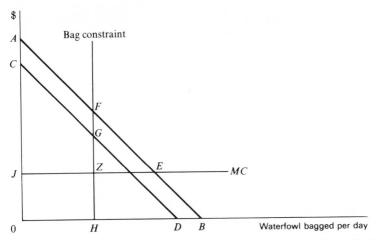

*Figure 6.1.* A hunter's demand and cost curves for bagged waterfowl.

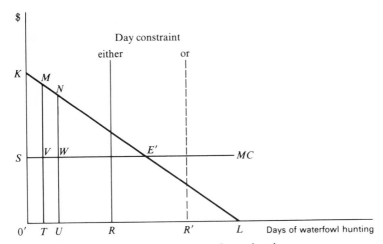

*Figure 6.2.* The same individual's demand and cost curves
for waterfowl hunting days.

Alternatively, as in Figure 6.2, the net benefits and costs may be attributed to the recreation day, where $KL$ represents the income-compensated demand curve of the hunter for hunting days during the season, and $O'T$ represents the first day of hunting. $O'SVT$ represents the cost of

tween what an individual would be willing to pay for a product or service rather than do without it and what he does pay. For a thorough treatment of the subject, see Don Patinkin, "Demand Curves and Consumer's Surplus," *Measurement in Economics*, by Carl F. Christ and others (Stanford: Stanford University Press, 1963), pp. 83–112.

the day's hunting and equals the area $OJZH$ in Figure 6.1. Similarly, area $SKMV$ represents the net benefits from the day's hunting and corresponds to $JAFZ$ in Figure 6.1.[7]

If the hunter faces no constraint, he will hunt the number of days required to reach equilibrium $E'$. However, a constraint related to the season's day limit may (or may not) operate. The number of days an individual hunter will engage in the recreational activity is a function of the day limit and of his entire preference field for the use of his time. Hence his hunting days will be determined either by the constraint or by his having reached the unconstrained equilibrium, whichever occurs first. The constraint may also be considered a cost constraint, where marginal cost suddenly becomes infinite, e.g., if the individual spends one more day hunting he will lose his job or intolerable marital conflict will ensue. In Figure 6.2, the constraint would be operative at $R$ and irrelevant at $R'$.

The second day of hunting is represented in Figure 6.2 by $TU$. Since the demand curve is downward-sloping and the marginal cost per day is assumed constant, the net benefits must be less on the second day than on the first day. Hence, in Figure 6.1 the demand curve for bagged waterfowl on the second day, $CD$, must lie below the demand curve for the first day, $AB$. The net benefits from the second day of hunting, represented as $JCGZ$ in Figure 6.1, correspond to $VMNW$ in Figure 6.2. Although only two demand curves are shown in Figure 6.1, a curve exists for each day of hunting and each curve is lower than the preceding.[8]

Let us assume that the constraints in each graph are operative for the representative hunter and then observe the results of relaxing one limitation while holding the other constant.[9] If the bag limit is increased (or more waterfowl are available) while the season length remains the

---

[7] Thus the net benefit from hunting is attributed to the waterfowl bagged, even though the hunter may obtain other, secondary satisfactions during the recreation day, such as exercise and exposure to natural surroundings. Consumer's surplus, and therefore the measured net benefit, will not include the "secondary" benefit. To measure the surplus in the manner described in footnote 6, the recreationist would be confronted with the possibility of doing without waterfowl hunting, but *not* with the possibility of doing without alternative activities, such as hunting upland birds, which have similar secondary satisfactions associated with them. Hence the net benefit from waterfowl hunting may be attributed to the waterfowl bagged.

An exception would occur if the various satisfactions of the recreation day are synergistic, i.e., if the satisfaction from the other activities and experiences of the day are greater when they are combined with waterfowl hunting than when hunting is missing. In such case, the "synergistic benefit" unavoidably would be included in the measured net benefit.

[8] In theory, the curves could intersect. To simplify, it is assumed arbitrarily they do not.

[9] The assumption of independence is, of course, artificial. It does, however, produce a situation that readily can be analyzed.

same, the constraint in Figure 6.1 shifts to the right, and (assuming that curves in Figure 6.1 do not shift as a result) the demand curve in Figure 6.2 shifts outward, as each recreation day brings greater net benefits than it did before. This effect may be thought of as a quality change; the quality of the recreation day has benefited from the increased number of waterfowl bagged per day.

Alternatively, if the authorities increase the season length while holding bag limits constant, it is assumed that this will shift the constraint in Figure 6.2 to the right. The hunter will hunt more days, and additional demand curves on Figure 6.1 will become relevant. We can consider this a quantity change; the increased number of hunting days results in a greater number of waterfowl bagged.

Since many hunters are subject to one or both constraints, the net benefits to them of the marginal waterfowl will be positive. A peculiar situation exists in that a single item, an additional waterfowl, can affect each of two margins: a "quality margin" and a "quantity margin." The bird may be taken either as an additional bird shot on one of the (constant number of) hunting days, or as a benefit resulting from shooting (a fraction of) an additional day, with kill per day constant. Which margin is affected depends upon which constraint has been relaxed.

## A Mathematical Formulation

The material discussed above can be developed in mathematical form:

$$(1) \qquad V_i = f(Y_i, T_i, K_i/D_i, D_i) \qquad (i = 1, 2, ..., n)$$

where $V$ is a measure of consumer's surplus, $Y$ is a measure of income, preferably discretionary income, $T$ represents some measure or measures of taste, $K$ is bagged waterfowl kill for the season, and $D$ is the number of days of waterfowl hunting during the season. The symbol $i$ represents an individual hunter of which there are $n$.

The functional form of equation (1) is subject to certain constraints: namely, that the first partial derivatives of $V$ with respect to the first, third, and fourth independent variables are positive, and the second partial derivatives with respect to the last two variables are negative.

The first partial derivative of $V_i$ with respect to $(K_i/D_i)$, implicitly multiplied by the finite number one, is an approximation of the marginal value of an additional waterfowl taken on *each* day that individual $i$ hunts during the season. To obtain the approximation of the marginal value of one additional waterfowl, the partial must be divided by $D_i$. Hence

$$\frac{\partial V_i}{\partial (K_i/D_i)} \cdot \frac{1}{D_i},$$

represents the "quality margin"; the quality of the recreation day has increased by shooting a probabilistic fraction of an additional waterfowl per day, with the number of days held constant.

By similar reasoning, the value of a *marginal waterfowl* due to a change in $D$,

$$\frac{\partial V_i}{\partial D_i} \cdot \frac{1}{(K_i/D_i)},$$

approximates the "quantity margin"; the additional waterfowl has been taken by shooting an additional fraction of a day, holding constant the number of waterfowl killed on each hunting day.

There is no a priori reason why the two marginal valuations will be equal for any given hunter or for a number of hunters taken as a group. Which constraint is the more binding depends upon the functional forms of the demand curves in Figures 6.1 and 6.2.

## VALUATION OF WATERFOWL: AN EMPIRICAL TEST

### The Hunter Sample

Estimating the model developed in the last section requires data on the variables in equation (1)—consumer's surplus, income, tastes, waterfowl bagged per day, days of hunting.

Available resources restricted the study to the waterfowl hunters in the seven western states that lie wholly within the boundaries of the Pacific Flyway: namely, Arizona, California, Idaho, Nevada, Oregon, Utah, and Washington. The necessary data were obtained through questionnaires sent to a sample of 5,000 hunters randomly selected from a list provided by the U.S. Bureau of Sport Fisheries and Wildlife. The list contained names of individuals who purchased federal waterfowl hunting stamps during the 1967–68 season, and many of them had responded to the Bureau's waterfowl kill survey for the same year.

### The Questionnaire Format

A waterfowl hunting questionnaire pertaining to 1968–69 was developed, inquiring directly or indirectly about the number of seasons of hunting, the purchase of a waterfowl hunting stamp, waterfowl species preference, waterfowl bagged during the season and number of days of hunting, costs, consumer's surplus, age, education, number in family, income after taxes, and hunting on private land. The questionnaire is reproduced in Appendix A.

In the belief that hunters would be more likely to respond to a brief questionnaire, questions were carefully restricted in number and most were designed to be answered with no more than a number or a check mark. Obviously an information cost is incurred in minimizing the number of questions. For instance, a breakdown of costs attributable to killing a bird, to a hunting day, to the season as a whole, and to more than one season would have been of interest. But because these questions would have increased the length of the questionnaire considerably, they were not asked. The reader is warned that the cost question asked was somewhat novel: in seeking information on the hunter's own apperception of his costs, it is implied that hunters make decisions based on what they consider their costs to be, rather than on what an economist believes should be included or excluded.

In the middle of February 1969, printed copies of the questionnaire, each identified by number, were mailed to the hunters in the sample. In the first week of April, another copy was mailed to those who had not responded.

### Consistency of Theoretical Assumptions with Empirical Analysis

A number of simplifying assumptions were made for ease in presentation of theory. Their consistency with an empirical analysis requires discussion.

The assumption that waterfowl are homogeneous to the hunter permits all kill to be reported on the questionnaire as a single item. Separate estimates by hunters of dabbling duck kill, diving duck kill, and goose kill might have been subject to considerable memory bias. Furthermore, this assumption allows a single marginal valuation.

In the empirical analysis, as in the theoretical presentation, all costs for the season are treated as variable costs and are therefore reflected in the marginal cost curves both for waterfowl per day and for hunting days. This maintains the equivalence of the consumer's surplus from waterfowl bagged per day and from the hunting days.

In the theoretical section it was assumed that each hunter shot at but one site and that the kill probabilities at that site were known and constant for that hunter throughout the season. A single pair of graphs with stable constraints (Figure 6.1 and Figure 6.2) could then be used to illustrate the situation faced by the representative hunter. But these assumptions, particularly that of hunting at a single site, are untenable in reality. In the key Pacific Flyway state of California, for instance, the number of hunting days per hunter is restricted on state and federal refuges where the kill probabilities are excellent. The assumptions are retained in the empirical analysis but in specialized form. It is assumed that data from each hunter's questionnaire response reflects a single (composite) hunting ground and incorporates weighted averages of the differing characteristics of the sites actually hunted and weighted averages of the kill probabilities if they changed throughout the season on any site.

*The Questionnaire Results*

The questionnaire produced 2,455 usable responses for a response rate of nearly 50 percent. The first mailing resulted in 1,792 responses and the second in 663.

It was of particular interest to check the validity of equation (1), namely,

$$V_i = f(Y_i, T_i, K_i/D_i, D_i), \qquad (i = 1, 2, ..., n)$$

by regression of data obtained from the questionnaire response, and then to quantify the marginal value of a waterfowl to the hunter, using the parameter estimates from the regression.

*Choice of the Consumer's Surplus Measure*

The questionnaire attempted to elicit an estimate of both the equivalent and the compensating variations of consumer's surplus from each respondent who hunted in 1968. The question dealing with the equivalent variation through a hypothetical sale of hunting rights for a season provoked a highly emotional response in many individuals, as they objected even to the thought of selling their right. The percentage of hunters who wrote that they would not sell their right at any price was 12.4, and the percentage who named a very high figure such as one million dollars was 1.4 percent. Eliminating these responses, the mean value was $1,044.

The compensating variation question elicited no discernible emotional response in the large majority of respondents. The question asked the minimum amount costs would have had to have risen before the individual would have decided not to have gone hunting at all during the season, assuming general hunting conditions remained unchanged. Many individuals who said they would not sell their right to hunt at any price indicated without comment relatively low and seemingly quite rational dollar amounts to the increased cost question; the mean amount was $247.

The valuation of the compensating variation is the one of primary interest in this study and was used as $V_i$ in all regressions. Since ponds and potholes that produce waterfowl may be drained for other uses, the relevant consumer's surplus measure is the additional amount that individuals would be willing to pay to continue to hunt.

Measures of both valuations were attempted for two reasons: (1) asking the equivalent variation question before the more important compensating variation question allowed some prior psychological adjustment to a hypothetical question on the part of the respondents; (2) comparison of accurate measures of the two consumer's surpluses would provide information regarding the income-elasticity of the good.[10] In this particular instance, the good is probably best defined as hunting days. If the equivalent variation is greater than the compensating variation, the income elasticity is greater than one.[11] However, the dollar amount of the equivalent variation reported is felt to be emotionally biased, and no claim is made even to a first approximation of the true valuation. On the other hand, claim *is* made to having obtained a first approximation of the compensating variation consumer's surplus of the questionnaire respondents. (And the term consumer's surplus henceforth will refer to this valuation only.)

*Regression Results*

Multiple linear regression analysis was performed using data from the questionnaire responses, and the most satisfactory equation form and fitting was

(2) $\ln V = 1.44 + 0.466 \ln Y + 0.168 \ln S + 0.141 \ln E$
(t values)　　(8.7)　　　(4.5)　　　(5.3)

$$+ 0.308 \ln (K/D) + 0.480 \ln D$$
(7.0)　　　　　(12.5)

$$R^2 = 0.222, \qquad s^2 = 1.70, \qquad n = 1511,$$

where $S$ is number of seasons of waterfowl hunting, $E$ represents hunter costs for the season, and $Y$ is household income (after taxes) in thousands.[12] The other variables are as previously defined.

All variables are significant at the 0.001 level, and the significance of the last two supports the theoretical formulation. Although a higher $R^2$ would be desirable, the result obtained here is acceptable for a cross-section study involving no aggregation. The signs and magnitudes of the regression parameters are encouraging, as they meet the restrictions on the functional form stated earlier: namely, that the first partial deriva-

[10] Income elasticity is the percentage change of the quantity of a good purchased divided by the percentage change in income (that caused the quantity of the good purchased to change in the first place).
[11] Patinkin, pp. 94–95.
[12] Many of the questions called for a response in terms of checking a range of values —e.g., income within the range of $5,000 to $7,499. The means of the ranges were used in the regression analysis.

Table 6.1. Means of Untransformed Variables

| Variable | Sym-bol | Sample size[a] | | |
|---|---|---|---|---|
| | | 1,692 | 1,511 | 1,122 |
| Consumer's surplus ($) | $V$ | 247 | 256 | 257 |
| Household income after taxes ($1,000) | $Y$ | 11.9 | 12.1 | 12.2 |
| No. of seasons hunted | $S$ | 16.1 | 16.2 | 16.7 |
| Hunter's cost per season ($) | $E$ | 337 | 322 | 301 |
| Bagged kill per day (no.) | $K/D$ | 2.19 | 2.46 | |
| No. of days of hunting per person | $D$ | 9.7 | 10.5 | |
| Seasonal bagged waterfowl kill (no.) | $K$ | 21.4 | 23.9 | 25.0 |
| Bagged kill in 1967 (no.) | $K_{67}$ | | | 25.7 |

[a] Of the 1,692 active hunters who gave responses to consumer's surplus, costs, income, and number of seasons of hunting, 1,511 reported at least one kill in 1968, and 1,122 reported at least one kill in both 1967 and 1968.

tives of $V$ with respect to the first, fourth, and fifth independent variables must be positive and that the second partials of the fourth and fifth independent variables must be negative.

Of the 2,455 questionnaire respondents, 2,013 potential hunters had purchased a waterfowl hunting stamp, and of these 1,861 were active hunters engaging in at least one day of sport. Of the active hunters, 1,692 also gave responses to consumer's surplus, costs, income, and number of seasons of hunting.[13]

The successful hunters who shot and retrieved at least one bird and who gave responses to the other variables numbered 1,511. The sample used in equation (2) comprises the individuals in this last group. The means for selected variables for this and the preceding group are given in Table 6.1.

*Choice of Independent Variables*

The use of hunting costs of waterfowl as a variable determining consumer's surplus may cause some readers considerable uneasiness. It is argued that costs are used in the regression as a taste variable and hence are plausible and acceptable as an independent variable. The regression results show a positive relationship between consumer's surplus and costs; there is no a priori reason why the relationship must be positive or negative.

The ideal measure of income for explanation of recreation values would be discretionary income, i.e., income remaining after purchase of essentials (however defined). The best available substitute, household income after taxes, was used instead.

[13] Because the values of costs and income were the midpoints of ranges, the values could not be zero, although they could be quite low. Since seasons of hunting included 1968, its value could not be less than one.

On first glance, multicollinearity between variables $K/D$ and $D$ might be thought high, as $D$ appears in both. That this may not be the case is perhaps best illustrated by example. A person's daily wage rate and the number of days he works per week may be considered largely independent of each other, yet the daily wage rate might be expressed as the weekly wage divided by the number of days worked. The weekly wage may be thought of as a composite of two independent variables, and seasonal kill may be thought of as a composite of daily retrieved kill $(K/D)$ and days hunted. In the logarithmic transformation used in equation (2), the correlation coefficient between $K/D$ and $D$ was $-0.15$.

A number of sets of dummy variables were tested as additions to equation (2). Each set was added separately. The chosen dummy variable form affected the value of the intercept of the logarithmic transformation.

Dummy variables rejected as not having significance were those representing level of education, the fact of having paid to hunt on private land, state of residence, and response to first mailing.[14] That the dummy variable representing mailing response was not significant ($t$ value = 0.57) is of interest. Mean values of the independent variables differed considerably in magnitude from the first mailing response to the second. For instance, the mean number of waterfowl was 4.8 birds greater for the first-mailing respondents than for their second-mailing counterparts, and the mean consumer's surplus was greater by $54. That the dummy variable was not significant lends some support to the hypothesis that the regression parameters are valid over a broad range of successful hunters, perhaps including those who did not respond to the questionnaire.

*Substitution of Seasonal Waterfowl Kill as an Independent Variable*

Seasonal retrieved waterfowl kill, $K$, was added to the regression equation and retrieved kill per day, $K/D$, and hunting days, $D$, were removed. As explained previously, the added variable represents a composite of the two removed.

The regression results were:

$$(3) \quad \ln V = 1.54 + 0.443 \ln Y + 0.163 \ln S + 0.149 \ln E + 0.409 \ln K$$

$$(t \text{ values}) \qquad (8.4) \qquad\quad (4.4) \qquad\quad (5.6) \qquad\quad (12.9)$$

$$R^2 = 0.217, \qquad s^2 = 1.71, \qquad n = 1511.$$

[14] The significance was based on examination of $t$ values. All dummy variables could be rejected at the 0.10 level except the set representing the seven states, where one pairing was significant at the 0.05 level. It is recognized that the $t$ test is inappropriate where multiple comparisons are made, as is done with the states. The use of the $t$ test in such cases tends to bias toward acceptance of the significance of some pairing. Considering the bias and the exceedingly high significance of the other variables, the dummy variables related to states were rejected.

Comparison with regression equation (2) shows that the substitution causes no untoward change in the magnitude of the regression parameters assigned to the independent variables common to both equations. The marginal waterfowl valuations implicit in equations (3) and (2) are now compared.

*Comparisons of Marginal Valuations*

The logarithmic linear regression transformation indicates a multiplicative relationship among the independent variables in their untransformed state. For instance, the untransformed counterpart of equation (3) is

(4) $$V = A Y^{\beta_1} S^{\beta_2} E^{\beta_3} K^{\beta_4}$$

or, substituting the parameter estimates,

(5) $$V = e^{1.54} Y^{0.443} S^{0.163} E^{0.149} K^{0.409}.$$

Thus, the marginal value of a waterfowl is the value of the partial derivative of $V$ with respect to $K$, implicitly multiplied by the finite number one:[15]

---

[15] Comparison of equations (4) and (5) shows that $A$ is assumed equal to $e^{1.54}$ where 1.54 is the value of the intercept in the logarithmic transformation regression (3). This means that a conditional median function of the variables in their untransformed state has been determined, rather than a conditional mean function. This has been shown by Arthur S. Goldberger in his article, "The Interpretation and Estimation of Cobb-Douglas Functions," *Econometrica*, vol. 35 (July 1968), 464–72. Let us take the simplest case where a multiplicative relationship is assumed between a variable $Y$ and a variable $X$:

$$Y = AX^{b_1}.$$

Parameter estimation is attempted by a least-squares logarithmic transformation regression. From standard assumptions, the observed values of ln $Y$ are normally distributed at each value of ln $X$; the mean and median of a normal distribution are of course equal. But from the log normal assumption it follows that in the untransformed state the distribution of $Y$ values at each $X$ value is skewed towards the higher values of $Y$, and the mean is greater than the median.

The conditional median function may be approximated by setting $A = e^{b_0}$ where $b_0$ is the value of the intercept determined by the logarithmic regression. If the conditional mean function is desired, it may be approximated by setting

$$A = e^{b_0} e^{1/2 s^2}.$$

(Both functions are approximations, as both estimators of $A$ are biased.) From equation (6) it is obvious that the value of $A$ enters into the value of the partial derivative and hence into the marginal valuation of a waterfowl. Since from equation (3)

$$s^2 = 1.71,$$

the marginal valuation estimated from the conditional mean function would be approximately 2.3 times that estimated from the condition median function. As the relatively high value of $s^2$ and the relatively low value of $R^2$ are closely related, there is great reluctance to adopt the conditional mean function, and the conditional median function therefore is accepted.

(6)
$$\frac{\partial V}{\partial K} = A\beta_4 \ Y^{\beta_1} \ S^{\beta_2} \ E^{\beta_3} \ K^{\beta_4-1}.$$

In a similar fashion, although somewhat less directly, the two marginal valuations of waterfowl developed above,

$$\frac{\partial V}{\partial(K/D)} \cdot \frac{1}{D} \quad \text{and} \quad \frac{\partial V}{\partial D} \cdot \frac{1}{K/D},$$

may be taken using equation (2). Calculated at the mean values of the untransformed independent variables, the three marginal valuations are $3.29, $2.38, and $3.70, respectively.

Use of either of the second and third valuations derived from equation (2) would pose a problem for work in sections that follow. If more (or fewer) waterfowl were available and their value were to be approximated, a decision would have to be made regarding how much each margin was affected by the change. The value of $\partial V/\partial K$ for equation (3) lies between the two values for equation (2) and does not pose the problem directly. Therefore, the calculated value of $3.29 is accepted as a first approximation of the marginal value of a waterfowl to the hunter, and hence as an approximation of a "market purchase price."[16]

### The Addition of 1967 Waterfowl Kill

Marion Clawson "hazarded the judgment that more than half of the total satisfactions" of recreational experiences occur through recollection.[17] If so, it would appear that hunters may include in their estimates of net benefits from the present year's hunting the benefits they receive this year from waterfowl bagged in previous years.[18]

[16] Were there a market for nontransferable rights to hunt and shoot a waterfowl, sold, let us say, by the United States government, the relevant price would be the equilibrium price, or the price that "cleared the market." Everyone who wished to buy *at that price* could do so, and precisely the number of rights to birds the government desired to sell would be sold. Each individual would purchase rights until the gross benefits from the last right purchased equaled the cost (sales price); marginal net benefits for each hunter would be zero. If at the last minute, after all rights had been sold and distributed, the government waived payment for the rights, each hunter would have a marginal net benefit from waterfowl in dollar terms equal to that of every other hunter.

The ideal valuation of a waterfowl from an economic standpoint would be the market-clearing price described above, but this cannot be determined in the absence of a market. Under present institutional arrangements, marginal net benefits from waterfowl may vary from individual to individual. Thus a single value taken as the marginal net benefit can be only an approximation, and the value is not necessarily the market-clearing price.

[17] Marion Clawson, "Economic Aspects of Sport Fishing," *Canadian Fisheries Reports*, No. 4 (Ottawa: The Department of Fisheries of Canada, 1965), p. 15.

[18] And a hunter who did *not* hunt in the present year but did in previous years would have a positive net benefit in the present year from past waterfowl hunting.

The hypothesis can be tested since the hunters in this study who were queried as to their 1968 waterfowl kill were also queried a year earlier by the Bureau of Sports Fisheries and Wildlife as to their 1967 kill. The 1967 kill of each hunter who responded to the Bureau's survey was available in coded form. Each code number represented a range of kill, such as 6–10 birds. The means of the ranges were used, and the open-ended range (òver 100 birds) was arbitrarily assigned the value of 125.

Each successful hunter in the sample of 1,511 had his 1967 retrieved kill ($K_{67}$) added to the data from his questionnaire response in this study. Those who did not respond to the 1967 survey and those who reported zero kill in 1967 were eliminated, leaving 1,122 hunters who were successful in both years. A regression similar to that in equation (3) was run:

(7)   $\ln V = 1.50 + 0.402 \ln Y + 0.166 \ln S + 0.143 \ln E$
       ($t$ values)        (6.6)              (3.7)              (4.5)

$$+ 0.315 \ln K + 0.152 \ln K_{67}$$
$$(7.2) \qquad\qquad (3.8)$$

$$R^2 = 0.228, \qquad s^2 = 1.63, \qquad n = 1122.$$

All variables are significant at the 0.001 level, which lends support to the spirit of Clawson's remarks.

The implications as to marginal valuation are interesting. The total marginal value of a waterfowl bagged in 1967, for instance, would be the sum of its discounted marginal values in 1967 and subsequent years. The partial derivative of $V$ with respect to $K_{67}$ in each year includes the regression parameter assigned to $K_{67}$ as one of the multiplicative terms. From an examination of parameter values assigned to $K$ and $K_{67}$ in equation (7), it appears likely that the marginal value of $K_{67}$ could be neglected after two or three years. Needless to say, data collection for the actual use of such a valuation scheme would be most difficult. It would be even more difficult if a notion of option value were introduced because it would have to be segregated from recollection value. The means of the variables used in equation (7) are reported in the last column of Table 6.1. The reader may suspect that the closeness of the means for the kill of waterfowl in 1967 and in 1968 indicates that hunters report the same number of bagged waterfowl each year, regardless of actual kill, but the correlation coefficient for the two variables in logarithmic form is 0.59, which does not seem high enough to support that hypothesis. Undoubtedly a true correlation does exist between the two variables.

*Response Bias*

There is reason to believe that hunters in our sample did not report their season's waterfowl kill on the average in the same way that hunters reported in the survey conducted by the Bureau of Sport Fisheries and Wildlife. After all plausible adjustments have been made, average kill in the government survey seems to be 25 percent lower than that shown herein.[19]

BIOLOGICAL EQUATIONS FOR DABBLING DUCKS

Prior to this section attention has focused on waterfowl valuation. Here we describe biological relationships pertaining to dabbling ducks. Later, the equations developed here will be linked to those on valuation.

*A Biological Production Function*

Most mathematical population models for wildlife and fish state a functional relationship between the breeding (spawning) population and the number of young that would be produced at various levels of the breeding population. Often it is assumed, implicitly or explicitly, that the breeding environment is sufficiently stable that it need not enter directly into the model.

However, in the case of dabbling ducks the breeding environment, of which ponds in the prairies are so important a part, decidedly is unstable. The number of ponds capable of support of breeding waterfowl and their young varies from year to year depending upon climatological conditions.

For a given species of dabbling ducks, let us say mallards, it is hypothesized that:

$$(8) \qquad\qquad I = h(W, P)$$

where $I$ is the number of immature birds that survive in September, $W$ is the number of adults in May, and $P$ is the measure of suitable wetlands.[20] It is assumed that (1) as the breeding population increases, the marginal (or additional) immatures resulting become fewer and fewer for each additional increase in the number of breeders, and (2) the immatures exhibit compensatory mortality in the early weeks of their lives. Hence,

$$\frac{\partial I}{\partial W} > 0 \quad \text{and} \quad \frac{\partial^2 I}{\partial W^2} < 0$$

over some range.

For ease in use in regression analysis, the multiplicative relationship

$$(9) \qquad\qquad I = A W^{\gamma_1} P^{\gamma_2}$$

[19] For a complete discussion of this problem see Judd Hammack, *Toward an Economic Evaluation of a Fugitive Recreational Resource: Waterfowl*, Ph.D. thesis, University of Washington (Ann Arbor: University Microfilms, 1969), pp. 64–69.

[20] The importance of incorporating a wetland factor in the determination of waterfowl production was demonstrated statistically by Crissey, pp. 161–71.

Table 6.2. Mallard Population Statistics and Canadian Prairie Pond Indices
*(millions)*

| Year | Continental mallard breeding population, May | Number of immature birds, September | Ponds, July |
|------|------|------|------|
| 1955 | 11.0 | 15.6 | 5.0 |
| 1956 | 12.2 | 13.9 | 3.6 |
| 1957 | 11.6 | 18.7 | 2.2 |
| 1958 | 14.5 | 11.0 | 1.7 |
| 1959 | 11.6 | 6.6 | 1.2 |
| 1960 | 9.7 | 11.0 | 1.7 |
| 1961 | 9.0 | 6.0 | 0.6 |
| 1962 | 6.9 | 6.6 | 0.8 |
| 1963 | 8.0 | 7.6 | 1.7 |
| 1964 | 7.9 | 6.0 | 1.1 |
| 1965 | 6.1 | 9.3 | 2.2 |
| 1966 | 7.8 | 8.9 | 2.0 |
| 1967 | 8.6 | 9.8 | 1.5 |
| 1968 | 8.3 | 6.2 | 0.85 |

Source: Estimates from Migratory Bird Populations Station, U.S. Bureau of Sport Fisheries and Wildlife, Laurel, Maryland. The estimates are subject to revision. For data of a comparable nature, see Aelred D. Geis, R. Kahler Martinson, and David R. Anderson, "Establishing Hunting Regulations and Allowable Harvest of Mallards in the United States," *The Journal of Wildlife Management*, vol. 33 (October 1969), pp. 848–59.

is taken as the specific functional form of equation (8). To meet the assumptions about the partial derivatives, we assume $0 < \gamma_1 < 1$.

A logarithmic transformation of mallard data for the years 1955–68 inclusive, shown in original form in Table 6.2, was regressed with the following results:

$$(10) \qquad \ln I = 1.07 + 0.413 \ln W + 0.479 \ln J$$
$$(t \text{ values}) \qquad (1.7) \qquad\quad (4.7)$$

$$R^2 = 0.76, \qquad s^2 = 0.039, \qquad n = 14$$

where $J$ represents July pond data.[21] However, an outlier test on the $I$ residuals requires rejection of the data for the year 1957 at the 0.10 level.[22] As can be seen from Table 6.2 the production of immature birds in that year was very high.

[21] The pond estimates are for central and southern Alberta, Saskatchewan, and Manitoba, and are employed as a proxy measure for continental wetlands relevant to breeding mallards. Pond values for the month of May are also available. They are an arguably appropriate substitute for the July pond variable. For further details see Hammack, pp. 87–92.

[22] The test used is that of W. J. Dixon, "Processing Data for Outliers," *Biometrics*, vol. 9 (March 1953), pp. 74–89.

The regressions were run again, this time with the 1957 data omitted. The results were:

(11)  $\ln I = 1.36 + 0.269 \ln W + 0.460 \ln J$
      ($t$ values)      (1.6)           (6.7)

$R^2 = 0.86$,      $s^2 = 0.018$,      $n = 13$

with no further outliers. Hence

(12)                    $I = 1.36 \, W^{0.269} J^{0.460}$

is accepted as the estimated production function in this preliminary study.

## A Difference Equation

An additional biological relationship determining the number of breeding mallards in any year will be stated here and used in modified form in the analytical model in the next section:

(13)                    $W_{t+1} = s_2 \left[ (I_t + s_1 W_t) - X_t \right].$

The number of mallards killed by hunters, but not necessarily bagged, is denoted by $X$. The symbol $s_1$ denotes the survival fraction of adult birds during the May to September period, which is equal to one minus the natural mortality fraction during that period. The symbol $s_2$ denotes the survival fraction of the entire population not killed by hunters from September to the following May. The beginning year is represented by $t$, and the following year by $t + 1$. During the hunting season it is assumed that hunter mortality is so dominant that other sources of mortality may be neglected. It is further assumed that the instantaneous rate of subsequent natural mortality is independent of the instantaneous rate of hunting mortality.[23]

The value of $s_1$ has been estimated at 95 to 96 percent. The value of 0.95 will be used here. A value for $s_2$ is considerably more difficult to determine. Natural mortality figures for mallards during the fall, winter, and spring periods combined have been estimated by the Migratory Bird Populations Station, U.S. Bureau of Sport Fisheries and Wildlife. The natural mortality is calculated by subtracting from the estimated fall mallard population both the estimated annual Canadian and United States kill and the breeding population of the subsequent spring; hence, natural mortality is not estimated independently. When the mean number of birds thought to have died from natural causes during fall, winter,

[23] Indebtedness is acknowledged to Gerald J. Paulik for aid in formulating equation (13).

and spring for the years 1955–65 is divided by the mean number of birds estimated to have been in the fall population over the same years, the natural mortality fraction is 0.16, which would set $s_2$ at approximately 0.84. The natural mortality fraction estimated for each of the years ranges from 0.07 to 0.27.[24]

## Optimum Economic Management

In the following discussion it is assumed that those charged with managing the mallard population seek to find that level of mallard population and supporting breeding habitat which maximizes the hunters' net willingness to pay for the hunting service through time.[25] Net willingness to pay is the difference between the hunter's valuation of his activity above his costs and the cost of obtaining additional wetlands.

### The Analytical Model

The net value of hunting during a season is the product of $N$ hunters and their individual valuation functions,

$$(14) \qquad\qquad NV(K, Y, S, E).$$

The second ingredient of the story is a pond cost function denoted by

$$(15) \qquad C(P), \frac{\partial C}{\partial P} > 0 \text{ for } P \geq \bar{P}, \qquad C(P) = 0 \text{ for } P < \bar{P}.$$

In this scenario it is assumed that a given amount of wetlands, $\bar{P}$, is freely available because the land has no alternative productive use. The term $\partial C/\partial P$ is the marginal cost of ponds, expressed as an annual rental rate; it is therefore the annual easement value of the pond.

Canadian and U.S. farmers will claim that the cost function has been misspecified because it fails to include annual crop damages. Presumably crop damage varies directly with the size of the fall flight and with the size of the population on the wintering habitat, although present crude statistical evidence will not support this view. Crop damage in Canada is related most fundamentally to the date and length of the crop harvesting activity relative to the time when waterfowl begin migrating south. If the internal mechanism governing time of fall flight in the mallards sends an immense population southward before grain crops have been swathed or after the crops have been combined, damage will be insig-

---

[24] Data in the paragraph were derived from Crissey, p. 163.

[25] The subsequent analysis assumes unrealistically that breeding habitat is not a random variable.

BROWN AND HAMMACK 191

nificant; but if even a small waterfowl population arrives just after swathing, crop damage will be severe.[26] Farther south, damage on crop-land may vary with the number of waterfowl wintering in the area, but we have been unable to estimate the relationship. Hence, our formulation of the cost relationship, which omits crop damage as a function of water-fowl population, is consistent with present knowledge.[27]

Specification of the value and cost functions alone is not sufficient be-cause waterfowl managers cannot act as free economic spirits with their enthusiasm for correct policy decisions tempered only by dollar com-parisons. Managers must also recognize that the mallard population at any point in time is governed by the following differential equation:

(16) $$\dot{W} = -W + s_2[I + s_1 W - c_3 NK].$$

This expression is equivalent to (13) with the following exceptions. The framework of the analysis has shifted from discrete to continuous time. The change simplifies the notation without loss of content, but the reader should bear in mind that all variables are dated implicitly. A third parameter, $c_3$, has been added in explicit recognition that not all birds killed are bagged birds. Total hunter ($N$) related physical losses to the system including crippling losses and unretrieved kill are estimated to be 1.25 times reported bag.[28] In review, reading from left to right within the brackets, the young ($I$) plus the surviving breeders ($s_1 W$) make up the fall flight from which the total kill ($c_3 NK$) is subtracted to obtain the wintering population. Some fraction ($s_2$) of the wintering population sur-vives to return to the northern breeding grounds in the spring. If this number is greater than the original number of breeders ($W$), clearly there has been a positive change; that is, the time derivative, $\frac{dW}{dt}$ or $\dot{W}$, is positive.[29]

Since those in charge of maximization have a many-period problem they must pick a discount rate ($\rho$) that describes the tradeoff between present and future valuable goods and services. Then, with knowledge

[26] Renewable Resources Consulting Services Limited, "A Study of Waterfowl Damage to Commercial Grain Crops in Alberta," Edmonton, Alberta, October 1969, pp. 51–52, 57, 59, 69.

[27] If crop damage is a function of population, the economic consequences of this fact are: (1) the optimal size of the population will be lower; (2) the marginal value of a bagged duck will be higher, so the number of ducks killed per season will be lower; and (3) the breeder/pond factor proportions will be lower than the results described below.

[28] The expression for total hunter losses in this section ($c_3 NK$) corresponds to the shorthand expression $X$ in an earlier section of the paper.

[29] The time derivative of any variable will be denoted by "·".

of the existing waterfowl population, $W(0)$, the problem is to find the sequence of $P$ and $K$ that maximizes

$$(17) \qquad \int_0^\infty [NV(K, Y, S, E) - C(P)]e^{-\rho t}$$

subject to (16).[30]

Formally the expression to be maximized is

$$(18) \quad H = \{NV(K, Y, S, E) - C(P) - \lambda[W - s_2(I + s_1 W - c_3 NK)]\}e^{-\rho t}$$

where $\lambda$ is an auxiliary variable. The functions have been specified in such a way that there is a solution and therefore an optimal management program.[31] The necessary conditions for maximization of $H$ are

$$(19a) \qquad \frac{\partial H}{\partial K} = \frac{\partial V}{\partial K} - \lambda s_2 c_3 = 0,$$

$$(19b) \qquad \frac{\partial H}{\partial P} = -\frac{\partial C}{\partial P} + \lambda s_2 \frac{\partial I}{\partial P} = 0,$$

$$(19c) \qquad -\lambda[1 - s_2 \partial I / \partial W - s_1 s_2] = -\dot{\lambda} + \rho \lambda.$$

The imputed value of a marginal change in the waterfowl population is the economic interpretation given to $\lambda$. For those trained in economics, think of waterfowl in general and mallards in particular as capital that combines with ponds (labor) to produce young (output). Verbally stated, expression (19a) says that hunters should kill up to the point where their marginal valuation is just equal to the economic loss to the system if capital is reduced by one unit. Since a fraction ($s_2$) of that mallard population would have died naturally, the hunter should only pay $s_2 \lambda$ where $s_2 \lambda$ is less than $\lambda$. But because he cripples some birds his charge is increased by $c_3$. Nowhere in the formulation of this model are words or equations to the effect that beneficiaries must pay. Only if we believe this principle should hunters pay $\lambda s_2 c_3$. On the other hand, if hunters do not pay, rather elaborate physical restrictions on hunting will have to be promulgated in order to obtain an optimal result.

Expression (19b) gives the standard economic result that factors ought

---

[30] In reality, knowledge about the variables $Y$, $S$, and $E$ is also needed. Since hunters' income, seasons hunted, and costs will change through time, estimates of these changes would have to be made if policies are formulated on the basis of this model. In the present paper the empirical illustrations follow from the use of mean sample values for $Y$, $S$, $E$. This is a substantive simplifying assumption.

[31] One of the best treatments of optimal control problems in economics may be found in Kenneth Arrow and Mordecai Kurz, *Public Investment, the Rate of Return and Optimal Fiscal Policy* (Baltimore: Johns Hopkins Press for Resources for the Future, 1970).

to be hired up to the point where the price of the factor, $\dfrac{\partial C}{\partial P}$, equals the value of its marginal product.

It is interpretively helpful to rewrite (19c) as

(20) $$\lambda g = \rho\lambda - \dot{\lambda}$$

where $g = -1 + s_2\partial I/\partial W + s_1 s_2$ (the own net rate of return on the natural resource). In a stationary state, when $\dot{\lambda} = 0$, equation (20) says, quite simply, that the best natural resource stock level is that for which the rate of discount equals the rate of growth of the natural resource. If one kind of capital is less productive than another kind, we should consume the less productive capital, say waterfowl, and get satisfaction in so doing, until the return on waterfowl capital equals the return on capital elsewhere in the economy. When the stock of waterfowl is smaller than optimal, the marginal price of $W$ is high and falls through time to its steady-state value. Hence, when $g$ is greater than $\rho$, $W$ is less than $W^*$, the optimal value, and $\dot{\lambda}/\lambda < 0$. As is true for most types of capital the marginal productivity of waterfowl is high for "small" amounts of $W$ because time has built this survival mechanism into most animals. This explanation makes sense to an economist. In biological terms, the mallards exhibit compensatory mortality. The average young per breeder surviving until the fall flight rises with decreases in the number of breeders.[32]

*Empirical Results*

The transition from the analytical model to empirical results involves bridging a chasm and an abyss, both of which require discussion at the outset. We tackle the chasm first—a pond must be well defined in terms of productivity, and ideally the cost of ponds should be estimated carefully. Our analysis is inadequate on both counts. In the model, wetlands are assumed to be homogeneous in the productivity of both waterfowl and grain crops. In reality, ponds vary in their ability to support waterfowl just as the dry depressions vary in their ability to support agricultural crop growth.

Suppose the solution calls for saving wetlands from drainage, through, say, an easement program. It is not sufficient to know the productivity of wetlands that remain in their natural state because of government easement. One must also know the productivity of these wetlands relative to

---

[32] Since the mallard production function is concave, a falling marginal function implies a falling average function. Species survival contracts with nature are not unqualified. When the population level of some species falls below a critical minimum, instantaneous death rates dominate instantaneous birth rates and the species becomes extinct.

the waterfowl productivity of the other wetlands. If easement ponds are less productive than ones that are freely available because they are not threatened by drainage, policy prescriptions will be biased. A researcher who wishes to plow this field will find fertile soil larded with boulders. The Canadian government support program for wetland easements provides suggestive data. Average annual payments made on recently acquired easement land are $5.60 per acre for land in Alberta, an area that provides waterfowl shot by Pacific Flyway hunters in the United States.[33] Since there is about 0.85 acre in a pond and its supporting wetlands, ponds have an easement cost of $4.76 per pond, on the basis of recent experience. How many wetlands could be obtained at this price is not a number known to every or any Canadian schoolboy.

Alternatively, one can try to estimate the opportunity cost of wetlands by investigating representative farm or crop budgets. A recent study of the Alberta region produced estimates in the neighborhood of $17 per wetland acre.[34]

The costs mentioned thus far refer only to maintaining the permanency of existing wetlands, but new wetlands can be created. According to Ducks Unlimited:

> Simple earth dams on the outlet of marshes store additional water to outlast periods of drought. Restriction of evaporation area is also effective. Dikes built across shallow marshes or lakes which are frequently dry, confine the water to half or less of the former area. There are also many large shallow prairie lakes too salty to be of much value to breeding waterfowl. Often inflowing creeks enter these lakes through shallow bays of lower salinity. A dam across the neck of the bay where it joins the lake proper develops the bay into good duck-breeding habitat. An inflowing creek can also be diverted through a series of natural basins en route to the lake. Creeks and other flowages, less well defined, can also be diverted into marshes and shallow lakes which lack sufficient water. New marshes can be created by diverting water to natural depressions in the terrain through the use of dams and other controls. Many fine areas have been developed in southern Alberta by using waste irrigation waters.[35]

[33] Average annual payments for the Canadian Prairies as a whole are $4.73 per acre. The information is derived from Canadian Wildlife Service, "Dollars From Wetlands" (leaflet), and from A. S. Goodman, Canadian Wildlife Service, in a personal communication dated October 7, 1969. In the United States, breeding-ground purchases have been made predominantly in North Dakota, South Dakota, and western Minnesota. Present wetland values in the area range from $25 per acre to $85 or so. Information was obtained from Burton W. Rounds, U.S. Bureau of Sport Fisheries and Wildlife, in a personal communication dated August 8, 1969.

[34] Prairie Agri-Management Consultants, Ltd., "Sensitivity Analysis of the Estimated Opportunity Cost of Maintaining Wetlands, Reports I and II," prepared for the Canadian Wildlife Service, February 20, 1970.

[35] Ducks Unlimited (Canada), "Information: A History of Ducks Unlimited," p. 5.

Ducks Unlimited estimates that its recent projects cost it slightly more than $1 per acre. The low figure is largely attributed to the fact that it buys no land.[36]

In summary, estimates of the costs of a pond vary from about $1 to $17. Fortunately, the choice of an estimate is considerably narrowed. In the case described below, a pond cost of $4.76 produced an optimum number of ponds greatly exceeding the historical average, indicating that new ponds should be created. In our judgment, Ducks Unlimited does not have sufficient moral suasion to coax that much land out of current production. Therefore, cases assuming values of $17 per pond and $12 per pond are illustrated as well. The latter figure was chosen arbitrarily.

Having bridged the chasm with a frayed rope, we now face the abyss. On the economic side, only hunters in the Pacific Flyway were studied. The physical relations are continental. Joining the two parts requires either that the economic relations be broadened or that the physical functions be reduced from the continent to the Pacific Flyway. However, decomposition of the continental physical relationship into subregional relationships, one of which might be the Pacific Flyway, is possible only if nature is kind enough to yield constant returns to scale; that is, if equal proportionate increases in both breeders and ponds produce the same proportionate increase in young. Since the multiplicative production function does not exhibit this property, the decomposition is precluded, and the economic relationships therefore are broadened to continental scope. Although a rigorous decomposition is not possible, we illustrate the numerical results for the Pacific Flyway by apportioning waterfowl kill on the basis of that flyway's hunter population to the total North American hunter population. It is assumed that all hunters in Canada and the United States have the same tastes, average income, average seasons hunted, and average costs as those hunters sampled in our Pacific Flyway. Admittedly these are heroic assumptions. For purposes of analysis, we have also assumed that total kill, $K$, is equal to $3.33B$, where $B$ equals the number of mallards bagged. This relationship was estimated from data in the *Waterfowl Status Reports*.

Table 6.3 summarizes the stationary values for waterfowl, ponds, implicit prices, and seasonal bag assuming 1968 economic conditions, an arbitrarily chosen discount rate of 8 percent and the following parameter values: $s_1 = 0.95$, $s_2 = 0.84$, $c_3 = 1.25$, the number of hunters in the Pacific Flyway is 0.279 million and the total number of hunters is 1.715 million.[37]

[36] Personal communication from Ducks Unlimited (Canada), January 22, 1971.

[37] A lower discount rate typically means that an economy accumulates a greater store of wealth including, in this case, more waterfowl. More waterfowl produce a

Table 6.3. Illustrative Stationary Economic Optimal Values

|  | Historical values, 1961–68[a] | Cost of pond = $4.76 | Cost of pond = $12.00 | Cost of pond = $17.00 |
|---|---|---|---|---|
| $W$<br>Breeders<br>(millions) | 7.8 | 33 | 15.2 | 11.4 |
| $P$<br>July ponds<br>(millions) | 1.3 | 22 | 6.3 | 4.0 |
| $\lambda$<br>Marginal value<br>of a waterfowl<br>(dollars) |  | 1.90 | 3.10 | 3.70 |
| $B$<br>Mallard kill per<br>hunter, Pacific<br>Flyway | 3.5[b] | 16 | 7.1 | 5.3 |
| Total mallard<br>kill, Pacific<br>Flyway (millions) | 0.9 | 4.5 | 2.0 | 1.5 |
| Total kill per<br>hunter, Pacific<br>Flyway | 11[b] | 53 | 24 | 18 |
| Total kill,<br>Pacific Flyway<br>(millions) | 3.5[b] | 14.8 | 6.6 | 4.9 |
| Total conti-<br>nental mallard<br>kill (millions) | 3.7 | 27.4 | 12.2 | 9.1 |

*Note:* Assumptions were as follows: discount rate = 8%; $s_1$ = 0.95, $s_2$ = 0.84; $c_3$ = 1.25; number of hunters in the Pacific Flyway = 0.279 million; total number of hunters = 1.715 million.

[a] Data computed from United States Department of the Interior, Bureau of Sport Fisheries and Wildlife, *Waterfowl Status Report*, Annual Series.

[b] Average for years 1965–69.

Given these assumptions and estimates, how does the recent historical average compare with the economic optimum? From 1961 to 1968 the estimated average breeders and July ponds were 7.8 million and 1.3 million respectively, while the economic optimum (pond cost equals $12) calls for 15.2 million breeders and 6.3 million ponds, a sizable difference indeed. Historically, the continental mallard harvest averaged nearly 4

larger stationary yield, implying a lower stationary marginal value for the waterfowl harvested. Moreover, a lower discount rate for a given pond cost induces a change in the factor proportions, increasing the ratio of $W$ to $P$.

million, whereas the optimum produces about 12 million, again a very sizable difference.[38]

Optimal paths of $W$, $P$, $\lambda$, and $B$ through time can be calculated given initial values for $W$ and the (19) equation system, together with the differential equation governing the waterfowl population. It is a tedious and unwarranted task. While the model is strong analytically, existing data probably are too frail to give substantial support to the illustrative numerical exercises already presented. Nevertheless, just as thought games give us a glimpse of productive ways to look at unsolved problems, empirical analysis reveals the variables requiring more accurate measurement and often produces results that induce one to reformulate his conceptual apparatus. In view of the dangers of misplaced specificity, further qualifications of our numerical illustrations are in order.

First, the empirical model is cast in terms of mallards, whereas only approximately 30 percent of the waterfowl bagged in the Pacific Flyway are mallards. Implicitly it is assumed that changing mallards by a given proportion also changes the availability of the other species in the same proportion, and the share of each species in the bag remains the same.[39]

Second, production is estimated on the basis of prairie ponds, regarded as a proxy variable for continental ponds. If, on the average, nature and drainage activities by man in the prairies and in the larger region are harmonious, there is no cause for concern. But increasing the amount of wetlands in the Canadian prairies by artificial means by some multiple of the historic average implies in our model that an unknown amount of wetlands has been added elsewhere at an unknown cost. Therefore, the data in Table 6.3, based on costs of wetlands in the prairies only, must be considered as illustrative examples.

A summary of this section is easy. The model basically is a time-dependent analysis of a single plant producing one good with two factors of production. The good is purchased in a single market. There is no uncertainty. The real world calls for a multistage, spatially differentiated, stochastic production process yielding many goods from many inputs. The goods are sold in many spatially differentiated markets. The real world calls for a rich institutional clothing whereas our approach is starkly naked in this respect. There is a good deal to be done, most of it by the physical scientists. Much of this research should be done in con-

[38] The historical average was computed from the U.S. Department of the Interior, Bureau of Sport Fisheries and Wildlife, *Waterfowl Status Report*, Annual Series.

[39] Two reasons why change in species composition might result in changed estimates of parameter values are: (1) possible differences among species with respect to fertility rates; and (2) differences among species with respect to wetlands environment preferences. Mallards are thought to prefer parklands and pintails to prefer grasslands. See Crissey, p. 164.

junction with economists. We need to know much more about what determines the routes and destinations of the fall flights of many if not all of the species of dabblers, divers, and geese. We need careful, independent identification of crucial rates of natural mortality. We must learn more about interspecies competition for available hunting grounds. How do individual species respond to changes in wintering habitat? How alike are hunter valuations across flyways and across states within a flyway? At present there are no satisfactory answers to these questions. But they are worth answering, not because they are intellectually challenging, which they are, but rather because waterfowl are too valuable to be mismanaged.

# *Appendix A*

## WATERFOWL HUNTING QUESTIONNAIRE AND TRANSMITTAL LETTERS

UNIVERSITY OF WASHINGTON
Seattle, Washington
98105

Department of Economics

Dear Waterfowl Hunter:

The University of Washington is engaged in a study of waterfowl and waterfowl hunting in the Western States. We hope the results of the study will help to improve the management of waterfowl resources. Through a random selection process you have been chosen to receive our questionnaire.

Only you, the waterfowl hunter, can give us the answers we need. Will you please help us by filling out the enclosed questionnaire and returning it in the self-addressed envelope which requires no postage? We have tried to make the questionnaire as short as possible. Although some of the questions may be difficult for you to answer accurately, please try to give your best guess.

You have our word that your individual answers will be held in strict confidence and will be used only for the purposes of this study. Your response will be combined with many others and only group totals will be used in the study results. The number that appears on your questionnaire allows us to remove your name from our list when the questionnaire is returned, so that we may avoid bothering you again.

If you have any comments you would like to make about the questionnaire, feel free to do so on the back of this letter and return it along with the questionnaire.

Thank you for your cooperation.

Best wishes for good hunting,

Dr. Gardner Brown, Jr.
Assistant Professor of Economics,
Institute for Economic Research

UNIVERSITY OF WASHINGTON
Seattle, Washington
98105

Department of Economics

Dear Waterfowl Hunter:

We seem not to have received back the waterfowl hunting questionnaire sent to you a few weeks ago. We enclose another copy in case something happened to the first one. Won't you take a few minutes to fill it out and return it to us in the self-addressed postage-paid envelope? *Your* answers *are* important.

We emphasize that your individual answers will be held in strict confidence and will be used only for the purposes of this study. Your response will be combined with many others and only group totals will be used in the study results. The number that appears on your questionnaire allows us to remove your name from our list when the questionnaire is returned, so that we may avoid bothering you again. If you have any comments you would like to make, feel free to do so on the back of this letter and return it along with the questionnaire.

If you have already mailed the original copy back to us, we are sorry to have bothered you again.

Thank you once more for your help.

Best wishes for good hunting,

Dr. Gardner Brown, Jr.
Assistant Professor of Economics
Institute for Economic Research

## WATERFOWL HUNTING QUESTIONNAIRE

We use the term "waterfowl hunting season" or just "hunting season" often in our questions. By this we mean the open waterfowl hunting period usually starting in October of one year and ending in many areas in January of the following year. To emphasize that a single season may overlap two calendar years we refer, for instance, to the "1968–69 hunting season."

Question 1.   During approximately how many seasons have you hunted waterfowl, *including* the 1968–69 season?

        _____ seasons

Question 2.   Did you purchase a Migratory Bird Hunting Stamp ("Duck Stamp") for the 1968–69 season? Please indicate your answer by a check mark below.

    \_\_\_\_ Yes           \_\_\_\_ No

IF YES, please go on to Question 3.

IF NO, please check the reason why you did not purchase a stamp. (Please check *only* the major reason.) Then skip directly to *Question 9a* and answer the remaining questions.

    \_\_\_\_ Waterfowl hunting too expensive

    \_\_\_\_ Not enough time available to hunt

    \_\_\_\_ Too far to drive to hunting area

    \_\_\_\_ Insufficient number of waterfowl

    \_\_\_\_ Areas of waterfowl hunting too crowded with other people

    \_\_\_\_ Other reason (please explain) _____

    _____

    _____

Question 3.   Kindly indicate below the kinds of waterfowl you prefer to hunt. Use a "1" for your *first* choice, a "2" for your *second* choice (if any), etc. Please do not go beyond your third choice.

    \_\_\_\_ American Widgeon

    \_\_\_\_ Mallard

    \_\_\_\_ Pintail

    \_\_\_\_ Shoveler       Ducks

    \_\_\_\_ Teal

    \_\_\_\_ Goldeneye, Redhead
           or Scaup

    \_\_\_\_ Other varieties of ducks not listed above

    \_\_\_\_ Ducks in general, don't particularly care what variety

_____ Geese

_____ Coots

Question 4.  Approximately how many waterfowl did you shoot and retrieve
during the 1968–69 season? (If the answer is zero, please enter "0.")

_____ waterfowl

Question 5.  On about how many days did you hunt waterfowl during the 1968–
69 season? (If the answer is zero, please enter "0.")

_____ days

Next, we would like to ask you a question involving an entirely fictitious
situation; it is the only way we can obtain the desired information. The question
may seem difficult and may take some thought, but we would like your best
guess.

Question 6.  Suppose you have the right to hunt waterfowl just as you have had
that right during the last season and the seasons before it. But also
suppose that you could sell your right to hunt waterfowl for *a season*, and if you did sell the right, you yourself could not hunt waterfowl during that season. You would set your own price and the
choice would be entirely up to you whether or not you sold this
right.

We emphasize that this situation is entirely fictitious—no one is going to
restrict waterfowl hunting on the basis of this questionnaire and no one could
actually buy or sell this natural right.

But, WHAT IS THE *SMALLEST* AMOUNT YOU THINK YOU
WOULD TAKE TO GIVE UP YOUR RIGHT TO HUNT WATERFOWL
FOR A SEASON—SAY, 1968–69? Please check the most appropriate answer
below.

| | |
|---|---|
| _____ $0.00 to $2.49 | _____ $100 to $199 |
| _____ $2.50 to $4.99 | _____ $200 to $299 |
| _____ $5.00 to $9.99 | _____ $300 to $399 |
| _____ $10.00 to $19.99 | _____ $400 to $499 |
| _____ $20.00 to $29.99 | _____ $500 to $749 |
| _____ $30.00 to $49.99 | _____ $750 to $1000 |
| _____ $50.00 to $74.99 | _____ Over $1000 |
| _____ $75.00 to $99.99 | (please specify amount |
| | $ _____ ) |

Question 7.  About how much do you figure your total waterfowl hunting costs
were for the 1968–69 season? (An obvious cost would be shotgun
shells. We are interested in what *you* consider your costs to be. We

therefore prefer not specifying cost categories, thus leaving the matter up to you.)

After you have given the question a little thought, please check the answer which you feel best represents your *total* costs *for the season.*

| | |
|---|---|
| ___ $0.00 to $2.49 | ___ $100 to $199 |
| ___ $2.50 to $4.99 | ___ $200 to $299 |
| ___ $5.00 to $9.99 | ___ $300 to $499 |
| ___ $10.00 to $19.99 | ___ $500 to $749 |
| ___ $20.00 to $34.99 | ___ $750 to $999 |
| ___ $35.00 to $49.99 | ___ $1000 to $1499 |
| ___ $50.00 to $74.99 | ___ $1500 to $1999 |
| ___ $75.00 to $99.99 | ___ $2000 or more |
| | (please specify amount |
| | $ _____ ) |

Since we have been talking about costs, we would now like to ask you another question on the same subject, but this one again involves an entirely fictitious situation. Again, the question may seem difficult and take some thought, but we would like your best guess.

Question 8.  Suppose that your waterfowl hunting costs for the 1968–69 season were greater than you estimated in Question 7.

*Assume these increased costs in no way affected general hunting conditions.*

ABOUT *HOW MUCH GREATER* DO YOU THINK YOUR COSTS WOULD HAVE HAD TO HAVE BEEN BEFORE YOU WOULD HAVE DECIDED NOT TO HAVE GONE HUNTING *AT ALL* DURING THAT SEASON?

We emphasize that the dollar amounts given below are intended to represent imaginary increased costs, that is, costs over and above the actual costs you estimated in Question 7. Please check the answer below that you consider most appropriate.

| | |
|---|---|
| ___ $0.00 to $2.49 | ___ $100 to $199 |
| ___ $2.50 to $4.99 | ___ $200 to $299 |
| ___ $5.00 to $9.99 | ___ $300 to $399 |
| ___ $10.00 to $19.99 | ___ $400 to $499 |
| ___ $20.00 to $29.99 | ___ $500 to $749 |
| ___ $30.00 to $49.99 | ___ $750 to $1000 |
| ___ $50.00 to $74.99 | ___ Over $1000 |
| ___ $75.00 to $99.99 | (please specify amount |
| | $ _____ ) |

Question 9a. Please indicate your approximate age:

_____ Under 16 years                    _____ 45–54 years

_____ 16–24 years                       _____ 55–64 years

_____ 25–34 years                       _____ 65 years or more

_____ 35–44 years

Question 9b. Kindly indicate the category that represents your highest level of formal education:

_____ 8th grade or under (elementary school)

_____ 9th through 12th grade (high school)

_____ Beyond 12th grade (college)

Question 10. The number of persons in my household, including myself, is

_____ 1                                 _____ 5

_____ 2                                 _____ 6

_____ 3                                 _____ 7

_____ 4                                 _____ Over 7 persons
                                        (please specify
                                        number _____)

Question 11. The annual income after taxes in my household is about

_____ Under $2500                       _____ $10,000 to $14,999

_____ $2500 to $4999                    _____ $15,000 to $19,999

_____ $5000 to $7499                    _____ $20,000 to $29,999

_____ $7500 to $9999                    _____ $30,000 or more (please
                                        specify to nearest
                                        $10,000  $_____)

Question 12. During the 1968–69 season did you at any time hunt for waterfowl on private property or a private club where you, yourself, had to pay in some way for the right to hunt?

_____ Yes              _____ No

IF YES, will you please give your estimates on the items below?

The number of waterfowl I shot and retrieved on private "pay land" during the 1968–69 season was about _____ waterfowl. (If zero, please enter "0.")

The number of days I hunted on private "pay land" during the 1968–69 season was about _____ days.

My *total* costs for hunting on private "pay land" during the 1968–69 season were about $_____.

# 7

# A Quantitative Approach to the Classification of Inland Waters

ANDREW L. SHELDON *

The inland waters of the United States range from the Laurentian Great Lakes to ponds in which small boys pursue frogs and salamanders. Mountain trout streams and the Mississippi are two extremes on the spectrum of flowing waters. Man-made lakes are a recent feature of the landscape while Great Salt Lake is a dwindling remnant of a lake with nearly one million years of history (Bradley, 1963). Such comparisons could be extended to emphasize the number and variety of inland waters. Regardless of their nature and location, all lakes and streams are exposed to some degree of human influence and all represent resources of differing quality and magnitude. The nature of the resource is variable and complex. Transportation, sport and commercial fishing, power generation, industrial, municipal and agricultural water supply, scenic and recreational qualities, or unique biological and geological features, or combinations of these are attributes of many lakes and streams. Decisions concerning items in this resource complex may be made following intensive planning or, more frequently, result from cumulative small decisions or inadvertent side effects of unrelated operations.

Adequate information is a prerequisite for decision making. The pressure of conflicting demands on a single water body sometimes generates enough information to permit a rational allocation of uses within a lake basin or watershed, but comparative information for between-lake decisions is fragmentary and not readily available. There is some virtue in

* Department of Zoology, University of Montana; formerly biologist with Natural Environments Program, Resources for the Future, Inc.

205

meeting problems one at a time, but decisions made in isolation are likely to reduce all aquatic systems to some common denominator. This common level need not be the lowest, but the results are likely to be far from optimal no matter how we define the optimum. Decisions made in isolation are especially inefficient when many small actions lead to an unanticipated and undesired result. Such "tyranny of small decisions" (Kahn, 1966) determines the fate of many of our smaller lakes and streams.

This multitude of smaller water bodies is the primary concern of my report. These lakes and streams are relegated to minor rank in most resource planning yet, by virtue of their wide dispersion and great variety, form a resource whose aggregate value is considerable. In addition, certain uses are possible and reasonable for these minor aquatic environments but are out of the question for larger systems. It is not likely that the lower course of any major river will ever be designated a primitive area or natural environment to serve as an ecological standard, yet allocation of certain smaller streams for these purposes is legitimate and logical.

Decision making requires information that is not only adequate and accurate but digestible. The number of lakes, streams, springs, and swamps is enormous, and any administrator forced to read descriptions of each and every one of them before making a decision would probably resort to a random numbers table. Some means of organizing and condensing this information is required.

In this report I have attempted to review and apply procedures useful in handling and synthesizing information about aquatic environments. Much of the methodology and philosophy is borrowed from other fields, and it is likely that some of the results can be extended to areas other than the one under consideration.

Emphasis is on procedures, since the shortage of comparable data precludes anything more than a first generation effort. I view this study as autocatalytic, because improved methods of handling data should lead to increased use of and demand for information. Availability of test data will then permit refinement of classification techniques and their interpretation, leading eventually to systems of classification of aquatic environments to meet various resource management objectives.

## METHODS

Classification is a defense mechanism triggered by a surfeit of information. Telephone directories, taxonomic keys, and lake typologies are some of the symptoms. In other cases classification is a substitute for knowledge, since naming something implies that we know something about it. This aspect of classification is more akin to witchcraft than science.

Many attempts have been made to classify or order information about aquatic environments. Hutchinson (1957, 1967, and in the projected third volume of the Treatise) has reviewed most of them and Jarnefelt (1958), Round (1958), Rodhe (1958), Margalef (1958), Findenegg (1964), Larkin and Northcote (1958), Elster (1958), and Pennak (1958) have discussed particular aspects. The typology of running waters has been considered by Kuehne (1962), and Illies and Botosaneanu (1963). Regional and descriptive limnology of North American waters forms the core of Frey (1963). In related fields, Whittaker (1962) has reviewed the multitude of schemes applied to plant communities and assemblages and Clements and Shelford (1939) have typified a variety of plant and animal communities.

The most striking feature of limnological classifications is not the difficulty of producing some sort of arrangement, but the multiplicity of arrangements that have been proposed. The wide variety of criteria and the importance accorded them have led to a bewildering array of types, series, and arrangements. Each proposal will provoke strong disagreement both within the ranks of those who believe some sort of ordering possible and necessary and from those who see any kind of classification as an attempt to reduce the natural world to artificial and abstract categories.

There is little likelihood that any formula for classifying lakes and streams will gain wide acceptance among limnologists, much less those concerned with particular uses and aspects of water bodies. Arrangement, terminology, and the requisite information are all subject to disagreement. Any attempt to impose such a formula will probably be unsuccessful unless produced and supported by some large and prestigious scientific body or a government agency whose practices would, by sheer mass, entrain those of other users.

I do not believe that the time is right for a universal classification of water bodies. There will always be a need for special-use arrangements, and the criteria used to define one classification may have no bearing on another problem. Combinations may be useful in some cases, and a whole array of classifications may be focused on decisions concerning a single body of water. For example, biologists, water supply engineers, and water skiers might construct classifications indicating that one lake was of exceptional value to each. Conflicts over use would not be resolved by classification. Instead, the classifications would provide information of aid to the decision process.

Rather than attempt to discover a universal formula, a sort of limnological philosopher's stone, I have concentrated on methods useful for various purposes. Most of the examples have been drawn from physical and biological limnology. The techniques are the methods of numerical taxonomy, which have found application in a number of fields including ecology, economics, and medical diagnosis. I have emphasized numerical methods for several reasons. I believe that the methodology is refined and powerful enough to serve a useful purpose in limnology and related areas. While numerical methods are examples of the "rational idiot" approach to science, their reliance on a known and understandable logic produces usable and informative results and highlights the strengths and weaknesses of the more subjective methods. Inventories of large numbers of lakes and streams will produce masses of complex data requiring mechanical processing. These are valid reasons for approaching limnological classification as a problem in multivariate analysis.

*Criteria for and Uses of Classifications*

The adequacy of a classification can be evaluated by a number of criteria. The first, and in the minds of some the most important, criterion is theoretical justification. Biological taxonomy is judged by the way in which it reflects evolutionary history and genetic relationships. While theoretical and abstract considerations have played a part in many classifications, most systems lack the coherence of phylogenetic patterns.

However, most ecologists have taken a more pragmatic approach to classification. Many systems have been developed for use in such applied fields as forest management, trout stocking, or waste disposal. The major criterion has been that of usefulness rather than theoretical soundness. The inevitable, but not necessarily undesirable, result is an almost infinite number of classifications for the same array of streams or lakes. Regardless of the nature of the inputs and importance accorded to each, all such classifications must walk the fine line between simplicity and reality. The desire to pigeonhole is natural, yet natural variability is often great enough so that classifications produced by splitters and lumpers will be very different. If the objectives of the classifiers are different and the information is weighted in different ways, the variety of classifications increases still further. One measure of the "goodness" of a classification is its concordance with other independently derived arrangements. Thus Webb et al. (1967) compared a floristic classification of Australian rainforest vegetation with one based on soils and climate of the same sites. An alternative criterion is the degree to which the classification can be used to predict variables not used in its construction.

Intended use determines both the form of the classification and the information used in its construction. In some cases, including telephone directories, consolidation of information for easy retrieval is the main objective. In other cases the classification is expected to produce groups with enough characteristics in common so that a name or number will convey information to a person who is not familiar with every individual or item in the group. Classifications can also be used to simplify large bodies of data to the point where the natural range of variation is readily perceived and rare or unusual items detected.

Management or use may be influenced by classification. An unusual site may be accorded special treatment or management simply because it is rare. If some typological scheme is used to assign management procedures, it can lead to a simplification of management or, if the diagnosis or typing is incorrect, to the extension of blanket rules to situations in which they do not apply. If experimental or management procedures are being evaluated, it may be desirable to replicate the experiment within types in order to gain precision or to spread the observations over several types in order to broaden the range of interpretation and applicability.

*Peculiarities of Aquatic Systems*

Although soil types, moisture regime, etc., have been put to good use by plant ecologists, much of the classification of terrestrial areas has been based on the structure or composition of the plant assemblages found in those areas. Although both macrophytes and algae have been the basis of lake typologies, the results have not been entirely satisfactory for several reasons. The most obvious is the importance, visibility, and relative permanence of vascular plants on land and their relative unimportance in lakes and streams. Contrast a forest of oak trees with a bloom of blue-green algae which is a transitory phenomenon whose specific composition can be identified only by a specialist. Although land plant communities do vary seasonally in structure and composition, such variation is much less pronounced than the rapid fluctuations in the composition and density of limnetic algae and zooplankton.

In the aquatic environment, factors such as stream gradient, lake basin morphometry, and water chemistry have the upper hand and the living components of the system are less massive and visible than on land. This is not to say that the biological features are unimportant or that biological processes do not influence the course of future events. The classical pattern of succession from lake to marsh to dry land is one example of changes brought about, at least in part, by living things. Brooks and Dodson (1965) have described a case where the introduction of a planktivorous fish led to drastic changes in zooplankton populations.

A further difficulty lies in the incomplete taxonomic knowledge of

many aquatic groups. The taxonomic history of North American *Daphnia*
as reviewed by Brooks (1957) provides a good, although extreme, example. This important group of zooplankters has been divided, lumped, and
redivided so that during this century as many as fifty and as few as four
distinct entities have been recognized. The currently recognized number
of species is thirteen. This chaotic history has resulted both from changes
in biological and taxonomic viewpoints and from the extraordinary
variability of many freshwater organisms. The plasticity under different
environmental conditions is well exemplified by cyclomorphosis in
*Daphnia*, and Drouet's (1968) recent work on the blue-green algae indicates that the 3,500 named species in this group are but environmentally
induced variants (often highly distinctive) of twenty-six widespread
species. The opposite side of the coin is indicated by Hutchinson's re-
mark (in Frey, 1963) that "It is hard to avoid wondering whether many
other species of small freshwater animals actually are composite entities,
separated beyond the dreams of the wildest schizotaxonomist." He cites
Price's (1958) work on the copepod *Cyclops* as one example. To the non-
biologist, taxonomy often appears as something of a biological parlor
game. However, the establishment of names and reliable identification
procedures is essential if biological classification of water bodies is to be
really feasible. Much of the disagreement about the importance of indicator species and what they indicate may be resolved by schizotax-
onomy.

Forbes (1925) described a lake as a microcosm, but water bodies are
far from being closed systems. A stream obviously has continuity, and
direction and events in one section are influenced by upstream sections.
In the same way, lakes and their connecting streams (Cushing, 1963)
interact to form a complex system. This is demonstrated especially well
by a series of reservoirs such as those on the Little Tennessee River
(Gerking, 1963). Although lakes and stream sections cannot be considered as independent of their drainage areas, inventory and classifications schemes will probably be applied to such small units. In contrast,
systems models probably will give greater weight to inputs from an
entire watershed.

*The Process of Classification*

The essential steps in any classification are description, comparison,
and synthesis. These steps, their importance to the problem of lake
classification, and their relationship to numerical classificatory techniques will be discussed in the following sections.

*Description.* Description is the characterization of one or more attributes of a lake or other object by words or numbers. The common

expedient of verbal description is imprecise and also confounds the three steps of classification. The description of a lake as "large" and "blue" illustrates the problem. The color variable implies the existence of a quantitative color scale and the naming (classification) of some range on that scale as blue rather than green. The color description has the virtue of independence from the description of other lakes since the existence of a color spectrum could be deduced from physical principles. The size variable condenses all three steps into one, since the term "large" implies a rough estimate of area, comparison with other lakes, and synthesis of a group of lakes of some size into the category "large." While such descriptions are common, definition, synthesis, and interpretation are determined by the collector and recipient of the data.

Numerical methods of classification require quantitative descriptions rather than words. The simplest description is of the binary sort in which arbitrary categories are recorded in a series of yes or no statements. Since the boundaries may be subjective, binary statements may be little more than camouflage for fuzzy verbal descriptions. If distinctive boundaries exist, as between most biological species, binary descriptions gain precision.

Ordinal or ranked descriptions assign an ordered series of numbers to categories or to the individuals described. Ordinal scales have obvious advantages both in classifying individuals as part of some larger universe and in comparing individuals within a set of lakes.

Interval measurement is possible for many of the variables measured in lake surveys. While many characteristics can be measured with high precision, some attributes may vary greatly in time. Such data may be more honestly given on an ordinal scale unless time series of observations are available.

The change from interval to ordinal scaling is an example of one common transformation. Other transformations, such as the logarithmic, may be used, and some common limnological measurements, such as transparency and light extinction coefficient, are simply transformed measurements of the same phenomenon.

Since numerical methods of classification operate on the variances of attribute distributions, transformations that alter the variance will obviously have some effect on the classification that is the ultimate objective.

A further set of transformations may be necessary if the individuals or lakes are specified by many attributes with different units of measurement. Normally these attributes must be reduced to some standard form with mean zero and unit variance or range. The choice of standardization procedures will alter the resulting classifications.

The theory of measurement and of transformations is important, but arithmetic will not compensate for data inputs that have no bearing on objectives. Examples in later sections use variables important to the person who collected the data or considered to be important by most limnologists. In some cases, importance reflects the ease with which the variable could be measured.

Most of the material in this report is drawn from the literature of physical and biological limnology. Such data, although not always comparable, are available for many inland waters. Information on the social aspects of lakes and streams is in short supply, and the problem of comparability is especially severe.

Water bodies can be, and have been, classified in many ways. It would be difficult or impossible to produce a single arrangement that would reconcile all the existing or proposed classifications. It would seem preferable to develop a set of arrangements that could be used independently of one another.

The common denominator of aquatic environments is water, regardless of the nature of its container, and one logical classification would be of water types based on such attributes as chemistry, temperature, transparency, etc. A classification of lakes and streams would be based on the attributes of the water as well as stream and lake morphometry, climatic variables, etc. At a still higher level, it might be possible to classify whole watersheds.

The attributes used in classification may be social, biological, or environmental. Environmental variables are readily measured, and most limnological surveys have emphasized environmental characteristics. Lakes can be classified by morphometric criteria, chemistry, or thermal characteristics, or by combinations of these attributes.

Many limnologists believe that biological characteristics are the best measures of the environment. This may be true, yet biological sampling for composition or quantity encounters taxonomic problems and seasonal variability at least as great as the variation in environmental characteristics. If a biological classification is desired, there seem to be three possible types. The first would be based on a limited number of indicator species in one or more taxonomic groups. The second, probably based on presence/absence data, would be similar to the floristic classifications used by plant ecologists. The third would incorporate bulk or macroscopic properties such as annual primary productivity, standing crops of particular groups of organisms, species diversities, again by major groups, pigment ratios (Margalef, 1968), etc. A classification independent of specific composition could be used to compare lakes from widely separated regions. The ideal classification, if such a thing is possible, should include both biological data and the environmental background. Any of these biological classifications could be applied to entire lakes or components such as the plankton, benthos, or littoral biota.

*Comparison: Similarity and Difference.* A statement that two individuals are members of the same class implies that they resemble one another more than they resemble members of another class or, conversely, that the difference between classes is greater than the difference between members of a class. Although the verbal statements are two sides of the same coin, mathematical measures of similarity and difference lead to somewhat different results. A variety of resemblance measures have been reviewed by Sokal and Sneath (1963). Given a set of $m$ individuals (lakes), each described by $n$ attributes where the attributes may be binary, ranked, or continuous variates, we can present the information in an $m \times n$ matrix, as in Figure 7.1.

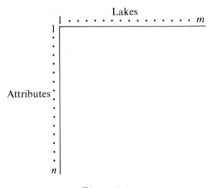

*Figure 7.1.*

If the attributes are binary, the between-lake comparisons may be summarized in the conventional $2 \times 2$ table.

|   | + | − |
|---|---|---|
| + | a | b |
| − | c | d |

One measure of similarity is the correlation coefficient—product-moment, rank, or the $\phi$ coefficient for nominal data. (Note that this is a between-lake rather than a between-attribute correlation.) Related measures include the similarity coefficient of Sokal and Sneath (1963). The major difference between the $\phi$ coefficient and the measure of Sokal and Sneath (1963) is that the former counts negative matches as evidence of similarity while Sokal and Sneath believe that characters lacking in both individuals (lakes) should not be used in classification. Other contingency measures have properties similar to those of the $\phi$ coefficient. In taxonomic terms, the correlation measures are shape measures.

The most widely used difference measure is Euclidean distance

$$\Delta_{ij}^2 = \sum^n (X_{ij} - X_{ik})^2,$$

which is simply an extension of the Pythagorean theorem to points in a multidimensional space. For binary variates in a $2 \times 2$ table, the formula reduces to $b + c$. Euclidean distance is a size measure.

Similarity and difference are relative measures and have value only as comparative statistics. Computation of resemblances yields an $m \times n$ matrix of resemblances between individuals (Figure 7.2).

*Synthesis.* The philosophy of classification (Gilmour and Walters, 1964) is largely independent of its application, and the following discussion—although the examples are limnological—could apply to biological systematics or library science. The simplest arrangement is one based on a single attribute of the items to be ranked or classified. Rodhe's (1958) suggestion that lakes be classified by their primary productivity ($gC/m^2/yr$) is of this type, as are some of the salinity classifications which have been proposed. The first result is simply an ordered sequence. To classify items in this sequence, we are forced to devise criteria for separating class $A$ from $B$, $B$ from $C$, and so on. This is the central problem of all taxonomy, and various procedures have been developed to accomplish this division. One method is to decide that $n$ classes are needed for what-

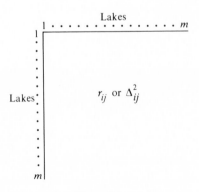

*Figure 7.2.*

ever purpose we have in mind, and divide the salinity or productivity scale into $n$ equal intervals, which will contain varying numbers of lakes. Another method would be to divide the scale at some points which, from outside evidence or by intuition, mark a significant transition in the general nature of the classified items. Thus Rawson and Moore (1944) selected 300 parts per million (ppm) total dissolved solids as the boundary between fresh and saline waters, while Whittaker and Fairbanks (1958) chose 1,000 ppm as the critical concentration.

Another procedure utilizes the frequency distribution of the items along the attribute scale to effect divisions that are in some way efficient. Thus a bimodal distribution would be divided at some point between the modes. In statistical terms, such a division rule would be designed to maximize the between-group variance and minimize the within-group variance. Since division rules of this type are the basis of the more complex techniques, their advantages and failings are critically important in the interpretation of results. The first characteristic of such rules is their dependence on the numbers of items in each mode (Figure 7.3). In this example, a single division would fall at position 1, although outlying members $c$, $d$, $e$ are more distant from mode $b$ than $a$ is from $b$. Divisions 2 and 3 would follow and produce a four-class grouping that, intuitively at least, is quite satisfactory. However, lakes $c$, $d$, and $e$ would still be regarded as somewhat aberrant outliers of the main groups $a$ and $b$. On the other hand, item $c$, which is closer to $d$ than the outliers of group $a$ are to each other, will be raised to class level merely because it is isolated. Figures 7.4 and 7.5 show alternative distributions with the same range of values. If the division rules are weighted by frequency, the classes that emerge are quite different from those in Figure 7.3. In the one-dimensional case, it is easy to see that the members of the minor classes are really quite distinct. However, in the more complex multidimensional situation, frequency-weighted rules will discriminate against the single outlying individual no matter how unique it may be.

Weighted division rules have another drawback. In the examples, I have assumed that the items represent a closed universe and that no sampling errors or bias are involved. In some experimental or management situations, this presents no problem since the universe is closed and no inferences about the items not included will be required. However, if we wish to classify a large group of items from the characteristics of a sample, sample variability and bias become important. Few limnological surveys are complete censuses of all the lakes in a given region. The situation is still more uneven when larger areas are considered.

Classification by a single attribute has the virtue of simplicity, but lakes and other entities are normally much too complex to describe by

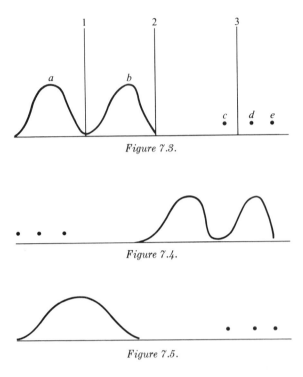

Figure 7.3.

Figure 7.4.

Figure 7.5.

one number or statement. Multivariate classification presents all the problems of the simple case and additional ones as well. Consider a group of lakes characterized by three variables, $A$, $B$, and $C$, each of which exists in two states, $A$ and $\bar{A}$, $B$ and $\bar{B}$, etc. If the attributes are independent, eight possible classes exist:

$$A \quad A \quad A \quad A \quad \bar{A} \quad \bar{A} \quad \bar{A} \quad \bar{A}$$
$$B \quad B \quad \bar{B} \quad \bar{B} \quad B \quad B \quad \bar{B} \quad \bar{B}$$
$$C \quad \bar{C} \quad C \quad \bar{C} \quad C \quad \bar{C} \quad C \quad \bar{C}$$

This is a simple classification and the choice of a division rule is no more difficult than in the case of a single attribute. However, if we wish to create a hierarchic classification in which the ultimate divisions are subsets of some larger group, six different hierarchies are possible. We must now choose a sequence as well as a division rule. Looking at the hierarchy as a series of divisions, one might decide that one factor was more important, and make the primary division on that factor and succeeding divisions in the order of importance. Alternatively, the factors may be ordered by the magnitude of their between-group variances. Another alternative is a division on the factor most highly correlated with the remaining ones (Williams and Lambert, 1959).

## Hierarchic Classification

A resemblance matrix of any size is an intractable object; some method of summarizing or ordering the matrix is needed. Many ecologists have relied on visual scanning to detect and form groups of similar items, and computer programs have been developed to do the same thing (Pfister, 1967).

An alternative to the clustered matrix is the hierarchy. The construction of such a classification involves a series of decisions of the type: "$A$ is most similar to $C$, $B$ most like $D$, and the average characteristics of the groups $AC$ and $BD$ are more like one another than either is to $E$." The result of this set of decisions is the hierarchy shown in Figure 7.6.

A variety of grouping strategies have been proposed and a general formulation derived by Lance and Williams (1967). The simplest grouping rule is that of nearest-neighbor sorting, where individuals are added to groups on the basis of their resemblance to the most similar individual in that group. Other rules, such as group average or centroid, compare the individual to be added with the average or median characteristics of each of the formed groups and all remaining individuals. Dendrograms produced this way form more coherent groups while nearest-neighbor sorting often yields chains in which each individual is added to the first group (pair) formed. The general model of Lance and Williams provides a weighting scheme to yield dendrograms of any desired degree of coherence. The obvious problem is that strong grouping power increases the risk of misclassification of intermediate individuals. In fact, all hierarchic methods share this problem since each individual must be assigned some

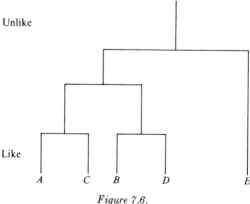

*Figure 7.6.*

specific position in the tree. The hierarchic schemes have another weakness when built in an additive fashion. Each individual is paired with another individual or group on the basis of limited information, and the decision is irrevocable. Certain sorting rules such as centroid will produce reversals in which fusion of two groups may occur at a level lower than the levels of the last individuals added to those groups. Dendrograms, while constructed from multivariate statistics, are not multidimensional figures. At the very most they resemble decorative mobiles that are free to pivot at a number of points. Hierarchies do not portray inter-group relationships at all well.

In spite of these drawbacks, hierarchic methods have some prominent advantages. Storage requirements and computer running time are relatively small. Hierarchic schemes are useful for rapid exploratory sorting and may be the only practical approach to large bodies of data. Brown (1969) has made effective use of one of these methods for sorting phytoplankton samples.

*Ordination*

Hierarchic methods are a rather heavy-handed approach to the reduction of multidimensional systems to some simpler form. A more elegant method is that of Gower (1966). Gower ordination has much in common with principal components and other standard multivariate methods (Anderson, 1958; Seal, 1964). Relationships are projected on a series of orthogonal axes and the original interindividual distances are preserved. The basic similarity matrix may be of the correlation or distance type.

Emphasis in this report is on ordination of individuals (lakes) rather than attributes. Attribute ordination by principal components has been used as a preliminary step, but it should be noted that principal components reduction retains the ordering of attributes, which is largely destroyed by ordination of individuals. Thus principal components reduction of attributes is useful in its own right. If the number of dimensions is low, principal components ordination is a usable substitute for Gower ordination of individuals.

Ordination retains the original information much better than do the hierarchic methods. However, storage requirements and running time are greatly increased. In some cases the added information may not warrant the effort. Webb et al. (1967) have compared and evaluated several classification and ordination techniques.

*Uniqueness*

Rarity is often a synonym of value, and the unusual lake or stream may be given special attention by managers. Leopold and Marchand

(1968) developed a uniqueness measure that they applied to data from a group of California streams. The Leopold-Marchand measure is defined as the reciprocal of the number of individuals possessing a character or falling in a particular category of a character scale. Thus their uniqueness ratio is applicable to nominal data only and discards the information contained in ordinal or interval scales.

The following definition of uniqueness can be applied to nominal or ordered data and utilizes Euclidean distance as its metric:

$$U_i = 2n\sqrt{\prod_{j=1}^{n} \triangle_{ij}^2},$$

where $\triangle_{ij}^2$ is the squared distance between $i$ and $j$ and $n$ is the number of inter-individual distances in the system which, of course, will be one less than the number of individuals.

```
                      · 2
                                     · 5
       · 1            · 3
                                  · 6
                      · 4
```

In the two-dimensional example item 1 ranks highest on the uniqueness scale followed by the pair 5, 6, the pair 2, 4, and the least unique item 3. This geometric definition of uniqueness is intuitively satisfactory and the distance measures can be prefaced by principal components reduction to remove redundancy.

*The Universe Problem*

Most of the limnological classifications proposed are regional in scope and most of the disagreement about lake typology has arisen from this fact. Within any geological and climatic region certain attributes may dominate, e.g., high salinity, high flushing rates, phosphorus deficiency, etc., while in other areas an entirely different set of key factors will be used in the construction of a regional typology. Such classifications are seldom comparable between regions except in a very general way. Regional distinctions increase the power of multivariate classifications since correlations between attributes diminish with increased heterogeneity. This gain in power is one advantage to extending the universe to be classified. The larger universe is also more likely to contain closely similar lakes, thus reducing the number of forced and unnatural combinations.

If computationally practical, larger and more varied universes will yield more realistic and powerful classifications. Important as this technical point may be, the real gain from increasing the universe lies in the wider base for making decisions. An unusual or valuable lake may be unique at the local level but replicated many times on the national scene, while another may be unique at the national level as well. Peterken (1968) has discussed this problem with reference to the selection of terrestrial areas for preservation. If rarity is equated with value, then the second is worth more than the first. On the other hand, management decisions, especially those related to preservation, are often made at the local or regional level. In the future it will be small comfort for the inhabitant of New York or Wisconsin to know that wilderness lakes have been preserved in Florida and California. The distribution of people is as important as the distribution of resources.

*Special Procedures*

In the following examples I have used several unconventional techniques. These modifications will not be acceptable to all workers. I have used them because they appear to have some utility or because they are less objectionable than the alternatives.

Similarity measures have proliferated to the point where it is almost criminal to propose another, but I have found the following measure quite useful:

$$D = 2\triangle_{ij}^2 - r_{ij}\,\triangle_{ij}^2.$$

This measure was developed for use in hierarchic sorting methods. The initial fusions in a hierarchy are based on minimal information, and any device that will improve the first allocations seems worthwhile. The $D$ measure includes both size and shape information and I developed it with the idea that both magnitude and arrangement of environmental factors are determinants of biological attributes. In a few cases I have entered the $D$ measure in the Gower method, although the geometric interpretation of this procedure is not readily apparent.

Principal components reduction of environmental data (attributes) will show that much of the information is redundant. The first one or two vectors include characters that are correlated because they are associated in members of a group and other characters that were measured several times under different names. Because it is undesirable to give weight to redundancy, I have adopted the following procedure. Apply principal components reduction to the standardized attributes. Consider only those vectors whose cumulative contribution to the total variance exceeds some level, say 95 percent, or which include at least some minimal proportion of the variance of all single characters. Standardize these reduced attributes and use them as the basis for the similarity matrix. The original data and the components may be standardized to zero mean and unit variance or range. I prefer the range alternative.

This entire procedure is wasteful of information and gives undesirable weight to minor components and random elements. However, the procedure is conservative—i.e., less likely to produce a strong classification —and seems preferable to methods that over-value redundancy. There is no need to manipulate biological presence-absence data in this way.

## A Critique of Numerical Methods

Numerical methods of classification have been applied to a variety of subjects and materials—taxonomic, ecological, and economic (Williams, 1967). Most of the problems are independent of the application, although the greatest controversy has focused on the use of numerical methods in biological systematics. As a perusal of any recent issue of *Systematic Zoology* will show, taxonomists are divided in their views. Some claim that numerical methods do not reveal phylogeny while others believe the opposite. These polemics have little relevance to the present problem since the objective of ecological and most other classifications is simply to group like with like. The problem of successional states, such as the stages in eutrophication, may require special handling (Williams et al., 1969). With this exception, similarity through descent is not at issue and a purely phenetic classification is appropriate.

Numerical classifications are not unique. Alternatives exist at every stage, from the selection and treatment of attributes through the choice of similarity measure and grouping or ordination method. Choice of a method or methods from this array of possibilities is probably the most difficult step in the whole process. Empirical (Webb et al., 1967) and analytic (Gower, 1967) comparisons of various techniques have been made, but choice of method is still as much a matter of informed judgment as a science. The optimal procedure will vary from problem to problem, although all methods can be expected to produce results with some degree of resemblance. Cole (1969) and Pielou (1969) have reviewed the methods discussed here and a number of others.

The real problem in multivariate classification is not the method but the original data and their preliminary treatment. All multivariate grouping techniques are designed to minimize within-group variances or distances and maximize those between groups. This perfectly rational objective gives rise to a number of problems.

The data must be given in some standardized units such as standard deviations or ranges. Transformations such as the logarithmic will alter the variances and the resulting classification. In some cases we may have a good reason to prefer one transformation over another, but often we do not. Sampling variances and errors can be expected to vary between attributes.

The most serious problem is character redundancy. Suites of redundant characters will dominate a classification since, simply by repetition, they will make a large contribution to the total variance. The difficulty lies in distinguishing between attributes measured several times under different names, e.g., lake "size" as area, mean depth, maximum depth, and those correlated by some causal mechanism, e.g., phosphorus, chlorophyll. Principal components reduction and canonical analysis (Brezonik et al., 1969) identify such attribute clusters but do not tell one what to do with them. Factor analysis (rotation) increases the problem. Redundancy completely invalidates the use of the eigenvalues as measures of importance.

Presence-absence data for biological species are free of the redundancy problem to a large extent. There exists a logical dividing line between the attributes, and the common possession of a group of species is a valid criterion of similarity. In spite of this logical, if not statistical, independence of presence-absence data, difficulties may arise. If presence-absence data for a large group of organisms (diatoms) are combined with data for a smaller group (copepods), the resulting classification will be based on diatoms and tell little about copepods unless the two groups are highly concordant.

Methods that operate on within- and between-group variances will confound relative abundance with degree of difference. In ordination procedures a rare but unusual individual may not appear in the first few vectors. Thus a single eutrophic or transitional lake in a collection of oligotrophic lakes might not be detected. Hierarchic methods have the advantage of isolating rare but distinctive items in a residual group where they are readily detected.

The frequency-dependence of the numerical methods limits the inferences to be drawn about items not included in the sample. Proper sampling design will be vital if large-scale use is to be made of numerical methods. In the examples following below I have taken the view that the sample represents a closed universe and all positions in a classification or ordination are relative.

The user of any type of multivariate procedure runs the risk of being carried away by his enthusiasm for the power of the techniques and their ease of execution. There is a tendency to add variables beyond reason. This proliferation of attributes can lead to two undesirable results. If the number of independent dimensions is large, individuals may be over-defined and no grouping will be possible. The extra variables are simply noise in the system. Even without over-definition, addition of extra or irrelevant variables will weaken the classification. The diatom-copepod example given above is a case of this kind.

Added variables may be new or they may be derived from previous entries in the attribute list. Ratios and products are two types of derived variables that are not simple linear combinations of the original data. The use of derived variables is legitimate, but some a priori hypothesis or model is required if the number of derived variables is to be kept within reasonable bounds.

Numerical methods of classification have many shortcomings, but these deficiencies do not invalidate their use. More subjective and traditional methods operate within the same limitations. Numerical methods are certainly no worse than subjective methods and may be better in many cases. Numerical classifications can be evaluated and compared if the logic of their construction is understood. The limitations follow directly from the operating rules. Numerical methods have their place in limited analysis of simple systems, and for large and complex situations there is no other choice.

## Classifications, Predictions, and Models

Modern science emphasizes process rather than appearance, so classification would seem a step in the wrong direction. However, since an understanding of system dynamics is far more difficult to attain than an assessment of appearance, most inferences about dynamics will be based on appearance. The comparable problem in biological systematics has been discussed by Sokal and Crovello (1970). Classification is necessary if the results of detailed studies are to be extrapolated to other systems.

Classification and dynamics have another more fundamental linkage. The choice of attributes from an infinite array of descriptors is determined by our views on importance of the attributes. Limnological data, such as phosphate concentrations, morphometry, and species diversities, are collected because they are believed to influence or reflect the dynamics of lacustrine ecosystems. Thus a model, if only of the most general sort, is a prerequisite for meaningful classification.

The connection between models and classification is a reciprocal one since classification provides information for improved dynamic models. Experimental limnology is an underdeveloped science although Vallentyne (1969) has described the initiation of an extensive project of this type. [See also Johnson and Vallentyne (1971) and Hall, Cooper, and Werner (1970).] Classification or ordination can aid in experimental design and analysis. Allocation of treatments, replication, and tests of factor interactions are standard statistical problems that can be handled only when within- and between-group variability is defined. Green and Hobson (1970) have made interesting application of numerical methods in allocating sampling in marine areas.

In a nonexperimental approach to dynamics, multiple correlation and regression analysis (Brezonik et al., 1969) can be used to develop empiri-

cal models. Since nonlinear and nonadditive effects and interactions are
all too common in complex systems, there would seem to be some value
in analyses in which at least some of the variables are constant rather
than merely adjusted through partial regression techniques. Goldman
et al. (1968) have used a hierarchic sorting strategy to examine and simplify factor interactions within a single lake. Classification and ordination
provide the tools for this purpose.

Improved models and understanding of the relevant variables should
generate more realistic and accurate classifications, which in turn will
provide the background for improved experimental and analytical approaches to dynamics. Ultimately these models, and a knowledge of the
conditions under which they apply, will provide powerful tools for prediction and for the management of aquatic systems.

EXAMPLES

The examples below have been selected because they illustrate certain
features of various numerical techniques as they can be applied to

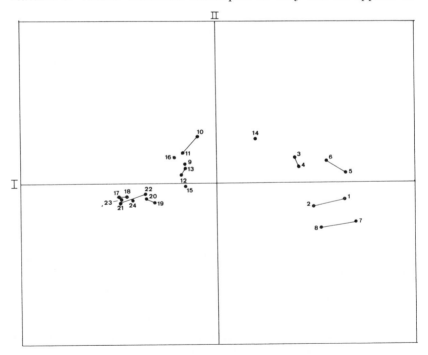

*Figure 7.7.* Vectors I and II of principal components ordination of physical and
chemical data for Swedish lakes. Observations on the same lake are connected.

limnological data. None of the examples is especially modern, but there is a shortage of recent work extensive enough for the purpose. Biological nomenclature and limnological techniques have changed but I have retained the names and units of the original worker.

*Swedish Lakes*

Thunmark (1945) measured a few chemical and physical variables on fifteen Swedish lakes, studied the algal flora, and identified the dominant plankters at the time of the survey. Several of the lakes were examined at other seasons and other years to give a total of twenty-four observations. The lakes were classified as very eutrophic (four lakes, numbers 1–8), weakly eutrophic (six lakes, 9–16), and oligotrophic (five lakes, 17–24). Hutchinson (1967, pp. 389–90) has summarized and discussed Thunmark's observations.

Thunmark's data for transparency, color, $KMnO_4$ demand, pH, and conductance (see Appendix Table 1) were used as inputs for multivariate analysis. Principal components reduction (Figures 7.7 and 7.8) shows that most of the information can be presented in a single dimension.

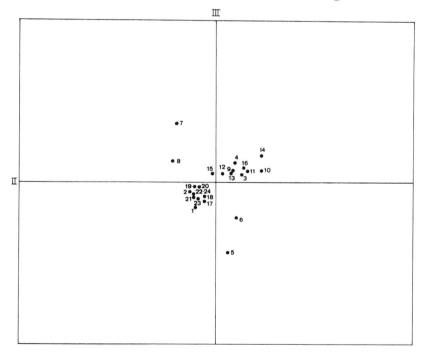

*Figure 7.8.* Vectors II and III of principal components ordination of physical and chemical data for Swedish lakes.

Vector I accounts for 82 percent and the first three for 96 percent of the total variance. Cumulative values for the five individual attributes ranged from 91 percent to 99 percent over the first three vectors. Vectors I–III were standardized by their eigenvalues and similarity matrices were computed from these reduced and standardized attributes.

Figure 7.9 is the hierarchy developed from the D measure explained earlier. The oligotrophic lakes appear as a single cohesive group. The weakly eutrophic lakes form another cluster. Lake 3–4 appears as an outlier of this group. The remaining eutrophic lakes are quite heterogeneous, as indicated by the principal components.

Thunmark's plankton data are tabulated for comparison with the arrangements generated from the physical and chemical data (Table 7.1). Thunmark emphasized the ratio # species Chlorococcales/Desmideae as a means of separating trophic categories. The ratios are consistent with the grouping and Lake 3–4 is clearly intermediate. The dominant plankters are less consistent with the grouping, but some trends are discernible.

Thunmark's data provide a simple test of the usefulness of numerical

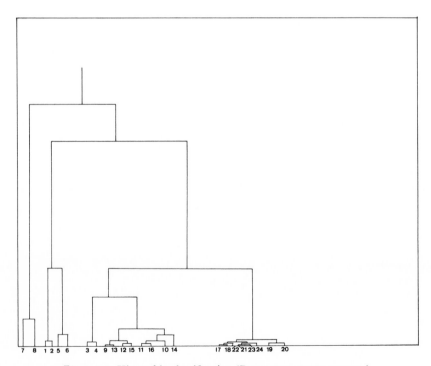

*Figure 7.9.* Hierarchic classification (D measure, group average) of Swedish lakes.

Table 7.1. Comparison of Plankton Distributions and Diversity with the
Environmental Classification of Figure 7.9 [From Thunmark (1945)]

| Lake | # Chloro-coccales | # Desmideae | Ratio | Dominant Phytoplankter | Dominant Zooplankter |
|------|------|------|------|------|------|
| 7 | 41 | 6 | 6.8 | Melosira ambigua | Daphnia cucullata |
| 8 | 36 | 3 | 12.0 | Melosira ambigua | Daphnia cucullata |
| 5 | 42 | 7 | 6.0 | Microcystis viridis | Chydorus sphaericus |
| 6 | 23 | 3 | 7.7 | Microcystis viridis | Filinia longiseta |
| 1 | 38 | 7 | 5.4 | Microcystis viridis | Daphnia cucullata |
| 2 | 28 | 2 | 14.0 | Scenedesmus naegeli | Daphnia cucullata |
| 3 | 39 | 15 | 2.6 | Microcystis aeruginosa | Daphnia cucullata |
| 4 | 26 | 5 | 5.2 | Microcystis aeruginosa | Cyclops leuckarti |
| 14 | 14 | 7 | 2.0 | Pediastrum clathratum | Chydorus sphaericus |
| 9 | 18 | 6 | 3.0 | Fragellaria crotonensis | Diaptomus gracilis |
| 13 | 27 | 12 | 2.2 | Microcystis flos-aquae | Cyclops leuckarti |
| 10 | 19 | 7 | 2.7 | Anabaena spiroides | Chydorus sphaericus |
| 11 | 28 | 17 | 1.6 | Melosira ambigua | Diaphanasoma brachyurum |
| 16 | 15 | 15 | 1.0 | Microcystis aeruginosa | Diaphanasoma brachyurum |
| 12 | 19 | 14 | 1.4 | Microcystis flos-aquae | Daphnia cristata |
| 15 | 25 | 12 | 2.1 | Melosira ambigua | Cyclops leuckarti |
| 22 | 9 | 27 | .3 | Tabellaria flocculosa | Diaptomus gracilis |
| 17 | 13 | 27 | .5 | Botryococcus brauni | Cyclops leuckarti |
| 18 | 12 | 29 | .4 | Botryococcus brauni | Cyclops leuckarti |
| 19 | 10 | 29 | .3 | Microcystis flos-aquae | Holopedium gibberum |
| 20 | 14 | 35 | .4 | Microcystis flos-aquae | Holopedium gibberum |
| 21 | 10 | 27 | .4 | Anabaena flos-aquae | Holopedium gibberum |
| 23 | 4 | 20 | .2 | Botryococcus brauni | Diaptomus gracilis |
| 24 | 6 | 27 | .2 | Cyclotella bodanica | Bosmina spp. |

techniques in limnology. Visual inspection of the data indicates three groups of lakes and these groups were recovered by the procedure used. The numerical methods also give some indication of within-group heterogeneity. The number of dimensions in this case is low and the numerical methods can be expected to give the same results as a more subjective approach. More complicated examples will be presented in later sections.

*North American Lakes*

Detailed limnological data are available for only a few regions in North America, and the methods and measurements are not always comparable. In an attempt to achieve a wide geographic coverage, I have reduced the data from a number of limnological surveys to their lowest common denominator. The data in Appendix Table 2 are drawn from Narver (1967) and Sparrow (1966) (British Columbia), Berg (1963) (New York), Reimers et al. (1955) (California), and the long series of New Hampshire lakes from Newell (1960, 1963). Figure 7.10 is the hierarchy formed with

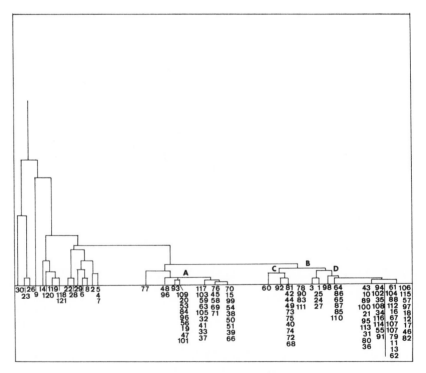

*Figure 7.10.* Hierarchic classification (Euclidean distance, group average) of selected North American lakes.

a group average sorting strategy and Euclidean distance as the difference measure. A number of lakes, including the slightly saline lakes of British Columbia and the alpine California lakes, are isolated at a high level. Group A consists of unstratified lakes with subgroups based on chemical and morphometric criteria. Group B contains thermally stratified lakes and distinguishes those with little or no profundal oxygen (D) from those in which oxygen is not depleted. Additional subgroups and isolated individuals can be distinguished as well. Regardless of the subject matter, Figure 7.10 shows the major feature of hierarchic classifications. A heterogeneous residual group containing about 15 percent of the lakes is isolated first. The remaining larger divisions are based on characters that define coherent and, in this case, meaningful groups.

Gower ordination applied to the same data and measure gives slightly different results (Figures 7.11 and 7.12). Vector I distinguishes thermally stratified from unstratified lakes, and Vector II primarily reflects differences in hypolimnetic oxygen. Vector III emphasizes the chemical aspects. Members of the residual group in the hierarchic scheme are not readily distinguished in the ordination, although all appear in one or more of the higher vectors. Ordination depicts the interrelationship of the lakes in a more detailed way than the hierarchy, although at some cost in interpretability. Balanced against the added information and complexity is a tenfold increase in computing time.

*Finnish Lakes*

Jarnefelt (1956) examined over 400 Finnish lakes and grouped them in various trophic categories. I have selected seventy of these for which physical, chemical (Appendix Table 3), and biological (phytoplankton, fishes) data are recorded. Jarnefelt's algal records are condensed and abbreviated to such an extent that recovery of the information is extremely difficult. His trophic classification is based largely on these data, and it is of some interest to see how much information can be obtained from the physical and chemical data. Figure 7.13 shows the first two vectors of the Gower ordination on the distance measure of the reduced and standardized attributes. No distinctive groups are indicated but the trophic series is partially recovered. Several explanations are available for the non-appearance of well-defined trophic categories: (a) Jarnefelt utilized biological information that may provide more sensitive criteria for delimiting trophic groups; (b) trophic state may lie on a continuum with no sharp demarcations; (c) some of the attributes, such as the morphometric data, may be irrelevant to the question of trophic state, and the variability shown by ordination may result from added noise in the system; (d) the use of reduced and standardized attributes may dis-

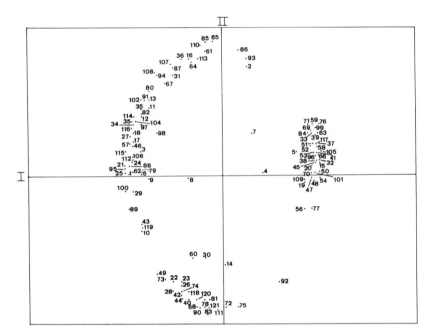

*Figure 7.11.* Gower ordination (Euclidean distance) of North American lakes.

card useful information and emphasize random differences between the lakes.

A hierarchic arrangement (not shown) of these data was no more successful in recovering the trophic groups, although many of the subgroups consisted of lakes in a single trophic category. Ordination, which portrays the reticulate nature of the similarities between the lakes, is more useful than classification of this rather homogeneous group of lakes.

*English Tarns*

Macan (1950, 1963) and Mackereth et al. (1957) have studied the biology and chemistry of a series of small ponds in the English Lake District. Macan's data (Appendix Table 4) provide an opportunity to evaluate the use of multivariate techniques in interpreting biological data.

Most of the variables Macan and his co-workers measured were chemical; consequently, Vector I of the principal components reduction (Figures 7.14 and 7.15) is dominated by chemical attributes, although altitude makes some contribution. Vector II isolates some of the minor ions and a component of area. Vector III is dominated by plant growth and to a lesser extent, by area. Vector IV emphasizes area, plant growth, and

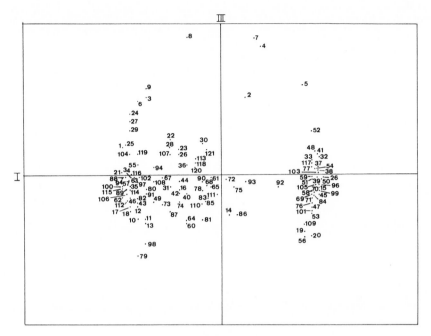

*Figure 7.12.* Gower ordination (Euclidean distance) of North American lakes.

altitude. Higher vectors pick up the effects of minor ions and the residuals associated with the other variables. The first seven vectors account for 97 percent of the total variance and 92 percent or more of the variances of individual attributes. Standardization of the components is obviously necessary since the large eigenvalue of component I reflects redundancy. Standardization gives greater weight to the lesser components (which presumably include most of the sampling error) than is desirable, but the inclusion of random noise seems preferable to overvaluing a set of redundant characters.

Figures 7.14 and 7.15 plot the first three attribute vectors. The occurrence of a few selected species is superimposed to show that their distribution can be related to the environmental background. Taken in pairs and examined in detail, the principal components provide no great insight into the composition of the entire fauna.

A hierarchic classification (Figure 7.16) was constructed using the D measure and group average sorting on the first five components standardized to unit variance. This classification is compared (Table 7.2) with species distributions and part of the original physical and chemical data. The classification has ordered the raw data fairly well, although some

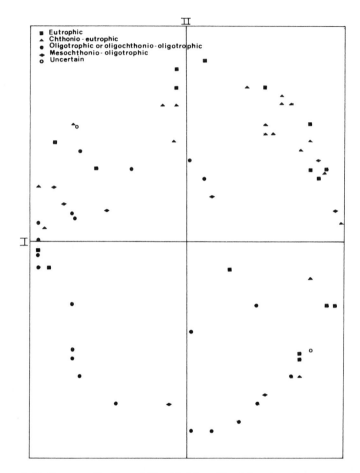

*Figure 7.13.* Gower ordination of Finnish lakes. Trophic categories superimposed on
the environmental ordination.

groups (e.g., 4, 25) differ substantially in one attribute. Others, such as
the pair 17, 30, are alike only in sharing extreme values of a single character. The tarns are a rather homogeneous lot and most have at least
one character in common with at least one other pond. The biological
data are grouped to some extent, although transitional cases occur. The
classification as drawn in Figure 7.16 is one of many possible ones since
all the fusions are free to pivot. The biological data have been used to
order the entries in Table 7.2.

The classification of Figure 7.16 has a tendency to chain, adding

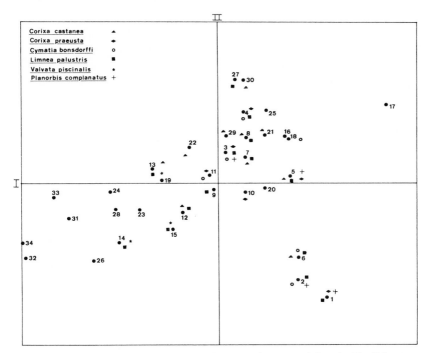

*Figure 7.14.* Principal components ordination of environmental data for English tarns. Distribution of selected species indicated.

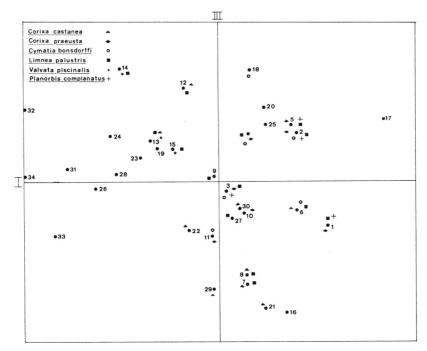

*Figure 7.15.* Principal components ordination of environmental data for English tarns. Distribution of selected species indicated.

Table 7.2. Comparison of Biological Data for English Tarns with the Environmental Classification of Figure 7.16
(Major Divisions of the Classification Are Indicated)

| | 5 | 6 | 1 | 2 | 4 | 25 | 18 | 27 | 17 | 30 | 8 | 22 | 7 | 11 | 21 | 16 |
|---|---|---|---|---|---|---|---|---|---|---|---|---|---|---|---|---|
| Corixa praeusta | + | | + | | + | | | | | | | | | | | |
| Cymatia bonsdorffi | | + | | + | | | + | | | | | | | + | | |
| Corixa linnei | + | | + | | + | | | | | | + | + | | + | + | |
| Corixa fossarum | | | | + | | | | | + | | + | | | | | + |
| Corixa distincta | + | | | | + | | | | + | | + | | | + | | |
| Corixa scotti | + | + | + | + | | + | + | | | + | + | + | | | | |
| Corixa castanea | + | + | | | | | + | + | | + | + | + | + | | + | |
| Limnea stagnalis | | | | + | | | | | | | | | | | | |
| Planorbis crista | | | | + | + | | | | | | | | | | | |
| Planorbis complanatus | + | | + | + | | | | | | | | | | | | |
| Limnea palustris | + | + | | | + | | | | | | + | | + | | | |
| Valvata piscinalis | | | | | | | | | | | | | | | | |
| Physa fontinalis | | | | | | | | | | | | | | | | |
| Planorbis contortus | | | | | | | | | | | | | | | | |
| Planorbis albus | + | | + | + | + | | + | | + | | + | + | + | + | + | + |
| Limnea pereger | + | + | + | + | + | + | + | + | + | + | | + | + | + | + | + |
| Area | 55 | 334 | 64 | 210 | 83 | 104 | 308 | 42 | 6 | 8 | 16 | 8 | 8 | 52 | 30 | 28 |
| Plant stage | 1 | 3 | 2 | 1 | 1 | 1 | 1 | 2 | 1 | 2 | 3 | 2 | 3 | 2 | 3 | 3 |
| Altitude | 2 | 1 | 1 | 1 | 1 | 1 | 1 | 1 | 1 | 2 | 2 | 2 | 1 | 1 | 1 | 1 |
| Calcium | 14.7 | 16.3 | 20.0 | 19.8 | 6.0 | 6.6 | 5.9 | 4.1 | 11.7 | 4.7 | 10.5 | 4.7 | 8.5 | 6.5 | 7.7 | 9.6 |

Table 7.2. (cont'd)

| | 3 | 23 | 29 | 10 | 9 | 20 | 14 | 15 | 12 | 13 | 19 | 24 | 28 | 31 | 33 | 32 | 34 | 26 |
|---|---|---|---|---|---|---|---|---|---|---|---|---|---|---|---|---|---|---|
| *Corixa praeusta* | + | | | + | | | | | | | | | | | | | | |
| *Cymatia bonsdorffi* | + | | | | | | | | | | | | | | | | | |
| *Corixa linnei* | | | | + | | | | | | | | | | | | | | |
| *Corixa fossarum* | | + | | | + | | | | + | + | | | | | | | | |
| *Corixa distincta* | | + | | + | + | | | | + | + | | + | | | | | | |
| *Corixa scotti* | + | + | + | + | | + | + | + | + | + | + | + | + | + | + | | | + |
| *Corixa castanea* | | | + | | | | | | + | + | | | + | | | | | |
| *Limnea stagnalis* | | | | | | | | | | | | | | | | | | |
| *Planorbis crista* | | | | | | | + | | | | | | | | | | | |
| *Planorbis complanatus* | + | | | | | | | | | | | | | | | | | |
| *Limnea palustris* | | | | | + | + | + | + | + | + | | | | | | | | |
| *Valvata piscinalis* | | | | | | | + | + | + | + | | | | | | | | |
| *Physa fontinalis* | | | | | | | + | + | | | | | | | | | | |
| *Planorbis contortus* | | | | | | | + | | + | + | | | | | | | | |
| *Planorbis albus* | + | + | | + | + | + | + | + | + | | + | + | | | | | | |
| *Limnea pereger* | + | + | + | | | + | + | + | + | + | + | + | + | | | | | + |
| Area | 186 | 352 | 150 | 48 | 48 | 213 | 430 | 128 | 440 | 116 | 83 | 160 | 42 | 62 | 52 | 372 | 150 | 25 |
| Plant stage | 2 | 2 | 3 | 2 | 1 | 1 | 2 | 1 | 1 | 1 | 1 | 1 | 2 | 3 | 2 | 1 | 1 | 1 |
| Altitude | 1 | 2 | 1 | 2 | 1 | 1 | 2 | 2 | 2 | 2 | 2 | 2 | 1 | 3 | 3 | 2 | 2 | 3 |
| Calcium | 6.2 | 5.2 | 6.4 | 9.8 | 8.8 | 9.7 | 5.3 | 7.4 | 4.9 | 5.0 | 5.3 | 3.9 | 4.1 | 2.8 | 2.8 | 1.3 | 1.5 | 5.1 |

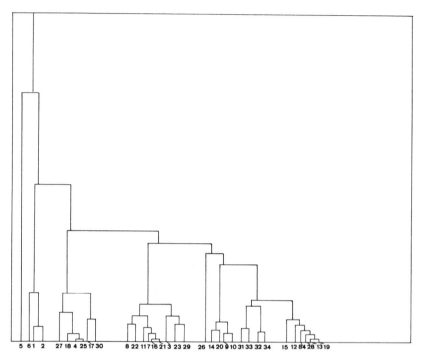

*Figure 7.16.* Hierarchic classification (D measure, group average) of English tarns.

weakly differentiated groups at each stage, rather than forming distinctive subgroups. This is characteristic of data sets with reticulate and complex relationships between individuals. Ordination is indicated. The Gower procedure was entered with the D measure in the similarity matrix. As mentioned earlier, I am uncertain about the geometric interpretation of this procedure. However, the D ordination, which differs from both the correlation and distance ordinations, seems to account for the distributional data somewhat better. The first three vectors of the ordination are shown in Figures 7.17 and 7.18 and the distributions of various species are superimposed.

The tendency for ordination to submerge the extreme individuals in the major groups of the first few vectors is a disadvantage, but it is obvious that particular biological attributes do tend to fall in definite regions of the ordination. Given the ordination on physical and chemical characters, but no biological information, we could still select ponds that would provide most of the biological variety or pick groups of similar ponds with some assurance of biological homogeneity.

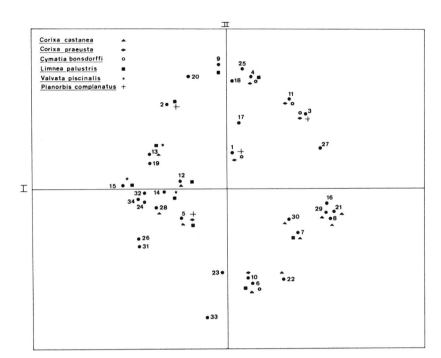

*Figure 7.17.* Gower ordination (D measure) of environmental data for English tarns.

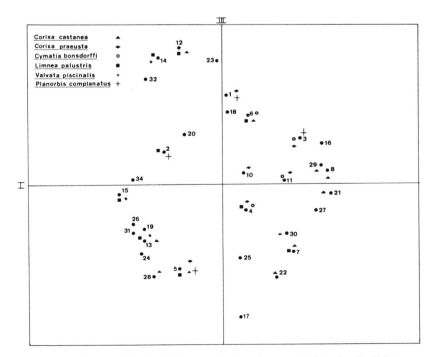

*Figure 7.18.* Gower ordination (D measure) of environmental data for English tarns.

Many biologists would argue that the organisms are the best measure of the environment. Gower ordination of the presence-absence data is shown in Figures 7.19 (distance) and 7.20 (correlation). The biological groups do conform to certain features of the environment and suggest the existence of factors other than the ones measured. The two measures produce different pictures of the relationships between the ponds. Correlation ordination emphasizes similarities while distance ordination emphasizes differences. The distance measure is, in part, a diversity measure (McIntosh, 1967) and is sensitive to differences in faunal richness. This dependence on diversity may make the distance measure unsuitable for some purposes and highly useful for others. Reduction in diversity is often correlated with environmental disturbance or rigor, and distance classification or ordination may be especially useful in eutrophication and pollution studies. In this example there is no reason to choose one over the other.

The vectors shown here are only part of the picture since the eigenvalues fall very slowly and seven vectors are needed to account for 95

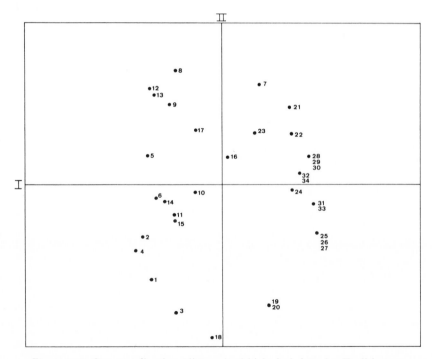

*Figure 7.19.* Gower ordination (distance) of biological data for English tarns.

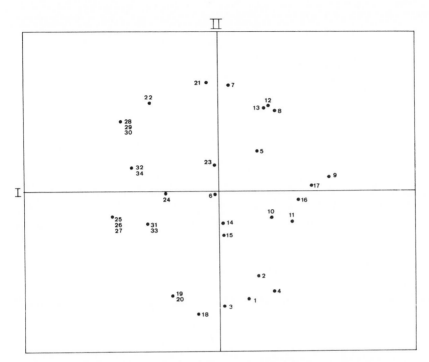

*Figure 7.20*. Gower ordination (φ coefficient) of biological data for English tarns.

percent of the total variance. In more descriptive terms, the individuals are overdefined and the unique elements make a large contribution to the total variance.

This analysis indicates some of the strengths, weaknesses, and possibilities of multivariate methods when applied to data from a limited lake district.

*Washington Lakes*

Biological studies on lakes are more likely to involve the planktonic fauna than littoral invertebrates. The distribution of zooplankton in a series of lakes in the state of Washington was studied by Whittaker and Fairbanks (1958), and I have subjected their data to several multivariate procedures. The physical and chemical data in Appendix Table 5 were standardized by range both in the original and reduced attributes and the D measure computed. The D measure was entered in the Gower procedure, yielding the vectors shown in Figure 7.21. The distribution of selected copepods is superimposed and those lakes with but a single

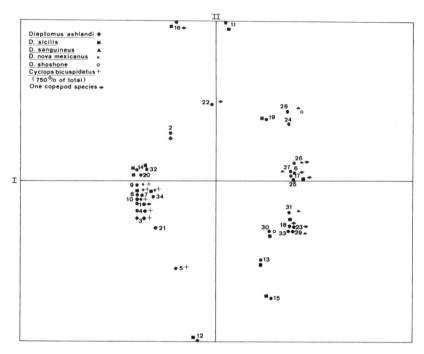

*Figure 7.21.* Gower ordination (D measure) of environmental data for Washington lakes. Distribution of selected species superimposed.

species, regardless of its identity, are indicated. Figure 7.22 is the correlation ordination of the relative abundance data for the zooplankton. Figure 7.23 represents a deliberate attempt to use every bit of information and the most powerful method to construct a classification of the lakes.

The ordination on physical and chemical variables produces an arrangement that groups lakes occupied by the same species and those lakes of low diversity. The lakes are extremely variable in salinity, permanence, and morphometry, and ordination on environmental variables should tell one something about the biological attributes. Higher vectors distinguish environmental subgroups and regions that correlate with the copepod distributions. The biological ordination distinguishes a single group dominated by *Diaptomus sicilis* and several other less strongly defined groups. In general, these groups are similar to those proposed by Whittaker and Fairbanks, although the internal variability is better portrayed by the ordination. It should be noted that the "*D. sicilis* group" is physically quite variable. Lake 16 is saline (12,100 ppm)

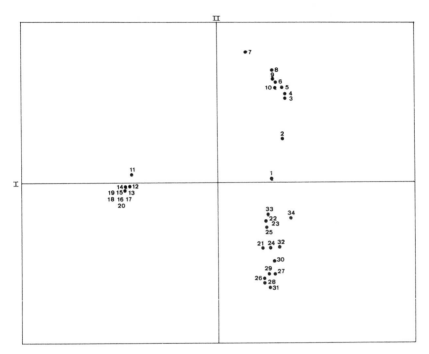

*Figure 7.22.* Ordination (correlation coefficient) of zooplankton relative abundance data for the Washington lakes.

and permanent, while lake 17 is fairly fresh (305 ppm) and temporary. The combined classification in Figure 7.23 could be used to allocate typical or unusual lakes for preservation or experimental purposes, although considerable variability, both biological and environmental, remains.

## CONCLUSIONS

Aquatic environments are but a small fraction of the total picture of natural resources. However, the heterogeneity of the resource and the varied demands placed upon it complicate both management and scientific investigation. If this report has a dominant theme, it is the idea that natural diversity exists and managers and scientists should take advantage of this variation. Complete disorder, however, is intolerable, and the numerical techniques explored here are capable of reducing this disorder to manageable proportions.

Numerical methods are not unique; an almost infinite number of classifications is possible. Flexibility and computational ease make the

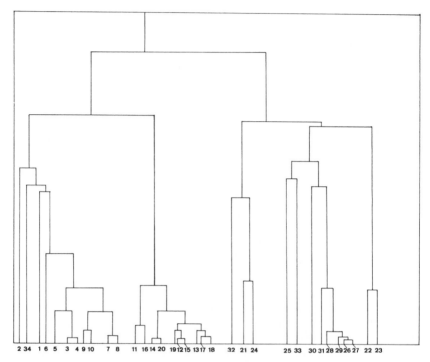

*Figure 7.23.* Combined environmental-biological (D-sort) classification
of Washington lakes.

technique applicable to a wide variety of subjects and materials. Methodology and data inputs should be governed by applications. Although
useful, the methods used in this report are not necessarily the most
powerful and efficient ones available. The intent has not been the development of perfect methods, if such exist, but rather to explore the
usefulness and disadvantages of numerical classifications of limnological
data.

The numerical methods and computer applications discussed in this
paper can be useful for the following purposes: (a) information retrieval,
(b) rapid organization of large data sets, (c) rapid identification of unusual or unique items in large arrays of data, (d) objective arrangement
of limnological data, which may lead to new insights, (e) experimental
design, (f) extrapolation of the results of natural and man-caused events
to similar environments.

In a time of mounting pressure on wild lands and natural areas, the
preservation of variety and of areas of esthetic, recreational, and scien-

tific purposes (Bormann, 1966; Sheldon, 1970) takes on increasing urgency. It is true that large, spectacular, and unusual lakes such as Lake Michigan, Lake Tahoe, and Crater Lake will be managed, abused, or preserved quite independently of the fate of other water bodies. However, lesser lakes and streams must be viewed as part of a larger system. It can be argued that preservation is an issue best handled at the local or regional level and based on local opportunity, informed judgment, considerations of land tenure, and the practicality of watershed control. In the absence of a national overview, local action is the only possibility. A national viewpoint has prominent advantages and in special cases, such as water bodies on the federal lands, is a necessity. While the subjective approach can work in small regions, automated techniques will be required if large quantities of survey data are to be processed and acted upon with any speed.

A system of information storage and processing is a necessity for good management and might have a pronounced effect on modern limnology. Early limnologists emphasized the comparative aspects of their science and, in so doing, defined a set of problems that still occupy their successors. It seems to me that the gains in understanding and techniques could be used in a new round of comparative studies, which would not only provide information for management and document historical changes in aquatic environments but also define a new framework for detailed investigations. In the long run, the contrasts provided by the comparative approach may be the most powerful tool available in the search for general principles.

At the present time the greatest problem is the shortage of comparable data from large numbers of lakes and streams. Because comparative limnology is much less fashionable than it was thirty years ago, few large-scale surveys have utilized modern techniques. The speed and reliability of modern instrumentation, coupled with an arrangement for taxonomic consultation with, for example, the Smithsonian Oceanographic Sorting Center, would make high-quality surveys possible. A data bank such as those projected for the Flora North America or the proposed Ecological Institute would be necessary.

The kinds of information needed for classificatory purposes have not been well defined. Physical and biological limnologists have defined the problems of interest to them and have developed and applied techniques of measurement. The social aspects of this finely divided and widely dispersed resource are less well understood. While of both theoretical and practical importance, such things as hypolimnetic oxygen deficits and the diatom flora are no more important than esthetic aspects or projected demands for recreation.

# Appendix

Appendix Table 1. Swedish Lakes [after Thunmark (1945)]

| Observa-tion | Trans-parency (cm) | Color | KMnO$_4$ demand | pH | Conductance |
|---|---|---|---|---|---|
| 1 | 42 | 35 | 246.7 | 8.4 | 170.5 |
| 2 | 46 | 31 | 198.2 | 7.8 | 189.0 |
| 3 | 50 | 22 | 135.6 | 8.4 | 158.0 |
| 4 | 46 | 24 | 119.1 | 8.4 | 163.6 |
| 5 | 38 | 22 | 328.7 | 8.4 | 186.7 |
| 6 | 45 | 19 | 248.9 | 8.4 | 200.0 |
| 7 | 82 | 41 | 122.7 | 8.3 | 296.2 |
| 8 | 65 | 43 | 157.2 | 8.1 | 154.8 |
| 9 | 236 | 10 | 39.6 | 7.3 | 79.9 |
| 10 | 180 | 7 | 35.0 | 7.8 | 66.4 |
| 11 | 208 | 7 | 32.7 | 7.4 | 68.9 |
| 12 | 305 | 11 | 39.6 | 7.3 | 82.1 |
| 13 | 301 | 9 | 36.1 | 7.4 | 92.0 |
| 14 | 141 | 10 | 62.3 | 8.2 | 178.4 |
| 15 | 270 | 14 | 45.4 | 7.2 | 75.3 |
| 16 | 248 | 6 | 19.0 | 7.3 | 82.1 |
| 17 | 585 | 5 | 24.8 | 7.0 | 39.0 |
| 18 | 505 | 6 | 30.4 | 6.8 | 42.7 |
| 19 | 448 | 11 | 36.9 | 6.9 | 60.3 |
| 20 | 462 | 10 | 32.2 | 6.9 | 53.6 |
| 21 | 604 | 6 | 26.1 | 6.9 | 55.8 |
| 22 | 494 | 7 | 38.2 | 7.0 | 53.4 |
| 23 | 575 | 6 | 26.4 | 6.9 | 43.2 |
| 24 | 542 | 7 | 29.2 | 6.9 | 54.3 |

Appendix Table 2. North American Lakes

| Observation | 1 Area (acres) | 2 Mean depth (ft) | 3 pH | 4 Alkalinity (ppm) | 5 Temperature (°F) at maximum depth | 6 Oxygen (ppm) at maximum depth | 7 Transparency (ft) | 8 Transparency/mean depth | Source |
|---|---|---|---|---|---|---|---|---|---|
| 1 | 120 | 57 | 7.7 | 60 | 44 | 0.0 | 11 | 0.19 | Narver 1967 |
| 2 | 10 | 17 | 8.2 | 47 | 67 | 0.0 | 15 | 0.88 | Sparrow 1966 |
| 3 | 30 | 32 | 8.8 | 73 | 50 | 0.0 | 13 | 0.41 | |
| 4 | 68 | 34 | 8.7 | 123 | 54 | 5.0 | 30 | 0.88 | |
| 5 | 52 | 24 | 8.5 | 145 | 67 | 6.0 | 24 | 1.00 | |
| 6 | 24 | 43 | 8.5 | 189 | 44 | 0.0 | 14 | 0.32 | |
| 7 | 78 | 35 | 8.9 | 132 | 60 | 3.0 | 30 | 0.86 | |
| 8 | 66 | 38 | 8.8 | 249 | 50 | 3.0 | 24 | 0.63 | |
| 9 | 55 | 27 | 9.2 | 356 | 48 | 0.0 | 5 | 0.18 | |
| 10 | 114 | 62 | 6.3 | 3 | 50 | 4.0 | 16 | 0.26 | Berg 1964 |
| 11 | 329 | 37 | 5.5 | 2 | 50 | 0.0 | 15 | 0.40 | |
| 12 | 33 | 38 | 5.9 | 10 | 50 | 0.0 | 14 | 0.37 | |
| 13 | 26 | 41 | 5.4 | 2 | 50 | 0.0 | 19 | 0.46 | |
| 14 | 762 | 190 | 4.9 | 1 | 50 | 7.0 | 85 | 0.45 | |
| 15 | 260 | 23 | 6.0 | 11 | 65 | 7.0 | 18 | 0.78 | |
| 16 | 5 | 19 | 5.9 | 10 | 50 | 0.0 | 13 | 0.68 | |
| 17 | 25 | 58 | 5.9 | 3 | 50 | 0.0 | 16 | 0.28 | |
| 18 | 148 | 29 | 5.8 | 14 | 50 | 0.0 | 8 | 0.28 | |
| 19 | 44 | 10 | 6.0 | 8 | 68 | 7.0 | 4 | 0.40 | |
| 20 | 27 | 7 | 5.3 | 2 | 68 | 7.0 | 3 | 0.52 | |
| 21 | 640 | 83 | 7.0 | 28 | 50 | 0.0 | 13 | 0.16 | |
| 22 | 10,624 | 274 | 8.1 | 103 | 50 | 7.0 | 12 | 0.04 | |
| 23 | 42,496 | 435 | 7.4 | 106 | 50 | 7.0 | 17 | 0.04 | |
| 24 | 3,328 | 59 | 7.7 | 108 | 50 | 0.0 | 21 | 0.36 | |
| 25 | 1,856 | 66 | 7.3 | 111 | 50 | 0.0 | 10 | 0.15 | |
| 26 | 43,328 | 618 | 7.1 | 105 | 50 | 7.0 | 27 | 0.04 | |
| 27 | 768 | 37 | 7.5 | 80 | 50 | 0.0 | 16 | 0.43 | |
| 28 | 8,896 | 297 | 7.5 | 93 | 50 | 7.0 | 34 | 0.11 | |
| 29 | 67 | 192 | 7.5 | 157 | 50 | 0.0 | 31 | 0.16 | |
| 30 | 51,200 | 55 | 7.8 | 66 | 65 | 6.0 | 8 | 0.14 | |

Newell 1960 →

| | | | | | | | | |
|---|---|---|---|---|---|---|---|---|
| 31 | 309 | 26 | 6.8 | 6 | 64 | 1.5 | 10 | 0.38 |
| 32 | 358 | 14 | 7.0 | 23 | 69 | 7.5 | 13 | 0.93 |
| 33 | 22 | 5 | 6.8 | 25 | 75 | 6.6 | 5 | 1.00 |
| 34 | 25 | 10 | 6.8 | 45 | 56 | 1.2 | 3 | 0.30 |
| 35 | 25 | 20 | 6.4 | 33 | 52 | 0.0 | 6 | 0.30 |
| 36 | 118 | 22 | 6.9 | 7 | 60 | 0.8 | 11 | 0.50 |
| 37 | 10 | 7 | 6.6 | 13 | 72 | 7.2 | 7 | 1.00 |
| 38 | 4 | 14 | 6.3 | 6 | 58 | 7.4 | 14 | 1.00 |
| 39 | 87 | 4 | 6.2 | 10 | 64 | 7.0 | 4 | 1.00 |
| 40 | 170 | 60 | 6.8 | 10 | 49 | 7.0 | 15 | 0.25 |
| 41 | 25 | 7 | 7.3 | 25 | 74 | 7.5 | 7 | 1.00 |
| 42 | 2,807 | 142 | 7.0 | 7 | 47 | 8.0 | 10 | 0.07 |
| 43 | 1,286 | 61 | 6.8 | 7 | 54 | 3.9 | 8 | 0.13 |
| 44 | 179 | 117 | 7.2 | 16 | 49 | 7.7 | 15 | 0.13 |
| 45 | 15 | 4 | 5.2 | 2 | 68 | 9.0 | 4 | 1.00 |
| 46 | 117 | 36 | 6.3 | 9 | 51 | 0.8 | 11 | 0.30 |
| 47 | 40 | 15 | 6.2 | 10 | 68 | 7.2 | 8 | 0.53 |
| 48 | 20 | 8 | 7.2 | 26 | 63 | 7.0 | 5 | 0.62 |
| 49 | 254 | 110 | 6.6 | 6 | 49 | 5.7 | 15 | 0.14 |
| 50 | 3 | 4 | 6.3 | 4 | 56 | 8.7 | 4 | 1.00 |
| 51 | 6 | 6 | 6.0 | 2 | 57 | 6.8 | 6 | 1.00 |
| 52 | 11 | 11 | 7.4 | 60 | 68 | 5.5 | 8 | 0.73 |
| 53 | 37 | 11 | 5.7 | 4 | 69 | 6.4 | 7 | 0.64 |
| 54 | 8 | 6 | 6.6 | 23 | 60 | 9.6 | 6 | 1.00 |
| 55 | 47 | 22 | 6.7 | 20 | 58 | 0.4 | 7 | 0.32 |
| 56 | 19 | 11 | 6.1 | 5 | 60 | 6.4 | 5 | 0.45 |
| 57 | 43 | 35 | 6.6 | 10 | 45 | 0.5 | 14 | 0.40 |
| 58 | 12 | 2 | 5.4 | 2 | 70 | 7.5 | 2 | 1.00 |
| 59 | 49 | 7 | 6.2 | 5 | 71 | 5.7 | 7 | 1.00 |
| 60 | 7,850 | 48 | 6.7 | 6 | 63 | 5.2 | 8 | 0.17 |
| 61 | 142 | 28 | 6.8 | 5 | 57 | 3.6 | 14 | 0.50 |
| 62 | 6 | 42 | 6.2 | 5 | 44 | 0.4 | 7 | 0.17 |
| 63 | 7 | 5 | 6.1 | 5 | 76 | 6.8 | 5 | 1.00 |
| 64 | 10 | 14 | 5.4 | 4 | 55 | 0.0 | 8 | 0.57 |
| 65 | 10 | 22 | 6.0 | 10 | 58 | 0.0 | 15 | 0.68 |
| 66 | 27 | 8 | 6.1 | 3 | 62 | 7.3 | 8 | 1.00 |
| 67 | 37 | 30 | 6.3 | 3 | 48 | 0.5 | 19 | 0.63 |

Appendix Table 2. (cont'd)

| Observation | 1 Area (acres) | 2 Mean depth (ft) | 3 pH | 4 Alkalinity (ppm) | 5 Temperature (°F) at maximum depth | 6 Oxygen (ppm) at maximum depth | 7 Transparency (ft) | 8 Transparency/ mean depth | Source |
|---|---|---|---|---|---|---|---|---|---|
| 68 | 4,106 | 168 | 6.9 | 6 | 45 | 9.4 | 26 | 0.15 | Newell 1960 |
| 69 | 11 | 13 | 5.2 | 2 | 64 | 6.3 | 13 | 1.00 | |
| 70 | 11 | 28 | 6.2 | 2 | 55 | 5.9 | 20 | 0.71 | |
| 71 | 6 | 4 | 5.2 | 3 | 60 | 5.7 | 4 | 1.00 | |
| 72 | 6,765 | 98 | 7.0 | 20 | 52 | 9.7 | 22 | 0.22 | |
| 73 | 346 | 75 | 6.6 | 11 | 48 | 6.0 | 14 | 0.19 | |
| 74 | 315 | 60 | 6.8 | 6 | 52 | 6.3 | 13 | 0.22 | |
| 75 | 46 | 51 | 6.9 | 9 | 52 | 8.2 | 17 | 0.33 | |
| 76 | 6 | 6 | 5.2 | 14 | 73 | 5.8 | 5 | 0.83 | |
| 77 | 7 | 38 | 6.4 | 8 | 56 | 9.2 | 33 | 0.87 | |
| 78 | 408 | 126 | 6.8 | 6 | 51 | 8.2 | 25 | 0.20 | |
| 79 | 48 | 39 | 5.4 | 7 | 48 | 2.8 | 13 | 0.33 | |
| 80 | 538 | 41 | 6.6 | 9 | 62 | 0.4 | 14 | 0.34 | |
| 81 | 3,091 | 61 | 6.0 | 6 | 44 | 8.9 | 12 | 0.20 | |
| 82 | 210 | 39 | 6.3 | 9 | 54 | 0.9 | 15 | 0.38 | |
| 83 | 995 | 158 | 6.6 | 8 | 50 | 9.5 | 18 | 0.11 | |
| 84 | 14 | 8 | 6.0 | 3 | 74 | 5.3 | 5 | 0.63 | Newell 1963 |
| 85 | 24 | 18 | 6.2 | 30 | 62 | 1.5 | 9 | 0.50 | |
| 86 | 7 | 16 | 5.2 | 2 | 59 | 0.5 | 12 | 0.75 | |
| 87 | 180 | 30 | 5.9 | 9 | 58 | 0.3 | 14 | 0.47 | |
| 88 | 150 | 62 | 6.6 | 4 | 47 | 1.6 | 25 | 0.40 | |
| 89 | 68 | 61 | 6.8 | 9 | 48 | 2.7 | 11 | 0.18 | |
| 90 | 4,058 | 142 | 7.0 | 10 | 52 | 8.3 | 22 | 0.15 | |
| 91 | 26 | 19 | 6.6 | 14 | 57 | 1.4 | 7 | 0.37 | |
| 92 | 49 | 42 | 6.6 | 10 | 50 | 11.0 | 20 | 0.48 | |
| 93 | 41 | 20 | 6.6 | 9 | 73 | 1.2 | 10 | 0.50 | |
| 94 | 62 | 23 | 6.8 | 7 | 56 | 0.2 | 11 | 0.48 | |
| 95 | 31 | 43 | 7.1 | 9 | 48 | 0.3 | 6 | 0.14 | |
| 96 | 42 | 8 | 6.2 | 12 | 72 | 6.9 | 6 | 0.75 | |
| 97 | 11 | 32 | 6.4 | 2 | 46 | 0.0 | 15 | 0.47 | |

Reimers et al. 1955 →

| | 1 | 2 | 3 | 4 | | 5 | 6 | 7 |
|---|---|---|---|---|---|---|---|---|
| 98 | 14 | 14 | 5.2 | 12 | 57 | 0.3 | 2 | 0.14 |
| 99 | 41 | 15 | 6.3 | 11 | 62 | 5.0 | 10 | 0.67 |
| 100 | 472 | 43 | 6.8 | 7 | 52 | 3.0 | 14 | 0.32 |
| 101 | 99 | 20 | 6.4 | 3 | 66 | 6.0 | 10 | 0.50 |
| 102 | 280 | 29 | 6.8 | 7 | 55 | 0.8 | 12 | 0.41 |
| 103 | 31 | 13 | 6.4 | 9 | 71 | 8.7 | 13 | 1.00 |
| 104 | 121 | 46 | 7.0 | 13 | 54 | 1.7 | 20 | 0.43 |
| 105 | 19 | 9 | 5.8 | 1 | 74 | 8.0 | 9 | 1.00 |
| 106 | 14 | 70 | 6.0 | 4 | 44 | 0.0 | 21 | 0.30 |
| 107 | 228 | 30 | 6.6 | 5 | 51 | 0.2 | 20 | 0.67 |
| 108 | 2 | 10 | 6.4 | 21 | 53 | 0.0 | 5 | 0.50 |
| 109 | 83 | 9 | 6.0 | 8 | 78 | 7.4 | 3 | 0.33 |
| 110 | 39 | 11 | 6.1 | 10 | 60 | 0.8 | 6 | 0.54 |
| 111 | 1,111 | 122 | 6.7 | 9 | 50 | 10.0 | 20 | 0.16 |
| 112 | 85 | 52 | 6.3 | 6 | 50 | 2.2 | 22 | 0.42 |
| 113 | 11 | 13 | 7.0 | 26 | 65 | 0.9 | 6 | 0.46 |
| 114 | 62 | 18 | 6.6 | 12 | 54 | 0.9 | 6 | 0.33 |
| 115 | 14 | 48 | 6.4 | 13 | 46 | 0.0 | 15 | 0.31 |
| 116 | 6 | 16 | 6.9 | 36 | 55 | 0.0 | 4 | 0.25 |
| 117 | 43 | 23 | 6.4 | 2 | 70 | 5.6 | 23 | 1.00 |
| 118 | 34 | 170 | 7.0 | 17 | 40 | 7.6 | 60 | 0.35 |
| 119 | 18 | 110 | 7.0 | 13 | 40 | 2.8 | 46 | 0.42 |
| 120 | 152 | 290 | 7.0 | 11 | 40 | 9.2 | 67 | 0.23 |
| 121 | 168 | 140 | 7.0 | 67 | 44 | 8.8 | 51 | 0.36 |

Attribute Correlation Matrix

| Variable | 1 | 2 | 3 | 4 | 5 | 6 | 7 | 8 |
|---|---|---|---|---|---|---|---|---|
| 1 | 1.0000 | | | | | | | |
| 2 | 0.6321 | 1.0000 | | | | | | |
| 3 | 0.2047 | 0.2378 | 1.0000 | | | | | |
| 4 | 0.2158 | 0.2327 | 0.7380 | 1.0000 | | | | |
| 5 | -0.0503 | -0.4318 | -0.2279 | -0.1761 | 1.0000 | | | |
| 6 | 0.1624 | 0.2387 | -0.0782 | -0.1632 | 0.2674 | 1.0000 | | |
| 7 | 0.0503 | 0.5127 | 0.1599 | 0.1094 | -0.4636 | 0.1770 | 1.0000 | |
| 8 | -0.2951 | -0.5085 | -0.2207 | -0.1379 | 0.6508 | 0.2381 | -0.1626 | 1.0000 |

Appendix Table 3. Finnish Lakes [after Jarnefelt (1956)]

| Observation | Area (ha) | Maximum depth (meters) | Mean depth (meters) | Shoreline development | Transparency (meters) | Transparency/mean depth | Color | Cl (mg/l) | Fe (mg/l) | Alkalinity (mg/l) |
|---|---|---|---|---|---|---|---|---|---|---|
| 1 | 1,360 | 22.0 | 4.7 | 3.1 | 1.9 | 0.40 | 50 | 0.9 | 0.10 | 0.35 |
| 2 | 880 | 20.0 | 3.3 | 3.2 | 1.1 | 0.33 | 50 | 2.6 | 0.05 | 0.44 |
| 3 | 488 | 9.0 | 3.0 | 2.7 | 1.4 | 0.47 | 40 | 2.8 | 0.10 | 0.40 |
| 4 | 525 | 1.3 | 0.7 | 2.2 | 0.4 | 0.57 | 110 | 1.1 | 0.80 | 0.24 |
| 5 | 76 | 7.0 | 4.5 | 1.6 | 1.1 | 0.24 | 70 | 3.3 | 0.18 | 0.37 |
| 6 | 25 | 4.0 | 2.0 | 1.6 | 1.0 | 0.50 | 40 | 3.8 | 0.28 | 0.23 |
| 7 | 320 | 15.0 | 2.4 | 1.8 | 1.6 | 0.67 | 45 | 0.7 | 0.12 | 0.24 |
| 8 | 34 | 6.0 | 2.9 | 1.2 | 1.0 | 0.34 | 70 | 2.2 | 0.52 | 0.39 |
| 9 | 176 | 3.0 | 1.2 | 1.6 | 1.7 | 1.41 | 40 | 0.7 | 0.28 | 0.24 |
| 10 | 2,390 | 12.0 | 3.7 | 2.6 | 1.4 | 0.38 | 50 | 1.4 | 0.36 | 0.28 |
| 11 | 755 | 12.5 | 2.4 | 10.4 | 0.9 | 0.38 | 80 | 1.6 | 0.40 | 0.45 |
| 12 | 160 | 4.5 | 1.5 | 1.0 | 0.4 | 0.27 | 300 | 2.2 | 2.02 | 2.90 |
| 13 | 364 | 8.0 | 2.5 | 1.7 | 0.7 | 0.28 | 50 | 1.9 | 0.04 | 0.28 |
| 14 | 16 | 6.3 | 1.8 | 1.8 | 0.7 | 0.39 | 135 | 0.2 | 0.51 | 0.24 |
| 15 | 400 | 9.0 | 3.5 | 2.3 | 1.1 | 0.31 | 75 | 1.9 | 9.00 | 0.20 |
| 16 | 500 | 4.0 | 2.2 | 1.5 | 1.1 | 0.50 | 105 | 1.7 | 1.48 | 0.12 |
| 17 | 2,650 | 25.0 | 5.3 | 4.0 | 1.5 | 0.28 | 55 | 3.1 | 0.16 | 0.23 |
| 18 | 71 | 8.0 | 4.0 | 2.4 | 2.3 | 0.57 | 50 | 1.1 | 0.84 | 0.46 |
| 19 | 161 | 1.7 | 1.0 | 1.4 | 0.4 | 0.40 | 154 | 0.1 | 0.65 | 1.60 |
| 20 | 370 | 4.0 | 2.5 | 2.7 | 3.7 | 1.48 | 40 | 1.1 | 0.16 | 1.40 |
| 21 | 5,560 | 29.0 | 8.4 | 4.1 | 2.8 | 0.33 | 40 | 1.6 | 0.08 | 0.25 |
| 22 | 63 | 16.5 | 4.7 | 2.5 | 2.5 | 0.53 | 40 | 1.5 | 0.16 | 1.40 |
| 23 | 120 | 15.0 | 5.0 | 2.2 | 2.0 | 0.40 | 40 | 5.3 | 0.12 | 0.40 |
| 24 | 5,422 | 32.0 | 8.2 | 4.4 | 2.5 | 0.30 | 40 | 1.7 | 0.04 | 2.30 |
| 25 | 28 | 10.0 | 6.0 | 1.6 | 6.0 | 1.00 | 40 | 0.7 | 0.02 | 0.06 |
| 26 | 8,000 | 35.0 | 15.0 | 9.1 | 5.0 | 0.33 | 38 | 2.6 | 0.09 | 0.18 |
| 27 | 135 | 8.0 | 3.0 | 2.3 | 4.3 | 1.43 | 40 | 1.9 | 0.11 | 0.10 |
| 28 | 33 | 13.5 | 4.3 | 2.1 | 5.0 | 1.16 | 40 | 1.9 | 0.19 | 0.50 |
| 29 | 620 | 18.0 | 4.6 | 4.0 | 2.0 | 0.43 | 87 | 0.2 | 0.03 | 0.24 |
| 30 | 4 | 4.0 | 2.0 | 1.5 | 1.2 | 0.60 | 120 | 1.1 | 0.88 | 0.08 |
| 31 | 434 | 16.0 | 8.0 | 1.9 | 2.6 | 0.32 | 58 | 2.6 | 0.08 | 0.13 |
| 32 | 800 | 52.0 | 10.0 | 13.3 | 2.0 | 0.20 | 50 | 0.1 | 0.15 | 0.16 |

| | | | | | | | | | | |
|---|---|---|---|---|---|---|---|---|---|---|
| 33 | 258 | 12.0 | 7.0 | 2.2 | 3.8 | 0.54 | 70 | 2.8 | 0.09 | 0.15 |
| 34 | 30 | 6.0 | 2.5 | 1.5 | 1.2 | 0.48 | 170 | 1.9 | 0.96 | 0.06 |
| 35 | 7,900 | 28.0 | 9.5 | 6.8 | 1.5 | 0.16 | 76 | 1.9 | 0.23 | 0.19 |
| 36 | 170 | 18.0 | 5.0 | 1.8 | 2.3 | 0.46 | 40 | 3.1 | 0.04 | 0.54 |
| 37 | 30 | 1.0 | 1.0 | 1.4 | 1.0 | 1.00 | 53 | 1.9 | 0.83 | 0.22 |
| 38 | 1,700 | 30.0 | 8.6 | 2.8 | 2.9 | 0.34 | 40 | 2.5 | 0.14 | 0.22 |
| 39 | 260 | 24.0 | 5.3 | 2.4 | 1.3 | 0.24 | 40 | 2.1 | 0.06 | 0.44 |
| 40 | 175 | 5.0 | 2.0 | 2.5 | 2.0 | 1.00 | 38 | 3.9 | 0.08 | 0.26 |
| 41 | 4,260 | 17.0 | 5.0 | 4.2 | 2.5 | 0.50 | 40 | 2.1 | 0.16 | 0.13 |
| 42 | 3,050 | 38.0 | 8.9 | 3.6 | 1.3 | 0.15 | 40 | 3.3 | 0.02 | 0.34 |
| 43 | 150 | 15.0 | 7.0 | 1.6 | 1.3 | 0.18 | 40 | 4.1 | 0.09 | 0.36 |
| 44 | 57 | 12.0 | 5.8 | 1.7 | 2.0 | 0.22 | 80 | 0.7 | 0.60 | 0.26 |
| 45 | 23 | 12.0 | 4.0 | 1.4 | 2.2 | 0.50 | 40 | 0.7 | 0.12 | 0.80 |
| 46 | 130 | 3.0 | 1.5 | 1.3 | 2.0 | 1.46 | 70 | 0.7 | 0.50 | 0.33 |
| 47 | 2,815 | 44.0 | 10.0 | 3.9 | 2.8 | 0.20 | 40 | 0.6 | 0.02 | 0.31 |
| 48 | 716 | 32.0 | 9.8 | 1.6 | 0.8 | 0.28 | 50 | 1.6 | 0.08 | 0.46 |
| 49 | 84 | 2.0 | 1.2 | 1.4 | 1.5 | 0.71 | 105 | 1.7 | 0.62 | 0.17 |
| 50 | 420 | 8.0 | 4.5 | 2.0 | 1.1 | 0.33 | 70 | 0.9 | 2.12 | 0.08 |
| 51 | 180 | 11.0 | 3.7 | 1.1 | 0.9 | 0.30 | 85 | 1.3 | 0.04 | 0.20 |
| 52 | 110 | 11.0 | 3.3 | 2.0 | 2.0 | 0.27 | 180 | 0.9 | 1.97 | 0.21 |
| 53 | 220 | 24.0 | 5.0 | 2.1 | 4.0 | 0.32 | 43 | 4.5 | 0.67 | 0.36 |
| 54 | 55 | 30.0 | 13.6 | 1.6 | 3.8 | 0.15 | 50 | 2.6 | 0.70 | 0.18 |
| 55 | 750 | 31.0 | 9.5 | 2.3 | 4.2 | 0.42 | 40 | 0.9 | 0.04 | 0.30 |
| 56 | 879 | 23.0 | 6.3 | 2.4 | 3.0 | 0.60 | 40 | 2.2 | 0.09 | 0.16 |
| 57 | 3,591 | 30.0 | 5.2 | 4.6 | 3.5 | 0.81 | 50 | 2.3 | 0.08 | 0.16 |
| 58 | 115 | 7.0 | 4.0 | 1.6 | 2.3 | 0.75 | 43 | 1.9 | 0.09 | 0.17 |
| 59 | 510 | 21.0 | 10.0 | 2.1 | 2.4 | 0.35 | 40 | 2.6 | 0.10 | 0.19 |
| 60 | 50 | 15.0 | 10.0 | 1.8 | 3.0 | 0.23 | 37 | 8.6 | 0.06 | 0.44 |
| 61 | 526 | 19.0 | 5.2 | 2.7 | 2.9 | 0.46 | 40 | 0.3 | 0.80 | 0.25 |
| 62 | 1,735 | 25.0 | 10.0 | 1.6 | 3.9 | 0.30 | 40 | 2.0 | 0.04 | 0.20 |
| 63 | 2,400 | 91.0 | 25.0 | 2.1 | 2.4 | 0.12 | 40 | 1.5 | 0.00 | 0.19 |
| 64 | 1,600 | 35.0 | 7.3 | 3.2 | 2.0 | 0.53 | 50 | 0.1 | 0.07 | 0.24 |
| 65 | 232 | 12.0 | 3.1 | 2.8 | 2.3 | 0.77 | 40 | 1.5 | 1.80 | 0.10 |
| 66 | 73 | 14.5 | 6.9 | 1.8 | 2.8 | 0.29 | 40 | 1.3 | 0.12 | 0.12 |
| 67 | 267 | 45.5 | 8.1 | 2.5 | 2.0 | 0.28 | 40 | 0.4 | 0.16 | 0.21 |
| 68 | 490 | 14.0 | 4.2 | 1.5 | 1.0 | 0.67 | 63 | 1.6 | 0.10 | 0.15 |
| 69 | 4 | 5.0 | 2.0 | 1.3 | | 1.00 | 40 | 2.2 | 1.10 | 0.32 |
| 70 | 4,400 | 32.0 | 8.0 | 4.0 | | 0.13 | 105 | 9.9 | 1.60 | 0.00 |

Appendix Table 4. English Tarns [after Macan (1950) and Mackereth, Lund, and Macan (1957)]
I. Environmental Characteristics

| Observation | Area (Dm²) | Plant density[a] | Altitude[b] | Total dissolved solids (meq/l) | Ca (mg/l) | Mg (mg/l) | Na (mg/l) | K (mg/l) | Cl (mg/l) | SO₄ (mg/l) | Winter Ca (mg/l) | Winter alkalinity (mg/l) |
|---|---|---|---|---|---|---|---|---|---|---|---|---|
| 1 | 64 | 2 | 1 | 1.5 | 20.0 | 2.6 | 4.7 | 0.9 | 9.8 | 12 | 16.6 | 62.5 |
| 2 | 210 | 1 | 1 | 1.4 | 19.8 | 2.1 | 5.1 | 0.7 | 9.1 | 12 | 15.2 | 34.6 |
| 3 | 186 | 2 | 1 | 0.6 | 6.2 | 1.0 | 5.0 | 0.5 | 9.4 | 11 | 6.3 | 11.9 |
| 4 | 83 | 1 | 2 | 0.8 | 6.0 | 1.7 | 6.2 | 0.7 | 12.5 | 11 | 5.7 | 10.5 |
| 5 | 55 | 3 | 1 | 1.2 | 14.0 | 2.4 | 6.2 | 1.4 | 10.0 | 17 | 9.2 | 24.0 |
| 6 | 334 | 3 | 1 | 1.4 | 16.3 | 3.5 | 5.1 | 0.6 | 8.2 | 13 | 8.6 | 33.5 |
| 7 | 8 | 3 | 1 | 0.8 | 8.5 | 1.5 | 5.0 | 0.4 | 8.2 | 12 | 5.6 | 21.5 |
| 8 | 16 | 3 | 1 | 0.9 | 10.5 | 1.4 | 5.0 | 0.8 | 9.1 | 10 | 4.3 | 12.0 |
| 9 | 48 | 1 | 1 | 0.7 | 8.8 | 0.9 | 4.2 | 0.4 | 8.8 | 8 | 6.0 | 17.3 |
| 10 | 48 | 2 | 2 | 0.9 | 9.8 | 2.1 | 4.3 | 0.4 | 11.4 | 10 | 9.6 | 14.4 |
| 11 | 52 | 2 | 1 | 0.6 | 6.5 | 0.6 | 3.5 | 0.5 | 8.0 | 9 | 7.1 | 12.0 |
| 12 | 440 | 1 | 2 | 0.5 | 4.9 | 0.9 | 4.2 | 0.5 | 7.5 | 9 | 3.3 | 6.6 |
| 13 | 116 | 1 | 2 | 0.5 | 5.0 | 0.8 | 4.4 | 0.5 | 8.8 | 9 | 3.8 | 8.0 |
| 14 | 430 | 1 | 2 | 0.6 | 5.3 | 1.3 | 4.0 | 0.2 | 8.9 | 5 | 3.6 | 9.3 |
| 15 | 128 | 1 | 2 | 0.7 | 7.4 | 1.3 | 3.8 | 0.5 | 7.3 | 8 | 5.1 | 16.1 |

| | | | | | | | | | | | | |
|---|---|---|---|---|---|---|---|---|---|---|---|---|
| 16 | 28 | 3 | 1 | 0.8 | 9.6 | 1.5 | 4.1 | 0.6 | 12.3 | 9 | 5.5 | 18.9 |
| 17 | 6 | 1 | 1 | 1.1 | 11.7 | 2.4 | 7.8 | 0.8 | 11.4 | 15 | 7.6 | 15.0 |
| 18 | 308 | 1 | 1 | 0.7 | 5.9 | 1.6 | 5.5 | 0.6 | 11.4 | 12 | 5.2 | 7.3 |
| 19 | 83 | 1 | 2 | 0.6 | 5.3 | 1.1 | 4.5 | 0.6 | 8.1 | 7 | 4.0 | 8.5 |
| 20 | 213 | 1 | 1 | 0.9 | 9.7 | 1.9 | 5.3 | 0.3 | 10.6 | 9 | 6.7 | 12.7 |
| 21 | 30 | 3 | 1 | 0.7 | 7.7 | 1.3 | 5.1 | 0.5 | 9.2 | 10 | 6.0 | 15.7 |
| 22 | 32 | 2 | 2 | 0.6 | 6.2 | 1.1 | 4.7 | 0.5 | 8.7 | 10 | 3.8 | 8.6 |
| 23 | 352 | 2 | 2 | 0.5 | 5.2 | 1.0 | 4.2 | 0.4 | 6.8 | 9 | 3.4 | 8.6 |
| 24 | 160 | 1 | 2 | 0.5 | 3.9 | 0.9 | 4.3 | 0.1 | 6.1 | 10 | 3.0 | 3.9 |
| 25 | 104 | 1 | 1 | 0.7 | 6.6 | 1.2 | 6.0 | 0.6 | 11.2 | 13 | 5.7 | 12.2 |
| 26 | 25 | 1 | 3 | 0.5 | 5.1 | 0.6 | 3.3 | 0.3 | 6.1 | 6 | 4.4 | 27.0 |
| 27 | 42 | 2 | 1 | 0.6 | 4.1 | 1.1 | 5.5 | 0.8 | 10.5 | 10 | 4.2 | 4.8 |
| 28 | 47 | 1 | 2 | 0.5 | 4.9 | 1.1 | 3.7 | 0.2 | 4.9 | 9 | 3.8 | 6.5 |
| 29 | 150 | 3 | 1 | 0.6 | 6.4 | 0.8 | 4.2 | 0.5 | 8.2 | 13 | 4.3 | 10.7 |
| 30 | 8 | 2 | 2 | 0.7 | 4.7 | 1.3 | 6.2 | 0.6 | 12.9 | 10 | 5.2 | 7.1 |
| 31 | 62 | 1 | 3 | 0.4 | 2.8 | 0.5 | 3.2 | 0.5 | 5.8 | 7 | 2.7 | 10.5 |
| 32 | 372 | 1 | 2 | 0.3 | 1.3 | 0.5 | 2.6 | 0.4 | 3.9 | 4 | 1.8 | 4.7 |
| 33 | 52 | 2 | 3 | 0.3 | 2.2 | 0.7 | 3.3 | 0.3 | 5.9 | 6 | 1.9 | 4.6 |
| 34 | 150 | 1 | 2 | 0.2 | 1.5 | 0.4 | 2.1 | 0.1 | 3.4 | 4 | 1.8 | 2.5 |

a Arbitrary scale ranging from 1 (absent or sparse) to 3 (luxuriant).

b 1 = below 500 ft elevation; 2 = 500–1,000 ft; 3 = above 1,000 ft.

Appendix Table 4. (cont'd)
II. Biological Characteristics

| Lake | Limnea pereger | Planorbis albus | Planorbis contortus | Physa fontinalis | Valvata piscinalis | Limnea palustris | Planorbis complanatus | Planorbis crista | Limnea stagnalis | Corixa castanea | Corixa scotti | Corixa distincta | Corixa fossarum | Corixa linnei | Cymatia bonsdorffi | Corixa praeusta |
|---|---|---|---|---|---|---|---|---|---|---|---|---|---|---|---|---|
| 1 | + | + | | | | + | + | | | | + | | | | + | + |
| 2 | + | + | | | | + | + | + | + | | + | | + | | + | |
| 3 | + | + | | | | | + | | | | + | | | | + | + |
| 4 | + | + | | | | + | | + | | | + | + | | | + | + |
| 5 | + | + | | | | + | + | | | + | + | + | | + | | + |
| 6 | + | + | | | | + | | | | + | + | | | | + | |
| 7 | + | | | | | + | | | | + | | | | | | |
| 8 | | + | | | | + | | | | | + | + | + | | | |
| 9 | | + | | | | + | | | | | | + | + | | | |
| 10 | | + | | | | | | | | | | + | | + | | + |
| 11 | + | + | | | | | | | | | + | + | | + | + | + |
| 12 | + | + | + | | | + | | | | + | + | + | + | | | |
| 13 | + | + | + | | + | + | | | | + | + | + | + | | | |
| 14 | + | + | + | + | + | + | | + | | | + | | | | | |

| | | | | | | | | | | | | | | | | | | | |
|---|---|---|---|---|---|---|---|---|---|---|---|---|---|---|---|---|---|---|---|
| + | + | + | + | + | + | + | + | + | + | + | + | + | + | + | + | | | | |
| + | + | + | + | + | + | | | | | | | | | | | | | | |
| + | | | | | | | | | | | | | | | | | | | |
| + | | | | | | | | | | | | | | | | | | | |
| + | | | | | | | | | | | | | | | | | | | |
| | | | | | | + | + | | | | + | + | + | | | | | | |
| + | | | + | + | + | + | + | + | + | + | + | + | + | + | | | + | | |
| | | + | | | | + | | + | + | | | | | | | | | | |
| | + | + | | | | | | + | | | | | | | | | | | |
| | | | | | | + | + | | | | | | | | | | | | |
| | | | + | | | | | | | | | | | | | | | | |
| 15 | 16 | 17 | 18 | 19 | 20 | 21 | 22 | 23 | 24 | 25 | 26 | 27 | 28 | 29 | 30 | 31 | 32 | 33 | 34 |

meq/l = milliequivalents/liter.

Appendix Table 5. Washington Lakes [after Whittaker and Fairbanks (1958)]
I. Physical and Chemical Characteristics

| Lake | Area (ha) | Perma-nence[a] | Depth[b] | Transparency (ft) Max. | Transparency (ft) Min. | Total dissolved solids (ppm) | Na (ppm) | Mg (ppm) | K (ppm) | Ca (ppm) | B (ppb) | Fe (ppb) | Cu (ppb) |
|---|---|---|---|---|---|---|---|---|---|---|---|---|---|
| 1 | 860.00 | 3 | 3 | 1.0 | 0.5 | 170.0 | 15.0 | 5.0 | 4.8 | 0.7 | 0.16 | 1.44 | 0.90 |
| 2 | 39.00 | 3 | 3 | 10.5 | 8.5 | 235.0 | 26.0 | 11.0 | 7.6 | 1.4 | 0.64 | 0.17 | 0.40 |
| 3 | 140.00 | 3 | 3 | 14.0 | 2.5 | 265.0 | 48.0 | 13.0 | 11.0 | 2.3 | 0.87 | 0.84 | 0.50 |
| 4 | 210.00 | 3 | 3 | 12.0 | 1.8 | 305.0 | 70.0 | 24.0 | 13.2 | 4.0 | 0.85 | 0.50 | 0.50 |
| 5 | 27.00 | 3 | 3 | 10.5 | 2.5 | 230.0 | 34.0 | 15.0 | 6.4 | 1.6 | 1.04 | 0.37 | 0.10 |
| 6 | 0.40 | 1 | 1 | 2.5 | 2.5 | 330.0 | 46.0 | 27.0 | 5.0 | 3.4 | 0.68 | 2.51 | 1.50 |
| 7 | 85.00 | 3 | 2 | 1.2 | 0.2 | 250.0 | 26.0 | 13.0 | 12.0 | 2.6 | 0.21 | 0.32 | 1.10 |
| 8 | 2,060.00 | 3 | 2 | 3.0 | 1.0 | 210.0 | 40.0 | 11.0 | 11.2 | 1.8 | 1.12 | 0.40 | 0.10 |
| 9 | 735.00 | 3 | 2 | 2.5 | 2.0 | 335.0 | 24.0 | 19.0 | 9.4 | 1.4 | 0.29 | 0.70 | 0.40 |
| 10 | 97.00 | 3 | 3 | 6.0 | 1.5 | 425.0 | 94.0 | 7.0 | 21.2 | 6.3 | 0.08 | 0.21 | 0.10 |
| 11 | 225.00 | 3 | 2 | 0.5 | 0.2 | 2,350.0 | 705.0 | 10.0 | 122.0 | 28.0 | 1.64 | 3.36 | 12.20 |
| 12 | 25.00 | 2 | 1 | 0.1 | 0.1 | 1,040.0 | 268.0 | 14.0 | 29.6 | 12.2 | 1.85 | 5.78 | 1.10 |
| 13 | 36.00 | 2 | 2 | 0.3 | 0.1 | 4,270.0 | 1,480.0 | 6.0 | 210.0 | 57.0 | 0.63 | 0.54 | 0.40 |
| 14 | 43.00 | 3 | 2 | 1.5 | 1.2 | 4,290.0 | 1,480.0 | 7.0 | 169.0 | 28.0 | 1.60 | 0.81 | 1.50 |
| 15 | 4.40 | 2 | 1 | 3.0 | 0.3 | 875.0 | 302.0 | 15.0 | 42.4 | 11.4 | 0.41 | 4.16 | 3.30 |
| 16 | 963.00 | 3 | 2 | 2.5 | 2.5 | 12,100.0 | 4,140.0 | 38.0 | 364.0 | 148.0 | 9.07 | 1.81 | 20.00 |
| 17 | 0.20 | 1 | 1 | 2.5 | 2.5 | 305.0 | 21.0 | 10.0 | 6.6 | 2.6 | 0.50 | 0.46 | 1.20 |
| 18 | 2.50 | 1 | 1 | 2.5 | 0.1 | 630.0 | 126.0 | 23.0 | 55.2 | 5.4 | 0.35 | 0.09 | 0.06 |
| 19 | 48.00 | 2 | 1 | 0.3 | 0.1 | 1,140.0 | 166.0 | 21.0 | 35.0 | 7.2 | 3.13 | 5.95 | 11.30 |
| 20 | 43.00 | 3 | 2 | 2.5 | 2.0 | 2,290.0 | 715.0 | 10.0 | 54.0 | 30.0 | 0.76 | 0.55 | 0.20 |
| 21 | 48.00 | 2 | 2 | 2.5 | 1.0 | 415.0 | 96.0 | 32.0 | 15.2 | 2.8 | 0.20 | 0.67 | 0.40 |
| 22 | 1.50 | 2 | 1 | 2.5 | 0.5 | 8,710.0 | 2,600.0 | 283.0 | 210.0 | 98.0 | 3.70 | 1.13 | 2.00 |
| 23 | 1.20 | 1 | 1 | 3.0 | 0.5 | 610.0 | 126.0 | 34.0 | 19.2 | 9.0 | 1.07 | 3.90 | 1.80 |
| 24 | 1.30 | 2 | 1 | 2.5 | 3.0 | 310.0 | 49.0 | 6.0 | 22.8 | 2.0 | 1.13 | 1.01 | 2.50 |
| 25 | 0.20 | 1 | 1 | 2.5 | 2.5 | 1,245.0 | 224.0 | 66.0 | 131.0 | 12.4 | 1.86 | 2.34 | 0.20 |
| 26 | 0.01 | 1 | 1 | 2.5 | 2.5 | 390.0 | 59.0 | 26.0 | 61.0 | 2.8 | 0.72 | 0.15 | 1.30 |
| 27 | 2.40 | 1 | 1 | 3.0 | 3.0 | 290.0 | 45.0 | 22.0 | 24.8 | 2.0 | 0.29 | 2.90 | 3.30 |
| 28 | 0.54 | 1 | 1 | 2.0 | 2.0 | 600.0 | 200.0 | 29.0 | 33.8 | 7.6 | 0.72 | 0.78 | 11.20 |
| 29 | 0.60 | 1 | 1 | 2.5 | 0.1 | 1,305.0 | 365.0 | 16.0 | 124.0 | 16.6 | 0.38 | 0.37 | 0.40 |
| 30 | 0.40 | 1 | 1 | 2.5 | 2.5 | 1,320.0 | 84.0 | 63.0 | 18.8 | 6.4 | 4.28 | 13.20 | 3.20 |
| 31 | 14.00 | 2 | 1 | 2.5 | 2.5 | 410.0 | 33.0 | 11.0 | 8.6 | 3.9 | 0.09 | 1.50 | 0.04 |
| 32 | 200.00 | 2 | 1 | 3.0 | 3.0 | 370.0 | 66.0 | 28.0 | 18.0 | 2.7 | 0.05 | 1.33 | 1.70 |
| 33 | 8.50 | 2 | 1 | 2.5 | 1.5 | 155.0 | 35.0 | 13.0 | 6.8 | 3.2 | 0.24 | 1.05 | 0.50 |
| 34 | 340.00 | 3 | 2 | 20.0 | 2.5 | 38,700.0 | 13,000.0 | 22.0 | 1,190.0 | 470.0 | 8.28 | 3.90 | 4.90 |

[a] 1 = temporary or seasonal; 2 = semipermanent with fluctuating water levels; 3 = permanent and stable.
[b] 1 = <2 meters; 2 = 2–6 meters; 3 = >6 meters.

Appendix Table 5. (cont'd)
II. Copepod Distribution and Relative Abundance

(percent)

| Lake | 1 *Epischura nevadensis* | 2 *Diaptomus sicilis* | 3 *Diaptomus sanguineus* | 4 *Diaptomus ashlandi* | 5 *Diaptomus novar-mexicanus* | 6 *Diaptomus shoshone* | 7 *Diaptomus leptopus* | 8 *Cyclops bicuspidatus* | 9 *Cyclops vernalis* | 10 *Cyclops varicans* | 11 *Eucyclops agilis* | 12 *Tropo-cyclops prosinus* | 13 *Macro-cyclops albidus* |
|---|---|---|---|---|---|---|---|---|---|---|---|---|---|
| 1 | 37.0 | | | 100.0 | | | | | | | | | |
| 2 | 0.4 | | | 32.0 | | | | 30.0 | | | 0.6 | | |
| 3 | 1.0 | | | 44.0 | | | | 56.0 | | | 1.0 | | |
| 4 | | | | 41.0 | | | | 58.0 | | | 12.0 | | |
| 5 | | | | | | | | 88.0 | | | | | |
| 6 | | | | | | | | 100.0 | | | | | |
| 7 | | 28.0 | | | 1.0 | | | 71.0 | | | 0.1 | | |
| 8 | | 10.0 | | | 9.0 | | | 81.0 | | | | | |
| 9 | | | | | 21.0 | | | 79.0 | | | | | |
| 10 | | | | | 34.0 | | | 66.0 | | | 0.3 | | |
| 11 | | 91.0 | | | | | | 9.0 | | | | | |
| 12 | | 98.0 | | | | | | 2.0 | | | | | |
| 13 | | 98.0 | | | | | | 1.0 | 1.0 | | | | |
| 14 | | 98.0 | | | | | | 0.1 | | | | | 1.0 |
| 15 | | 99.0 | | | | | | 0.1 | | 0.4 | | | |
| 16 | | 100.0 | | | | | | | | | | | |
| 17 | | 100.0 | | | | | | | | | | | |
| 18 | | 100.0 | | | | | | | 3.0 | | | | |
| 19 | | 97.0 | | | | | | 3.0 | | | | | |
| 20 | | 87.0 | | | | | | 13.0 | | | | | |
| 21 | | | | | | | 65.0 | 20.0 | | | 100.0 | | 15.0 |
| 22 | | | | | | | | | | | 100.0 | | |
| 23 | | | | | | | | | | | | | |
| 24 | | | | | | | 18.0 | 27.0 | | | 46.0 | | 9.0 |
| 25 | | | | | | | | 100.0 | | | | | |
| 26 | | | 100.0 | | | | | | | | | | |
| 27 | | | 91.0 | | | | | 6.0 | | | 3.0 | | |
| 28 | | | 97.0 | | | 3.0 | | | | | | | |
| 29 | | | 94.0 | | | | | 6.0 | | | | | |
| 30 | | 69.0 | | | | 19.0 | | 12.0 | | | | | |
| 31 | | | 75.0 | | | | | 5.0 | | 8.0 | | | 12.0 |
| 32 | | 25.0 | | | | | | 15.0 | | 39.0 | 10.0 | | 11.0 |
| 33 | | | | | | | | 1.0 | | | | 99.0 | |
| 34 | | | | | | | | | | | | | |

LITERATURE CITED

Anderson, T. W. 1958. *An Introduction to Multivariate Statistical Analysis*. New York: Wiley.

Berg, C. O. 1963. Middle Atlantic states. In *Limnology of North America*, ed. D. G. Frey, pp. 191–237. Madison: University of Wisconsin Press.

Bormann, F. H. 1966. The need for a federal system of natural areas for scientific research. *BioScience* 16:585–86.

Bradley, W. H. 1963. Paleolimnology. In *Limnology of North America*, ed. D. G. Frey, pp. 621–52. Madison: University of Wisconsin Press.

Brezonik, P. L.; Morgan, W. H.; Shannon, E. E.; and Putnam, H. D. 1969. Eutrophication factors in north central Florida lakes. *Engineering Progress at the University of Florida* 23(8):1–101.

Brooks, J. L. 1957. The systematics of North American *Daphnia*. *Memoirs of the Connecticut Academy of Arts and Sciences* (New Haven) 13:1–180.

———, and Dodson, S. I. 1965. Predation, body size, and composition of plankton. *Science* 150:28–35.

Brown, D. C. 1969. Grouping plankton samples by numerical analysis. *Hydrobiologia* 33:289–301.

Clements, F. E., and Shelford, V. E. 1939. *Bio-Ecology*. New York: Wiley.

Cole, A. J. 1969. *Numerical Taxonomy*. New York: Academic Press.

Cushing, C. E. 1963. Filter feeding insect distribution and planktonic food in the Montreal River. *Transactions of the American Fisheries Society* 92:216–19.

Drouet, F. 1968. Revision of the classification of the *Oscillatoriaceae*. Academy of Natural Sciences of Philadelphia, Monograph 15.

Elster, H. J. 1958. Das limnologische Seetypensystem, Rückblick und Ausblick. *Verhandlungen der Internationalen Vereinigung für theoretische und angewandte Limnologie* (Stuttgart) 13:101–20.

Findenegg, I. 1964. Types of planktic primary production in lakes of the eastern Alps as found by the radioactive carbon method. *Verhandlungen der Internationalen Vereinigung für theoretische und angewandte Limnologie* (Stuttgart) 15:352–59.

Forbes, S. A. 1925. The lake as a microcosm. *Bulletin of the Illinois Laboratory of Natural History* (Urbana) 8:537–50.

Frey, D. G. (ed.) 1963. *Limnology of North America*. Madison: University of Wisconsin Press.

Gerking, S. D. 1963. Central states. In *Limnology of North America*, ed. D. G. Frey, pp. 239–68. Madison: University of Wisconsin Press.

Gilmour, J. S. L., and Walters, S. M. 1964. Philosophy and classification. *Vistas in Botany*, ed. W. B. Turrill, 4:1–22.

Goldman, C. R.; Gerletti, M.; Javornicky, P.; Melchiorri-Santolini, V.; and de Amezaga, E. 1968. Primary productivity, bacteria, phyto- and zooplankton in Lake Maggiore: Correlations and relationships with ecological factors. *Memoria dell'Istituto di Idrobiologia* (Pallanza, Italy) 23:49–127.

Gower, J. C. 1966. Some distance properties of latent root and vector methods used in multivariate analysis. *Biometrika* 53:325–38.

———. 1967. A comparison of some methods of cluster analysis. *Biometrics* 23:623–37.

Green, R. H., and Hobson, K. D. 1970. Spatial and temporal structure in a temperate intertidal community with special emphasis on *Gemma gemma* (Pelecypoda: Mollusca). *Ecology* 51:999–1011.

Hall, D. J.; Cooper, W. E.; and Werner, E. T. 1970. An experimental approach to the production dynamics and structure of freshwater animal communities. *Limnology and Oceanography* 15:839–928.

Hutchinson, G. E. 1957. A treatise on limnology. Volume 1. *Geography, Physics and Chemistry.* New York: Wiley.

———. 1967. A treatise on limnology. Volume 2. *Introduction to Lake Biology and the Limnoplankton.* New York: Wiley.

Illies, J., and Botosaneanu, L. 1963. Problèmes et méthodes de la classification et de la zonation écologique des eaux courantes considérées surtout du point de vue faunistique. *Mitteilungen der Internationalen Vereinigung für theoretische und angewandte Limnologie* (Stuttgart) 12:1–57.

Jarnefelt, H. 1956. Zur Limnologie einiger Gewässer Finnlands. XVI. Mit besonderer Berücksichtigung des Planktons. *Annals Zoological Society of Vanamo* (Finland) 17, 201 pp.

———. 1958. On the typology of northern lakes. *Verhandlungen der Internationalen Vereinigung für theoretische und angewandte Limnologie* (Stuttgart) 13:228–35.

Johnson, W. E., and Vallentyne, J. R. 1971. Rationale, background, and development of experimental lake studies in northwestern Ontario. *Journal of the Fisheries Research Board of Canada* (Ottawa) 28:123–28.

Kahn, A. E. 1966. The tyranny of small decisions: Market failures, imperfections and the limits of economics. *Kyklos* 19(1):23–47.

Kuehne, R. A. 1962. A classification of streams illustrated by fish distribution in an eastern Kentucky creek. *Ecology* 43:608–14.

Lance, G. N., and Williams, W. T. 1967. A general theory of classificatory sorting strategies. 1. Hierarchical systems. *Computer Journal* 9:373–80.

Larkin, P. A., and Northcote, T. G. 1958. Factors in lake typology in British Columbia. *Verhandlungen der Internationalen Vereinigung für theoretische und angewandte Limnologie* (Stuttgart) 13:252–63.

Leopold, L. B., and Marchand, M. O. 1968. On the quantitative inventory of the riverscape. *Water Resources Research* 4:709–17.

Macan, T. T. 1950. Ecology of freshwater mollusca in the English Lake District. *Journal of Animal Ecology* (U.K.) 19:124–46.

———. 1963. *Freshwater Ecology.* New York: Wiley.

McIntosh, R. P. 1967. An index of diversity and the relation of certain concepts to diversity. *Ecology* 48:392–404.

Mackereth, F. J. H.; Lund, J. W. G.; and Macan, T. T. 1957. Chemical analysis in ecology illustrated from Lake District tarns and lakes. *Proceedings of the Linnean Society of London* (U.K.) 167:159–75.

Margalef, R. 1958. "Trophic" typology versus biotic typology, as exemplified in the regional limnology of northern Spain. *Verhandlungen der Internationalen Vereinigung für theoretische und angewandte Limnologie* (Stuttgart) 13:339–49.

———. 1968. *Perspectives in Ecological Theory.* Illinois: University of Chicago Press.

Narver, D. W. 1967. Primary production in two small lakes of the northern interior plateau of British Columbia. *Journal of the Fisheries Research Board of Canada* (Ottawa) 24:2189–93.

Newell, A. E. 1960. Biological survey of the lakes and ponds in Coos, Grafton and Carroll Counties. New Hampshire Fish and Game Department, Survey Report No. 8a:1–297.

———. 1963. Biological survey of the lakes and ponds in Sullivan, Merrimack, Belknap and Strafford Counties. New Hampshire Fish and Game Department, Survey Report No. 8b:1–276.

Pennak, R. W. 1958. Regional lake typology in northern Colorado, U.S.A. *Verhandlungen der Internationalen Vereinigung für theoretische und angewandte Limnologie* (Stuttgart) 13:264–83.

Peterken, G. F. 1958. International selection of areas for reserves. *Biological Conservation* 1:55–61.

Pfister, R. M. 1967. A microbiological contribution to a systems approach to water quality in Lake Erie and other bodies of water. In *Systems Approach to Water Quality in the Great Lakes.* Proceedings of the Third Annual Symposium on Water Resources Research of the Ohio State University Water Resources Center, September 1967.

Pielou, E. C. 1969. *An Introduction to Mathematical Ecology.* New York: Wiley-Interscience.

Price, J. L. 1958. Cryptic speciation in the vernalis group of cyclopididae. *Canadian Journal of Zoology* (Ottawa) 36:285–303.

Rawson, D. S., and Moore, J. E. 1944. The saline lakes of Saskatchewan. *Canadian Journal of Research* (Ottawa) D 22:141–201.

Reimers, N.; Maciolek, J. A.; and Pister, E. P. 1955. Limnological study of the lakes in Convict Creek Basin, Mono County, California. U.S. Fish and Wildlife Service, *Fisheries Bulletin* 56:437–503.

Rodhe, W. 1958. Primärproduktion und Seetypen. *Verhandlungen der Internationalen Vereinigung für theoretische und angewandte Limnologie* (Stuttgart) 13:121–41.

Round, F. E. 1958. Algal aspects of lake typology. *Verhandlungen der Internationalen Vereinigung für theoretische und angewandte Limnologie* (Stuttgart) 13:306–10.

Seal, H. L. 1964. *Multivariate statistical analysis for biologists.* London: Methuen.

Sheldon, A. L. 1970. Streams for research. In *Proceedings of the 19th Southern Water Resources and Pollution Control Conference*, Durham, N.C.: Department of Civil Engineering, Duke University, pp. 127–31.

Sokal, R. R., and Crovello, T. J. 1970. The biological species concept: A critical evaluation. *American Naturalist* 104:127–53.

———, and Sneath, P. H. 1963. *Principles of Numerical Taxonomy.* San Francisco: Freeman.

Sparrow, R. A. H. 1966. Comparative limnology of lakes in the southern Rocky Mountain Trench, British Columbia. *Journal of the Fisheries Research Board of Canada* 23:1875–95.

Thunmark, S. 1945. Zur Soziologie des Süsswasser-planktons. Eine methodo-logischökologische Studie. *Folia Limnologica Scandinavica* (Sweden and Denmark) 3:1–66.

Vallentyne, J. R. 1969. Experimental lakes in Northwest Ontario. *Biological Conservation* 1:257–58.

Webb, L. J.; Tracey, J. G.; Williams, W. T.; and Lance, G. N. 1967. Studies in the numerical analysis of complex rain-forest communities. I. A comparison of methods applicable to site/species data. *Journal of Ecology* (U.K.) 55:171–91.

Whittaker, R. H. 1962. Classification of natural communities. *Botanical Review* 28:1–239.

———, and Fairbanks, C. W. 1958. A study of the plankton copepod communities in the Columbia Basin, southeastern Washington. *Ecology* 39:46–65.

Williams, W. T. 1967. The computer botanist. *Australian Journal of Science* (Sydney) 29:266–71.

———; Lance, G. N.; Webb, L. J.; Tracey, J. G.; and Dale, M. B. 1969. Studies in the numerical analysis of complex rain-forest communities. III. The analysis of successional data. *Journal of Ecology* (U.K.) 57:515–35.

———, and Lambert, J. M. 1959. Multivariate methods in plant ecology, I: Association-analysis in plant communities. *Journal of Ecology* (U.K.) 47:83–101.

# 8
## Aesthetic Dimensions of the Landscape

R. BURTON LITTON, JR.*

Mining, logging, and dam building, all accompanied by road construction, are some of the more conspicuous kinds of resource use activities. They share some common characteristics: they usually occur in wildlands; they have become most obvious in the recent past;[1] they can be executed at a fast rate; they change the way the landscape looks; they are subject to considerable public criticism.[2] The arena within which these activities may occur is especially concentrated in the western states. Excluding Alaska, a line from the Texas Panhandle to the boundary between Montana and North Dakota shears off eleven western states, and almost half of their total area (760 million acres) is in federal ownership, most of it subject to developmental change. In these same states, nearly one-fifth of their whole area is under U.S. Forest Service administration. This is the particular scene for this paper on the landscape— the visual resources. The National Forest lands present an enormous range of landscape available for research; their administration offers a promising opportunity for control of the visual environment. Yet concentrating on these wildlands in no way restricts the implications for better visual control in other lands, whether private or public.

This study is not biased against the needs to produce timber, to store water, to make electricity, or build roads. It is based on direct field

---

* Landscape architect, University of California, Berkeley.
[1] U.S. Forest Service, Wyoming Forest Study Team, *Forest Management in Wyoming* (Ogden, Utah: Intermountain Region, USFS, 1971), p. 4.
[2] Dale A. Burk, *The Clearcut Crisis* (Great Falls, Mont.: Jursnick Printing, 1970).

observation of what has been happening to the landscape—the scenic resource—during the last ten years. There is no doubt that the landscape of wildlands has been and is being visually degraded by effects of use that range in function from recreation,[3] to timber cutting.[4] What happens is that some of the integrity of the landscape as a continuum is disrupted and some of the variety it offers is lost. With loss of variety we become less able to provide for the varied expectations of users. We are adept at replacing quality with mediocrity.

As the landscape that can be seen deteriorates, there is also the equivalent of generalized reduction in environmental quality, especially for the sightseer and the recreationalist. Yet the fault is not wholly that of the resource manager or his staff. He is now being asked to be more sensitive about the landscape and to engage in a new kind of intensive management that seeks compatibility with the environment, both generally and visually.

Unfortunately, tangible means of responding to the landscape as a resource in its own right—hence to the esoteric area of aesthetics—has a long way to go. In this particular thrust calling for better relationships between resource use and the native landscape, management does need assistance. This study attempts to provide some of that assistance. It starts with ways of recognizing and evaluating the landscape as something that is seen as a visual experience and that can be instrumental in guiding a better fit for resource use activities.

Beginning with the mid-1960s, a number of political responses indicate reaction to generalized concern for quality of the environment issues. Some of these have been the 1965 White House Conference on Natural Beauty[5] with its attendant Citizens' Council, the Highway Beautification Act, the 1969 President's Council on Environmental Quality, and the National Environmental Policy Act of 1969. Various states have held somewhat similar conferences and have established councils or commissions. The number of environmentally oriented legislative bills has grown prodigiously, especially since such crises as the Santa Barbara oil spill. Increases, real or proposed, in the expenditure of federal and state funds also indicate the strength of a growing conviction that better environments for recreation and habitation need to be created or protected.

At another level, there is the pressure exerted by private individuals

[3] Robert Cahn, "Will Success Spoil the National Parks?" *Christian Science Monitor* (May–June 1968).

[4] Raymond F. Dasmann, *The Destruction of California* (Macmillan, 1965).

[5] White House Conference on Natural Beauty, *Beauty for America, Proceedings* (U.S. Government Printing Office, 1965).

and conservation groups who are keenly aware and assertive about specific acts and projects affecting the landscape. The list is long and includes situations in practically every part of the country: Hells Canyon, Storm King, Bitterroot Forest, White Cloud Peaks, Mineral King, the Wyoming Forests, to name only a few.

In all these expressions of concern, the visible landscape plays a key role. Not infrequently, the impacts on the environment that are perceived trigger the first critical responses, to be followed by a search for other, less conspicuous effects.[6] Critics' actions may range from physical confrontations to well-documented demands for managerial improvement, including greater sensitivity to a full range of outdoor resources and the installation of better controls. Yet all the while the notion of a landscape as a special kind of visual composition that creates an environment seldom emerges with clarity. Nor is the landscape necessarily protected from visual deterioration even if all remedies for pollution were to be successful overnight.

Neither extractive industries in particular nor resource management efforts in general have given much recognition to the visual modifications in the landscape that are the outcome of their actions or decisions. However, the demands that they consider such effects are of recent origin, and techniques for their response have been less than coherent. Yet there is evidence that visual end-products could have been more accurately predicted and that alternative choices might have offered results more compatible with aesthetics. Certain terms familiar in land management can suggest some of the goals that might be valid when we treat the landscape as a visual resource.

*Preservation* may be as clear as any managerial goal, but it is dynamic and several possibilities are indicated. It can mean encouraging the normal changes associated with ecological succession, or it can mean the preservation of a selected stage of succession such as that of the California coast redwoods—a goal that is strongly influenced by a dominant visual theme.[7]

*Protection* and *maintenance* are objectives which will allow compatible alterations in the landscape. These goals can be met with several levels in intensity of change. Alterations may be kept small in scale or there may be careful and complete design solutions for larger alterations that will conform to the major structure of the landscape. But to accomplish this kind of protection requires that the landscape framework be recognized in the beginning.

[6] Orris C. Herfindahl and Allen V. Kneese, *Quality of the Environment* (Resources for the Future, 1965).

[7] Edward C. Stone, "Preserving Vegetation in Parks and Wilderness," *Science*, vol. 150, no. 3701 (1965), pp. 1263–64.

*Enhancement* is a favorite word for justifying changes in the outdoors, but it should logically apply only to those man-made modifications that offer relief from a monotonous or deteriorating landscape. *Degradation* is no managerial objective, but it should be recognized as the easiest thing to accomplish by making changes; it needs to be countered by a goal of *rehabilitation*. *Restoration* is a another possibility, suggesting a comprehensive and difficult goal of replacing the whole set of relationships that made up some landscape of the past. It would also be possible to *remodel* a landscape that had been destroyed, not necessarily to resemble some earlier state but to bring about something new and stabilized—ready to start again on a cycle of change.

. The accomplishment of these managerial objectives could be served in part by using the existent landscape as a visual display against which impacts could be gauged and predicted. But the landscape is nothing if not complicated and at times seems inscrutable. What is needed is a concept that characterizes the landscape in terms concrete enough to be instrumental in helping to fix resource management goals and resulting end-products. Recognition of the characteristics of the visual landscape is a basic concept in this study. From such a beginning, incomplete though it may be, it is assumed that constraints and alternatives in development can be explored before choices are made. In this way there is an opportunity to avoid those visible mistakes that are unanticipated and degrading—those that the land manager is forced to live with but would wish to avoid in the future.

### ATTRIBUTES OF THE LANDSCAPE

Using design[8] as a field of knowledge and drawing specifically upon the discipline of landscape architecture, it has been my research endeavor to give definition to certain characteristics found in the landscape. The approach has been to set hypotheses, making use of extensive field observations, most of which have been in National Forest lands of the western states. In discovering what appear to be generalized attributes of the landscape, I divide and call them *factors of recognition* and *compositional types*. Six of each are identified. Primary recognition factors are form, space, and time variability; these exist essentially beyond the capacity of the observer to change them, yet it has been shown that they can be degraded. Secondary recognition factors are observer position, distance, and sequence; they describe relationships between observer and the landscape and are subject to certain manipulations. From these means of recognition and their combination, it becomes possible to identify com-

[8] "Design," as a term used in this study, implies arrangement that is both functionally adequate and aesthetically pleasing as a visual composition.

positions and to suggest classification types. The six landscape types or compositional units consist of: (1) panoramic landscape, (2) feature landscape, (3) enclosed landscape, (4) focal landscape, (5) forest (canopied) landscape, and (6) detail landscape.

Making use of these factors and landscape types, it should theoretically be possible for resource management people to come to some agreement about what landscape resources consist of, to document and evaluate scenic resources in a more rational way, and to respond more sensitively to the landscape in general. But the real substance of this study goes beyond hypothetical identification of recognition factors and landscape types. Is our representation of designers' concepts highly personalized despite the background of a particular field of knowledge? Or have we something more universal, capable of objective use for appraisal and evaluation of the landscape? We are looking for a system of landscape identification and description that enjoys common reliability across a broad range of different participants.

Kenneth H. Craik, associate professor of psychology and associate research psychologist in the Institute of Personality Assessment and Research at the University of California, Berkeley, has developed a test set of landscape dimensions based upon the factors and types. With the aid of panels of observers, he has examined the objective validity or invalidity of the dimensions—hence has examined the hypotheses that lie behind them. Photo-color transparencies of wildland scenes were used to suggest the landscape. Results of that testing are contained in "Appraising the Objectivity of Landscape Dimensions," a companion paper to mine, which appears later in this volume. Craik concludes that for most of the dimensions tested there does exist a basis in objective reality.

So far as I know, this interdisciplinary research linkage between landscape architecture and psychology, represented by our collaboration, has had no precedent. What people as individuals see in their environment has produced a vast number of assumptions to which neither his nor my study will add. The entire emphasis here is on the question of objectivity concerning visual dimensions of the landscape, not on the matter of "like-dislike" preferences, nor, at this point, on other matters dealing with human responsiveness to landscape. Craik's dimensions are of greatest use as tools that will help in the study of preferences and behavioral or attitudinal response for research yet to be undertaken.

RECOGNITION FACTORS

A set of recognition factors can lay a common foundation so that the landscape may be seen as a visual composition, with physical dimensions, and as containing positive aesthetic qualities. I have already identified primary recognition factors as consisting of form, space, and time variability.

Secondary recognition factors—observer position, distance, and sequence—share a common range of change based upon the actions of the human observer as his relationship to surroundings is altered. An observer's position, his distance from a feature, or the sequential pattern of his travel may be influential forces in giving him either a vivid or a dull impression of the landscape. Because these factors are subject to manipulation by design and represent ways of establishing better rapport between sightseer and landscape, it is, perhaps, misleading to refer to them as secondary factors. Both primary and secondary groups of recognition factors reinforce one another and offer us greater choice in how we wish to approach aesthetic analysis of the landscape. We can start with an examination of what is present, and consider the relationships that can be discovered between user and landscape.

Together, form and space are the two overriding factors that help describe the structure of landscape within the confines of visual composition. General modes of design organization involving space and form include three other basics: lines, surfaces, and color. Lines and surfaces have direction and attitude; surfaces are further distinguished by color and texture. Color is expressed by its own special qualities, such as hue and value. In short order, it is apparent that an infinite number of relationships are possible and normal. With this in mind, it is only a convenient simplification to talk about individual or isolated characteristics. Nothing we see, particularly in the landscape, is simple or disconnected, and no time need be wasted in looking for absolute design rules or guides.[9] So it is for convenience and as a short cut to understanding that the somewhat pragmatic discussions follow; I do not intend them to be dogmatic even if their brevity suggests it.

*Form*

Form in the landscape is defined here as it relates particularly to the convex elements of land form—ranges, mountains, mesas, hills. At larger scale, these are positive and upright parts of the physiographic base, with form defined primarily as solid volumes or masses. At smaller scale, the idea is extended to include the volume of plants, whether that of individual trees or, especially, that collective volume of the forest. More accurately, forest volumes are semisolids, and their form-giving characteristics are most apparent at the outside edge seen in elevation.

[9] Gyorgy Kepes, *Language of Vision* (Chicago: Paul Theobald Co., 1944).

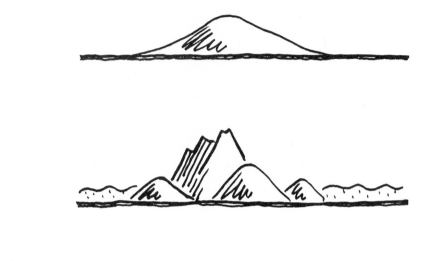

*Figure 8.1.* Diagrams showing the characteristics of isolation, scale, silhouette, and surface variance.

This concept of form as a positive thing can also be thought of as the counterpart of space being a negative thing.[10] Space is identified with concave physiographic elements—basins, valleys, canyons, swales. In this sense the two are apt to be interdependent, but some kind of contrast must be present if either form or space is to be obvious and compositionally lucid. Dominating contrasts giving distinction are isolation, relative size or scale, contour distinction or silhouette, and surface variance (Figure 8.1). These are some of the ways in which aesthetic quality may be perceived. (Also, see the section on aesthetic criteria, which appears later in this paper.)

*Isolation* gives prominence through simple separation from surround-

---

[10] Henry V. Hubbard and Theodora Kimball, *An Introduction to the Study of Landscape Design* (Macmillan, 1917).

ings. An unusual land form set by itself has extraordinary visual distinction, but even an ordinary single form, such as a rock or tree ("Lone Pine"), will seemingly gain in stature as it becomes a positive thing against a neutral ground. In its simplicity, isolation is powerful and clear.

*Dominance by relative size* is probably more often encountered than is simple isolation. It is rather more subtle because judgment as to degree of difference is involved. On a grand scale, the volcanic cones of the Middle Cascade Range are examples: Mt. Hood or Mt. Rainier. While these mountain forms also have other means of significant visual expression, they do dominate by their sheer mass. This sense of immensity applies as well to a mountain range. On a more modest scale, as commonplace a name as "Big Rock" indicates that discrimination is made because of size comparison. *Scale* (the attribute of related and sensed sizes of elements) is ultimately sensed as a relationship to the human figure.[11] Visual clues are important to relate one thing to another; for example, trees of a familiar size range can be helpful to us in gauging the scale of a hill or mountain. The Grand Canyon imparts to us a sense of grandeur in part because of our difficulty in sensing its size and unusual scale.

*Contour distinction* is apt to be most significant where the edge of a solid is played against the fluid color of the sky. Marked irregularity or change from some expected outline is the contrast that marks this skyline or silhouette characteristic. Its source may often be some geological anomaly. Skyline edge is not the only place where this condition can be expected or observed. Strong edge contrasts can also emerge from spatial separation (distance between edges) or change of material (earth and water, grassland and forest). Another kind of contour distinction can emerge from the repetition of similar land forms. This has a strength of its own that builds upon geological conformity rather than anomaly.

*Surface variance* is an overlay modification of both form and spatial units. It is particularly expressed in an overview as two-dimensional shapes, patterns or textures based upon the vegetative skin of the terrain and upon differences of soil or mineralization. Such terms as shape, pattern, and texture need some definitive clarification: shape is concerned with singular areas, texture involves simple repetition, and pattern is a complex fabric made up of shapes, textures, surfaces, and lines.

For distinction, surface variance will come from contrasting edges and areas with definite differences. These differences may involve color or textural changes, such as barren rock faces against grass cover or conifer forest.

---

[11] Heath Licklider, *Architectural Scale* (New York: Braziller, 1965).

*Space*

Space in the landscape is that spatial definition made up of concave elements of land form—basins, valleys, canyons, swales. These may be called the negative parts of the physiographic base and can be thought of as voids; at a smaller scale Simonds calls them "site volumes."[12] Their definition is made by the faces of land form, by vegetation, or by a combination of the two. The two basic parts of outdoor space may also be compared in principle to the floor and walls of architectural space. There is always some interdependence between space and form with an infinite number of dominate-subordinate relationships possible between them.

Spatial distinction comes in part from the elements of contrast previously discussed. Additionally, space is further modified by four factors: proportions (floor and walls), constitution (floor and walls), configuration, and scale or relative size.

Proportions stated as limits of enclosure can be set in this way: the lesser the floor extent and the higher the walls, the greater the spatial definition; the greater the floor extent and the lower the walls, the lesser the spatial definition. Muir commented that he saw Yosemite Valley as a great hall.[13] Examining it, we find a cross section with a floor-wall proportion of about $1:1\frac{1}{2}$. This may seem to be a sterile observation, but it indicates a condition of awesome enclosure. Other more usual kinds of valley definitions may be visualized for comparison. As the distance between walls is increased, the sense of space enclosed also begins to break down. Eventually the confinement of two sides gives way to that of the closer side only, making one-sided space (see Figure 8.2).

*Constitution*—the materials that make up floor and walls, their slope and degree of continuity—also contributes to the degree of spatial definition and to quality. Sheer rock walls are more powerful, more impressive than sloping, wooded faces. Discontinuities in walls and floors alike give particular direction and compel attention. Water, forming either the plane of a lake or the visual tension line of a stream, can become the dominating characteristic of the floor, especially rich since it is normally accompanied by changes of vegetation.

*Configuration* of space is concerned with horizontal shape or the nature of its "floor plan." Perception of it is concentrated visually about the junction between floor and walls. Should the meeting of the two be sharp, through marked change of material or slope, then the definition will be correspondingly sharp. Simplicity of configuration, such as a small oval meadow, is clear and easily recognized. It can yield to the senses a degree

[12] John O. Simonds, *Landscape Architecture* (New York: F. W. Dodge Corp., 1961).
[13] John Muir, *The Mountains of California* (Doubleday, 1961).

of strength, but a more complex figure, which unfolds its variety through a series of subspaces, is apt to arouse greater sustained interest. Time is necessary to unravel the more intricate space.

Scale and relative size have already been briefly mentioned as they

Yosemite Valley Section, 1:1½ floor-wall proportions

Luray, Va. Section, 15:1 floor-wall proportions

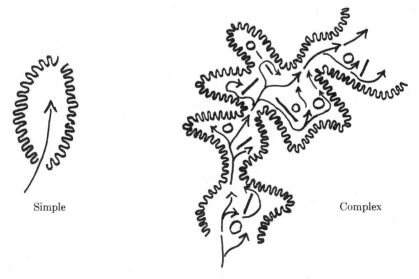

Simple                                                                    Complex

*Figure 8.2.* Spaces indicating proportions and plan configurations.

apply to form, but the boundaries of space become a special limitation within which scale can be most readily appreciated. While scale is apt to be abstract in the outdoors, spatial enclosure at least restricts the extent of an area, organizes it, and seemingly reduces the number of elements that compete for attention. Visual clues again come into play as familiar objects suggest a comparison based upon sizes. Results of that comparison will have an influence as to whether we find a space dramatic or merely usual to our experience.

*Time Variability*

Time variability is the term chosen to represent the primary factor of short-term change. It is the effect of natural phenomena occurring at a given point in time, producing a visual product that is characteristic of that moment. The observer is essentially a captive of those conditions that occur as he finds them. It is major source of variation, both enrichment and dearth, acting upon form and space.

This is a broad factor which includes (1) light and color, and (2) ephemeral influences related to meteorological and diverse other conditions. These occur regardless of any movement on the part of the observer although it is true that his choice of advantageous locations and orientations can influence his ability to see certain of these time-linked effects. Only short intervals are considered—those that are seasonal, diurnal, or momentary. It sets aside the long-term perspective of the forester or the geologist. This conforms to the here and now for the sightseer. Fleeting images gathered by the wildlands visitor in the course of a brief stay must be considered to create lasting impressions, good or bad.

*Light* we take for granted and do not usually spend time thinking of the relationship between sunlight and our fundamental capacity to see. Apart from uncontrolled modification, such as smog, we have not the ability to modify natural light in the landscape, but it is important to recognize the profound effects and changes that occur during the day or season. Constructive responses, such as advantageous locations and orientations for viewing stations, can be made in planning and design as light effects are recognized.

*Color* is the basic manifestation of light that is familiar in daily experience. In a simplified way, its compound characteristics are expressed by hue, concerning named properties, and value, concerning darkness or lightness.[14] Hue is the attribute of color which is said to be green or greenish, red or reddish, or any other color identified in the spectrum. Pure colors are rare in the landscape except as they are represented in the

[14] Rudolf Arnheim, *Art and Visual Perception* (University of California Press, 1954).

rainbow. We are apt to be impressed by the striking and saturated hues of spring chartreuse or autumn yellows. Normal colors for the landscape during other times of the year are more somber, more gray, thus less impressive. Color value is the resemblance of a tonal quality that can be compared to white, some shade of gray, or black. In general impressions of the landscape, value contrasts are likely to be important means through which something is made conspicuous. Conversely, two elements of similar value, even though of different hues, will not be so readily seen. Some of the more conspicuous value differences are sky and earth elements seen together, grassland and forest, or disturbed earth seen against undisturbed earth.

*Directions* of light, indicating how light strikes the surface of objects, are usually described as front, side, or back lighting.[15] In the landscape, particular lighting conditions tend to be related to time of day; but they are also the modifications obtained through changes in the observer's orientation, different directional relationships between earth surfaces and sun, and the varied facings of land surfaces. North faces in the Northern Hemisphere, for example, tend to be obscured by shade and shadow—a characteristic of backlighting. This is in sharp contrast to the very different condition found among typically more fully lit south faces. Front lighting is obtained when the sun is directly behind the observer. He stands with his shadow ahead and sees a fully lit landscape. Shadows and shade tend to be at a minimum since they fall away on the off side. This produces apparent flatness, and three dimensional modeling is at a minimum. Good color distinction should be possible. Side lighting occurs when the sun is to one side or the other of the observer—for example, when the light direction is at a 90° angle to the line of sight. Sharp modeling will result from the combination of direct lighting and the definite shades and shadows. Three-dimensionality and a sense of depth should be most apparent. By itself, this one viewing condition is apt to give the most comprehensive sense of the landscape. Backlighting takes place when the sun is in front of the observer. Then surface details are obscured in shade and top or edges are rims of light. The effect is to reveal the main structure of form without detail distractions. It tends to hide a great deal, yet it can be dramatic.

High light intensity is not necessarily the most revealing. Strong shadows can obscure detail, while reflected light from highlighted surfaces can burn out nuances of shading. Lower light intensity or shadowless, overcast atmosphere can offer advantages in the capacity to see color.

*Ephemeral influences* are those diverse and transitory effects that defy

[15] M. Minnaert, *The Nature of Light and Color in the Open Air* (Dover Press, 1954).

cataloguing. Some of them are positively related to light but represent
somewhat more unusual phenomena; they could be described as "double
take" effects. As factors they are divided into four groupings: (1) meteorological conditions, (2) seasonal expectations, (3) projected and reflected images, and (4) animal occupancy and signs.

Meteorological conditions can be further broken down to include subdivisions such as cloud and fog formations, precipitation, light vagaries,
and wind motion. It is a mistake to assume that fog, for example, is an
unfortunate condition which detracts from the attractions of a landscape; rather, as fog drifts it can dramatize the landscape, imparting to
it emphasis and simplification. Clouds can be the most arresting elements of some landscapes; here, seasonal and regional effects should be
anticipated.

Seasonal expectations are most apt to suggest conspicuous changes in
vegetation, but they also include cyclic patterns involving typical regional weather and wildlife. Even fallen leaves at the ebb of autumn
mark a sight worth the seeing.

Projected and reflected images, while aspects of light, are secondary
images that reinforce the impact of the landscape. These are the shadows
projected on solid surfaces and the mirror reflections cast on water.
Although shadows command little attention, they are two-dimensional
expressions of objects or form seen in the round. Reflections do command
attention, abstracting from their subject and providing a softly darkened
commentary on the nature of their color and main lines of composition.[16]

Animal occupancy and signs are subtle kinds of landscape enrichment
that are chiefly enjoyed by walkers. Except for those with special knowledge, the experience of sighting wildlife is fleeting and the occurrence of
chance. The aesthetic appeal of animals has been well recognized, and
the relationship of animals to habitat suggests an interesting harmony
between aesthetics and ecology.[17] However, game management con-
tinues to emphasize production and harvest, placing little effort on the
"nonproductive" opportunities of simply observing birds and animals.
The term signs, as used here, is meant to encompass a wider and more
diverse group of indications than animal tracks alone. These can be symbolic and filled with implication.[18] Snake skins and bird feathers, ghost
trees and the dried stalks of dead annuals suggest such varied wonders
as visual jewels, abstract sculpture, or next year's life to come. In man-

[16] Henry D. Thoreau, *Walden* (New American Library of World Literature, 1960).
[17] A. Starker Leopold, "Quantitative and Qualitative Values in Wildlife Management," in *Natural Resources—Quality and Quantity* (University of California Press,
1967).
[18] Jiro Harada, *A Glimpse of Japanese Ideals* (Tokyo: Kokusai Bunka Shinkokai,
1937).

agement or inventory considerations, it is well to bear in mind that because of time variability even the most ordinary of landscapes can have momentary distinction.

## Secondary Recognition Factors

Secondary recognition factors—observer position, distance, and sequence—join the primary ones as different means, sometimes auxiliary means, of examining the landscape for analytical and managerial purposes. They stress the observer's relationships to surroundings.

*Observer position* is a term employed here to describe the observer's elevational relationship between himself and the landscape he sees. It is used to indicate if he is essentially below, essentially at the same level, or essentially above the visual objective. Three specific terms are used to be more precise: (1) observer inferior, (2) observer normal, and (3) observer superior. This is apart from orientation since it is assumed that a sightseer will gravitate to a directional line of sight that is tied to the compositional structure of the landscape, desirably a unified image.[19] The term has a number of advantages: it emphasizes the viewer, and it helps integrate distance with form and space. It can suggest, for example, a conscious choice of placing the viewer in a variety of different positions as, for example, when design of a scenic road or trail is contemplated. If you have ever moved along the rim of the Grand Canyon, always looking down or across, could you have failed to wonder what its space and qualities might be like when seen from the river bottom?

Observer inferior position can be described as being at the "bottom" of the landscape. Literally, this may be inaccurate because the standing observer will always find some part of his surroundings below eye level. But categories of position cannot have absolute limitations, and it is a normal visual consistency that more distant objects are seen higher in the field of vision. This position is most restrictive with respect to screening and the emphasis of spatial enclosure. (Landscapes of open plains or expansive water planes—boundless circumstances—are exceptions to this.) It tends to draw attention to the facades of surrounding walls. There is a likelihood of shortened viewing distances while in this position.

Observer normal position occurs on a sidehill location, where a level line of sight can coincide roughly with the central mass or void of landscape beyond. Attention is expected to be concentrated on solids rather than voids.[20] The normal position is somewhat of a compromise between the higher and lower viewing stations—it may have typical effects of either. Moderate screening may be expected, as may intermediate view-

[19] Kurt Koffka, *Principles of Gestalt Psychology* (Harcourt Brace, 1935).
[20] Ibid.

ing distances. It can provide a reasonably good overview while still potentially able to provide a sense of boundary walls if they are present. It is apt to be a somewhat commonplace viewing relationship, satisfactory only if not overdone.

Observer superior position allows the viewer to look out above the landscape. Or at least he seems to be above his surroundings. The mountaintop station point is implied. There is an opportunity to see maximum distances and with minimum likelihood of screening or enclosure. Some quality of detachment, the characteristics of an airplane view, can occur. It is good for introduction and general orientation as to how elements in the landscape are disposed. Gross structure should be most clearly revealed. As an initiation to surroundings it is ideal.

*Distance*, like scale, is abstract until some comparison or measurement is made. It raises a basic question: What is the best distance from which to see a landscape? The answer must be: What do you expect to see if a place is named and a distance set? This needs to be structured with direct intention. In the example of planning for a scenic road, the objective should be the conscious assembly of a variety of viewing distances put together in an interesting sequence. Man-made alterations in the landscape and their different versions need to be understood from a distance before (or if) they are executed. Examination from a distance should constitute a test of possibilities, not just a rerun of what has happened or what can be seen.

Three conventional terms in painting—foreground, middleground, and background—can be helpful in describing distance relationships.[21] While these imply no specific ranges of distance, they can be used to suggest some related distances. Though arbitrary, these are based on field observations and comparisons in the National Forests of the western United States.

| | Near Boundary (in miles) | Far Boundary (in miles) |
|---|---|---|
| Foreground distance.......... | 0 | $\frac{1}{4}$–$\frac{1}{2}$ |
| Middleground distance........ | $\frac{1}{4}$–$\frac{1}{2}$ | 3–5 |
| Background distance.......... | 3–5 | ∞ |

These categories should have credence only as they represent an idea. They do have certain flexibility built in that can allow variations of

[21] Another system for determining distance relationships and supportive of the concepts given here is described in Hubert D. Burke, Glenn H. Lewis, and Howard R. Orr, "A Method for Classifying Scenery from a Roadway," reprinted from *Park Practice Program Guideline* (Washington: National Park Service and National Conference on State Parks, March 1968), pp. 125–41.

atmosphere or seasonal influences. Others could be developed for a particular region. The following discussion implies use of the distance zones given.

Foreground can be designated with clarity and simplicity not possible in middle and background because the observer is present—a direct participant. He can have the impressions of immediate details—bark pattern, boulder forms, or degraded parts. The motion of wind in trees or grass will be apparent. This is a zone of important linkage because it sets a tone of quality or its absence, and there is the tangible beginning of a sense of scale through touchable objects. Intensity of color and its value will be at a maximum level. This is to say that aerial perspective is undeveloped in the foreground, lacking the effect of color diminution due to atmospheric scattering of light rays. At greater distances, the intensification of aerial perspective becomes an important means of discrimination.

Middleground is critical for two reasons. This is where the parts of the landscape can be seen to join together, where hills become a range or trees make a forest. This is also where man-made changes may be revealed as sitting comfortably upon the landscape. Or where conflicts of form, color, shape, or scale show up. Aerial perspective should be distinctly developed within this intermediate distance. Colors will be unmistakable but they will be more blue, softer than those of the foreground. Some of the sharpness of value contrasts will be reduced.

Background distance effects are primarily those explained by aerial perspective. Surfaces of land forms will lose detail distinctions, emphasis will be on outline or edge. Color will be softly unreal and its actual identification will be in doubt. There is a total simplification, with background becoming an effective foil against which foreground or background is more clearly seen—a figure-ground relationship.[22] Silhouettes and ridges of one land mass against another are the conspicuous visual parts of the background. Their expression will be by simple planes with strong edges. And skyline as the function of solid against film color of the sky will be the strongest line of all.

*Sequence* is the factor of the observer's movement through the landscape, the order and timing applied to various visual and spatial experiences and effects.[23] It can be conceived of as the mixing together, in a fashioned order, of all the factors of recognition and the landscape types as well. This is the complicated but normal way in which the landscape—or a building—is seen bit by bit. We see it from a distance, from close up,

[22] James J. Gibson, *Perception of the Visual World* (Houghton Mifflin, 1950).
[23] Philip Thiel, "A Sequence Experience Notation for Architectural and Urban Spaces," *The Town Planning Review*, vol. 32, no. 1 (1961).

from above and below;[24] we go around it and through it; light gives way to darkness and clear sky gives way to clouds. We see it in movement and from static points. Memory and anticipation mix with the experience of the present. Because of its extraordinary level of complexity compared to other factors, it was not appraised in Craik's research.

Sequence is what we find as we set out across an area that allows choice of movement. Consider a road or trail again. Importantly, it can be manipulated or designed in a chosen way. Sequential handling should be considered as the ultimate end-product that gives a desirable and interesting experience to the user. Additionally, what a particular sequence consists of can be a measure of quality. A rich and varied series of experiential effects can be said to have a high interest index or a high density of richness. Either a monotonous landscape or an unimaginative routing displays a low richness index—a low density of interest.

## Landscape Compositional Types

The recognition factors that have been described may now be used as tools to define landscape compositional types. Certain kinds of natural landscapes do demonstrate strong visual coherence and appear to be found universally, this forming one basis for their being called types. Compositions are identified here as composed organizations displaying an integrated and balanced structure, such as those within a work of art or that are the product of design.[25] Six compositional types are identified and proposed: panoramic, feature, enclosed, focal, forest or canopied, and detail landscapes. Subtypes are also recognized, as are a host of variants. This, as any classification scheme, attempts to recognize and place together those combinations of elements dominated by common characteristics. Through establishment and recognition of landscape types, comparisons can more readily weigh likenesses or differences.

By designating landscape types as conspicuous and limited visual nodes, it should be noted that most of the undifferentiated continuum of the landscape is seemingly omitted from consideration. The landscape types, however, depend upon this continuum as the foil against which they are displayed (the figure-ground relationship again). The total landscape does consist of an extensive fabric enlivened by concentrated points of visual interest. One cannot exist satisfactorily without the other if aesthetic quality is to be found in the larger landscape.

*The panoramic landscape* is based on Webster's definition of panoramic: "an unobstructed or complete and comprehensive view of a region in

[24] Clarence King, *Mountaineering in the Sierra Nevada* (University of Nebraska Press, 1970). Note observations made in the 1860s in approaching Mt. Shasta.
[25] Herbert Read, *The Meaning of Art* (Baltimore: Penguin Books, 1959).

every direction." Standing upon the Great Plains comes to mind—a 360° void of space defined only by the level horizon line where base plane and line of sight intersect. Absence of enclosure is implied. Less abstractly, an angular limitation closer to 180°, a response to peripheral vision, seems more typical. Dominant line quality is that of horizontality. The panoramic landscape is expanding, reaching out without bounds. It is not a horizontal composition contained by screening edges nor is it one of restricted distances. It is a placid arrangement of great stability, a simple foil against which subordinate forms, edges, or minor enclosures at foreground or middleground distances are seen. The outside limits appear static while close-in elements appear to move in response to the traveling viewer.[26] Because the sky constitutes a major part of the total image area, cloud formations and atmospheric color changes can be dominating.

Three subdivisions are identified: panoramas of water bodies, plains, and ranges. Those of water bodies and plains are most nearly similar. The water-dominated type has a special interest zone which corresponds to the linear junction of water and shore. Two different characteristics are especially associated with the panoramic-range landscape: the observer position is high (observer superior) and marked aerial perspective is common.

*A feature landscape* (or feature-dominated landscape) is one in which a single thing or a cohesive set of related elements dominates their surroundings. Those convex elements of land form, especially considered in the discussion of form, are one key to this type, but tree forms and vivid expressions of water are also included. Features, the heart of feature landscapes, are easy to identify as concrete and specific things which have distinction. The attributes of contrast apply: isolation, conspicuous size, distinct silhouette, and obvious surface pattern. Attention to rather ordinary place names suggests qualities and characteristics that stand out with respect to surroundings: Black Mountain, Great Falls, Big Pine, or Cedar Grove are examples.

As the names of the places above suggest, three kinds of feature landscapes can be identified: those dominated by land form, by water expression, and by tree form or collectively grouped (grove) tree forms. There is a general hierarchy in the three subclasses. Land forms, because of their three-dimensionality and tendency to be the largest sized components of their environment, are apt to assume visual superiority.[27]

[26] Donald Appleyard, Kevin Lynch, and John R. Myer, *The View From the Road* (M.I.T. Press, 1964).

[27] Research Planning and Design Associates, Inc., *Study of Visual and Cultural Environment*, North American Regional Water Resources Study, preliminary issue (Amherst, Mass., 1967).

Water body features show subservience to land form but yet are in contrast to earth surface. They appear often as two-dimensional shapes, but assert themselves through motion, color, and light reflection.[28] Plant form features are most limited by subtlety, sheer size potentials, and probable subordination to both land form and water. Old growth hardwood coves of the Blue Ridge or the Mariposa Redwood Grove of the Sierra Nevada suggest two divergent samples, each with its own strong and distinct design quality.

*The enclosed landscape* is marked by its concavity, becoming an integrated unit because of basin-like containment of floor by surrounding walls. Space or spatial definition is to the enclosed landscape what individual projecting forms and dominating elements are to the feature landscape. But the presence of spatial definition, using the recognition factors concerned with space, is not precisely the same in an enclosed landscape. Indistinction because of relatively low walls, relatively broad floors, or both gives weakest expression to this particular landscape type. Even though enclosed landscapes tend to be more passive compositions than do feature landscapes, the more vivid examples indicate higher quality and easier recognition.[29] Two words, "canyon" and "swale," suggest a visual comparison between powerful and weak expressions of the type.

Three subclasses are distinguished, depending upon the nature of the enclosing elements: (1) slope-face enclosure, (2) cliff-face enclosure, and (3) vegetation-face enclosure. Although the vertical face is used as the primary means of differentiation, the floor with its variations will also aid discrimination. Floor classes (elongated, circular, simple, complex, etc.) could be described but are not developed here. The sloping terrain face with angular surface is common and apt to be covered by vegetation; easy transition with the floor is common. Cliff-face enclosure, with near-vertical surfaces is the most positive visual limitation, but occurs infrequently. It will tend to be sparsely vegetated or barren, potentially contrasting in color and sharply joined with the floor. Trees grouped together or a forest edge mark the vegetation-face enclosure. Smallest in scale compared with the other two, plant walls will also range from apparent solidity to near transparency.

*The focal landscape* is a composition of nearly parallel lines or a series of aligned objects which appear to converge upon a point or locus; parallelism and aligned points indicate two different divisions in the classification. It is assumed that the observer is so located that his line of sight generally coincides with the compositional alignment. Most often

[28] Mirei Shigemori, *Gardens of Japan* (Kyoto: Nissha Printing Co., 1949).
[29] Simonds, *Landscape Architecture.*

associated with river and stream courses, drainage defiles, or elongated strips of riparian vegetation, the type can also be based upon faults, scarps, and other linear expressions of geological structure. Varying degrees of enclosure from very open to tightly closed can be expected. Man-made focal compositions in the landscape can also emerge from straight road segments, long flat curves, or corridor clearings. Axial design and planning such as that of the Italian Renaissance period has consciously exploited this arrangement. We still use it but are no longer wedded to it.

The focal landscape automatically emphasizes the point of convergence or the focal area, and four different terminal alternatives can occur. They consist of: (1) convergence point or area, (2) terminal feature, (3) open portal, and (4) screened closure. These terminal areas represent a particularly significant part of the visual composition, and their sensitivity to impacts of change should be obvious.

*Forest or canopied landscape* is that arrangement within the forest itself, under the envelopment of leaf canopy and upon the ground plane. In addition to the overhead limitation, it is further defined by tree stem scale, their character and density, and by the nature of the forest floor with its undergrowth complex.

Stem and stand characteristics can be hinted at by such terms as old growth hardwood, young mixed conifers, or mature ponderosa pine forest. Yet to the inexperienced these provide no sense of composition. Visual analysis can provide another set of discriminations such as vertical order, variation, scale, bole color contrasts, or darkness and lightness from the canopy. Floor and undergrowth components join those of stem and stand, making up plant communities that may be examined for their visual rather than ecological relationships.[30] The simple, open floor complements large-scale vertical stems. To pose another example, an uneven floor with heavy undergrowth reduces visual penetration and can obscure the relationship to trunks to the ground plane. The forest landscape, containing detail richness, is better the province of pedestrian than passing motorist. This landscape type, while including any number of different scale relationships tends to be modest in scale as seen from within, yet more than a third of North America is covered by forest.

*Detail landscapes* (or details of the landscape) are a small world of visual compositions that accompany each of the larger landscape types. They are local but regional clues to surroundings—the building units from which the larger landscape is finally constructed. A detail is a visual fragment that can, in turn, be identified as belonging to a specific and

[30] Rexford Daubenmire, *Plant Communities* (Harper & Row, 1968).

larger landscape which is its source. Or which is the source? The larger landscape and its little details are critically joined in mutual support.[31]

Landscape detail as seen with the naked eye is a limitation set here, although others have explored visual compositions of microscopic size. Again this is an environment largely reserved for the pedestrian. And some sightseers may find this small-scale world more to their liking, more provocative than that of the larger types. Small compositions can be identified that depend upon the minutia of plant forms and parts; of rock, earth, and weathering and water detail. Their variations defy any attempt to categorize what these compositions may be, but they embrace all of the line-surface-color elements found in design. Because of the range of variations, the detail landscape was not included in the Craik study. It is interesting to note that these motifs found in nature have served as a source of design inspiration for man throughout his recorded history. And now most ecological research tends to come out of minute relationships, some of it directly visible but much of it microscopic or submicroscopic. Here again, perhaps we may be able to discover some ties between aesthetics and ecology.

How does the detail landscape fit into resource management concerns? Involved are such diverse possibilities as ecological linkage, awareness and development of sensitivity to the landscape resource, or ideas suggested for the design refinement of buildings and structures in the landscape.

## Aesthetic Criteria

Awareness should be the first product coming out of the recognition factors and landscape types—awareness that such a thing as a landscape resource may exist and that it may have aesthetic quality in some measure. Beginning with awareness as the start of aesthetic perception, several steps follow.[32] Recognition of material qualities such as line, form, color, and other more complex elements follows after awareness or may even contribute to development of initial sensing. Then there is the observation that parts or qualities are composed into satisfying collective forms, patterns, and other unified arrangements. This section suggests several means of evaluating the landscape for aesthetic quality, an area of concern that seems to have been marked only by confusion and a reluctance to treat the subject as if it has any substance.

The National Environmental Policy Act now calls for considering the

[31] Kevin Lynch, *Site Planning* (M.I.T. Press, 1968).
[32] Read, *The Meaning of Art.*

environment in terms of "esthetically pleasing surroundings. . . . [one] which supports diversity and variety of individual choice." Furthermore it calls for procedures "—which will insure that presently unquantified environmental amenities and values may be given appropriate consideration in decision making along with economic and technical consideration . . ."[33] If the subject is dealt with directly and honestly, it will no longer be satisfactory to generalize about aesthetics or natural beauty and assume that the matter has been covered.[34]

Another tendency in landscape appraisal has been to present an evaluation of recreational opportunities as the equivalent of an aesthetic appraisal. Particular recreational activities may be enhanced by environments of high quality, but recognition of active pursuits in the landscape tells us absolutely nothing of aesthetic quality. This may be understandable if we remember Dasmann's observation that it has not been considered "good form" to consider aesthetics in western resource management.[35] Gifford Pinchot's guiding principles used in structuring the Forest Service did not—perhaps could not—become involved with matters of natural amenity. But now some discussion about aesthetic values and criteria is needed.

Aesthetic value that is seen to exist in perceptual objects, including the landscape as such an object, is "value that an object has on account of its beauty."[36] This seems to be the generalization behind "natural beauty." However, it should be more helpful to consider aesthetic quality of the landscape in the same light as Stephen Pepper considers art. As he says: "Paradoxically, the greatest enhancement of quality [incorporates] in art those very activities which are hostile to quality." The activities referred to are: (1) practical activity (serving utilitarian need), (2) intellectual analytical activity (scientific division and isolation), and (3) regular activity (the routine and commonplace).[37] These are aspects that should be apparent to land managers who must think of the many attributes of the land and landscape, including, in the Forest Service, the effects of multiple use. While Pepper's observations do not eliminate dilemmas, they have the desirable effect of saying that quality will not result if it is merely reserved for objects of exquisite uselessness, if it is

[33] Public Law 91-190, Jan. 1, 1970, Sec. 101 (b) and Sec. 102.
[34] "Really, there is lost only the aesthetics of a flowing river." Pacific Northwest Power Co., *Environmental Statement—Middle Snake River* (July 1971), p. 61. What will be lost can only be guessed at because the report does not attempt to define "aesthetics."
[35] Raymond F. Dasmann, *A Different Kind of Country* (Macmillan, 1968).
[36] Monroe C. Beardsley, *Aesthetics: Problems in the Philosophy of Criticism* (Harcourt Brace, 1958), p. 507.
[37] Stephen C. Pepper, *Aesthetic Quality* (Scribner's, 1937), p. 44.

cosmetic or superficial, or if it is separated from function. It then becomes a valid proposition that protection of quality in the landscape is a goal that needs to be directly coordinated with other goals of resource use and manipulation. These goals need joining, not separation.

To find aesthetic quality and judge it requires appropriate criteria. These are not defined by recreational opportunities, nor by personal opinions; neither are they a rationale made to support whatever kinds of developmental needs that may be identified. Three basic criteria are generally recognized: unity, vividness, and variety. They may be applied to a painting, to music, or to the landscape. These criteria do not exist in isolation, they overlap one another. Through all of the preceding discussions, these criteria have been the sources of directing critical discrimination. The factors of recognition have the combined aim of recognizing the landscape resource and its aesthetic quality.

*Unity* is that quality of wholeness in which all parts cohere, not merely as an assembly but as a single harmonious unit. The sum of the parts adds up to more than a simple total. Five of the landscape types and their subclasses—panoramic, feature, enclosed, focal, and forest landscapes—represent compositions that illustrate this cohesive state. The detail landscape is omitted because it is subordinate to the other types and is a fragment; even so, it has a special kind of unity connected with locality and suggesting force of particular environmental influences. The landscape continuum, the natural fabric between visual nodes (landscape types), also has unity because it is a connected set of patterns and textures. Manipulative alterations have a tendency to disrupt natural continuities and thus may result in loss of unity.

Dominance and subordination concern the proportions found among parts and whole so that unity is affected. A landscape type contains an expression of dominance and unity; man-made changes have the potential for breaking that unity and diminishing quality. Also, the landscape types will appear whole so long as subordinate parts do not reach proportions approaching equality and chaotic competition. Parts can reach a state of merely repeating one another to the point of monotony—a state of unity but one lacking quality. This may also help describe the nature of the continuum: placidly uniform (for a given region), perhaps monotonous, but yet displaying unity. Pattern development has been described as an aspect of surface variance. It is organization, providing harmony (unity) among shapes, edges, lines, colors, and textures. We need to design man-made patterns that tie to this particular unity of the landscape. Pattern has a subordinate role as it conforms to the dominating form—space structure of landscape. By itself, it cannot constitute a full measure of quality, but it contributes and especially relates to changes in vegetative cover. Elements concerned with pattern (as related to unity) also overlap into the criterion of variety.

In summary, just as the absence of unity (fragmentation) indicates absence of aesthetic quality, so different amounts of disruption and lack of balance among parts related to the whole indicate various levels of quality.

*Vividness* is that quality in the landscape which gives distinction and makes it visually striking. It refers primarily to the strength of a single composition but could as well apply to the total impression built up over time and in sequence. The implication is that most sightseers will be aware of obvious compositions, separating them from those landscapes that command scant attention: Lynch uses the word "imageability" to portray strength of visual identity.[38] Other words, such as "clarity," "apparency," "intensity," or "novelty," are also useful and used.

Vividness grows out of the relationships of the individual parts that come together to make a conspicuous, yet whole, landscape. There are three ways in which formal relationships are established within design components: by similarity, by contrast, and by indifferent difference.[39] Similarity involves the repetition of like or similar characteristics. It achieves vividness by reinforcement, bringing into association those things which bear an overriding and recognizable likeness. It succeeds or expresses quality so long as it also maintains unity (which it is most apt to do) and yet contains variety (which potentially threatens it). Similarity gives a passive kind of compositional strength. Man-made changes that depend upon concepts of similarity have a maximum opportunity of staying safely within this particular kind of vividness. Contrast, involving the conflict of dissimilarity as its means of producing vividness, puts sharply different things or qualities together. It is expressed simply as like qualities are contrasted, such as those of color (Red Hill, Black Hill)—an overlap with similarity. Or it is expressed in a complex way as compound characteristics are brought together (Big Humpback Mountain, Clear Creek, Green Meadow). Contrast is the most obvious source of vividness and quality, if it avoids confusion. Man-made changes in the landscape are apt to be noticed for their contrast, but are often negative in quality. We need to exercise the greatest care in designing changes that we know will become conspicuous because of contrasts. Indifferent difference, occupying a middle point between similarity and contrast, is prone to produce indistinction rather than vividness. It is made up of parts that can be recognized as neither much

[38] Kevin Lynch, *The Image of the City* (Cambridge, Mass.: Technology Press and Harvard University Press, 1960).

[39] Beardsley, *Aesthetics . . . Criticism.*

alike nor much different from one another. By itself, it does not logically constitute quality although it can make a contribution through being a visual foil—a base against which contrast may well be set. Here again, much of the nature of the landscape continuity is described. Both vagueness and complexity are involved. We may use this principle in avoiding competition with natural vividness.

*Variety*, in simple form, can be defined as an index to how many different objects and relationships are found present in a landscape. "Richness" and "diversity" are other words which carry the same sense, but "variety" is chosen here because it seems a sympathetic link between design and the ecological aspects of the landscape. It is expressed in environmental heterogeneity.[40] Greater variety is an indication of higher aesthetic quality.

But sheer number of objects as determined by counting them in the landscape does not constitute a good measure of how variety bears on quality. There needs to be order and control over numerous and diverse parts. Simplification through organization is necessary—an overlap with unity. The landscape types described compositionally represent frameworks into which variety may be visually integrated. There are also several themes of design by which elements of variety may be given order. They are repetition, segregation, and gradation.

Repetition, as observed on the surface of the landscape, is commonplace and attracts little attention until it reaches the point of excess, which produces monotony. Yet variety is present; it is merely subordinated into broad areas of texture or of pattern. Sometimes it may be beyond our level of attention. It is most obviously found in vegetative cover (surface variance) where relatively large areas are characterized by many repeated parts that are yet seen as continuous.

Segregation is a higher level of ordering variety. It begins at the margins of opposing kinds of texture, for example. It involves the contrast of several distinct arrangements of design components or patterns brought together. One arrangement alternately replaces another, or they repeat in random order. An analogy may be drawn with music in which rhythm represents changes of theme or accent while beat (repetition) is still maintained.

Gradation is that ordered variety which reaches toward a climax and which may include a climax. There is a directional thrust or build-up. It can be a compound arrangement in which both repetition and segregation take place. In the landscape, the presence of a feature would represent a climax and most evident proof of gradation. Additionally, grada-

---

[40] Dasmann, *A Different Kind of Country*.

tion could be encountered within the confines of a single landscape composition seen at a given point or as it developed over time with the progression of sequential views. Sequence, however, does not discriminate in the same way as gradation—it can as well be regressive. Quality can then be gauged through determining the presence of variety and, particularly, through recognizing the ways in which it is ordered.

To make an aesthetic evaluation of the landscape is to apply the criteria presented and their elaboration discussed in the recognition factors. To be sure, we have little more than an outline here, but the purpose is to define beginnings. The simplest application—the place to start— would be that of making a comparison among examples of the same kind of landscape type. A regional limitation should also be helpful[41]—the Grand Canyon as a paragon of enclosed landscapes does not necessarily diminish the local value of a small gorge landscape in Nebraska. This deliberate approach is needed before comparisons among different landscape types can be handled with any degree of competence. That the landscape is indeed a visual resource will depend in part on recognition of aesthetic quality.

## The Landscape as a Resource

How can resource management be improved by making use of scenic recognition factors and landscape types? An initiation of awareness and development of sensitivity toward the landscape is of first and general importance, especially to those disciplines which have, traditionally and practically, other concerns with resources. But to become conscious of the landscape as a resource is not enough; concrete evidence is needed. Evidence can be put together with an inventory of scenic elements that can apply the concepts given here. The landscape inventory becomes a document representing key points about our visual environment. Other pertinent decisions and interpretations may follow. Otherwise the landscape remains mute in the decisions that affect it. There have been, and are, eloquent spokesmen for the landscape. Aldo Leopold wrote movingly of Arizona's high country.[42] Thomas Moran's paintings of Yellowstone documented places not otherwise known. But records of less unusua, landscapes are needed if what is seen there is to be recognized, evaluatedl and sensitively used.

An analogy may be drawn between scenic inventories and those for other natural resources. Timber types or soils, for example, are usually

[41] Stanley A. Cain, "Ecological Impacts on Water Resources Development," *Water Resources Bulletin*, vol. 4, no. 1 (1968), pp. 57–71.
[42] Aldo Leopold, *A Sand County Almanac* (Oxford University Press, 1949).

portrayed on maps so that their presence, their extent, and their location and locational relationships are shown. Topographic maps, narrative reports, and other graphic representations can provide supporting information. The map (with topography) as a starting point for a landscape inventory is critical because it emphasizes a visual record for a visual resource. Whether the map inventory represents timber types or the landscape, the same principles of definition are involved. But timber types have long been defined, while agreement on what should be recorded in a landscape inventory is only now being developed. Craik and I feel confident that the factors of recognition and the landscape types have a measure of reliability that makes them appropriate for this purpose.

*A landscape inventory* is primarily dependent on the discoveries of field reconnaissance. Reluctance to go into the field thwarts the whole intent. Visual corridors, landscape types, and recognition elements are necessarily found through direct observations and then plotted. Some of this data can be developed from topographic maps and air photos. Standard $7\frac{1}{2}$ minute (1:24,000) U.S. Geological Survey maps are recommended as a base likely to be most compatible with the kind of detail to be obtained. The nature of the terrain, however, could make it desirable to use maps with either larger or smaller scale. Indications of landscape elements can be located directly on the base map. Photography, sketches, notes, and the use of abstract notation symbols[43] can all be employed in extracting and recording the necessary information. A narrative report will be needed to carry some of the data as it is finally assembled and weighed.

Two types of inventories can be considered: those that are route based and those showing reconnaissance areas. Both are assumed to include a map (or several for different data) and appropriate supporting information.

The route-based inventory is, first of all, a visual corridor.[44] It is mapped from a route, and its outside boundary line is the limit of the visible landscape (see Figure 8.3). It does not matter if the route is a road, a trail, or a stream. Both in the inventory construction and its later use, rate of travel speed suggests differing significance in the kind of detail recorded. A recording technique is best and most conveniently developed as related to an existing route. A series of these inventories on either existing or proposed routes can obviously be put together to form a comprehensive planning area. This kind of inventory tied to an existing

[43] Appleyard, Lynch, and Myer, *The View from the Road.*

[44] R. Burton Litton, Jr., *Forest Landscape Description and Inventories*, U.S. Forest Service Research Paper PSW-49 (Berkeley: Pacific Southwest Forest and Range Experiment Station, 1968).

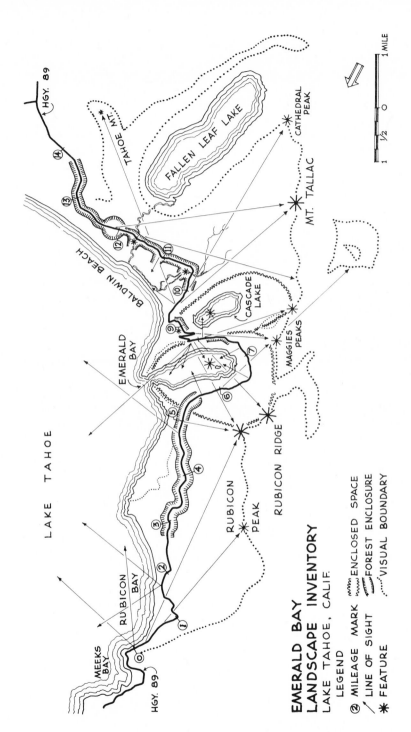

EMERALD BAY
LANDSCAPE INVENTORY
LAKE TAHOE, CALIF.

LEGEND

② MILEAGE MARK    〰〰 ENCLOSED SPACE
╱ LINE OF SIGHT    ⫴⫴ FOREST ENCLOSURE
✳ FEATURE         ⋯⋯ VISUAL BOUNDARY

LAKE TAHOE

MEEKS BAY

RUBICON BAY

HGY. 89

RUBICON PEAK

RUBICON RIDGE

EMERALD BAY

BALDWIN BEACH

CASCADE LAKE

MAGGIES PEAKS

MT. TALLAC

CATHEDRAL PEAK

FALLEN LEAF LAKE

TAHOE MT.

HGY. 89

1 ½ 0 1 MILE

*Figure 8.3.* A typical route inventory.

route (either a road or stream) is especially appropriate for intensive management problems within the specific visual corridor involved.[45]

An area inventory presumes the boundaries of an arbitrary unit, a number of watersheds, a physiographic unit, or a planning area.[46] It could be made from joined route inventories, but the usual start is with map and air photo examination, then to the field for orientation and sampling. Aerial examination gives the best introduction, but sampling must be done on the ground where the "real landscape" is discovered. With surface evidence providing a basis for accurate interpretation, it becomes possible to return again to air photos to give coverage that can be extended to a comprehensive area. Such a visual inventory is most appropriate as applied to extensive problems, including variables to be encountered in preliminary planning and consideration of broad alternative choices of design.

It is a certainty that all disciplinary branches of resource management will affect the way the landscape looks as they go about their particular endeavors. Thus the visual landscape is the responsibility of many; no single discipline can keep it from falling apart. While the landscape inventory offers some specific documentation of an elusive resource and its construction has value as a teaching device, it is not otherwise an end in itself. However, it helps make a case for the landscape. The following set of environmental objectives may aid in approaching the wildlands from the viewpoint of landscape:

- At the most general level, the landscape needs to be recognized for its contribution to the quality of the environment. Measures designed to combat pollution do not necessarily address protection of the landscape.
- Inclusion of the intangible values represented in the visual landscape will help set priorities in the use of wildlands.
- If the landscape is used as a display against which the objectives of different management disciplines may be better integrated, this will also help to clarify the direction taken in management—whether it is protective or deteriorative toward the landscape, whether it may enhance or be restorative, whether it is intensive and local, or extensive and broad, or both.

[45] U.S. Forest Service, Northern Region, *River Plan for Wild and Scenic Rivers* (Missoula, Mont., 1969).

[46] Philip H. Lewis, Jr., and Associates, *Regional Design for Human Impacts*, Upper Mississippi Comprehensive Basin Study (Madison, Wis.: Thomas Publications, 1968). R. Burton Litton, Jr., "Visual Landscape Units of the Lake Tahoe Region," in *Scenic Analysis of the Lake Tahoe Region* (South Lake Tahoe, Calif.: Tahoe Region Planning Agency and U.S. Forest Service, 1971).

- Landscapes should be compared and evaluated as representing a resource in their own right. Sensitive or resistant areas should be identified as they may be judged to result from manipulative changes.
- Plans for future changes should compare the projected impacts of various alternatives. This may be done by graphic portrayal of visual impacts. Visual end-products need to be anticipated; there is no excuse for their being unanticipated, unsavory surprises.

# 9

# *Appraising the Objectivity of Landscape Dimensions*

KENNETH  H.  CRAIK*

The objective assessment of landscape scenes along a standard set of visual dimensions will make important contributions to the scientific study of man-environment relations (Craik, 1968; 1969a; 1970) and to innovative practices in natural resources management (Litton and Twiss, 1966; Litton, 1968). The capacity to relate observers' descriptions and evaluations of landscapes to systematically varied landscape attributes opens up promising opportunities for research in environmental psychology. An objective system of landscape dimensions has value for natural resources management because of its immediate implications for improved methods of conducting landscape inventories and evaluating landscape resources.

The aims of the present study were to appraise the inter-observer objectivity of a comprehensive system of landscape dimensions and to illustrate its scientific application. It is useful to distinguish among at least three kinds of human response to landscape:

1) *descriptive assessments,* which simply seek to depict, rate, measure, etc., the attributes of specific landscapes;
2) *evaluative appraisals,* which judge the relative quality of specific landscapes against some implicit or explicit standard of comparison; and
3) *preferential judgments,* which express a wholly personal, subjective appreciation of (or repugnance for) specific landscapes.

The Landscape Rating Scales and Graphic Landscape Typology de-

* Department of Psychology, University of California, Berkeley.

veloped in this project are techniques for the descriptive assessment of landscapes. They do not entail evaluative or preferential judgments by observers.

Of course, these descriptive techniques can be employed in substantive research on the appraisal of landscape quality and in the study of landscape preferences. For example, as a descriptive task, observers can be asked to judge whether a landscape contains a surface shape. If in subsequent research, appraisals of the relative quality of, say, forty landscapes were related to independent descriptive assessments of them, it might be revealed that the presence of surface shapes tends to be positively associated with ratings of landscape quality. Consequently, presence of surface shapes might be appropriately assigned a positive weight in an index of landscape quality. But that is a different operation from the descriptive task of determining whether given landscapes do or do not contain surface shapes. Likewise, a study of the preferential ratings of a particular subgroup of the general public, e.g., Great Plains farmers, might indicate that the presence of surface shapes is negatively related to their preferences for landscapes. Again, the distinction between preferential ratings of landscapes and descriptive assessments of landscapes can be drawn.

## APPRAISAL OF INTER-OBSERVER OBJECTIVITY[1]

Since this system of landscape dimensions employs the human observer as a principal component of its measuring instrument, it is essential for informed practical and scientific application to appraise the extent to which it yields reproducible data that are not dependent upon a particular individual for their collection (Block, 1961). To achieve this purpose, (1) the initial conceptual dimensions were embodied in a standard set of landscape rating scales, (2) the overall level of agreement displayed by observers in the use of each rating dimension was tested, and (3) the degree of similarity in judgments made by experts and nonexperts and by conservation-oriented observers and other observers was examined.

### Constructing Landscape Rating Scales

Fortunately, an analytic and illustrative presentation of the system of landscape dimensions to be appraised in this study was available as a definitional resource (Litton, 1968). A more fully elaborated version of this analysis of landscape is included in this volume.

[1] This research was conducted with the valuable assistance of Arvalea Nelson and Helen Piotrkowski.

In collaboration with Litton, a set of Landscape Rating Scales was devised which embodied the principal elements of his system of landscape dimensions.

Landscape Rating 1 refers to observer position, i.e., "the location of the observer as he looks upon a visual objective" (Litton, 1968, p. 5).

1.  The observer is

    1.  looking down upon the scene
    2.  looking straight on at the scene
    3.  looking up toward the scene.

Landscape Ratings 2 and 3 deal with distance dimensions. The distance designations in Rating 2 were based upon Litton's boundaries for the foreground, middleground, and background zones (Litton, 1968, p. 3). Due to the configuration of landscape and relative observer position, the sense of foreground, middleground, or background can be absent from a landscape scene. Rating 3 taps this variable.

2.  Extent of view: the distance to the most remote elements in the scene is

    4.  less than $\frac{1}{4}$ mile
    5.  $\frac{1}{4}$ mile to 3 miles
    6.  greater than 3 miles.

3.  Indicate the presence of

    7.  foreground (encircle "7" if present)
    8.  middleground (encircle "8" if present)
    9.  background (encircle "9" if present).

Landscape Rating 4 distinguishes two principal variations in a compositional aspect of landscape form.

4.  Is the observer afforded a panoramic view?

    10.  Yes, a sweeping expanse, with the scene falling away from the observer.
    11.  Yes, a horizontal expanse, with the wide view straight on from the observer.
    12.  No.

Landscape Rating 5 treats the direction of lighting.

5.  The scene is lighted by

    13.  side light, with the sun low to either side of the observer
    14.  back light, with the sun low and shining toward the observer

15. front light, with the sun low behind the observer
16. direction of light indeterminate.

Landscape Rating 6 is directed to the spatial definition of landscape scenes, indexing the extent and kind of enclosure.

6. The scene presents a sense of vertical enclosure which blocks off the line of vision:
   (encircle all items that apply)

   17. In all directions and entirely surrounds the observer
   18. Directly ahead of the observer
   19. On the right side
   20. On the left side
   21. Does not apply—no sense of vertical enclosure.

Landscape Ratings 7 and 8 bear upon landscape forms which can become salient features.

7. Does the scene contain an isolated form, composed of a single element or a group of elements, seen in profile or silhouette against the sky or against a distant background?

   22. Definitely present
   23. Somewhat present
   24. Definitely absent.

8. Does the scene contain a surface shape, seen as an outline embedded in the landscape itself?

   25. Definitely present
   26. Somewhat present
   27. Definitely absent.

Landscape Rating 9 relates to compositional attributes which suggest a focal landscape.

9. Focal view: are there elements in the scene which direct the line of vision along a prescribed pathway?

   28. Definitely present
   29. Somewhat present
   30. Definitely absent.

Of the many ephemeral landscape features, e.g., fog, hoarfrost, reflected images, sunset coloration, Landscape Rating 10 considers variations in cloud formation.

10. The clouds in the scene have the appearance of

    31. delicate, feathery, sweeping fibers

    32. dense, billowing, white mounds, sharply outlined

    33. low, grey, thick, diffuse masses

    34. Does not apply—no clouds in the scene.

Throughout this report, the ten main categories will be referred to as Landscape Rating Scales (1 through 10), while the thirty-four specific attributes will be referred to as landscape dimensions (1 through 34).

Except as encompassed in Ratings 6, 7, and 8, the elements of undergrowth and landscape details (Litton, 1968, pp. 35–40) did not appear to warrant specific rating scales.

Sequence is a crucial factor in the experience of landscape (Craik, 1969b, Litton, 1968; Thiel, 1961, 1965). However, it functions as a higher-order variable, comprising the temporal patterning of attributes already embodied in the Landscape Rating Scales. Establishing adequate inter-observer objectivity for the present system of landscape dimensions is a prerequisite to field studies of the sequential experience of landscape.

Two panels of university students ($N = 9$; $N = 6$) served in pilot studies of the preliminary rating scales and graphic typology. On the basis of these results and after consultation with Litton, a final set of procedures was developed.

*Selecting a Test Set of Diverse Landscape Scenes*

If the test set of landscape scenes failed to possess sufficient diversity, certain components of the Landscape Rating Scales might be seldom employed by panels of observers and, consequently, their reliability would remain unappraised.

In a review of several thousand color photographic slides of landscape scenes, an initial set of 100 scenes was selected, representing varied landscapes and displaying minimal signs of human activity and artifacts. Review of the larger collection also led to the development of a Graphic Landscape Typology (Figure 9.1), capturing in a holistic manner the basic configurations of frequently occurring landscape compositions. As an indirect means of attaining diversity in the final test set of 50 scenes, the initial set of 100 were classified according to the Graphic Landscape Typology by a third panel of nine university students. Judged representatives of each graphic type were included in the final test set.

*Constituting Panels of Observers*

In addition to the three panels of university students participating in the pilot studies, the following panels served in the final testing:

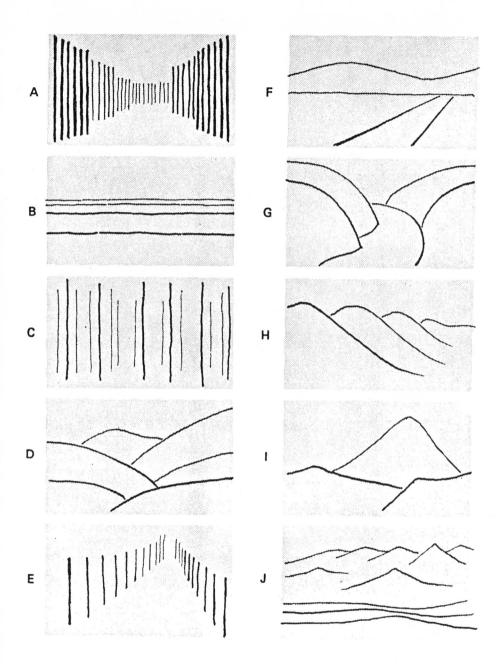

*Figure 9.1.* Graphic landscape typology.

1) Forestry and Conservation Panel ($N = 18$): This panel consisted of faculty and advanced students in the School of Forestry and Conservation, University of California, Berkeley.[2]

2) Landscape Architecture Panel ($N = 10$): This panel consisted of faculty and graduate students in the Department of Landscape Architecture, College of Environmental Design, University of California, Berkeley.[3]

3) Forest Service Panel ($N = 22$): This panel of younger Forest Service personnel (age range 22–38) participated in the study while attending a training program conducted by the U.S. Forest Service at Twain-Harte, California.[4]

4) University Student Panels I, II, III, and IV ($N$s = 21, 24, 25, 16 respectively): Students participating in these panels were recruited from the Placement Office of the University of California, Berkeley, and were paid on an hourly basis. They comprised a diverse sampling, including majors in anthropology, English, criminology, history, physics, geology, biological science, education, sociology, art and design, pre-nursing, comparative literature, speech, psychology, French, biochemistry, communication, political science, social welfare, mathematics, zoology, Slavic languages, engineering, architecture, chemistry, philosophy, geography, art history, and dramatic art.

5) Conservation Course Panel ($N = 90$). This panel consisted of class members of a course in open space offered by Daniel B. Luten, in the Department of Geography, University of California, Berkeley. In contrast to the other student panels, the members of this panel were more heavily drawn from such majors as zoology, forestry, geography, and architecture, but also included majors in English, political science, anthropology, psychology, sociology, economics, business administration, computer science, physics, journalism, and chemistry.[5]

*Procedure*

Each panel of observers was informed of the general purpose and nature of the project. Participants were given a set of Landscape Rating

[2] The cooperation of Henry Vaux, School of Forestry and Conservation, University of California, Berkeley, in making arrangements for this panel is gratefully acknowledged.

[3] The cooperation of David Streatfield, Department of Landscape Architecture, University of California, Berkeley, in enlisting the participation of this panel is gratefully acknowledged.

[4] The cooperation and hospitality extended by Wayne Iverson and Paul Madden, U.S. Forest Service, Region 5, are gratefully acknowledged.

[5] The cooperation of Daniel B. Luten, Department of Geography, University of California, Berkeley, in enlisting the participation of this panel is gratefully acknowledged.

Scales and a copy of the Graphic Landscape Typology (see Appendix A and Figure 9.1). Then they were instructed in their two tasks. For each landscape scene, they were first to decide which of the ten graphic types it best exemplified, recording their judgments by placing the appropriate letter ("A" through "J") on the rating form. Next, for the same scene, they were to work down the Landscape Rating Scales, encircling numbers to record their ratings of the scene on each landscape dimension.

The fifty landscape scenes of the test set were presented by means of 35 mm color photographic slides and a carousel projector. The experimenter sought to maintain a rapid work tempo while heeding the slower pace of stragglers. Judgment time tended to decrease progressively as the observers became familiar with the landscape dimensions.

A typical testing session required a two-hour period during which a panel would rate the first twenty-five landscape scenes on Landscape Scales 1–5 and the second twenty-five scenes on Landscape Scales 6–10, as well as making typological judgments for all fifty scenes. Appendix Table C.1 indicates the range of judgments made by the several panels participating in this study.

It should be noted that the amount of instruction provided the panelists was minimal, e.g., there was almost no verbal embellishment of the Graphic Landscape Typology and no substantive expansion of the content of the Landscape Rating Scales. Thus, the appraisal of the consensual validity of these procedures is a conservative one. A modest program of training in their use would be expected to increase the amount of agreement among observers over that found in the present study.

*Appraisal of the Reliability of the Landscape Rating Scales and Graphic Landscape Typology*

*1. Landscape Rating Scales: Findings for the Total Set of Panels.* If no agreement were displayed by the panels of observers in their use of Landscape Rating Scales for describing specific scenes, there would be a tendency for an equal number of observers to choose each option of a given rating. The $X^2$ one-sample test provides the appropriate statistical appraisal of agreement. The hypothetical results for Landscape Rating 5, presented in Appendix Table C.2, illustrate the application of this test. In the data for Scene 11, fourteen of the twenty-one observers agree upon dimension 14, while the other seven split their votes between dimensions 15 and 16. In randomly generated data, this level of agreement would occur less than once in a thousand times. The data for Scene 8 display considerably less agreement and that for Scene 13, essentially no agreement at all.

Appendix Table C.3 presents the combined results for all panels.[6] An impressive amount of agreement is indicated. Of the 800 statistical tests of consensual use of the Landscape Rating Scales, 576 are significant beyond the .001 level, 631 beyond the .01 level, and 690 beyond the .10 level.

The Landscape Rating Scales vary somewhat in the amount of agreement shown by observers in their descriptions of the test set of fifty landscape scenes. For each Landscape Rating Scale, Appendix Table C.4 presents the number of landscape scenes for which its use attained agreement beyond the .10 level of significance.

Disagreements in the use of the rating scales are spread rather evenly over the test set of fifty landscape scenes. Taking the .10 level as criterion for agreement, four scenes showed agreement on all sixteen statistical tests, sixteen scenes showed disagreement on only one, ten scenes showed disagreement on two, twelve scenes showed disagreement on three, five scenes showed disagreement on five, while one enigmatic scene showed disagreement on six of the sixteen statistical tests.

*2. Landsacpe Rating Scales: Comparisons among Expert and Nonexpert Panels.* Appendix Table C.5 presents separate analyses of the judgments made by the Landscape Architecture, Forest Service, and University panels. Close inspection of the table suggests that the Landscape Rating Scales operate similarly across panels. Disagreements among members within a panel tend to occur on the same combinations of ratings and scenes for all panels. For each of the sixteen statistical tests made for each landscape scene, Appendix Table C.6 lists the number of scenes on which each panel attained statistically significant agreement (beyond the .10 level), plus the rank order of this index for each panel.[7] The rank order correlations of this index of overall agreement are substantial both between the expert and nonexpert panels (Landscape Architecture and University panels: +.66; Forest Service and University panels: +.67; Combined Expert panels and University panel: +.72) and between the two expert panels (Landscape Architecture and Forest Service panels: +.83). Thus, the landscape ratings which are used with relatively high agreement by expert panels tend also to be those used with high agreement by nonexperts. Furthermore, when each panel displays internal agreement in rating a specific scene on a landscape dimension, the actual

---

[6] Appendix Table C.3 does not include the Landscape Architecture panel's Landscape Ratings 1–5 for Scenes 18–25 and Landscape Ratings 6–10 for Scenes 44–50.

[7] Because the Forestry panel did not rate all scenes, its judgments have been omitted from this analysis.

trend in the judgments is similar from panel to panel and typically yields the same modal rating by all panels (see Appendix Table C.5).

*3. Landscape Rating Scales: Comparison between Conservation-oriented Panelists and Other Panelists.* Each panelist was asked to indicate any memberships in conservation-oriented organizations. On this basis, the 177 members of the Landscape Architecture, Forestry, Forest Service, Conservation Course, and University I and IV panels were divided into two groups of judges: 53 members of conservation-oriented organizations and the remaining 124 panelists. Thirty-one of the conservation-oriented panelists were members of the Sierra Club, while smaller numbers were members of organizations such as the National Audubon Society, the Wilderness Society, the Nature Conservancy, Save the Bay, the National Wildlife Federation, the University of California Hiking Club, Active Conservation Tactics (ACT), and Ecology Action.

Appendix Table C.7 presents the results of a comparison between these two specially constituted panels. For this analysis, the $X^2$ test for two independent samples is appropriate for testing the hypothesis that conservation-oriented panelists differ from other panelists in their use of the Landscape Rating Scales. The sixteen distinct ratings made for Scenes 1 through 6 were analyzed. Of the ninety-six distinct statistical tests performed, only 12 findings support the hypothesis beyond the .10 level. Furthermore, in ninety-six independent statistical tests, 9.6 significant findings would be expected at the .10 level by chance alone. In summary, there is no statistical basis for supporting the hypothesis that conservation-oriented panelists differ from other panelists in their use of the Landscape Rating Scales.

*4. Graphic Landscape Typology.* For each of the fifty test scenes, Appendix Table C.8 presents the typological designations made by the Landscape Architecture, Forestry and Conservation, Forest Service, and University Student panels. A majority of the panelists agree upon a single classification for forty-one of the fifty test scenes. For most scenes, two typological designations account for a large proportion of the panelists' judgments. In some research and applied contexts, it would be appropriate to employ a double-code device, e.g., Scene 1 would be a J-A, Scene 2, an E-G.

Appendix Table C.9 presents the modal typological designation of the fifty scenes for several panels. Substantial agreement between expert and nonexpert panels and among expert panels is demonstrated. Complete agreement across panels is displayed for thirty-six of the fifty test scenes

and marked agreement for most of the remaining scenes. In six of the
latter scenes, Type A is involved, suggesting that some modifications in
that category may be warranted.

## THE RELATIONSHIP OF LANDSCAPE DIMENSIONS AND TYPES TO AESTHETIC APPEAL

The combined landscape ratings and typological judgments of all
panels provide the basis for classifying the test set of fifty landscape
scenes according to these known characteristics. A further analysis permits exploration of the relationship between landscape dimensions and
the aesthetic appeal of landscape scenes.

A panel of sixty university students enrolled in a geography course
appraised the aesthetic appeal of each of the fifty test scenes in accord
with the following directions: "Imagine yourself actually in each landscape setting and rate how aesthetically pleasing it would be by encircling
a number from '1' (low) through '7' (high) on the rating scale."[8] The
distribution of each judge's fifty ratings was divided into thirds, as
closely as possible, and the scenes within the low, middle, and high categories were reassigned values of "1," "2," and "3" respectively. Mean
values were computed separately for each scene based upon the ratings
of the twenty-four female judges and the thirty-six male judges. The
correlation between the two sets of ratings for the fifty test scenes was
+.94, which warranted computing a final set of mean aesthetic values
based upon the entire set of ratings.

A chi-square analysis of the relationship of each landscape dimension
to aesthetic appeal identified a set of weak but congruent findings:

1. at the .10 level of statistical significance:

    A. a sense of vertical enclosure which blocks off the line of vision
       directly ahead of the observer is *negatively* related to aesthetic
       appeal;
    B. the degree to which the scene contains a focal view, directing
       the line of vision along a prescribed pathway, is *positively* re-
       lated to aesthetic appeal;

2. at the .20 level of statistical significance:

    C. an extent of view greater than three miles is *positively* related to
       aesthetic appeal;

---

[8] Thanks are again expressed for the cooperation of Daniel B. Luten in enlisting
the participation of this panel.

    D. a panoramic view, either a sweeping or horizontal expanse, is
        *positively* related to aesthetic appeal;
    E. the presence of any kind of clouds is *positively* related to aes-
        thetic appeal.

The emphasis upon distant views is noteworthy.

In addition, the relationship of aesthetic appeal to graphic types of
landscape scenes was explored. First, the mean aesthetic ratings for the
modal representatives of each type were computed:

| Type | Number of Scenes | Mean Aesthetic Rating |
|------|------------------|-----------------------|
| A | 2 | 2.46 |
| B | 5 | 1.65 |
| C | 5 | 1.60 |
| D | 5 | 1.83 |
| E | 5 | 2.16 |
| F | 5 | 1.92 |
| G | 6 | 2.67 |
| H | 6 | 1.91 |
| I | 4 | 2.06 |
| J | 7 | 2.05 |

To obtain a graduated index of the relative strength of membership of
each scene within a given type, the scenes were rank ordered according to
the number of judges in the combined panel who assigned the scene to
that type. Thus, indices of A-ness, B-ness, etc., were derived for each
scene and then these indices were correlated separately with aesthetic
appeal:

| Index | Correlation with Aesthetic Appeal | Significance Level |
|-------|-----------------------------------|--------------------|
| A-ness | .08 | |
| B-ness | −.44 | .01 |
| C-ness | −.21 | .20 |
| D-ness | −.02 | |
| E-ness | .34 | .02 |
| F-ness | .13 | |
| G-ness | .36 | .01 |
| H-ness | −.06 | |
| I-ness | .06 | |
| J-ness | −.01 | |

The positive correlations between the aesthetic appeal of landscape
scenes and their degree of membership in Types G and E are consistent

with the relatively high mean aesthetic ratings of the modal representatives of those types. Similarly, the negative correlations between aesthetic appeal and degree of membership in Landscape Types B and C are consistent with the relatively low mean aesthetic ratings of the modal representatives of those types. The two modal scenes for Landscape Type A yielded the highest mean aesthetic rating (2.46), but the A-ness of the entire set of test scenes is not related to aesthetic appeal (.08). Clearly, improvement in the conception of this type and a larger set of modal representatives will be required before this discrepancy can be further examined.

## Development and Application of the Landscape Adjective Check List

Adjective checklists have been successfully used in the recording of impressions of persons, in personality research (Gough and Heilbrun, 1965). The development of techniques for the study of environmental descriptions is receiving attention from several researchers (Collins, 1968, 1969; Kasmar and Vidulich, 1968; Lowenthal et al., 1967; Canter, 1969; Hershberger, 1969; Sanoff, 1969; Sonnenfeld, 1969). However, no checklist has been available for use in research on landscape description.

The diverse collection of fifty landscape scenes established in other phases of this research was presented to a panel of thirty-five university freshmen and sophomores, who were requested to list ten adjectives descriptive of each scene.[9] They were asked to describe each scene independently of their descriptions of previous scenes, repeating adjectives whenever appropriate. An inclusive list of every adjective and descriptive phrase employed at least once by an observer in describing any scene was compiled.[10] A total of 1,196 distinct descriptive terms resulted. A tally of the frequency with which each term was employed in this descriptive study was then made. Examination of usage frequencies revealed that a selection of all adjectives employed six or more times yielded a reasonably comprehensive array of terms. By eliminating certain redundant terms and adding terms that would contribute to the breadth of coverage, the present preliminary version of the Landscape Adjective Check List (LACL) was constructed (Appendix B).

The advantages of the LACL are its use of everyday language, the brevity and ease with which judgments are made and recorded, its

---

[9] Thanks are due to Helen Piotrkowski for arranging the participation of this panel.
[10] Not every observer listed ten terms per scene.

breadth of coverage, and its wide and flexible application and forms of analysis. The LACL can be used to gather descriptive impressions of landscapes quickly from large samples of observers in the field. Descriptions of the same landscapes by systematically selected samples of observers can be statistically compared. Impressions of ideal and imaginary, as well as actual landscapes, can be recorded. The effects of changes in landscape conditions and features can be recorded through observers' LACL descriptions. The influence of weather conditions and variations in natural lighting upon impressions of landscape can be analyzed. The degree to which photographs, sketches, and other simulations yield LACL descriptions equivalent to those rendered of the same scenes in the field can be appraised. Although further developmental effort, employing a wider range of landscape scenes and diverse observers, will contribute to its improvement, the LACL can be counted upon to yield useful findings in its present form.[11]

In an illustrative application of the LACL, a panel of twenty-one university students enrolled in a landscape architecture course described six landscape scenes by means of the check list.[12] Scenes having the following ranks on the previously described mean ratings of aesthetic appeal were drawn, sight unseen, from the fifty test scenes for this study: the scenes with ranks of 1, 2, 16, 34, 49, and 50.

Adjectives checked in different frequencies (at the .001 level of statistical significance) in the descriptions of both the two aesthetically most appealing and least appealing scenes and the three most and least appealing scenes are listed on the following page. In addition, adjectives that differentiated (at the .001 level of significance) descriptions of the two most appealing scenes from the two moderately appealing scenes (ranks 1 and 2 versus ranks 16 and 34) and, in the same direction, differentiated the two moderately appealing scenes from the two least appealing scenes (ranks 16 and 34 versus 49 and 50) are identified by an asterisk.

In a complete research design, descriptions of the entire set of fifty landscape scenes would be related to the criterion measure of aesthetic appeal. Although based upon only six scenes selected along the dimension of aesthetic appeal, the present findings do serve to illustrate the application of the LACL.

[11] Development of the Landscape Adjective Check List has also been supported through a cooperative agreement with the U.S. Forest Service.
[12] The cooperation of Clare Cooper, Department of Landscape Architecture, University of California, Berkeley, in enlisting the participation of this panel is gratefully acknowledged.

*Attributes of Aesthetically Appealing Scenes*

| | | |
|---|---|---|
| *active | *fresh | rapid |
| *alive | *friendly | *refreshing |
| *Alpine | glacial | restful |
| beautiful | green | rich |
| bright | happy | rippled |
| brisk | high | rocky |
| *clean | impressive | romantic |
| *clear | inspiring | running |
| cold | *invigorating | rushing |
| colorful | *living | secluded |
| cool | lovely | spring-like |
| crashing | majestic | swift |
| crisp | moist | timbered |
| enclosed | *mountainous | unspoiled |
| exciting | natural | vegetated |
| flowing | *picturesque | watery |
| forceful | pleasant | wet |
| free | pretty | wild |
| *forested | pure | wooded |

*Attributes of Aesthetically Unappealing Scenes*

| | | |
|---|---|---|
| *arid | destroyed | scraggly |
| bare | dirty | ugly |
| barren | drab | unfriendly |
| bleak | *dry | uninspiring |
| brown | *dull | uninviting |
| burned | eroded | weedy |
| bushy | golden | windswept |
| colorless | hot | withered |
| depressing | lifeless | worn |
| deserted | monotonous | yellow |
| desolate | plain | |

## Conclusions

The results of this appraisal of the objectivity of a system of landscape dimensions are encouraging. Substantial consensus among panels drawn from forestry and conservation, landscape architecture, the U.S. Forest Service, and general university students has been demonstrated. In addition, these expert and nonexpert panels show impressive agreement in the way they employed the Landscape Rating Scales. Areas for improvement have also been identified, particularly in the operation of Landscape Rating Scales 7 and 8. A Graphic Landscape Typology has also shown promise as a useful supplement to the Landscape Rating Scales, although efforts to improve the functioning of Landscape Type A appear warranted.

This appraisal of the Landscape Rating Scales and Graphic Landscape Typology has been based upon assessments of simulated presentations of landscapes by means of 35 mm color photographic slides. Rather than further laboratory studies using this mode of presentation, the results strongly suggest the appropriateness of immediate field application of the techniques. Further improvement, refinement, and expansion of the two procedures can best occur within the context of field application.

The establishment of a series of standard viewing stations within a nonurban region affording a diversity of viewing potentials would offer a natural yet controlled field setting for checking the objectivity of the Landscape Rating Scales and Graphic Landscape Typology in the assessment of directly presented landscapes. On the basis of the present findings and previous research on observational descriptions of persons (Block, 1961; Cline, 1964), arithmetically combined judgments made by a small team of three or four observers working independently of each other can be expected to attain a level of reliability meeting scientific and practical requirements. The institution of brief training procedures may markedly enhance the objectivity of these observational assessments.

In addition to their applied use in natural resources management and regional landscape design (Litton and Twiss, 1967; Litton, 1968), the Landscape Rating Scales and Graphic Landscape Typology offer important aids to basic research on man-environment relations (Craik, 1970). The present findings illustrate the contribution they may make to increased understanding of the factors involved in the aesthetic appeal of landscape scenes. It will be possible to advance research relating the aesthetic preferences of various observer groups to systematic characteristics of landscape scenes (Shafer, Hamilton, and Schmidt, 1969). However, a major research effort will be required to further our knowledge of human responsiveness to landscape. For example, in the present exploratory study, only a single evaluative rating was obtained, i.e., the rating of aesthetic appeal. Yet, the evaluative response to landscape is potentially multidimensional, including a global subjective preference (i.e., "like-dislike"), an aesthetic appeal, and perhaps several others (Coughlin and Goldstein, 1970; Rabinowitz and Coughlin, 1970). The dimensionality of the criterion panels' evaluative judgments should be fully determined and a more precise index of aesthetic appeal developed (Child, 1969).

The Landscape Adjective Check List is another contribution to the technology of observational assessment of the environment. Its role in the study of aesthetic response to landscape has also been illustrated. Within the context of the present research, another appropriate analysis would identify adjectival terms related to variations among scenes on each of the Landscape Rating Scales and also those terms tending to be employed differentially in the description of scenes belonging to the various landscape types.

As the full potential of these three new techniques of environmental psychology is realized in programmatic research, we will ultimately be able to specify what landscapes are preferred or not preferred by various observer groups, what descriptive responses of the observers mediate their preferences, and what landscape characteristics are associated with both descriptive and evaluative appraisals.

# *Appendix A*

## LANDSCAPE RATING SCALES

### VIEWING NATURAL LANDSCAPES

Name _____ Age _____ Sex _____

College major _____

If a student, year in college _____

Occupation _____

What percentage of your early years (through 18) were spent in these settings?

_____ Urban

_____ Suburban

_____ Rural

How often did you spend summers in the country, or at the shore (e.g., camps, family vacations)?

_____ Frequently

_____ Sometimes

_____ Never

How often did your family move during your early years (through 18)?

_____ Never

_____ 1–5 times

_____ 6 or more times

List your major leisure time activities:

      Weekend activities:

      Vacation activities:

Do you belong to any voluntary or professional associations concerned with the natural landscape (e.g., Sierra Club, Audubon Society, hiking clubs)? Please list.

*Landscape Rating Scales*

Type: A through J:

Name _____

The observer is

1. looking down upon the scene
2. looking straight on at the scene
3. looking up toward the scene.

Extent of view: the distance to the most remote elements in the scene is

4. less than ¼ mile
5. ¼ mile to 3 miles
6. greater than 3 miles.

Indicate the presence of

7. foreground (encircle "7" if present)
8. middleground (encircle "8" if present)
9. background (encircle "9" if present).

Is the observer afforded a panoramic view?

10. Yes, a sweeping expanse, with the scene falling away from the observer
11. Yes, a horizontal expanse, with the wide view straight on from the observer
12. No.

The scene is lighted by

13. side light, with the sun low to either side of the observer
14. back light, with the sun low and shining toward the observer
15. front light, with the sun low behind the observer
16. direction of light indeterminate.

| Item | 1 | 2 | 3 | 4 | 5 | 6 | 7 | 8 | 9 | 10 | 11 | 12 | 13 |
|---|---|---|---|---|---|---|---|---|---|---|---|---|---|
| 1 | 1 | 1 | 1 | 1 | 1 | 1 | 1 | 1 | 1 | 1 | 1 | 1 | 1 |
| 2 | 2 | 2 | 2 | 2 | 2 | 2 | 2 | 2 | 2 | 2 | 2 | 2 | 2 |
| 3 | 3 | 3 | 3 | 3 | 3 | 3 | 3 | 3 | 3 | 3 | 3 | 3 | 3 |
| 4 | 4 | 4 | 4 | 4 | 4 | 4 | 4 | 4 | 4 | 4 | 4 | 4 | 4 |
| 5 | 5 | 5 | 5 | 5 | 5 | 5 | 5 | 5 | 5 | 5 | 5 | 5 | 5 |
| 6 | 6 | 6 | 6 | 6 | 6 | 6 | 6 | 6 | 6 | 6 | 6 | 6 | 6 |
| 7 | 7 | 7 | 7 | 7 | 7 | 7 | 7 | 7 | 7 | 7 | 7 | 7 | 7 |
| 8 | 8 | 8 | 8 | 8 | 8 | 8 | 8 | 8 | 8 | 8 | 8 | 8 | 8 |
| 9 | 9 | 9 | 9 | 9 | 9 | 9 | 9 | 9 | 9 | 9 | 9 | 9 | 9 |
| 10 | 10 | 10 | 10 | 10 | 10 | 10 | 10 | 10 | 10 | 10 | 10 | 10 | 10 |
| 11 | 11 | 11 | 11 | 11 | 11 | 11 | 11 | 11 | 11 | 11 | 11 | 11 | 11 |
| 12 | 12 | 12 | 12 | 12 | 12 | 12 | 12 | 12 | 12 | 12 | 12 | 12 | 12 |
| 13 | 13 | 13 | 13 | 13 | 13 | 13 | 13 | 13 | 13 | 13 | 13 | 13 | 13 |
| 14 | 14 | 14 | 14 | 14 | 14 | 14 | 14 | 14 | 14 | 14 | 14 | 14 | 14 |
| 15 | 15 | 15 | 15 | 15 | 15 | 15 | 15 | 15 | 15 | 15 | 15 | 15 | 15 |
| 16 | 16 | 16 | 16 | 16 | 16 | 16 | 16 | 16 | 16 | 16 | 16 | 16 | 16 |

## TYPE: A THROUGH J:

Name

| | 14 | 15 | 16 | 17 | 18 | 19 | 20 | 21 | 22 | 23 | 24 | 25 |
|---|---|---|---|---|---|---|---|---|---|---|---|---|
| **The observer is** | | | | | | | | | | | | |
| 1. looking down upon the scene | 1 | 1 | 1 | 1 | 1 | 1 | 1 | 1 | 1 | 1 | 1 | 1 |
| 2. looking straight on at the scene | 2 | 2 | 2 | 2 | 2 | 2 | 2 | 2 | 2 | 2 | 2 | 2 |
| 3. looking up toward the scene. | 3 | 3 | 3 | 3 | 3 | 3 | 3 | 3 | 3 | 3 | 3 | 3 |
| **Extent of view: the distance to the most remote elements in the scene is** | | | | | | | | | | | | |
| 4. less than ¼ mile | 4 | 4 | 4 | 4 | 4 | 4 | 4 | 4 | 4 | 4 | 4 | 4 |
| 5. ¼ mile to 3 miles | 5 | 5 | 5 | 5 | 5 | 5 | 5 | 5 | 5 | 5 | 5 | 5 |
| 6. greater than 3 miles. | 6 | 6 | 6 | 6 | 6 | 6 | 6 | 6 | 6 | 6 | 6 | 6 |
| **Indicate the presence of** | | | | | | | | | | | | |
| 7. foreground (encircle "7" if present) | 7 | 7 | 7 | 7 | 7 | 7 | 7 | 7 | 7 | 7 | 7 | 7 |
| 8. middleground (encircle "8" if present) | 8 | 8 | 8 | 8 | 8 | 8 | 8 | 8 | 8 | 8 | 8 | 8 |
| 9. background (encircle "9" if present). | 9 | 9 | 9 | 9 | 9 | 9 | 9 | 9 | 9 | 9 | 9 | 9 |
| **Is the observer afforded a panoramic view?** | | | | | | | | | | | | |
| 10. Yes, a sweeping expanse, with the scene falling away from the observer | 10 | 10 | 10 | 10 | 10 | 10 | 10 | 10 | 10 | 10 | 10 | 10 |
| 11. Yes, a horizontal expanse, with the wide view straight on from the observer | 11 | 11 | 11 | 11 | 11 | 11 | 11 | 11 | 11 | 11 | 11 | 11 |
| 12. No. | 12 | 12 | 12 | 12 | 12 | 12 | 12 | 12 | 12 | 12 | 12 | 12 |
| **The scene is lighted by** | | | | | | | | | | | | |
| 13. side light, with the sun low to either side of the observer | 13 | 13 | 13 | 13 | 13 | 13 | 13 | 13 | 13 | 13 | 13 | 13 |
| 14. back light, with the sun low and shining toward the observer | 14 | 14 | 14 | 14 | 14 | 14 | 14 | 14 | 14 | 14 | 14 | 14 |
| 15. front light, with the sun low behind the observer | 15 | 15 | 15 | 15 | 15 | 15 | 15 | 15 | 15 | 15 | 15 | 15 |
| 16. direction of light indeterminate. | 16 | 16 | 16 | 16 | 16 | 16 | 16 | 16 | 16 | 16 | 16 | 16 |

Name _____

TYPE: A THROUGH J:

The scene presents a sense of vertical enclosure which blocks off the line of vision: (encircle all items that apply)

| | 1 | 2 | 3 | 4 | 5 | 6 | 7 | 8 | 9 | 10 | 11 | 12 | 13 |
|---|---|---|---|---|---|---|---|---|---|---|---|---|---|
| 17. In all directions and entirely surrounds the observer. | 17 | 17 | 17 | 17 | 17 | 17 | 17 | 17 | 17 | 17 | 17 | 17 | 17 |
| 18. Directly ahead of the observer. | 18 | 18 | 18 | 18 | 18 | 18 | 18 | 18 | 18 | 18 | 18 | 18 | 18 |
| 19. On the left side. | 19 | 19 | 19 | 19 | 19 | 19 | 19 | 19 | 19 | 19 | 19 | 19 | 19 |
| 20. On the right side. | 20 | 20 | 20 | 20 | 20 | 20 | 20 | 20 | 20 | 20 | 20 | 20 | 20 |
| 21. Does not apply—no sense of vertical enclosure | 21 | 21 | 21 | 21 | 21 | 21 | 21 | 21 | 21 | 21 | 21 | 21 | 21 |

Does the scene contain an isolated form, composed of a single element or a group of elements, seen in profile or silhouette against the sky or against a distant background?

| | 1 | 2 | 3 | 4 | 5 | 6 | 7 | 8 | 9 | 10 | 11 | 12 | 13 |
|---|---|---|---|---|---|---|---|---|---|---|---|---|---|
| 22. Definitely present. | 22 | 22 | 22 | 22 | 22 | 22 | 22 | 22 | 22 | 22 | 22 | 22 | 22 |
| 23. Somewhat present. | 23 | 23 | 23 | 23 | 23 | 23 | 23 | 23 | 23 | 23 | 23 | 23 | 23 |
| 24. Definitely absent. | 24 | 24 | 24 | 24 | 24 | 24 | 24 | 24 | 24 | 24 | 24 | 24 | 24 |

Does the scene contain a surface shape, seen as an outline embedded in the landscape itself?

| | 1 | 2 | 3 | 4 | 5 | 6 | 7 | 8 | 9 | 10 | 11 | 12 | 13 |
|---|---|---|---|---|---|---|---|---|---|---|---|---|---|
| 25. Definitely present. | 25 | 25 | 25 | 25 | 25 | 25 | 25 | 25 | 25 | 25 | 25 | 25 | 25 |
| 26. Somewhat present. | 26 | 26 | 26 | 26 | 26 | 26 | 26 | 26 | 26 | 26 | 26 | 26 | 26 |
| 27. Definitely absent. | 27 | 27 | 27 | 27 | 27 | 27 | 27 | 27 | 27 | 27 | 27 | 27 | 27 |

Focal view: are there elements in the scene which direct the line of vision along a prescribed pathway?

| | 1 | 2 | 3 | 4 | 5 | 6 | 7 | 8 | 9 | 10 | 11 | 12 | 13 |
|---|---|---|---|---|---|---|---|---|---|---|---|---|---|
| 28. Definitely present. | 28 | 28 | 28 | 28 | 28 | 28 | 28 | 28 | 28 | 28 | 28 | 28 | 28 |
| 29. Somewhat present. | 29 | 29 | 29 | 29 | 29 | 29 | 29 | 29 | 29 | 29 | 29 | 29 | 29 |
| 30. Definitely absent. | 30 | 30 | 30 | 30 | 30 | 30 | 30 | 30 | 30 | 30 | 30 | 30 | 30 |

The clouds in the scene have the appearance of

| | 1 | 2 | 3 | 4 | 5 | 6 | 7 | 8 | 9 | 10 | 11 | 12 | 13 |
|---|---|---|---|---|---|---|---|---|---|---|---|---|---|
| 31. delicate, feathery, sweeping fibers | 31 | 31 | 31 | 31 | 31 | 31 | 31 | 31 | 31 | 31 | 31 | 31 | 31 |
| 32. dense, billowing, white mounds, sharply outlined | 32 | 32 | 32 | 32 | 32 | 32 | 32 | 32 | 32 | 32 | 32 | 32 | 32 |
| 33. low, grey, thick, diffuse masses. | 33 | 33 | 33 | 33 | 33 | 33 | 33 | 33 | 33 | 33 | 33 | 33 | 33 |
| 34. Does not apply—no clouds in the scene. | 34 | 34 | 34 | 34 | 34 | 34 | 34 | 34 | 34 | 34 | 34 | 34 | 34 |

Name

| | 14 | 15 | 16 | 17 | 18 | 19 | 20 | 21 | 22 | 23 | 24 | 25 |
|---|---|---|---|---|---|---|---|---|---|---|---|---|

TYPE: A THROUGH J:

The scene presents a sense of vertical enclosure which blocks off the line of vision: (encircle all items that apply)

| | 14 | 15 | 16 | 17 | 18 | 19 | 20 | 21 | 22 | 23 | 24 | 25 |
|---|---|---|---|---|---|---|---|---|---|---|---|---|
| 17. In all directions and entirely surrounds the observer. | 17 | 17 | 17 | 17 | 17 | 17 | 17 | 17 | 17 | 17 | 17 | 17 |
| 18. Directly ahead of the observer. | 18 | 18 | 18 | 18 | 18 | 18 | 18 | 18 | 18 | 18 | 18 | 18 |
| 19. On the left side. | 19 | 19 | 19 | 19 | 19 | 19 | 19 | 19 | 19 | 19 | 19 | 19 |
| 20. On the right side. | 20 | 20 | 20 | 20 | 20 | 20 | 20 | 20 | 20 | 20 | 20 | 20 |
| 21. Does not apply—no sense of vertical enclosure | 21 | 21 | 21 | 21 | 21 | 21 | 21 | 21 | 21 | 21 | 21 | 21 |

Does the scene contain an isolated form, composed of a single element or a group of elements, seen in profile or silhouette against the sky or against a distant background?

| | 14 | 15 | 16 | 17 | 18 | 19 | 20 | 21 | 22 | 23 | 24 | 25 |
|---|---|---|---|---|---|---|---|---|---|---|---|---|
| 22. Definitely present. | 22 | 22 | 22 | 22 | 22 | 22 | 22 | 22 | 22 | 22 | 22 | 22 |
| 23. Somewhat present. | 23 | 23 | 23 | 23 | 23 | 23 | 23 | 23 | 23 | 23 | 23 | 23 |
| 24. Definitely absent. | 24 | 24 | 24 | 24 | 24 | 24 | 24 | 24 | 24 | 24 | 24 | 24 |

Does the scene contain a surface shape, seen as an outline embedded in the landscape itself?

| | 14 | 15 | 16 | 17 | 18 | 19 | 20 | 21 | 22 | 23 | 24 | 25 |
|---|---|---|---|---|---|---|---|---|---|---|---|---|
| 25. Definitely present. | 25 | 25 | 25 | 25 | 25 | 25 | 25 | 25 | 25 | 25 | 25 | 25 |
| 26. Somewhat present. | 26 | 26 | 26 | 26 | 26 | 26 | 26 | 26 | 26 | 26 | 26 | 26 |
| 27. Definitely absent. | 27 | 27 | 27 | 27 | 27 | 27 | 27 | 27 | 27 | 27 | 27 | 27 |

Focal view: are there elements in the scene which direct the line of vision along a prescribed pathway?

| | 14 | 15 | 16 | 17 | 18 | 19 | 20 | 21 | 22 | 23 | 24 | 25 |
|---|---|---|---|---|---|---|---|---|---|---|---|---|
| 28. Definitely present. | 28 | 28 | 28 | 28 | 28 | 28 | 28 | 28 | 28 | 28 | 28 | 28 |
| 29. Somewhat present. | 29 | 29 | 29 | 29 | 29 | 29 | 29 | 29 | 29 | 29 | 29 | 29 |
| 30. Definitely absent. | 30 | 30 | 30 | 30 | 30 | 30 | 30 | 30 | 30 | 30 | 30 | 30 |

The clouds in the scene have the appearance of

| | 14 | 15 | 16 | 17 | 18 | 19 | 20 | 21 | 22 | 23 | 24 | 25 |
|---|---|---|---|---|---|---|---|---|---|---|---|---|
| 31. delicate, feathery, sweeping fibers | 31 | 31 | 31 | 31 | 31 | 31 | 31 | 31 | 31 | 31 | 31 | 31 |
| 32. dense, billowing, white mounds, sharply outlined | 32 | 32 | 32 | 32 | 32 | 32 | 32 | 32 | 32 | 32 | 32 | 32 |
| 33. low, grey, thick, diffuse masses. | 33 | 33 | 33 | 33 | 33 | 33 | 33 | 33 | 33 | 33 | 33 | 33 |
| 34. Does not apply—no clouds in the scene. | 34 | 34 | 34 | 34 | 34 | 34 | 34 | 34 | 34 | 34 | 34 | 34 |

## *Appendix B*

### THE LANDSCAPE ADJECTIVE CHECK LIST

Name _____ Age _____ Sex _____

Date _____ Occupation _____

Landscape to be described _____

DIRECTIONS: This booklet contains a list of adjectives. Please read them quickly and put an X on the line beside each one you would consider descriptive of the designated landscape. Do not worry about duplications, contradictions, and so forth. Work quickly and do not spend too much time on any one adjective.

| | | | |
|---|---|---|---|
| ____ active | ____ cold | ____ eternal | ____ harsh |
| ____ adventurous | ____ colorful | ____ exciting | ____ hazy |
| ____ alive | ____ colorless | ____ expansive | ____ high |
| ____ arid | ____ comfortable | ____ extensive | ____ hilly |
| ____ autumnal | ____ content | ____ falling | ____ hot |
| ____ awesome | ____ contrasting | ____ farmed | ____ humid |
| ____ bare | ____ cool | ____ fast | ____ icy |
| ____ barren | ____ crashing | ____ flat | ____ imposing |
| ____ beautiful | ____ crisp | ____ flowery | ____ inspiring |
| ____ big | ____ cut | ____ flowing | ____ invigorating |
| ____ black | ____ dangerous | ____ foamy | ____ inviting |
| ____ bleak | ____ dark | ____ forceful | ____ isolated |
| ____ blue | ____ dead | ____ forested | ____ jagged |
| ____ boring | ____ deep | ____ free | ____ large |
| ____ bright | ____ dense | ____ fresh | ____ lazy |
| ____ brisk | ____ depressing | ____ friendly | ____ leafy |
| ____ broad | ____ deserted | ____ gentle | ____ lifeless |
| ____ brown | ____ desolate | ____ glacial | ____ light |
| ____ burned | ____ destroyed | ____ gloomy | ____ living |
| ____ bushy | ____ dirty | ____ golden | ____ lonely |
| ____ calm | ____ distant | ____ good | ____ lovely |
| ____ challenging | ____ drab | ____ grassy | ____ low |
| ____ changing | ____ dry | ____ gray | ____ lumpy |
| ____ clean | ____ dull | ____ green | ____ lush |
| ____ clear | ____ empty | ____ happy | ____ majestic |
| ____ cloudy | ____ eroded | ____ hard | ____ marshy |

| | | | |
|---|---|---|---|
| ___ massive | ___ pure | ___ shallow | ___ tranquil |
| ___ meadowy | ___ quiet | ___ sharp | ___ tree-studded |
| ___ misty | ___ rainy | ___ sliding | ___ ugly |
| ___ moist | ___ rapid | ___ slippery | ___ unfriendly |
| ___ monotonous | ___ reaching | ___ sloping | ___ uninspiring |
| ___ motionless | ___ reflecting | ___ slow | ___ uninteresting |
| ___ mountainous | ___ refreshing | ___ smooth | ___ uninviting |
| ___ moving | ___ relaxing | ___ snowy | ___ unusual |
| ___ muddy | ___ remote | ___ soft | ___ vast |
| ___ mysterious | ___ restful | ___ spacious | ___ vegetated |
| ___ narrow | ___ rich | ___ sparse | ___ violent |
| ___ natural | ___ rocky | ___ spring-like | ___ warm |
| ___ nice | ___ rolling | ___ stark | ___ watery |
| ___ nocturnal | ___ rough | ___ steep | ___ weedy |
| ___ noisy | ___ round | ___ still | ___ wet |
| ___ old | ___ rugged | ___ stoney | ___ white |
| ___ open | ___ running | ___ stormy | ___ wide |
| ___ orange | ___ rushing | ___ straight | ___ wild |
| ___ pastoral | ___ rusty | ___ strange | ___ windy |
| ___ peaceful | ___ sad | ___ summery | ___ wintry |
| ___ placid | ___ sandy | ___ sunny | ___ wooded |
| ___ plain | ___ secluded | ___ swampy | ___ yellow |
| ___ pleasant | ___ secure | ___ tall | |
| ___ pointed | ___ serene | ___ thick | |
| ___ powerful | ___ shadowy | ___ threatening | |
| ___ pretty | ___ shady | ___ towering | |

Institute of Personality Assessment and Research
University of California, Berkeley

K. H. Craik
1969

# *Appendix C*

Table C.1.  Range of Judgments Made by Each Panel

Forestry and Conservation Panel: Graphic landscape typology: Scenes 1–50
Landscape rating scales 1–5: Scenes 1–18
Landscape rating scales 6–10: Scenes 26–43

Landscape Architecture Panel: Graphic landscape typology: Scenes 1–50
Landscape rating scales 1–5: Scenes 1–18
Landscape rating scales 6–10: Scenes 26–43

Forest Service Panel: Graphic landscape typology: Scenes 1–50
Landscape rating scales: Scenes 1–25
Landscape rating scales: Scenes 26–50

University Students Panels I and IV: Graphic landscape typology: Scenes 1–50
Landscape rating scales 1–5: Scenes 1–25
Landscape rating scales 6–10: Scenes 26–50

University Student Panels II and III: Graphic landscape typology: Scenes 1–50
Landscape rating scales 1–5: Scenes 26–50
Landscape rating scales 6–10: Scenes 1–25

Conservation Course Panel: Graphic landscape typology: Scenes 1–6
Landscape rating scales 1–5: Scenes 1–6
Landscape rating scales 6–10: Scenes 26–31

Table C.2.  Illustration of the $X^2$ One-sample Test

Rating 13–16: The scene is lighted by

13. side light, with the sun low to either side of the observer
14. back light, with the sun low and shining toward the observer
15. front light, with the sun low behind the observer
16. direction of light indeterminate.

| Scene 11 | Rating: | 13 | 14 | 15 | 16 |
|---|---|---|---|---|---|
| | Frequency: | 0 | 14 | 2 | 5 |

$X^2 = 21.86$  Level of significance: beyond .001

| Scene 8 | Rating: | 13 | 14 | 15 | 16 |
|---|---|---|---|---|---|
| | Frequency: | 6 | 8 | 4 | 2 |

$X^2 = 4.00$  Level of significance: beyond .30

| Scene 13 | Rating: | 13 | 14 | 15 | 16 |
|---|---|---|---|---|---|
| | Frequency: | 5 | 5 | 6 | 5 |

$X^2 = .14$  Level of significance: beyond .99

Table C.3. Landscape Rating Scales: Combined Analysis for All Panels

| Scene | RATING SCALE 1 | | | | RATING SCALE 2 | | | |
|---|---|---|---|---|---|---|---|---|
| | 1 | 2 | 3 | Significance level | 4 | 5 | 6 | Significance level |
| 1 | 21 | 63 | 4 | .001 | 0 | 16 | 72 | .001 |
| 2 | 21 | 59 | 7 | .001 | 24 | 36 | 27 | .30 |
| 3 | 11 | 71 | 4 | .001 | 63 | 20 | 3 | .001 |
| 4 | 9 | 46 | 32 | .001 | 61 | 24 | 1 | .001 |
| 5 | 2 | 75 | 10 | .001 | 0 | 1 | 86 | .001 |
| 6 | 8 | 76 | 2 | .001 | 4 | 5 | 77 | .001 |
| 7 | 35 | 33 | 20 | .20 | 10 | 55 | 23 | .001 |
| 8 | 16 | 47 | 25 | .001 | 31 | 55 | 2 | .001 |
| 9 | 83 | 6 | 0 | .001 | 0 | 42 | 47 | .001 |
| 10 | 12 | 14 | 63 | .001 | 20 | 55 | 14 | .001 |
| 11 | 3 | 28 | 58 | .001 | 76 | 13 | 0 | .001 |
| 12 | 57 | 29 | 3 | .001 | 72 | 17 | 0 | .001 |
| 13 | 18 | 71 | 0 | .001 | 0 | 6 | 83 | .001 |
| 14 | 45 | 36 | 10 | .001 | 7 | 57 | 25 | .001 |
| 15 | 8 | 42 | 39 | .001 | 8 | 68 | 13 | .001 |
| 16 | 3 | 84 | 2 | .001 | 2 | 10 | 76 | .001 |
| 17 | 84 | 4 | 1 | .001 | 1 | 12 | 76 | .001 |
| 18 | 14 | 70 | 5 | .001 | 2 | 8 | 79 | .001 |
| 19 | 54 | 6 | 0 | .001 | 5 | 35 | 20 | .001 |
| 20 | 5 | 50 | 5 | .001 | 27 | 26 | 7 | .01 |
| 21 | 1 | 51 | 8 | .001 | 3 | 38 | 19 | .001 |
| 22 | 5 | 25 | 30 | .001 | 5 | 42 | 13 | .001 |
| 23 | 56 | 2 | 2 | .001 | 0 | 2 | 58 | .001 |
| 24 | 35 | 20 | 5 | .001 | 0 | 6 | 53 | .001 |
| 25 | 3 | 48 | 9 | .001 | 1 | 31 | 28 | .001 |
| 26 | 1 | 41 | 8 | .001 | 1 | 24 | 25 | .001 |
| 27 | 35 | 12 | 3 | .001 | 2 | 24 | 24 | .001 |
| 28 | 8 | 38 | 4 | .001 | 2 | 20 | 28 | .001 |
| 29 | 5 | 41 | 4 | .001 | 30 | 16 | 4 | .001 |
| 30 | 16 | 22 | 12 | .30 | 0 | 2 | 48 | .001 |
| 31 | 21 | 27 | 1 | .001 | 49 | 1 | 0 | .001 |
| 32 | 10 | 33 | 7 | .001 | 0 | 31 | 19 | .001 |
| 33 | 1 | 44 | 5 | .001 | 2 | 31 | 17 | .001 |
| 34 | 45 | 5 | 0 | .001 | 0 | 0 | 50 | .001 |
| 35 | 4 | 43 | 3 | .001 | 3 | 27 | 20 | .001 |
| 36 | 33 | 12 | 6 | .001 | 2 | 12 | 36 | .001 |
| 37 | 6 | 27 | 17 | .01 | 28 | 20 | 2 | .001 |
| 38 | 3 | 41 | 6 | .001 | 32 | 16 | 1 | .001 |
| 39 | 18 | 32 | 0 | .001 | 0 | 4 | 46 | .001 |
| 40 | 2 | 47 | 1 | .001 | 3 | 27 | 20 | .001 |
| 41 | 22 | 9 | 20 | .10 | 7 | 27 | 16 | .01 |
| 42 | 0 | 39 | 10 | .001 | 0 | 2 | 47 | .001 |
| 43 | 22 | 26 | 1 | .001 | 0 | 27 | 22 | .001 |
| 44 | 3 | 44 | 2 | .001 | 0 | 6 | 43 | .001 |
| 45 | 43 | 6 | 0 | .001 | 26 | 19 | 4 | .001 |
| 46 | 14 | 26 | 9 | .01 | 0 | 8 | 41 | .001 |
| 47 | 13 | 34 | 2 | .001 | 0 | 4 | 45 | .001 |
| 48 | 1 | 44 | 4 | .001 | 44 | 5 | 0 | .001 |
| 49 | 32 | 5 | 14 | .001 | 1 | 37 | 12 | .001 |
| 50 | 3 | 23 | 22 | .001 | 16 | 29 | 4 | .001 |

Table C.3. (cont'd)

RATING SCALE 3

| Scene | 7 | Significance level | 8 | Significance level | 9 | Significance level |
|---|---|---|---|---|---|---|
| 1 | 40 | .50 | 78 | .001 | 81 | .001 |
| 2 | 70 | .001 | 79 | .001 | 60 | .001 |
| 3 | 75 | .001 | 52 | .10 | 25 | .001 |
| 4 | 44 | .99 | 67 | .001 | 25 | .001 |
| 5 | 54 | .05 | 74 | .001 | 82 | .001 |
| 6 | 80 | .001 | 69 | .001 | 72 | .001 |
| 7 | 31 | .01 | 68 | .001 | 45 | .90 |
| 8 | 64 | .001 | 80 | .001 | 44 | .99 |
| 9 | 13 | .001 | 78 | .001 | 76 | .001 |
| 10 | 44 | .99 | 74 | .001 | 40 | .50 |
| 11 | 68 | .001 | 71 | .001 | 27 | .001 |
| 12 | 78 | .001 | 70 | .001 | 12 | .001 |
| 13 | 69 | .001 | 72 | .001 | 80 | .001 |
| 14 | 59 | .01 | 85 | .001 | 53 | .10 |
| 15 | 7 | .001 | 61 | .001 | 51 | .20 |
| 16 | 77 | .001 | 80 | .001 | 80 | .001 |
| 17 | 52 | .10 | 82 | .001 | 79 | .001 |
| 18 | 77 | .001 | 64 | .001 | 82 | .001 |
| 19 | 42 | .01 | 57 | .001 | 40 | .01 |
| 20 | 51 | .001 | 48 | .001 | 23 | .10 |
| 21 | 36 | .20 | 55 | .001 | 53 | .001 |
| 22 | 28 | .70 | 53 | .001 | 44 | .001 |
| 23 | 29 | .80 | 51 | .001 | 56 | .001 |
| 24 | 8 | .001 | 48 | .001 | 55 | .001 |
| 25 | 25 | .20 | 40 | .01 | 48 | .001 |
| 26 | 30 | .20 | 47 | .001 | 44 | .001 |
| 27 | 27 | .70 | 47 | .001 | 41 | .001 |
| 28 | 35 | .01 | 48 | .001 | 47 | .001 |
| 29 | 42 | .001 | 43 | .001 | 25 | .99+ |
| 30 | 44 | .001 | 49 | .001 | 47 | .001 |
| 31 | 39 | .001 | 32 | .05 | 2 | .001 |
| 32 | 21 | .30 | 40 | .001 | 44 | .001 |
| 33 | 42 | .001 | 46 | .001 | 43 | .001 |
| 34 | 22 | .50 | 50 | .001 | 50 | .001 |
| 35 | 30 | .20 | 42 | .001 | 42 | .001 |
| 36 | 21 | .30 | 47 | .001 | 49 | .001 |
| 37 | 12 | .001 | 41 | .001 | 14 | .01 |
| 38 | 41 | .001 | 45 | .001 | 24 | .80 |
| 39 | 40 | .001 | 48 | .001 | 50 | .001 |
| 40 | 38 | .001 | 42 | .001 | 43 | .001 |
| 41 | 14 | .01 | 39 | .001 | 32 | .05 |
| 42 | 41 | .001 | 49 | .001 | 47 | .001 |
| 43 | 37 | .001 | 46 | .001 | 37 | .001 |
| 44 | 33 | .05 | 42 | .001 | 47 | .001 |
| 45 | 42 | .001 | 42 | .001 | 22 | .80 |
| 46 | 14 | .01 | 33 | .05 | 39 | .001 |
| 47 | 25 | .99 | 45 | .001 | 47 | .001 |
| 48 | 49 | .001 | 35 | .01 | 14 | .01 |
| 49 | 23 | .70 | 49 | .001 | 35 | .01 |
| 50 | 23 | .70 | 42 | .001 | 24 | .80 |

Table C.3. (cont'd)

| | RATING SCALE 4 | | | | RATING SCALE 5 | | | | |
|---|---|---|---|---|---|---|---|---|---|
| Scene | 10 | 11 | 12 | Significance level | 13 | 14 | 15 | 16 | Significance level |
| 1 | 13 | 62 | 12 | .001 | 41 | 7 | 30 | 8 | .001 |
| 2 | 6 | 8 | 71 | .001 | 25 | 44 | 8 | 9 | .001 |
| 3 | 0 | 16 | 70 | .001 | 49 | 14 | 14 | 9 | .001 |
| 4 | 2 | 11 | 73 | .001 | 34 | 2 | 24 | 26 | .001 |
| 5 | 15 | 70 | 3 | .001 | 10 | 8 | 29 | 40 | .001 |
| 6 | 30 | 40 | 16 | .01 | 65 | 9 | 6 | 6 | .001 |
| 7 | 9 | 7 | 72 | .001 | 64 | 6 | 11 | 7 | .001 |
| 8 | 5 | 15 | 66 | .001 | 26 | 28 | 8 | 24 | .01 |
| 9 | 45 | 32 | 13 | .001 | 42 | 13 | 19 | 13 | .001 |
| 10 | 8 | 30 | 51 | .001 | 22 | 17 | 23 | 27 | .70 |
| 11 | 5 | 14 | 70 | .001 | 2 | 44 | 8 | 35 | .001 |
| 12 | 7 | 3 | 79 | .001 | 56 | 8 | 10 | 14 | .001 |
| 13 | 30 | 50 | 11 | .001 | 18 | 13 | 16 | 42 | .001 |
| 14 | 23 | 17 | 48 | .001 | 39 | 6 | 36 | 8 | .001 |
| 15 | 9 | 22 | 58 | .001 | 25 | 18 | 17 | 28 | .30 |
| 16 | 25 | 49 | 15 | .001 | 72 | 2 | 7 | 6 | .001 |
| 17 | 71 | 9 | 9 | .001 | 22 | 10 | 20 | 37 | .001 |
| 18 | 25 | 59 | 5 | .001 | 14 | 37 | 10 | 27 | .001 |
| 19 | 14 | 5 | 41 | .001 | 30 | 11 | 17 | 2 | .001 |
| 20 | 6 | 5 | 49 | .001 | 36 | 6 | 9 | 9 | .001 |
| 21 | 6 | 18 | 36 | .001 | 27 | 9 | 13 | 11 | .01 |
| 22 | 6 | 21 | 32 | .001 | 29 | 3 | 18 | 9 | .001 |
| 23 | 45 | 11 | 5 | .001 | 19 | 13 | 16 | 12 | .70 |
| 24 | 29 | 26 | 4 | .001 | 18 | 8 | 22 | 12 | .10 |
| 25 | 4 | 40 | 16 | .001 | 6 | 29 | 7 | 17 | .001 |
| 26 | 16 | 21 | 12 | .30 | 18 | 3 | 15 | 14 | .02 |
| 27 | 19 | 19 | 12 | .50 | 36 | 3 | 5 | 5 | .001 |
| 28 | 18 | 13 | 19 | .70 | 11 | 14 | 12 | 12 | .98 |
| 29 | 2 | 6 | 42 | .001 | 38 | 5 | 2 | 5 | .001 |
| 30 | 20 | 18 | 14 | .70 | 15 | 6 | 7 | 20 | .02 |
| 31 | 0 | 5 | 46 | .001 | 12 | 25 | 4 | 9 | .001 |
| 32 | 8 | 35 | 7 | .001 | 12 | 14 | 12 | 10 | .90 |
| 33 | 15 | 21 | 15 | .50 | 29 | 7 | 6 | 8 | .001 |
| 34 | 38 | 12 | 1 | .001 | 8 | 21 | 11 | 9 | .05 |
| 35 | 10 | 37 | 4 | .001 | 7 | 6 | 8 | 29 | .001 |
| 36 | 20 | 13 | 18 | .50 | 18 | 15 | 8 | 8 | .10 |
| 37 | 2 | 16 | 32 | .001 | 2 | 3 | 33 | 12 | .001 |
| 38 | 4 | 9 | 37 | .001 | 7 | 14 | 7 | 22 | .01 |
| 39 | 24 | 27 | 0 | .001 | 14 | 24 | 4 | 9 | .001 |
| 40 | 6 | 38 | 5 | .001 | 9 | 6 | 14 | 20 | .05 |
| 41 | 17 | 4 | 29 | .001 | 26 | 5 | 4 | 15 | .001 |
| 42 | 22 | 25 | 4 | .001 | 22 | 9 | 15 | 3 | .01 |
| 43 | 22 | 18 | 10 | .20 | 16 | 7 | 10 | 16 | .20 |
| 44 | 12 | 29 | 7 | .001 | 8 | 7 | 19 | 15 | .05 |
| 45 | 7 | 9 | 34 | .001 | 11 | 15 | 14 | 9 | .80 |
| 46 | 22 | 17 | 10 | .20 | 6 | 35 | 2 | 7 | .001 |
| 47 | 11 | 37 | 1 | .001 | 15 | 15 | 7 | 12 | .50 |
| 48 | 0 | 6 | 43 | .001 | 13 | 6 | 14 | 16 | .30 |
| 49 | 25 | 6 | 18 | .01 | 19 | 7 | 11 | 12 | .20 |
| 50 | 7 | 6 | 36 | .001 | 29 | 9 | 6 | 5 | .001 |

Table C.3. (cont'd)

RATING SCALE 6

| Scene | 17 | Significance level | 18 | Significance level | 19 | Significance level |
|-------|-----|------|-----|------|-----|------|
| 1 | 9 | .001 | 21 | .30 | 9 | .001 |
| 2 | 16 | .02 | 14 | .01 | 29 | .30 |
| 3 | 7 | .001 | 37 | .001 | 3 | .001 |
| 4 | 4 | .001 | 44 | .001 | 0 | .001 |
| 5 | 5 | .001 | 18 | .05 | 1 | .001 |
| 6 | 2 | .001 | 3 | .001 | 18 | .05 |
| 7 | 2 | .001 | 39 | .001 | 1 | .001 |
| 8 | 4 | .001 | 22 | .50 | 21 | .30 |
| 9 | 1 | .001 | 8 | .001 | 2 | .001 |
| 10 | 2 | .001 | 22 | .50 | 0 | .001 |
| 11 | 1 | .001 | 11 | .001 | 2 | .001 |
| 12 | 9 | .001 | 14 | .01 | 39 | .001 |
| 13 | 0 | .001 | 5 | .001 | 0 | .001 |
| 14 | 6 | .001 | 23 | .70 | 5 | .001 |
| 15 | 3 | .001 | 43 | .001 | 4 | .001 |
| 16 | 0 | .001 | 6 | .001 | 13 | .001 |
| 17 | 4 | .001 | 4 | .001 | 11 | .001 |
| 18 | 2 | .001 | 2 | .001 | 4 | .001 |
| 19 | 21 | .30 | 11 | .001 | 22 | .50 |
| 20 | 14 | .01 | 18 | .05 | 36 | .01 |
| 21 | 18 | .05 | 26 | .80 | 26 | .80 |
| 22 | 1 | .001 | 34 | .02 | 15 | .01 |
| 23 | 5 | .001 | 13 | .001 | 9 | .001 |
| 24 | 4 | .001 | 12 | .001 | 2 | .001 |
| 25 | 0 | .001 | 35 | .01 | 0 | .001 |
| 26 | 13 | .001 | 40 | .50 | 69 | .001 |
| 27 | 6 | .001 | 38 | .20 | 61 | .001 |
| 28 | 18 | .001 | 41 | .70 | 35 | .10 |
| 29 | 23 | .001 | 5 | .001 | 65 | .001 |
| 30 | 0 | .001 | 14 | .001 | 4 | .001 |
| 31 | 37 | .20 | 9 | .001 | 51 | .20 |
| 32 | 7 | .001 | 46 | .70 | 3 | .001 |
| 33 | 5 | .001 | 42 | .70 | 13 | .001 |
| 34 | 1 | .001 | 6 | .001 | 0 | .001 |
| 35 | 1 | .001 | 3 | .001 | 4 | .001 |
| 36 | 1 | .001 | 24 | .001 | 79 | .001 |
| 37 | 0 | .001 | 85 | .001 | 1 | .001 |
| 38 | 26 | .001 | 54 | .05 | 12 | .001 |
| 39 | 4 | .001 | 20 | .001 | 7 | .001 |
| 40 | 2 | .001 | 3 | .001 | 1 | .001 |
| 41 | 1 | .001 | 49 | .30 | 9 | .001 |
| 42 | 1 | .001 | 16 | .001 | 28 | .001 |
| 43 | 2 | .001 | 6 | .001 | 1 | .001 |
| 44 | 1 | .001 | 17 | .001 | 5 | .001 |
| 45 | 13 | .001 | 22 | .05 | 27 | .50 |
| 46 | 3 | .001 | 16 | .001 | 1 | .001 |
| 47 | 0 | .001 | 19 | .01 | 1 | .001 |
| 48 | 39 | .05 | 22 | .05 | 7 | .001 |
| 49 | 11 | .001 | 17 | .001 | 42 | .01 |
| 50 | 2 | .001 | 47 | .001 | 6 | .001 |

Table C.3. (cont'd)

| | | RATING SCALE 6 (CONT'D) | | |
| | | Significance | | Significance |
| Scene | 20 | level | 21 | level |
|---|---|---|---|---|
| 1 | 34 | .02 | 2 | .001 |
| 2 | 25 | .99 | 0 | .001 |
| 3 | 1 | .001 | 4 | .001 |
| 4 | 2 | .001 | 1 | .001 |
| 5 | 0 | .001 | 26 | .80 |
| 6 | 6 | .001 | 28 | .50 |
| 7 | 5 | .001 | 7 | .001 |
| 8 | 21 | .30 | 4 | .001 |
| 9 | 1 | .001 | 40 | .001 |
| 10 | 0 | .001 | 25 | .99 |
| 11 | 2 | .001 | 38 | .001 |
| 12 | 40 | .001 | 0 | .001 |
| 13 | 0 | .001 | 45 | .001 |
| 14 | 8 | .001 | 16 | .02 |
| 15 | 0 | .001 | 3 | .001 |
| 16 | 29 | .30 | 16 | .02 |
| 17 | 0 | .001 | 32 | .05 |
| 18 | 8 | .001 | 35 | .01 |
| 19 | 14 | .01 | 2 | .001 |
| 20 | 33 | .05 | 1 | .001 |
| 21 | 20 | .20 | 0 | .001 |
| 22 | 14 | .01 | 5 | .001 |
| 23 | 10 | .001 | 28 | .50 |
| 24 | 3 | .001 | 34 | .02 |
| 25 | 1 | .001 | 14 | .01 |
| 26 | 29 | .01 | 1 | .001 |
| 27 | 1 | .001 | 12 | .001 |
| 28 | 12 | .001 | 17 | .001 |
| 29 | 66 | .001 | 0 | .001 |
| 30 | 64 | .001 | 18 | .001 |
| 31 | 49 | .30 | 0 | .001 |
| 32 | 1 | .001 | 32 | .02 |
| 33 | 15 | .001 | 32 | .02 |
| 34 | 2 | .001 | 82 | .001 |
| 35 | 1 | .001 | 82 | .001 |
| 36 | 7 | .001 | 3 | .001 |
| 37 | 1 | .001 | 4 | .001 |
| 38 | 13 | .001 | 8 | .001 |
| 39 | 8 | .001 | 62 | .001 |
| 40 | 0 | .001 | 83 | .001 |
| 41 | 56 | .02 | 8 | .001 |
| 42 | 2 | .001 | 48 | .50 |
| 43 | 8 | .001 | 74 | .001 |
| 44 | 4 | .001 | 35 | .20 |
| 45 | 10 | .001 | 8 | .001 |
| 46 | 35 | .20 | 15 | .001 |
| 47 | 2 | .001 | 40 | .01 |
| 48 | 7 | .001 | 0 | .001 |
| 49 | 28 | .70 | 5 | .001 |
| 50 | 3 | .001 | 9 | .001 |

Table C.3. (cont'd)

| | RATING SCALE 7 | | | | RATING SCALE 8 | | | |
|---|---|---|---|---|---|---|---|---|
| Scene | 22 | 23 | 24 | Significance level | 25 | 26 | 27 | Significance level |
| 1 | 17 | 19 | 12 | .80 | 26 | 14 | 9 | .01 |
| 2 | 16 | 16 | 16 | .99 | 13 | 16 | 20 | .50 |
| 3 | 20 | 14 | 15 | .70 | 14 | 11 | 24 | .10 |
| 4 | 17 | 11 | 19 | .50 | 21 | 12 | 15 | .30 |
| 5 | 31 | 10 | 9 | .001 | 27 | 9 | 14 | .01 |
| 6 | 40 | 8 | 2 | .001 | 30 | 12 | 8 | .001 |
| 7 | 18 | 5 | 26 | .01 | 21 | 15 | 13 | .50 |
| 8 | 35 | 10 | 4 | .001 | 32 | 11 | 6 | .001 |
| 9 | 10 | 8 | 31 | .001 | 24 | 17 | 7 | .02 |
| 10 | 12 | 11 | 26 | .02 | 9 | 18 | 22 | .10 |
| 11 | 46 | 2 | 2 | .001 | 19 | 23 | 8 | .05 |
| 12 | 5 | 5 | 40 | .001 | 25 | 11 | 14 | .05 |
| 13 | 7 | 9 | 34 | .001 | 8 | 23 | 19 | .05 |
| 14 | 6 | 19 | 25 | .01 | 14 | 25 | 11 | .05 |
| 15 | 28 | 16 | 6 | .001 | 20 | 20 | 10 | .20 |
| 16 | 34 | 12 | 4 | .001 | 30 | 16 | 4 | .001 |
| 17 | 12 | 16 | 22 | .30 | 25 | 18 | 7 | .01 |
| 18 | 19 | 15 | 16 | .80 | 31 | 13 | 6 | .001 |
| 19 | 9 | 18 | 21 | .10 | 27 | 15 | 7 | .01 |
| 20 | 10 | 12 | 28 | .01 | 19 | 15 | 16 | .80 |
| 21 | 28 | 19 | 3 | .001 | 29 | 14 | 7 | .001 |
| 22 | 21 | 18 | 11 | .30 | 22 | 19 | 9 | .10 |
| 23 | 21 | 15 | 13 | .50 | 31 | 16 | 2 | .001 |
| 24 | 6 | 17 | 27 | .01 | 11 | 19 | 20 | .50 |
| 25 | 25 | 13 | 11 | .05 | 17 | 19 | 14 | .70 |
| 26 | 23 | 36 | 30 | .30 | 47 | 29 | 13 | .001 |
| 27 | 41 | 31 | 17 | .01 | 55 | 25 | 7 | .001 |
| 28 | 24 | 25 | 39 | .10 | 43 | 20 | 25 | .01 |
| 29 | 10 | 14 | 63 | .001 | 21 | 13 | 55 | .001 |
| 30 | 52 | 23 | 14 | .001 | 69 | 11 | 9 | .001 |
| 31 | 3 | 3 | 82 | .001 | 35 | 11 | 42 | .001 |
| 32 | 69 | 10 | 9 | .001 | 43 | 26 | 19 | .01 |
| 33 | 28 | 38 | 23 | .20 | 44 | 27 | 18 | .01 |
| 34 | 11 | 28 | 50 | .001 | 32 | 38 | 19 | .05 |
| 35 | 60 | 16 | 13 | .001 | 26 | 32 | 31 | .80 |
| 36 | 63 | 18 | 18 | .001 | 50 | 32 | 7 | .001 |
| 37 | 27 | 10 | 52 | .001 | 24 | 33 | 32 | .50 |
| 38 | 39 | 22 | 28 | .10 | 19 | 31 | 39 | .05 |
| 39 | 31 | 32 | 26 | .80 | 50 | 28 | 11 | .001 |
| 40 | 59 | 21 | 9 | .001 | 22 | 31 | 35 | .30 |
| 41 | 15 | 21 | 54 | .001 | 44 | 31 | 14 | .001 |
| 42 | 85 | 2 | 2 | .001 | 49 | 32 | 8 | .001 |
| 43 | 10 | 38 | 51 | .001 | 48 | 32 | 9 | .001 |
| 44 | 18 | 25 | 16 | .50 | 20 | 24 | 15 | .50 |
| 45 | 6 | 9 | 45 | .001 | 27 | 21 | 12 | .10 |
| 46 | 19 | 9 | 32 | .01 | 3 | 15 | 42 | .001 |
| 47 | 24 | 23 | 13 | .20 | 34 | 20 | 6 | .001 |
| 48 | 11 | 8 | 41 | .001 | 12 | 18 | 29 | .05 |
| 49 | 15 | 23 | 22 | .50 | 42 | 14 | 4 | .001 |
| 50 | 40 | 17 | 3 | .001 | 21 | 24 | 15 | .50 |

Table C.3. (cont'd)

| | RATING SCALE 9 | | | | RATING SCALE 10 | | | | |
| Scene | 28 | 29 | 30 | Significance level | 31 | 32 | 33 | 34 | Significance level |
|---|---|---|---|---|---|---|---|---|---|
| 1 | 14 | 27 | 8 | .01 | 3 | 1 | 0 | 44 | .001 |
| 2 | 38 | 8 | 3 | .001 | 3 | 0 | 0 | 45 | .001 |
| 3 | 13 | 18 | 18 | .70 | 4 | 0 | 5 | 39 | .001 |
| 4 | 17 | 10 | 22 | .20 | 2 | 0 | 0 | 46 | .001 |
| 5 | 4 | 16 | 30 | .001 | 20 | 25 | 4 | 1 | .001 |
| 6 | 46 | 1 | 3 | .001 | 10 | 1 | 37 | 2 | .001 |
| 7 | 34 | 9 | 6 | .001 | 2 | 0 | 2 | 45 | .001 |
| 8 | 18 | 20 | 11 | .30 | 6 | 1 | 7 | 35 | .001 |
| 9 | 8 | 16 | 25 | .02 | 5 | 0 | 2 | 42 | .001 |
| 10 | 8 | 12 | 29 | .001 | 1 | 0 | 0 | 48 | .001 |
| 11 | 6 | 14 | 30 | .001 | 6 | 0 | 8 | 35 | .001 |
| 12 | 45 | 4 | 1 | .001 | 0 | 0 | 0 | 50 | .001 |
| 13 | 6 | 11 | 32 | .001 | 11 | 2 | 35 | 2 | .001 |
| 14 | 12 | 30 | 8 | .001 | 6 | 0 | 0 | 44 | .001 |
| 15 | 6 | 22 | 22 | .01 | 1 | 0 | 0 | 49 | .001 |
| 16 | 41 | 9 | 0 | .001 | 13 | 11 | 25 | 1 | .001 |
| 17 | 12 | 17 | 21 | .30 | 0 | 0 | 50 | 0 | .001 |
| 18 | 18 | 23 | 7 | .02 | 11 | 1 | 30 | 8 | .001 |
| 19 | 18 | 23 | 8 | .05 | 1 | 1 | 1 | 45 | .001 |
| 20 | 46 | 0 | 4 | .001 | 0 | 0 | 1 | 49 | .001 |
| 21 | 24 | 18 | 8 | .02 | 38 | 8 | 1 | 3 | .001 |
| 22 | 8 | 27 | 15 | .01 | 0 | 0 | 0 | 50 | .001 |
| 23 | 33 | 14 | 3 | .001 | 7 | 0 | 4 | 39 | .001 |
| 24 | 14 | 19 | 17 | .70 | 10 | 22 | 19 | 1 | .001 |
| 25 | 6 | 13 | 31 | .001 | 7 | 3 | 1 | 39 | .001 |
| 26 | 63 | 25 | 1 | .001 | 88 | 0 | 0 | 0 | .001 |
| 27 | 17 | 40 | 30 | .02 | 4 | 0 | 25 | 58 | .001 |
| 28 | 44 | 34 | 10 | .001 | 10 | 0 | 7 | 70 | .001 |
| 29 | 80 | 6 | 3 | .001 | 0 | 0 | 5 | 84 | .001 |
| 30 | 27 | 35 | 27 | .50 | 8 | 31 | 50 | 0 | .001 |
| 31 | 81 | 6 | 2 | .001 | 1 | 0 | 3 | 83 | .001 |
| 32 | 15 | 42 | 32 | .01 | 0 | 1 | 2 | 85 | .001 |
| 33 | 69 | 17 | 3 | .001 | 60 | 2 | 5 | 22 | .001 |
| 34 | 14 | 45 | 30 | .001 | 69 | 3 | 12 | 4 | .001 |
| 35 | 7 | 28 | 54 | .001 | 5 | 3 | 82 | 0 | .001 |
| 36 | 71 | 18 | 0 | .001 | 70 | 5 | 3 | 9 | .001 |
| 37 | 7 | 8 | 74 | .001 | 0 | 1 | 0 | 88 | .001 |
| 38 | 9 | 23 | 56 | .001 | 2 | 0 | 20 | 65 | .001 |
| 39 | 71 | 14 | 4 | .001 | 59 | 26 | 1 | 3 | .001 |
| 40 | 18 | 31 | 38 | .05 | 0 | 6 | 83 | 0 | .001 |
| 41 | 25 | 43 | 21 | .01 | 22 | 1 | 8 | 57 | .001 |
| 42 | 35 | 32 | 22 | .30 | 1 | 2 | 0 | 86 | .001 |
| 43 | 8 | 29 | 52 | .001 | 1 | 0 | 0 | 88 | .001 |
| 44 | 7 | 30 | 23 | .001 | 32 | 16 | 1 | 11 | .001 |
| 45 | 41 | 15 | 4 | .001 | 0 | 1 | 0 | 59 | .001 |
| 46 | 5 | 22 | 33 | .001 | 2 | 0 | 5 | 53 | .001 |
| 47 | 5 | 20 | 35 | .001 | 31 | 21 | 5 | 3 | .001 |
| 48 | 8 | 19 | 33 | .001 | 0 | 0 | 2 | 58 | .001 |
| 49 | 59 | 6 | 1 | .001 | 0 | 0 | 0 | 59 | .001 |
| 50 | 9 | 10 | 41 | .001 | 4 | 0 | 1 | 55 | .001 |

Table C.4. Landscape Rating Scales: Extent of Agreement in the Use of Each Scale

| Landscape Rating Scale | Number of Scenes Consensually Rated* |
|---|---|
| 1 (1–2–3) | 48 |
| 2 (4–5–6) | 49 |
| 3 (7) | 34 |
| (8) | 50 |
| (9) | 42 |
| 4 (10–11–12) | 42 |
| 5 (13–14–15–16) | 30 |
| 6 (17) | 48 |
| (18) | 39 |
| (19) | 44 |
| (20) | 43 |
| (21) | 44 |
| 7 (22–23–24) | 36 |
| 8 (25–26–27) | 38 |
| 9 (28–29–30) | 43 |
| 10 (31–32–33–34) | 50 |

* That is, for which agreement was attained beyond the .10 level of statistical significance.

Table C.5. Landscape Rating Scales: Comparisons among Expert and Nonexpert Panels

RATING SCALE 1

| Scene | Forestry and Conservation |||| Landscape Architecture |||| Forest Service |||| University Students I ||||
|---|---|---|---|---|---|---|---|---|---|---|---|---|---|---|---|---|
| | 1 | 2 | 3 | p | 1 | 2 | 3 | p | 1 | 2 | 3 | p | 1 | 2 | 3 | p |
| 1 | 4 | 13 | 1 | .01 | 4 | 6 | 0 | .10 | 2 | 20 | 1 | .001 | 5 | 15 | 1 | .001 |
| 2 | 1 | 16 | 1 | .001 | 2 | 7 | 1 | .05 | 7 | 14 | 2 | .01 | 6 | 13 | 1 | .01 |
| 3 | 3 | 15 | 0 | .001 | 1 | 8 | 1 | .01 | 3 | 20 | 0 | .001 | 2 | 16 | 2 | .001 |
| 4 | 2 | 9 | 7 | .20 | 1 | 7 | 2 | .05 | 0 | 12 | 11 | .01 | 3 | 9 | 8 | .30 |
| 5 | 0 | 18 | 0 | .001 | 0 | 10 | 0 | .001 | 1 | 18 | 4 | .001 | 0 | 17 | 3 | .001 |
| 6 | 6 | 18 | 0 | .001 | 0 | 9 | 1 | .001 | 4 | 18 | 1 | .001 | 3 | 17 | 0 | .001 |
| 7 | 6 | 7 | 5 | .90 | 5 | 4 | 1 | .30 | 12 | 9 | 2 | .05 | 8 | 6 | 7 | .90 |
| 8 | 1 | 6 | 11 | .02 | 3 | 5 | 2 | .50 | 5 | 14 | 4 | .02 | 1 | 14 | 6 | .01 |
| 9 | 16 | 2 | 0 | .001 | 11 | 0 | 0 | .001 | 21 | 2 | 0 | .001 | 20 | 1 | 0 | .001 |
| 10 | 1 | 3 | 14 | .001 | 0 | 0 | 11 | .001 | 3 | 4 | 16 | .01 | 7 | 2 | 12 | .05 |
| 11 | 0 | 5 | 13 | .001 | 0 | 2 | 9 | .01 | 1 | 6 | 16 | .001 | 1 | 8 | 12 | .02 |
| 12 | 9 | 8 | 1 | .05 | 8 | 3 | 0 | .02 | 19 | 4 | 0 | .001 | 10 | 9 | 2 | .10 |
| 13 | 1 | 17 | 0 | .001 | 0 | 11 | 0 | .001 | 6 | 17 | 0 | .001 | 4 | 17 | 0 | .001 |
| 14 | 7 | 10 | 3 | .20 | 9 | 1 | 1 | .01 | 16 | 7 | 0 | .001 | 10 | 6 | 5 | .50 |
| 15 | 0 | 6 | 12 | .01 | 0 | 5 | 6 | .10 | 1 | 16 | 6 | .001 | 5 | 7 | 9 | .70 |
| 16 | 0 | 18 | 0 | .001 | 0 | 11 | 0 | .001 | 1 | 21 | 1 | .001 | 2 | 19 | 0 | .001 |
| 17 | 17 | 1 | 0 | .001 | 11 | 0 | 0 | .001 | 23 | 0 | 0 | .001 | 18 | 2 | 1 | .001 |
| 18 | 1 | 15 | 2 | .001 | 0 | 11 | 0 | .001 | 3 | 19 | 1 | .001 | 3 | 16 | 2 | .001 |
| 19 | | | | | 11 | 0 | 0 | .001 | 23 | 0 | 0 | .001 | 17 | 4 | 0 | .001 |
| 20 | | | | | 1 | 10 | 0 | .001 | 1 | 18 | 4 | .001 | 3 | 18 | 0 | .001 |
| 21 | | | | | 0 | 9 | 2 | .01 | 0 | 20 | 3 | .001 | 1 | 16 | 4 | .001 |
| 22 | | | | | 0 | 6 | 5 | .10 | 1 | 10 | 12 | .02 | 4 | 8 | 9 | .50 |
| 23 | | | | | 11 | 0 | 0 | .001 | 23 | 0 | 0 | .001 | 18 | 1 | 2 | .001 |
| 24 | | | | | 8 | 3 | 0 | .02 | 14 | 9 | 0 | .01 | 11 | 7 | 3 | .20 |
| 25 | | | | | 0 | 10 | 1 | .001 | 0 | 18 | 5 | .001 | 2 | 17 | 2 | .001 |

Table C.5. (cont'd)

RATING SCALE 2

| Scene | Forestry and Conservation | | | | Landscape Architecture | | | | Forest Service | | | | University Students I | | | |
|---|---|---|---|---|---|---|---|---|---|---|---|---|---|---|---|---|
| | 4 | 5 | 6 | p | 4 | 5 | 6 | p | 4 | 5 | 6 | p | 4 | 5 | 6 | p |
| 1 | 0 | 3 | 15 | .001 | 0 | 0 | 10 | .001 | 0 | 6 | 17 | .001 | 0 | 4 | 17 | .001 |
| 2 | 4 | 8 | 6 | .70 | 3 | 6 | 1 | .20 | 10 | 6 | 7 | .70 | 2 | 12 | 6 | .05 |
| 3 | 13 | 5 | 0 | .001 | 8 | 2 | 0 | .01 | 20 | 2 | 1 | .001 | 11 | 9 | 0 | .01 |
| 4 | 12 | 6 | 0 | .01 | 8 | 2 | 0 | .01 | 16 | 7 | 0 | .001 | 14 | 5 | 1 | .01 |
| 5 | 0 | 0 | 18 | .001 | 0 | 0 | 10 | .001 | 0 | 1 | 22 | .001 | 0 | 0 | 20 | .001 |
| 6 | 1 | 0 | 17 | .001 | 0 | 0 | 10 | .001 | 3 | 2 | 18 | .001 | 0 | 2 | 18 | .001 |
| 7 | 3 | 11 | 4 | .05 | 1 | 6 | 3 | .20 | 1 | 19 | 3 | .001 | 2 | 11 | 8 | .05 |
| 8 | 7 | 11 | 0 | .01 | 7 | 3 | 0 | .05 | 7 | 16 | 0 | .001 | 3 | 17 | 1 | .001 |
| 9 | 0 | 11 | 8 | .01 | 0 | 2 | 8 | .01 | 0 | 12 | 11 | .001 | 0 | 9 | 12 | .01 |
| 10 | 7 | 11 | 0 | .01 | 0 | 6 | 5 | .10 | 2 | 18 | 3 | .001 | 6 | 11 | 4 | .20 |
| 11 | 18 | 0 | 0 | .001 | 11 | 0 | 0 | .001 | 19 | 4 | 0 | .001 | 15 | 6 | 0 | .001 |
| 12 | 16 | 2 | 0 | .001 | 11 | 0 | 0 | .001 | 20 | 3 | 0 | .001 | 14 | 7 | 0 | .001 |
| 13 | 0 | 1 | 17 | .001 | 0 | 7 | 11 | .001 | 0 | 2 | 21 | .001 | 0 | 1 | 20 | .001 |
| 14 | 2 | 11 | 5 | .05 | 1 | 8 | 3 | .10 | 3 | 17 | 3 | .001 | 1 | 10 | 10 | .05 |
| 15 | 2 | 14 | 2 | .001 | 2 | 1 | 1 | .05 | 0 | 23 | 0 | .001 | 3 | 11 | 7 | .20 |
| 16 | 1 | 1 | 16 | .001 | 0 | 1 | 10 | .001 | 1 | 6 | 16 | .001 | 0 | 2 | 18 | .001 |
| 17 | 0 | 2 | 16 | .001 | 0 | 1 | 10 | .001 | 0 | 7 | 16 | .001 | 1 | 1 | 19 | .001 |
| 18 | 1 | 1 | 16 | .001 | 0 | 1 | 10 | .001 | 1 | 3 | 19 | .001 | 0 | 2 | 19 | .001 |
| 19 | | | | | 0 | 10 | 1 | .001 | 3 | 15 | 5 | .01 | 0 | 12 | 9 | .01 |
| 20 | | | | | 7 | 4 | 0 | .05 | 15 | 8 | 0 | .001 | 6 | 11 | 4 | .20 |
| 21 | | | | | 0 | 9 | 2 | .01 | 2 | 16 | 5 | .001 | 1 | 11 | 9 | .02 |
| 22 | | | | | 1 | 8 | 2 | .05 | 1 | 19 | 3 | .001 | 2 | 13 | 6 | .02 |
| 23 | | | | | 0 | 0 | 11 | .001 | 0 | 0 | 23 | .001 | 0 | 2 | 19 | .001 |
| 24 | | | | | 0 | 1 | 10 | .001 | 0 | 3 | 20 | .001 | 1 | 1 | 19 | .001 |
| 25 | | | | | 0 | 7 | 4 | .05 | 0 | 15 | 8 | .001 | 1 | 8 | 12 | .02 |

Table C.5. (cont'd)

RATING SCALE 3

| Scene | Forestry and Conservation | | Landscape Architecture | | Forest Service | | University Students I | |
|---|---|---|---|---|---|---|---|---|
| | 7 | p | 7 | p | 7 | p | 7 | p |
| 1 | 9 | .99 | 7 | .50 | 8 | .20 | 8 | .30 |
| 2 | 17 | .001 | 9 | .05 | 19 | .01 | 15 | .05 |
| 3 | 17 | .001 | 10 | .01 | 16 | .10 | 17 | .01 |
| 4 | 9 | .99 | 5 | .80 | 7 | .10 | 14 | .20 |
| 5 | 14 | .02 | 8 | .30 | 12 | .90 | 14 | .20 |
| 6 | 18 | .001 | 10 | .01 | 22 | .001 | 17 | .01 |
| 7 | 3 | .01 | 4 | .50 | 8 | .20 | 9 | .70 |
| 8 | 12 | .20 | 7 | .50 | 17 | .05 | 17 | .01 |
| 9 | 2 | .001 | 0 | .001 | 4 | .01 | 4 | .01 |
| 10 | 10 | .70 | 7 | .50 | 13 | .70 | 5 | .02 |
| 11 | 17 | .001 | 9 | .05 | 16 | .10 | 15 | .05 |
| 12 | 18 | .001 | 10 | .01 | 21 | .001 | 18 | .01 |
| 13 | 17 | .001 | 9 | .05 | 18 | .01 | 14 | .20 |
| 14 | 14 | .02 | 8 | .30 | 13 | .70 | 16 | .02 |
| 15 | 1 | .001 | 1 | .01 | 1 | .001 | 3 | .01 |
| 16 | 18 | .001 | 11 | .001 | 19 | .01 | 19 | .001 |
| 17 | 12 | .20 | 4 | .50 | 12 | .90 | 13 | .30 |
| 18 | 17 | .001 | 11 | .001 | 20 | .001 | 18 | .01 |
| 19 | | | 10 | .01 | 18 | .01 | 14 | .20 |
| 20 | | | 11 | .001 | 19 | .01 | 18 | .01 |
| 21 | | | 10 | .01 | 12 | .90 | 16 | .02 |
| 22 | | | 10 | .01 | 8 | .20 | 13 | .30 |
| 23 | | | 8 | .30 | 13 | .70 | 11 | .90 |
| 24 | | | 2 | .05 | 4 | .01 | 2 | .001 |
| 25 | | | 7 | .50 | 9 | .30 | 10 | .90 |

Table C.5. (cont'd)

RATING SCALE 3 (CONT'D)

| Scene | Forestry and Conservation 8 | $p$ | Landscape Architecture 8 | $p$ | Forest Service 8 | $p$ | University Students I 8 | $p$ |
|---|---|---|---|---|---|---|---|---|
| 1 | 17 | .001 | 10 | .01 | 16 | .10 | 20 | .001 |
| 2 | 17 | .001 | 10 | .01 | 19 | .01 | 19 | .001 |
| 3 | 11 | .50 | 7 | .50 | 12 | .90 | 14 | .20 |
| 4 | 11 | .50 | 8 | .30 | 22 | .001 | 12 | .70 |
| 5 | 16 | .001 | 10 | .01 | 17 | .05 | 17 | .01 |
| 6 | 15 | .01 | 7 | .50 | 16 | .10 | 16 | .02 |
| 7 | 14 | .02 | 7 | .50 | 18 | .01 | 16 | .02 |
| 8 | 17 | .001 | 9 | .05 | 22 | .001 | 18 | .01 |
| 9 | 16 | .001 | 9 | .05 | 18 | .01 | 19 | .001 |
| 10 | 15 | .01 | 8 | .30 | 19 | .01 | 19 | .001 |
| 11 | 16 | .001 | 9 | .05 | 17 | .05 | 16 | .02 |
| 12 | 17 | .001 | 9 | .05 | 17 | .05 | 15 | .05 |
| 13 | 16 | .001 | 8 | .30 | 16 | .10 | 18 | .01 |
| 14 | 16 | .001 | 11 | .001 | 22 | .001 | 20 | .001 |
| 15 | 11 | .50 | 8 | .30 | 10 | .70 | 19 | .001 |
| 16 | 17 | .001 | 10 | .01 | 21 | .001 | 17 | .01 |
| 17 | 17 | .001 | 11 | .001 | 20 | .001 | 19 | .001 |
| 18 | 14 | .02 | 5 | .80 | 12 | .90 | 18 | .01 |
| 19 | | | 11 | .001 | 22 | .001 | 20 | .001 |
| 20 | | | 10 | .01 | 19 | .01 | 15 | .05 |
| 21 | | | 9 | .05 | 23 | .001 | 17 | .01 |
| 22 | | | 11 | .001 | 21 | .001 | 17 | .01 |
| 23 | | | 11 | .001 | 20 | .001 | 15 | .05 |
| 24 | | | 9 | .05 | 15 | .20 | 19 | .001 |
| 25 | | | 6 | .80 | 11 | .90 | 16 | .02 |

Table C.5. (cont'd)

RATING SCALE 3 (CONT'D)

| Scene | Forestry and Conservation | | Landscape Architecture | | Forest Service | | University Students I | |
|---|---|---|---|---|---|---|---|---|
| | 9 | p | 9 | p | 9 | p | 9 | p |
| 1 | 16 | .001 | 10 | .01 | 21 | .001 | 19 | .001 |
| 2 | 13 | .10 | 5 | .80 | 16 | .10 | 16 | .02 |
| 3 | 4 | .02 | 3 | .30 | 5 | .01 | 8 | .30 |
| 4 | 4 | .02 | 4 | .50 | 8 | .20 | 5 | .02 |
| 5 | 18 | .001 | 10 | .01 | 20 | .001 | 19 | .001 |
| 6 | 18 | .001 | 10 | .01 | 15 | .20 | 15 | .05 |
| 7 | 12 | .20 | 8 | .30 | 11 | .90 | 11 | .90 |
| 8 | 12 | .20 | 7 | .50 | 10 | .70 | 7 | .20 |
| 9 | 16 | .001 | 11 | .001 | 20 | .001 | 17 | .01 |
| 10 | 10 | .70 | 1 | .01 | 10 | .70 | 13 | .30 |
| 11 | 7 | .50 | 2 | .05 | 9 | .30 | 5 | .02 |
| 12 | 1 | .001 | 0 | .001 | 5 | .01 | 4 | .01 |
| 13 | 18 | .001 | 10 | .01 | 17 | .05 | 20 | .001 |
| 14 | 14 | .02 | 8 | .30 | 13 | .70 | 9 | .70 |
| 15 | 12 | .20 | 5 | .80 | 15 | .20 | 11 | .90 |
| 16 | 18 | .001 | 9 | .05 | 20 | .001 | 18 | .01 |
| 17 | 18 | .001 | 10 | .01 | 18 | .01 | 18 | .01 |
| 18 | 18 | .001 | 10 | .01 | 20 | .001 | 19 | .001 |
| 19 | | | 9 | .05 | 12 | .90 | 16 | .02 |
| 20 | | | 3 | .30 | 8 | .20 | 10 | .90 |
| 21 | | | 10 | .01 | 20 | .001 | 19 | .001 |
| 22 | | | 8 | .30 | 21 | .001 | 14 | .20 |
| 23 | | | 10 | .01 | 21 | .001 | 19 | .001 |
| 24 | | | 10 | .01 | 20 | .001 | 19 | .001 |
| 25 | | | 10 | .01 | 20 | .001 | 17 | .01 |

Table C.5. (cont'd)

RATING SCALE 4

| Scene | Forestry and Conservation | | | | Landscape Architecture | | | | Forest Service | | | | University Students I | | | |
|---|---|---|---|---|---|---|---|---|---|---|---|---|---|---|---|---|
| | 10 | 11 | 12 | $p$ | 10 | 11 | 12 | $p$ | 10 | 11 | 12 | $p$ | 10 | 11 | 12 | $p$ |
| 1 | 2 | 13 | 3 | .01 | 3 | 4 | 3 | .95 | 2 | 20 | 1 | .001 | 3 | 15 | 2 | .001 |
| 2 | 0 | 0 | 18 | .001 | 0 | 0 | 10 | .001 | 0 | 1 | 22 | .001 | 2 | 5 | 12 | .02 |
| 3 | 0 | 4 | 14 | .001 | 0 | 0 | 10 | .001 | 0 | 4 | 19 | .001 | 0 | 5 | 15 | .001 |
| 4 | 0 | 3 | 15 | .001 | 0 | 0 | 10 | .001 | 0 | 2 | 21 | .001 | 0 | 5 | 15 | .001 |
| 5 | 0 | 18 | 0 | .001 | 0 | 9 | 1 | .001 | 5 | 17 | 2 | .001 | 7 | 13 | 0 | .01 |
| 6 | 4 | 11 | 3 | .05 | 1 | 8 | 1 | .01 | 9 | 8 | 6 | .80 | 9 | 9 | 2 | .10 |
| 7 | 1 | 0 | 17 | .001 | 2 | 0 | 8 | .01 | 2 | 4 | 17 | .001 | 3 | 2 | 16 | .001 |
| 8 | 1 | 3 | 14 | .001 | 0 | 1 | 9 | .001 | 2 | 5 | 16 | .001 | 1 | 6 | 13 | .01 |
| 9 | 8 | 8 | 3 | .30 | 7 | 2 | 2 | .20 | 13 | 6 | 4 | .10 | 11 | 8 | 2 | .05 |
| 10 | 1 | 0 | 15 | .001 | 0 | 3 | 8 | .02 | 3 | 9 | 11 | .20 | 4 | 8 | 9 | .50 |
| 11 | 2 | 0 | 16 | .001 | 0 | 2 | 9 | .01 | 2 | 3 | 18 | .001 | 1 | 6 | 14 | .01 |
| 12 | 1 | 0 | 17 | .001 | 0 | 0 | 11 | .001 | 1 | 1 | 21 | .001 | 4 | 1 | 16 | .001 |
| 13 | 5 | 14 | 0 | .001 | 0 | 1 | 10 | .001 | 11 | 12 | 1 | .01 | 8 | 13 | 0 | .001 |
| 14 | 4 | 2 | 12 | .01 | 4 | 1 | 6 | .20 | 10 | 3 | 10 | .20 | 4 | 7 | 10 | .30 |
| 15 | 2 | 3 | 13 | .01 | 2 | 2 | 7 | .20 | 2 | 8 | 14 | .02 | 3 | 4 | 13 | .02 |
| 16 | 4 | 9 | 5 | .50 | 0 | 8 | 3 | .02 | 9 | 12 | 2 | .05 | 8 | 11 | 2 | .05 |
| 17 | 15 | 2 | 1 | .001 | 10 | 0 | 1 | .001 | 17 | 3 | 3 | .001 | 15 | 4 | 2 | .001 |
| 18 | 3 | 15 | 0 | .001 | 0 | 10 | 1 | .001 | 6 | 16 | 1 | .001 | 10 | 10 | 1 | .05 |
| 19 | | | | | 3 | 1 | 7 | .10 | 5 | 2 | 16 | .001 | 6 | 2 | 13 | .02 |
| 20 | | | | | 0 | 0 | 11 | .001 | 1 | 2 | 20 | .001 | 3 | 2 | 16 | .001 |
| 21 | | | | | 0 | 0 | 11 | .001 | 2 | 5 | 16 | .001 | 2 | 7 | 12 | .001 |
| 22 | | | | | 0 | 4 | 7 | .05 | 3 | 8 | 12 | .10 | 1 | 8 | 11 | .05 |
| 23 | | | | | 11 | 0 | 0 | .001 | 18 | 5 | 1 | .001 | 15 | 5 | 1 | .02 |
| 24 | | | | | 9 | 2 | 0 | .01 | 8 | 14 | 1 | .01 | 13 | 7 | 1 | .001 |
| 25 | | | | | 0 | 7 | 4 | .05 | 1 | 18 | 5 | .001 | 3 | 13 | 4 | .02 |

Table C.5. (cont'd)

RATING SCALE 5

| Scene | Forestry and Conservation | | | | | Landscape Architecture | | | | | Forest Service | | | | | University Students I | | | | |
|---|---|---|---|---|---|---|---|---|---|---|---|---|---|---|---|---|---|---|---|---|
| | 13 | 14 | 15 | 16 | p | 13 | 14 | 15 | 16 | p | 13 | 14 | 15 | 16 | p | 13 | 14 | 15 | 16 | p |
| 1 | 6 | 2 | 7 | 3 | .30 | 7 | 0 | 3 | 0 | .01 | 9 | 0 | 11 | 3 | .01 | 9 | 4 | 5 | 2 | .20 |
| 2 | 5 | 9 | 0 | 3 | .02 | 5 | 5 | 0 | 0 | .02 | 5 | 13 | 2 | 3 | .01 | 8 | 9 | 2 | 1 | .02 |
| 3 | 11 | 3 | 2 | 2 | .01 | 7 | 1 | 2 | 0 | .01 | 11 | 6 | 3 | 3 | .10 | 13 | 3 | 4 | 0 | .001 |
| 4 | 7 | 0 | 7 | 4 | .10 | 5 | 0 | 2 | 3 | .20 | 6 | 0 | 3 | 14 | .001 | 11 | 0 | 7 | 2 | .01 |
| 5 | 3 | 0 | 3 | 12 | .001 | 1 | 0 | 3 | 6 | .05 | 1 | 1 | 6 | 15 | .001 | 1 | 7 | 9 | 3 | .05 |
| 6 | 16 | 0 | 0 | 2 | .001 | 9 | 0 | 1 | 0 | .001 | 17 | 2 | 1 | 3 | .001 | 14 | 5 | 1 | 0 | .001 |
| 7 | 18 | 0 | 0 | 0 | .001 | 9 | 0 | 0 | 1 | .001 | 16 | 3 | 2 | 2 | .001 | 13 | 2 | 5 | 1 | .001 |
| 8 | 9 | 2 | 0 | 7 | .01 | 2 | 5 | 1 | 2 | .50 | 4 | 5 | 2 | 12 | .02 | 6 | 8 | 4 | 2 | .30 |
| 9 | 11 | 2 | 2 | 2 | .01 | 6 | 2 | 3 | 0 | .10 | 9 | 2 | 4 | 8 | .20 | 10 | 3 | 4 | 3 | .10 |
| 10 | 6 | 0 | 2 | 10 | .01 | 4 | 2 | 2 | 3 | .80 | 3 | 1 | 6 | 13 | .01 | 5 | 9 | 6 | 1 | .20 |
| 11 | 0 | 6 | 0 | 12 | .001 | 0 | 2 | 3 | 6 | .10 | 0 | 16 | 0 | 7 | .001 | 0 | 14 | 2 | 5 | .001 |
| 12 | 12 | 1 | 0 | 5 | .001 | 7 | 0 | 2 | 2 | .05 | 12 | 3 | 1 | 6 | .01 | 12 | 4 | 4 | 1 | .01 |
| 13 | 2 | 0 | 0 | 16 | .001 | 2 | 2 | 0 | 7 | .05 | 4 | 3 | 3 | 13 | .01 | 5 | 5 | 6 | 5 | .99 |
| 14 | 13 | 1 | 4 | 0 | .001 | 3 | 0 | 8 | 0 | .01 | 7 | 1 | 12 | 3 | .01 | 10 | 1 | 6 | 5 | .05 |
| 15 | 7 | 3 | 1 | 7 | .20 | 3 | 3 | 2 | 3 | .98 | 3 | 5 | 3 | 12 | .05 | 6 | 5 | 5 | 4 | .95 |
| 16 | 18 | 0 | 0 | 0 | .001 | 11 | 0 | 0 | 0 | .001 | 16 | 0 | 2 | 4 | .001 | 15 | 1 | 3 | 2 | .001 |
| 17 | 2 | 3 | 1 | 12 | .001 | 6 | 0 | 1 | 4 | .05 | 7 | 2 | 3 | 11 | .05 | 6 | 2 | 6 | 7 | .50 |
| 18 | 4 | 1 | 2 | 10 | .01 | 1 | 5 | 0 | 5 | .10 | 2 | 10 | 1 | 10 | .01 | 5 | 12 | 4 | 0 | .01 |
| 19 | | | | | | 7 | 1 | 3 | 0 | .02 | 10 | 5 | 6 | 2 | .05 | 12 | 3 | 6 | 0 | .01 |
| 20 | | | | | | 9 | 2 | 0 | 0 | .001 | 9 | 3 | 4 | 7 | .30 | 14 | 3 | 2 | 2 | .001 |
| 21 | | | | | | 8 | 1 | 1 | 1 | .01 | 8 | 2 | 5 | 8 | .30 | 13 | 1 | 4 | 3 | .01 |
| 22 | | | | | | 4 | 1 | 4 | 1 | .50 | 10 | 1 | 5 | 7 | .10 | 9 | 1 | 9 | 1 | .01 |
| 23 | | | | | | 7 | 2 | 1 | 1 | .05 | 5 | 5 | 5 | 8 | .80 | 10 | 4 | 3 | 4 | .20 |
| 24 | | | | | | 6 | 1 | 1 | 3 | .20 | 6 | 1 | 9 | 7 | .20 | 8 | 3 | 8 | 2 | .20 |
| 25 | | | | | | 0 | 6 | 1 | 4 | .05 | 1 | 8 | 3 | 11 | .02 | 3 | 11 | 2 | 4 | .02 |

Table C.5. (cont'd)

RATING SCALE 6

| Scene | Forestry and Conservation | | Landscape Architecture | | Forest Service | | University Students I | |
|---|---|---|---|---|---|---|---|---|
| | 17 | p | 17 | p | 17 | p | 17 | p |
| 26 | 0 | .001 | 3 | .30 | 4 | .01 | 6 | .05 |
| 27 | 2 | .001 | 2 | .05 | 0 | .001 | 0 | .001 |
| 28 | 3 | .01 | 5 | .80 | 4 | .01 | 2 | .001 |
| 29 | 6 | .20 | 3 | .30 | 6 | .05 | 5 | .02 |
| 30 | 0 | .001 | 0 | .001 | 0 | .001 | 0 | .001 |
| 31 | 12 | .20 | 5 | .80 | 10 | .70 | 10 | .90 |
| 32 | 1 | .001 | 3 | .30 | 1 | .001 | 1 | .001 |
| 33 | 1 | .001 | 2 | .05 | 1 | .001 | 1 | .001 |
| 34 | 0 | .001 | 0 | .001 | 0 | .001 | 1 | .001 |
| 35 | 1 | .001 | 0 | .001 | 0 | .001 | 0 | .001 |
| 36 | 0 | .001 | 0 | .001 | 0 | .001 | 1 | .001 |
| 37 | 0 | .001 | 0 | .001 | 0 | .001 | 0 | .001 |
| 38 | 5 | .10 | 6 | .80 | 6 | .05 | 7 | .20 |
| 39 | 2 | .001 | 2 | .05 | 0 | .001 | 0 | .001 |
| 40 | 1 | .001 | 0 | .001 | 0 | .001 | 1 | .001 |
| 41 | 0 | .001 | 1 | .01 | 0 | .001 | 0 | .001 |
| 42 | 0 | .001 | 0 | .001 | 0 | .001 | 0 | .001 |
| 43 | 0 | .001 | 0 | .001 | 0 | .001 | 2 | .001 |
| 44 | | | 1 | .01 | 0 | .001 | 0 | .001 |
| 45 | | | 1 | .01 | 3 | .001 | 5 | .02 |
| 46 | | | 0 | .001 | 0 | .001 | 0 | .001 |
| 47 | | | 1 | .01 | 0 | .001 | 0 | .001 |
| 48 | | | 10 | .01 | 17 | .05 | 13 | .30 |
| 49 | | | 2 | .05 | 1 | .001 | 7 | .20 |
| 50 | | | 1 | .01 | 0 | .001 | 2 | .001 |

Table C.5. (cont'd)

RATING SCALE 6 (CONT'D)

| Scene | Forestry and Conservation | | Landscape Architecture | | Forest Service | | University Students I | |
|---|---|---|---|---|---|---|---|---|
| | 18 | $p$ | 18 | $p$ | 18 | $p$ | 18 | $p$ |
| 26 | 9 | .99 | 6 | .80 | 8 | .20 | 7 | .20 |
| 27 | 5 | .10 | 9 | .05 | 8 | .20 | 10 | .90 |
| 28 | 8 | .70 | 5 | .80 | 9 | .30 | 12 | .70 |
| 29 | 1 | .001 | 0 | .001 | 2 | .001 | 2 | .001 |
| 30 | 1 | .001 | 3 | .30 | 4 | .01 | 3 | .01 |
| 31 | 1 | .001 | 1 | .01 | 3 | .001 | 3 | .01 |
| 32 | 8 | .70 | 6 | .80 | 10 | .70 | 12 | .70 |
| 33 | 8 | .70 | 7 | .50 | 8 | .20 | 11 | .90 |
| 34 | 1 | .001 | 1 | .01 | 0 | .001 | 3 | .01 |
| 35 | 0 | .001 | 0 | .001 | 1 | .001 | 2 | .001 |
| 36 | 4 | .02 | 2 | .05 | 6 | .05 | 6 | .05 |
| 37 | 18 | .001 | 11 | .001 | 21 | .001 | 21 | .001 |
| 38 | 11 | .50 | 4 | .50 | 16 | .10 | 10 | .90 |
| 39 | 2 | .001 | 1 | .01 | 4 | .01 | 7 | .20 |
| 40 | 1 | .001 | 1 | .01 | 0 | .001 | 0 | .001 |
| 41 | 9 | .99 | 5 | .80 | 12 | .90 | 12 | .70 |
| 42 | 4 | .02 | 3 | .30 | 1 | .001 | 4 | .01 |
| 43 | 2 | .001 | 0 | .001 | 1 | .001 | 1 | .001 |
| 44 | | | 7 | .50 | 6 | .05 | 7 | .20 |
| 45 | | | 5 | .80 | 9 | .30 | 6 | .05 |
| 46 | | | 3 | .30 | 5 | .01 | 7 | .20 |
| 47 | | | 3 | .30 | 3 | .001 | 9 | .70 |
| 48 | | | 0 | .001 | 7 | .10 | 7 | .20 |
| 49 | | | 6 | .80 | 4 | .01 | 7 | .20 |
| 50 | | | 10 | .01 | 15 | .20 | 19 | .001 |

Table C.5. (cont'd)

RATING SCALE 6 (CONT'D)

| Scene | Forestry and Conservation | | Landscape Architecture | | Forest Service | | University Students I | |
|---|---|---|---|---|---|---|---|---|
| | 19 | $p$ | 19 | $p$ | 19 | $p$ | 19 | $p$ |
| 26 | 16 | .001 | 9 | .05 | 17 | .05 | 14 | .20 |
| 27 | 13 | .10 | 6 | .80 | 16 | .10 | 16 | .02 |
| 28 | 8 | .70 | 3 | .30 | 11 | .90 | 8 | .30 |
| 29 | 11 | .50 | 7 | .50 | 19 | .01 | 14 | .20 |
| 30 | 1 | .001 | 0 | .001 | 1 | .001 | 0 | .001 |
| 31 | 6 | .20 | 6 | .80 | 13 | .70 | 10 | .90 |
| 32 | 1 | .001 | 0 | .001 | 0 | .001 | 2 | .001 |
| 33 | 0 | .001 | 3 | .30 | 4 | .01 | 3 | .01 |
| 34 | 0 | .001 | 0 | .001 | 0 | .001 | 0 | .001 |
| 35 | 1 | .001 | 0 | .001 | 0 | .001 | 3 | .01 |
| 36 | 18 | .001 | 11 | .001 | 20 | .001 | 17 | .01 |
| 37 | 0 | .001 | 0 | .001 | 0 | .001 | 1 | .001 |
| 38 | 4 | .02 | 0 | .001 | 3 | .001 | 1 | .001 |
| 39 | 0 | .001 | 1 | .01 | 0 | .001 | 2 | .001 |
| 40 | 0 | .001 | 0 | .001 | 0 | .001 | 1 | .001 |
| 41 | 1 | .50 | 1 | .01 | 2 | .001 | 4 | .01 |
| 42 | 4 | .02 | 4 | .50 | 3 | .001 | 10 | .90 |
| 43 | 0 | .001 | 0 | .001 | 0 | .001 | 0 | .001 |
| 44 | | | 2 | .05 | 0 | .001 | 2 | .001 |
| 45 | | | 7 | .50 | 12 | .90 | 6 | .05 |
| 46 | | | 0 | .001 | 1 | .001 | 0 | .001 |
| 47 | | | 0 | .001 | 0 | .001 | 1 | .001 |
| 48 | | | 0 | .001 | 3 | .001 | 2 | .001 |
| 49 | | | 4 | .50 | 18 | .01 | 12 | .70 |
| 50 | | | 0 | .001 | 1 | .001 | 1 | .001 |

Table C.5. (cont'd)

RATING SCALE 6 (CONT'D)

| Scene | Forestry and Conservation | | Landscape Architecture | | Forest Service | | University Students I | |
|---|---|---|---|---|---|---|---|---|
| | 20 | p | 20 | p | 20 | p | 20 | p |
| 26 | 5 | .10 | 5 | .80 | 7 | .10 | 7 | .20 |
| 27 | 0 | .001 | 0 | .001 | 0 | .001 | 0 | .001 |
| 28 | 2 | .001 | 2 | .05 | 2 | .001 | 5 | .02 |
| 29 | 12 | .20 | 7 | .50 | 19 | .01 | 14 | .20 |
| 30 | 14 | .02 | 11 | .001 | 14 | .30 | 17 | .01 |
| 31 | 5 | .10 | 6 | .80 | 13 | .70 | 9 | .70 |
| 32 | 0 | .001 | 0 | .001 | 0 | .001 | 1 | .001 |
| 33 | 0 | .001 | 2 | .05 | 7 | .10 | 2 | .001 |
| 34 | 1 | .001 | 0 | .001 | 1 | .001 | 0 | .001 |
| 35 | 0 | .001 | 0 | .001 | 0 | .001 | 1 | .001 |
| 36 | 0 | .001 | 0 | .001 | 1 | .001 | 2 | .001 |
| 37 | 0 | .001 | 0 | .001 | 0 | .001 | 1 | .001 |
| 38 | 4 | .02 | 0 | .001 | 3 | .001 | 2 | .001 |
| 39 | 0 | .001 | 1 | .01 | 2 | .001 | 1 | .001 |
| 40 | 0 | .001 | 0 | .001 | 0 | .001 | 0 | .001 |
| 41 | 11 | .50 | 4 | .50 | 19 | .01 | 11 | .90 |
| 42 | 0 | .001 | 0 | .001 | 1 | .001 | 1 | .001 |
| 43 | 3 | .001 | 0 | .001 | 2 | .001 | 1 | .001 |
| 44 | | | 0 | .001 | 0 | .001 | 1 | .001 |
| 45 | | | 6 | .80 | 4 | .01 | 1 | .001 |
| 46 | | | 6 | .80 | 17 | .05 | 11 | .90 |
| 47 | | | 0 | .001 | 0 | .001 | 2 | .001 |
| 48 | | | 0 | .001 | 3 | .001 | 1 | .001 |
| 49 | | | 3 | .30 | 11 | .90 | 7 | .20 |
| 50 | | | 1 | .01 | 2 | .001 | 0 | .001 |

Table C.5. (cont'd)

RATING SCALE 6 (CONT'D)

| Scene | Forestry and Conservation | | Landscape Architecture | | Forest Service | | University Students I | |
|---|---|---|---|---|---|---|---|---|
|  | 21 | p | 21 | p | 21 | p | 21 | p |
| 26 | 0 | .001 | 0 | .001 | 1 | .001 | 0 | .001 |
| 27 | 3 | .01 | 0 | .001 | 4 | .01 | 2 | .001 |
| 28 | 3 | .01 | 0 | .001 | 5 | .01 | 5 | .02 |
| 29 | 0 | .001 | 0 | .001 | 0 | .001 | 0 | .001 |
| 30 | 4 | .02 | 0 | .001 | 5 | .01 | 4 | .01 |
| 31 | 0 | .001 | 0 | .001 | 0 | .001 | 0 | .001 |
| 32 | 8 | .50 | 1 | .01 | 12 | .90 | 7 | .20 |
| 33 | 9 | .99 | 1 | .01 | 10 | .70 | 6 | .05 |
| 34 | 17 | .001 | 11 | .001 | 22 | .001 | 17 | .01 |
| 35 | 17 | .001 | 11 | .001 | 22 | .001 | 16 | .02 |
| 36 | 0 | .001 | 0 | .001 | 2 | .001 | 1 | .001 |
| 37 | 0 | .001 | 0 | .001 | 2 | .001 | 0 | .001 |
| 38 | 2 | .001 | 1 | .01 | 1 | .001 | 4 | .01 |
| 39 | 14 | .02 | 8 | .30 | 18 | .01 | 13 | .30 |
| 40 | 16 | .001 | 10 | .01 | 23 | .001 | 19 | .001 |
| 41 | 2 | .001 | 3 | .30 | 1 | .001 | 1 | .001 |
| 42 | 10 | .70 | 5 | .80 | 19 | .01 | 7 | .20 |
| 43 | 14 | .02 | 11 | .001 | 20 | .001 | 17 | .01 |
| 44 |  |  | 0 | .001 | 17 | .001 | 12 | .70 |
| 45 |  |  | 1 | .01 | 2 | .001 | 5 | .02 |
| 46 |  |  | 4 | .50 | 4 | .01 | 5 | .02 |
| 47 |  |  | 7 | .50 | 20 | .001 | 11 | .90 |
| 48 |  |  | 1 | .01 | 0 | .001 | 0 | .001 |
| 49 |  |  | 2 | .05 | 3 | .001 | 1 | .001 |
| 50 |  |  | 0 | .001 | 6 | .05 | 0 | .001 |

Table C.5. (cont'd)

RATING SCALE 7

| Scene | Forestry and Conservation | | | | Landscape Architecture | | | | Forest Service | | | | University Students I | | | |
|---|---|---|---|---|---|---|---|---|---|---|---|---|---|---|---|---|
| | 22 | 23 | 24 | p | 22 | 23 | 24 | p | 22 | 23 | 24 | p | 22 | 23 | 24 | p |
| 26 | 5 | 7 | 6 | .90 | 5 | 3 | 3 | .70 | 3 | 10 | 10 | .20 | 6 | 9 | 6 | .70 |
| 27 | 12 | 2 | 4 | .01 | 7 | 4 | 0 | .05 | 7 | 10 | 6 | .70 | 10 | 8 | 3 | .20 |
| 28 | 6 | 4 | 8 | .70 | 4 | 2 | 5 | .70 | 4 | 6 | 13 | .10 | 7 | 6 | 7 | .95 |
| 29 | 2 | 3 | 13 | .01 | 1 | 1 | 8 | .01 | 3 | 4 | 16 | .01 | 3 | 4 | 13 | .02 |
| 30 | 15 | 1 | 2 | .001 | 9 | 2 | 0 | .01 | 12 | 7 | 4 | .20 | 9 | 7 | 5 | .70 |
| 31 | 0 | 2 | 16 | .001 | 0 | 0 | 10 | .001 | 1 | 0 | 22 | .001 | 0 | 1 | 20 | .001 |
| 32 | 16 | 0 | 2 | .001 | 10 | 0 | 0 | .001 | 19 | 2 | 2 | .001 | 14 | 4 | 3 | .01 |
| 33 | 6 | 7 | 5 | .90 | 4 | 5 | 2 | .70 | 8 | 8 | 7 | .98 | 8 | 10 | 3 | .20 |
| 34 | 1 | 4 | 13 | .01 | 3 | 3 | 5 | .70 | 1 | 8 | 14 | .01 | 2 | 7 | 12 | .05 |
| 35 | 11 | 3 | 4 | .05 | 9 | 2 | 0 | .01 | 14 | 4 | 5 | .02 | 14 | 5 | 2 | .01 |
| 36 | 15 | 2 | 1 | .001 | 7 | 3 | 1 | .10 | 20 | 1 | 2 | .001 | 10 | 9 | 2 | .10 |
| 37 | 5 | 1 | 12 | .01 | 3 | 1 | 7 | .10 | 12 | 1 | 10 | .02 | 4 | 5 | 12 | .10 |
| 38 | 8 | 4 | 6 | .70 | 5 | 3 | 3 | .70 | 10 | 4 | 9 | .20 | 9 | 7 | 5 | .70 |
| 39 | 5 | 8 | 5 | .70 | 3 | 5 | 3 | .70 | 9 | 7 | 7 | .20 | 7 | 7 | 7 | .99 |
| 40 | 15 | 3 | 0 | .001 | 8 | 3 | 0 | .02 | 16 | 2 | 5 | .001 | 10 | 9 | 2 | .10 |
| 41 | 2 | 3 | 13 | .01 | 2 | 2 | 7 | .20 | 5 | 9 | 9 | .50 | 3 | 5 | 13 | .02 |
| 42 | 16 | 3 | 2 | .001 | 10 | 1 | 0 | .001 | 23 | 0 | 0 | .001 | 20 | 1 | 0 | .001 |
| 43 | 2 | 6 | 10 | .10 | 3 | 3 | 5 | .70 | 2 | 8 | 13 | .02 | 2 | 6 | 13 | .02 |
| 44 | | | | | 4 | 4 | 2 | .70 | 8 | 10 | 5 | .50 | 7 | 8 | 6 | .90 |
| 45 | | | | | 2 | 1 | 8 | .05 | 3 | 1 | 19 | .001 | 0 | 5 | 16 | .001 |
| 46 | | | | | 3 | 4 | 4 | .95 | 7 | 3 | 13 | .05 | 7 | 3 | 11 | .20 |
| 47 | | | | | 4 | 3 | 4 | .95 | 6 | 11 | 6 | .50 | 10 | 8 | 3 | .20 |
| 48 | | | | | 2 | 1 | 8 | .05 | 5 | 2 | 16 | .001 | 4 | 2 | 15 | .001 |
| 49 | | | | | 5 | 4 | 2 | .70 | 6 | 13 | 4 | .10 | 5 | 6 | 10 | .50 |
| 50 | | | | | 9 | 2 | 0 | .01 | 20 | 3 | 0 | .001 | 11 | 7 | 3 | .20 |

Table C.5. (cont'd)

RATING SCALE 8

| Scene | Forestry and Conservation | | | | Landscape Architecture | | | | Forest Service | | | | University Students I | | | |
|---|---|---|---|---|---|---|---|---|---|---|---|---|---|---|---|---|
| | 25 | 26 | 27 | p | 25 | 26 | 27 | p | 25 | 26 | 27 | p | 25 | 26 | 27 | p |
| 26 | 11 | 5 | 2 | .05 | 3 | 5 | 3 | .70 | 11 | 11 | 1 | .02 | 14 | 4 | 3 | .01 |
| 27 | 12 | 5 | 1 | .01 | 9 | 0 | 2 | .01 | 15 | 8 | 0 | .001 | 17 | 3 | 0 | .001 |
| 28 | 11 | 2 | 5 | .05 | 8 | 1 | 2 | .05 | 9 | 8 | 6 | .80 | 12 | 5 | 3 | .05 |
| 29 | 3 | 2 | 13 | .01 | 2 | 2 | 7 | .20 | 6 | 1 | 16 | .001 | 8 | 7 | 6 | .90 |
| 30 | 17 | 1 | 0 | .001 | 11 | 0 | 0 | .001 | 15 | 3 | 5 | .01 | 18 | 2 | 1 | .001 |
| 31 | 10 | 1 | 7 | .05 | 5 | 0 | 5 | .10 | 8 | 2 | 13 | .02 | 10 | 6 | 5 | .50 |
| 32 | 12 | 4 | 2 | .01 | 6 | 2 | 2 | .30 | 10 | 10 | 3 | .20 | 9 | 7 | 5 | .70 |
| 33 | 10 | 6 | 2 | .10 | 4 | 2 | 5 | .70 | 9 | 8 | 5 | .50 | 14 | 6 | 1 | .01 |
| 34 | 7 | 5 | 6 | .90 | 4 | 4 | 3 | .95 | 7 | 9 | 5 | .50 | 7 | 13 | 1 | .01 |
| 35 | 6 | 8 | 4 | .70 | 3 | 7 | 1 | .10 | 7 | 6 | 10 | .70 | 9 | 7 | 5 | .70 |
| 36 | 13 | 4 | 1 | .01 | 4 | 5 | 2 | .70 | 15 | 7 | 1 | .01 | 13 | 7 | 1 | .01 |
| 37 | 4 | 10 | 4 | .20 | 2 | 3 | 6 | .50 | 8 | 6 | 9 | .80 | 6 | 8 | 7 | .90 |
| 38 | 3 | 6 | 9 | .30 | 1 | 3 | 7 | .10 | 5 | 7 | 11 | .30 | 5 | 11 | 5 | .20 |
| 39 | 13 | 2 | 3 | .01 | 8 | 3 | 0 | .02 | 13 | 7 | 3 | .05 | 12 | 7 | 2 | .05 |
| 40 | 4 | 6 | 8 | .70 | 3 | 4 | 3 | .95 | 9 | 7 | 7 | .20 | 5 | 9 | 7 | .70 |
| 41 | 10 | 5 | 3 | .20 | 6 | 4 | 1 | .20 | 12 | 8 | 3 | .10 | 10 | 8 | 3 | .20 |
| 42 | 8 | 8 | 2 | .20 | 7 | 4 | 0 | .05 | 15 | 6 | 2 | .01 | 13 | 7 | 3 | .01 |
| 43 | 10 | 6 | 2 | .10 | 8 | 2 | 1 | .05 | 12 | 7 | 4 | .20 | 10 | 10 | 1 | .01 |
| 44 | | | | | 4 | 2 | 4 | .70 | 9 | 7 | 7 | .20 | 6 | 10 | 5 | .05 |
| 45 | | | | | 7 | 1 | 3 | .10 | 11 | 7 | 5 | .30 | 10 | 8 | 3 | .50 |
| 46 | | | | | 2 | 1 | 7 | .05 | 0 | 8 | 15 | .001 | 1 | 6 | 14 | .20 |
| 47 | | | | | 8 | 3 | 0 | .02 | 13 | 8 | 2 | .02 | 14 | 5 | 2 | .01 |
| 48 | | | | | 1 | 0 | 10 | .001 | 4 | 4 | 15 | .01 | 5 | 10 | 6 | .50 |
| 49 | | | | | 9 | 1 | 1 | .01 | 16 | 5 | 2 | .001 | 16 | 5 | 0 | .001 |
| 50 | | | | | 4 | 3 | 4 | .95 | 8 | 8 | 7 | .98 | 10 | 7 | 4 | .30 |

Table C.5. (cont'd)

RATING SCALE 9

| Scene | Forestry and Conservation | | | | Landscape Architecture | | | | Forest Service | | | | University Students I | | | |
|---|---|---|---|---|---|---|---|---|---|---|---|---|---|---|---|---|
| | 28 | 29 | 30 | p | 28 | 29 | 30 | p | 28 | 29 | 30 | p | 28 | 29 | 30 | p |
| 26 | 12 | 6 | 0 | .01 | 10 | 1 | 0 | .001 | 17 | 6 | 0 | .001 | 17 | 4 | 0 | .001 |
| 27 | 2 | 9 | 7 | .20 | 3 | 3 | 5 | .70 | 5 | 11 | 7 | .30 | 6 | 12 | 2 | .05 |
| 28 | 11 | 6 | 1 | .02 | 6 | 5 | 0 | .10 | 11 | 8 | 4 | .20 | 11 | 6 | 3 | .10 |
| 29 | 17 | 1 | 0 | .001 | 11 | 0 | 0 | .001 | 20 | 2 | 1 | .001 | 17 | 3 | 1 | .001 |
| 30 | 6 | 8 | 4 | .70 | 5 | 3 | 3 | .70 | 6 | 6 | 11 | .50 | 5 | 13 | 3 | .02 |
| 31 | 17 | 1 | 0 | .001 | 11 | 0 | 0 | .001 | 18 | 3 | 2 | .001 | 19 | 2 | 0 | .001 |
| 32 | 4 | 13 | 1 | .01 | 2 | 8 | 1 | .05 | 6 | 7 | 10 | .70 | 1 | 9 | 11 | .02 |
| 33 | 16 | 1 | 1 | .001 | 9 | 2 | 0 | .01 | 21 | 2 | 0 | .001 | 13 | 8 | 0 | .01 |
| 34 | 3 | 11 | 4 | .05 | 2 | 6 | 3 | .50 | 6 | 8 | 9 | .80 | 3 | 11 | 7 | .20 |
| 35 | 3 | 3 | 12 | .02 | 1 | 6 | 4 | .20 | 1 | 4 | 18 | .001 | 1 | 9 | 11 | .02 |
| 36 | 15 | 3 | 0 | .001 | 10 | 1 | 0 | .001 | 16 | 7 | 0 | .001 | 15 | 6 | 0 | .001 |
| 37 | 0 | 2 | 16 | .001 | 1 | 1 | 9 | .01 | 2 | 0 | 21 | .001 | 3 | 4 | 14 | .01 |
| 38 | 2 | 3 | 13 | .01 | 2 | 3 | 6 | .50 | 2 | 1 | 20 | .001 | 2 | 9 | 9 | .10 |
| 39 | 18 | 0 | 0 | .001 | 9 | 1 | 1 | .01 | 17 | 6 | 0 | .001 | 15 | 4 | 2 | .001 |
| 40 | 4 | 4 | 10 | .30 | 4 | 4 | 2 | .70 | 4 | 10 | 9 | .20 | 4 | 10 | 7 | .30 |
| 41 | 8 | 6 | 4 | .70 | 5 | 3 | 3 | .70 | 6 | 12 | 5 | .20 | 3 | 14 | 4 | .01 |
| 42 | 10 | 4 | 4 | .30 | 5 | 3 | 3 | .70 | 6 | 10 | 7 | .70 | 7 | 12 | 2 | .05 |
| 43 | 4 | 7 | 7 | .70 | 1 | 3 | 7 | .10 | 1 | 5 | 17 | .001 | 0 | 12 | 9 | .01 |
| 44 | | | | | 11 | 6 | 3 | .20 | 2 | 9 | 12 | .05 | 4 | 13 | 4 | .05 |
| 45 | | | | | 11 | 0 | 0 | .001 | 15 | 6 | 2 | .01 | 13 | 7 | 1 | .01 |
| 46 | | | | | 4 | 1 | 6 | .20 | 2 | 10 | 11 | .05 | 2 | 5 | 14 | .01 |
| 47 | | | | | 2 | 6 | 3 | .50 | 0 | 5 | 18 | .001 | 4 | 10 | 7 | .30 |
| 48 | | | | | 2 | 0 | 9 | .01 | 1 | 4 | 18 | .001 | 3 | 11 | 7 | .20 |
| 49 | | | | | 11 | 0 | 0 | .001 | 18 | 5 | 0 | .001 | 18 | 3 | 0 | .001 |
| 50 | | | | | 3 | 2 | 6 | .50 | 4 | 4 | 15 | .01 | 3 | 5 | 13 | .02 |

Table C.5. (cont'd)

RATING SCALE 10

| Scene | Forestry and Conservation | | | | | Landscape Architecture | | | | | Forest Service | | | | | University Students I | | | | |
|---|---|---|---|---|---|---|---|---|---|---|---|---|---|---|---|---|---|---|---|---|
| | 31 | 32 | 33 | 34 | $p$ | 31 | 32 | 33 | 34 | $p$ | 31 | 32 | 33 | 34 | $p$ | 31 | 32 | 33 | 34 | $p$ |
| 26 | 17 | 0 | 0 | 0 | .001 | 11 | 0 | 0 | 0 | .001 | 23 | 0 | 0 | 0 | .001 | 21 | 0 | 0 | 0 | .001 |
| 27 | 1 | 0 | 9 | 8 | .01 | 0 | 0 | 2 | 9 | .001 | 2 | 0 | 8 | 13 | .001 | 1 | 0 | 3 | 17 | .001 |
| 28 | 4 | 0 | 2 | 12 | .001 | 0 | 0 | 1 | 10 | .001 | 1 | 0 | 2 | 20 | .001 | 5 | 0 | 0 | 15 | .001 |
| 29 | 0 | 0 | 3 | 15 | .001 | 0 | 0 | 0 | 11 | .001 | 0 | 0 | 1 | 22 | .001 | 0 | 0 | 1 | 20 | .001 |
| 30 | 3 | 4 | 11 | 0 | .01 | 0 | 3 | 7 | 0 | .01 | 0 | 7 | 16 | 0 | .001 | 2 | 10 | 10 | 0 | .01 |
| 31 | 1 | 0 | 1 | 16 | .001 | 0 | 0 | 0 | 10 | .001 | 0 | 1 | 1 | 22 | .001 | 0 | 0 | 1 | 20 | .001 |
| 32 | 0 | 0 | 0 | 18 | .001 | 0 | 0 | 0 | 11 | .001 | 0 | 1 | 0 | 22 | .001 | 0 | 0 | 2 | 19 | .001 |
| 33 | 15 | 0 | 0 | 3 | .001 | 8 | 0 | 1 | 2 | .01 | 11 | 0 | 3 | 9 | .01 | 14 | 2 | 1 | 4 | .001 |
| 34 | 13 | 0 | 1 | 3 | .001 | 9 | 0 | 2 | 0 | .001 | 19 | 1 | 3 | 0 | .001 | 15 | 2 | 3 | 1 | .001 |
| 35 | 0 | 1 | 17 | 0 | .001 | 0 | 0 | 11 | 0 | .001 | 0 | 2 | 21 | 0 | .001 | 4 | 0 | 18 | 0 | .001 |
| 36 | 16 | 0 | 0 | 2 | .001 | 9 | 0 | 0 | 1 | .001 | 15 | 1 | 2 | 5 | .001 | 17 | 3 | 0 | 0 | .001 |
| 37 | 0 | 0 | 0 | 18 | .001 | 0 | 0 | 4 | 7 | .01 | 0 | 0 | 0 | 23 | .001 | 0 | 1 | 1 | 20 | .001 |
| 38 | 1 | 0 | 8 | 9 | .01 | 8 | 3 | 0 | 0 | .01 | 0 | 3 | 0 | 20 | .001 | 1 | 0 | 1 | 18 | .001 |
| 39 | 13 | 4 | 0 | 1 | .001 | 0 | 0 | 11 | 0 | .001 | 8 | 8 | 0 | 0 | .001 | 15 | 4 | 1 | 1 | .001 |
| 40 | 0 | 1 | 17 | 0 | .001 | 2 | 0 | 2 | 7 | .05 | 0 | 4 | 19 | 0 | .001 | 0 | 1 | 20 | 0 | .001 |
| 41 | 3 | 0 | 1 | 14 | .001 | 0 | 0 | 0 | 11 | .001 | 3 | 1 | 2 | 16 | .001 | 8 | 0 | 2 | 11 | .001 |
| 42 | 0 | 0 | 0 | 18 | .001 | 0 | 0 | 0 | 11 | .001 | 1 | 1 | 0 | 21 | .001 | 0 | 1 | 2 | 20 | .001 |
| 43 | 0 | 0 | 0 | 18 | .001 | 4 | 4 | 0 | 1 | .20 | 0 | 0 | 0 | 23 | .001 | 1 | 0 | 0 | 20 | .001 |
| 44 | | | | | | 0 | 0 | 0 | 10 | .001 | 11 | 7 | 0 | 5 | .02 | 12 | 3 | 2 | 5 | .01 |
| 45 | | | | | | 0 | 0 | 4 | 10 | .001 | 0 | 1 | 0 | 22 | .001 | 0 | 0 | 1 | 21 | .001 |
| 46 | | | | | | 7 | 1 | 1 | 7 | .01 | 0 | 0 | 2 | 21 | .001 | 1 | 0 | 0 | 18 | .001 |
| 47 | | | | | | 0 | 0 | 1 | 1 | .02 | 13 | 4 | 4 | 2 | .01 | 11 | 8 | 2 | 1 | .01 |
| 48 | | | | | | 0 | 0 | 0 | 10 | .001 | 0 | 0 | 0 | 23 | .001 | 0 | 0 | 1 | 20 | .001 |
| 49 | | | | | | 0 | 0 | 0 | 9 | .001 | 0 | 0 | 0 | 23 | .001 | 0 | 0 | 1 | 21 | .001 |
| 50 | | | | | | 1 | 0 | 1 | 9 | .001 | 2 | 0 | 1 | 20 | .001 | 1 | 0 | 0 | 20 | .001 |

Table C.6. Landscape Rating Scales: Comparison of Agreement in the Use of Each Scale by Expert and Nonexpert Panels

| Landscape Rating Scale | Number of Scenes Consensually Rated* | | | | | | | |
|---|---|---|---|---|---|---|---|---|
| | Landscape Architecture | | Forest Service | | Combined Expert Panel** | | University Students | |
| | Number | Rank | Number | Rank | Number | Rank | Number | Rank |
| 1 (1–2–3) | 23 | 14.5 | 25 | 15.5 | 24.0 | 15.0 | 19 | 8.0 |
| 2 (4–5–6) | 23 | 14.5 | 24 | 13.5 | 23.5 | 14.0 | 22 | 12.0 |
| 3 (7) | 15 | 5.0 | 15 | 2.5 | 15.0 | 4.5 | 15 | 4.0 |
| (8) | 16 | 6.5 | 20 | 7.5 | 18.0 | 7.0 | 23 | 14.5 |
| (9) | 16 | 6.5 | 15 | 2.5 | 15.5 | 6.0 | 17 | 5.5 |
| 4 (10–11–12) | 21 | 13.0 | 22 | 10.0 | 21.5 | 12.0 | 23 | 14.5 |
| 5 (13–14–15–16) | 19 | 10.5 | 20 | 7.5 | 19.5 | 8.5 | 17 | 5.5 |
| 6 (17) | 19 | 10.5 | 24 | 13.5 | 21.5 | 12.0 | 21 | 11.5 |
| (18) | 12 | 1.0 | 17 | 5.5 | 14.5 | 2.5 | 12 | 1.0 |
| (19) | 17 | 8.0 | 22 | 10.0 | 19.5 | 8.5 | 19 | 8.0 |
| (20) | 18 | 9.0 | 22 | 10.0 | 20.0 | 10.0 | 19 | 8.0 |
| (21) | 20 | 12.0 | 23 | 12.0 | 21.5 | 12.0 | 20 | 10.0 |
| 7 (22–23–24) | 13 | 2.5 | 16 | 4.0 | 14.5 | 2.5 | 13 | 2.5 |
| 8 (25–26–27) | 14 | 4.0 | 13 | 1.0 | 13.5 | 1.0 | 13 | 2.5 |
| 9 (28–29–30) | 13 | 2.5 | 17 | 5.5 | 15.0 | 4.5 | 21 | 11.5 |
| 10 (31–32–33–34) | 24 | 16.0 | 25 | 15.5 | 24.5 | 16.0 | 25 | 16.0 |

* That is, for which agreement was attained beyond the .10 level of statistical significance. (Total number of scenes rated = 25.)

** Averaged results for the Landscape Architecture and Forest Service panels.

Table C.7. Landscape Rating Scales: Comparison between Conservation-oriented Panelists and Other Panelists

|  | Scene 1 | | Scene 2 | | Scene 3 | | Scene 4 | | Scene 5 | | Scene 6 | |
|---|---|---|---|---|---|---|---|---|---|---|---|---|
|  | $X^2$ | $p$ | $X^2$ | $p$ | $X^2$ | $p$ | $X^2$ | $p$ | $X^2$ | $p$ | $X^2$ | $p$ |
| Rating 1 | 0.41 | .90 | 6.66 | .05 | 2.03 | .20 | 4.64 | .10 | 0.01 | .95 | 0.19 | .70 |
| Rating 2 | 4.38 | .05 | 0.76 | .70 | 1.76 | .20 | 0.26 | .70 | 0.24 | .70 | 0.01 | .98 |
| Rating 3 |  |  |  |  |  |  |  |  |  |  |  |  |
| 7 | 0.17 | .70 | 4.43 | .05 | 1.57 | .30 | 0.11 | .80 | 0.01 | .95 | 0.26 | .70 |
| 8 | 3.15 | .10 | 1.78 | .20 | 2.65 | .20 | 1.18 | .30 | 0.35 | .70 | 5.35 | .05 |
| 9 | 2.62 | .20 | 6.80 | .01 | 0.24 | .70 | 0.01 | .95 | 0.94 | .50 | 0.01 | .95 |
| Rating 4 | 0.32 | .90 | 0.21 | .70 | 0.19 | .70 | 0.23 | .70 | 0.37 | .70 | 4.84 | .10 |
| Rating 5 | 3.98 | .30 | 1.94 | .70 | 2.92 | .50 | 2.67 | .30 | 5.53 | .20 | 1.11 | .80 |

|  | Scene 26 | | Scene 27 | | Scene 28 | | Scene 29 | | Scene 30 | | Scene 31 | |
|---|---|---|---|---|---|---|---|---|---|---|---|---|
|  | $X^2$ | $p$ | $X^2$ | $p$ | $X^2$ | $p$ | $X^2$ | $p$ | $X^2$ | $p$ | $X^2$ | $p$ |
| Rating 6 |  |  |  |  |  |  |  |  |  |  |  |  |
| 17 | 0.15 | .70 | 0.04 | .90 | 0.18 | .80 | 0.03 | .90 | 0.65 | .50 | 0.11 | .80 |
| 18 | 0.35 | .70 | 0.05 | .90 | 1.65 | .20 | 1.72 | .20 | 1.20 | .30 | 0.02 | .90 |
| 19 | 0.11 | .80 | 3.37 | .10 | 0.02 | .90 | 0.03 | .90 | 0.02 | .90 | 0.23 | .70 |
| 20 | 1.29 | .30 | 1.09 | .30 | 0.16 | .70 | 0.03 | .90 | 0.09 | .80 | 0.03 | .90 |
| 21 | 0.57 | .50 | 2.44 | .20 | 0.01 | .95 | 0.01 | .99 | 0.01 | .95 | 0.01 | .99 |
| Rating 7 | 3.86 | .20 | 7.65 | .05 | 0.63 | .80 | 2.01 | .50 | 3.24 | .20 | 0.02 | .90 |
| Rating 8 | 2.51 | .30 | 0.39 | .90 | 1.33 | .70 | 1.65 | .50 | 6.49 | .05 | 1.97 | .50 |
| Rating 9 | 0.21 | .70 | 2.05 | .50 | 5.14 | .10 | 0.01 | .98 | 0.18 | .95 | 0.22 | .70 |
| Rating 10 | 0.01 | .99 | 0.71 | .50 | 1.74 | .20 | 0.80 | .50 | 2.19 | .20 | 0.01 | .95 |

Table C.8. Graphic Landscape Typology: Typological Designations
for Fifty Test Scenes

| | Number of Panelists Allocating Scenes to Each Type | | | | | | | | | |
|---|---|---|---|---|---|---|---|---|---|---|
| Scenes | A | B | C | D | E | F | G | H | I | J |
| 1 | 38 | 1 | 0 | 5 | 0 | 1 | 0 | 0 | 0 | 89 |
| 2 | 8 | 0 | 1 | 1 | 90 | 6 | 30 | 0 | 0 | 0 |
| 3 | 12 | 1 | 118 | 0 | 2 | 3 | 0 | 0 | 1 | 1 |
| 4 | 5 | 15 | 101 | 0 | 0 | 1 | 0 | 4 | 5 | 4 |
| 5 | 0 | 4 | 0 | 1 | 1 | 2 | 0 | 1 | 1 | 126 |
| 6 | 1 | 2 | 1 | 0 | 18 | 110 | 2 | 0 | 1 | 1 |
| 7 | 1 | 0 | 20 | 5 | 5 | 3 | 3 | 9 | 93 | 0 |
| 8 | 12 | 1 | 7 | 20 | 5 | 4 | 64 | 6 | 14 | 2 |
| 9 | 0 | 4 | 0 | 107 | 0 | 0 | 0 | 5 | 0 | 22 |
| 10 | 4 | 108 | 12 | 5 | 0 | 4 | 1 | 3 | 1 | 1 |
| 11 | 4 | 103 | 12 | 6 | 0 | 2 | 1 | 1 | 4 | 5 |
| 12 | 1 | 0 | 0 | 0 | 108 | 16 | 13 | 0 | 0 | 0 |
| 13 | 1 | 119 | 0 | 1 | 0 | 2 | 0 | 0 | 0 | 15 |
| 14 | 2 | 0 | 1 | 116 | 0 | 0 | 5 | 8 | 3 | 3 |
| 15 | 2 | 1 | 10 | 2 | 1 | 1 | 0 | 12 | 101 | 8 |
| 16 | 15 | 3 | 0 | 1 | 13 | 81 | 4 | 0 | 0 | 19 |
| 17 | 1 | 0 | 0 | 52 | 0 | 1 | 0 | 81 | 1 | 2 |
| 18 | 6 | 21 | 1 | 0 | 2 | 56 | 4 | 3 | 0 | 45 |
| 19 | 39 | 1 | 9 | 31 | 10 | 2 | 36 | 3 | 4 | 2 |
| 20 | 2 | 0 | 2 | 1 | 122 | 4 | 6 | 0 | 1 | 0 |
| 21 | 45 | 0 | 22 | 2 | 25 | 4 | 16 | 3 | 13 | 7 |
| 22 | 1 | 4 | 2 | 5 | 0 | 1 | 1 | 109 | 1 | 14 |
| 23 | 2 | 0 | 1 | 46 | 4 | 1 | 57 | 4 | 9 | 14 |
| 24 | 2 | 0 | 1 | 106 | 0 | 2 | 4 | 3 | 10 | 10 |
| 25 | 0 | 4 | 0 | 7 | 0 | 3 | 0 | 3 | 3 | 117 |
| 26 | 12 | 0 | 1 | 9 | 3 | 1 | 75 | 17 | 10 | 7 |
| 27 | 25 | 1 | 0 | 12 | 0 | 2 | 3 | 40 | 14 | 37 |
| 28 | 34 | 2 | 1 | 20 | 8 | 9 | 16 | 3 | 4 | 41 |
| 29 | 2 | 0 | 9 | 0 | 120 | 2 | 1 | 0 | 0 | 0 |
| 30 | 1 | 2 | 1 | 8 | 0 | 2 | 1 | 108 | 10 | 3 |
| 31 | 3 | 0 | 3 | 0 | 116 | 0 | 11 | 1 | 0 | 0 |
| 32 | 0 | 4 | 0 | 0 | 0 | 3 | 0 | 1 | 6 | 122 |
| 33 | 9 | 2 | 0 | 4 | 25 | 56 | 26 | 1 | 1 | 12 |
| 34 | 3 | 1 | 0 | 118 | 0 | 1 | 1 | 0 | 3 | 9 |
| 35 | 0 | 133 | 0 | 0 | 1 | 2 | 0 | 0 | 0 | 0 |
| 36 | 4 | 0 | 0 | 3 | 15 | 7 | 62 | 37 | 8 | 0 |
| 37 | 1 | 11 | 88 | 7 | 0 | 1 | 0 | 5 | 14 | 9 |
| 38 | 46 | 4 | 83 | 0 | 1 | 0 | 0 | 0 | 0 | 2 |
| 39 | 4 | 0 | 0 | 5 | 3 | 71 | 37 | 0 | 0 | 16 |
| 40 | 0 | 132 | 0 | 1 | 0 | 0 | 0 | 0 | 0 | 2 |
| 41 | 1 | 1 | 26 | 9 | 2 | 2 | 3 | 82 | 10 | 0 |
| 42 | 1 | 0 | 1 | 4 | 1 | 6 | 0 | 10 | 103 | 10 |
| 43 | 0 | 0 | 0 | 121 | 0 | 0 | 0 | 6 | 6 | 3 |
| 44 | 3 | 2 | 0 | 12 | 0 | 6 | 0 | 6 | 10 | 107 |
| 45 | 17 | 3 | 4 | 1 | 28 | 6 | 76 | 1 | 0 | 0 |
| 46 | 5 | 18 | 5 | 16 | 0 | 0 | 1 | 87 | 2 | 2 |
| 47 | 0 | 7 | 0 | 1 | 0 | 3 | 0 | 1 | 0 | 124 |
| 48 | 23 | 0 | 109 | 0 | 2 | 0 | 0 | 0 | 0 | 1 |
| 49 | 1 | 0 | 0 | 11 | 3 | 4 | 109 | 4 | 4 | 0 |
| 50 | 0 | 4 | 15 | 5 | 0 | 2 | 0 | 6 | 76 | 25 |

Table C.9. Graphic Landscape Typology: Modal Typological Designations by Expert and Nonexpert Panels

| Scene | Forestry and Conservation | Landscape Architecture | Forest Service | I | II | III | IV | Total Panels |
|---|---|---|---|---|---|---|---|---|
| | | | | University Students | | | | |
| 1 | J | J | J | J | J | J | A | J |
| 2 | E | E | E | E | E | E | G | E |
| 3 | C | C | C | C | C | C | C | C |
| 4 | C | C | C | C | C | C | C | C |
| 5 | J | J | J | J | J | J | J | J |
| 6 | F | F | F | F | F | F | F | F |
| 7 | I | I | I | I | I | I | I | I |
| 8 | G | A | D | G | G | G | G | G |
| 9 | D | D | D | D | D | D | D | D |
| 10 | B | B | B | B | B | B | B | B |
| 11 | B | B | B | B | B | B | B | B |
| 12 | E | E | E | E | E | E | E | E |
| 13 | B | B | B | B | B | B | B | B |
| 14 | D | D | D | D | D | D | D | D |
| 15 | I | I | I | I | I | I | I | I |
| 16 | F | AF | F | F | F | F | F | F |
| 17 | H | D | H | H | H | H | H | H |
| 18 | J | FJ | F | J | F | F | F | F |
| 19 | A | A | D | D | G | G | A | A |
| 20 | E | E | E | E | E | E | E | E |
| 21 | E | A | A | G | I | A | A | A |
| 22 | H | H | H | H | H | H | H | H |
| 23 | D | G | G | D | DG | G | G | G |
| 24 | D | D | D | D | D | D | D | D |
| 25 | J | J | J | J | J | J | J | J |
| 26 | G | G | G | G | G | G | G | G |
| 27 | A | A | H | H | J | H | A | H |
| 28 | J | A | A | J | GJ | D | A | J |
| 29 | E | E | E | E | E | E | E | E |
| 30 | H | H | H | H | H | H | H | H |
| 31 | E | E | E | E | E | E | E | E |
| 32 | J | J | J | J | J | J | J | J |
| 33 | F | F | F | F | E | F | F | F |
| 34 | D | D | D | D | D | D | D | D |
| 35 | B | B | B | B | B | B | B | B |
| 36 | H | G | H | G | G | G | G | G |
| 37 | C | C | C | C | C | C | C | C |
| 38 | C | C | C | A | C | C | A | C | C |
| 39 | F | F | F | F | F | G | F | F |
| 40 | B | B | B | B | B | B | B | B |
| 41 | H | H | H | H | H | H | H | H |
| 42 | I | I | I | I | I | I | I | I |
| 43 | D | D | D | D | D | D | D | D |
| 44 | J | J | J | J | J | J | J | J |
| 45 | G | G | G | EG | G | G | E | G |
| 46 | H | H | H | H | H | H | H | H |
| 47 | J | J | J | J | J | J | J | J |
| 48 | C | C | C | C | C | C | C | C |
| 49 | G | G | G | G | G | G | G | G |
| 50 | I | I | I | I | I | I | I | I |

## References

Block, J. 1961. *The Q-sort Method in Personality Assessment and Psychiatric Research*. Springfield, Ill.: C. C. Thomas.

Canter, D. 1969. An intergroup comparison of connotative dimensions in architecture. *Environment and Behavior* 1:37–48.

Child, I. 1969. Esthetics. In G. Lindzey and A. Aronson (eds.), *Handbook of Social Psychology*, vol. III. Reading, Mass.: Addison-Wesley.

Cline, V. B. 1964. Interperson perception. In B. A. Maher (ed.), *Progress in Experimental Personality Research*, vol. 1. New York: Academic Press. Pp. 221–84.

Collins, J. B. 1968. Some verbal dimensions of architectural space perception. *Architectural Psychology Newsletter* 2:4–5.

———. 1969. Perceptual dimensions of architectural space validated against behavioral criteria. Unpublished doctoral dissertation, University of Utah.

Coughlin, R. E., and Goldstein, K. A. 1970. *The extent of agreement among observers on environmental attractiveness*. RSRI Discussion Paper Series, no. 37. Philadelphia, Pa.: Regional Science Research Institute.

Craik, K. H. 1968. The comprehension of the everyday physical environment. *Journal of the American Institute of Planners* 34:29–37.

———. 1969(a). Human responsiveness to landscape: An environmental psychological perspective. In K. Coates and K. Moffett (eds.), *Response to Environment*. Student Publication of the School of Design, vol. 18. Raleigh: North Carolina State University. Pp. 168–93.

———. 1969(b). Transportation and the person. *High Speed Ground Transportation Journal* 3:86–91.

———. 1970. Environmental psychology. In Craik et al., *New Directions in Psychology 4*. New York: Holt, Rinehart & Winston. Pp. 1–122.

Gough, H. G., and Heilbrun, A. B., Jr. 1965. *The Adjective Check List Manual*. Palo Alto, Calif.: Consulting Psychologists Press.

Hershberger, R. G. 1969. A study of meaning and architecture. Unpublished doctoral dissertation, University of Pennsylvania.

Kasmar, J. V., and Vidulich, R. N. 1968. *A factor analytic study of environmental description*. Unpublished report, Los Angeles, Medical Center, University of California.

Litton, R. B., Jr. 1968. *Forest Landscape Description and Inventories: A Basis for Land Planning and Design*. USDA Forest Service Research Paper PSW-49. Berkeley, California: Pacific Southwest Forest and Range Experiment Station.

———, and Twiss, R. H. 1967. The forest landscape: Some elements of visual analysis. *Proceedings of the Society of American Foresters: 1966*, Washington, D.C.: Society of American Foresters. Pp. 212–14.

Lowenthal, D., et al. 1967. An analysis of environmental perception. Unpublished. Washington, D.C.: Resources for the Future.

Rabinowitz, C. B., and Coughlin, R. E. 1970. *Analysis of landscape characteristics relevant to preference*. RSRI Discussion Paper Series, no. 38. Philadelphia, Pa.: Regional Science Research Institute.

Sanoff, H. 1969. Visual attributes of the physical environment. In K. Coates and K. Moffett (eds.), *Response to Environment.* Student Publication of the School of Design, vol. 18. Raleigh: North Carolina State University. Pp. 37–62.

Shafer, E. L., Jr., Hamilton, J. F., Jr., and Schmidt, E. A. 1969. Natural landscape preferences: A predictive model. *Journal of Leisure Research* 1:1–19.

Sonnenfeld, J. 1969. Equivalence and distortion of the perceptual environment. *Environment and Behavior* 1:83–100.

Thiel, P. A. 1961. A sequence-experience notation for architectural and urban space. *Town Planning Review* 32:33–52.

———. 1965. *Notes on environmental space and elementary space notation.* Seattle: University of Washington Press.

# Index

347